2006
Workflow Handbook

including

Business Process Management

2006
Workflow Handbook

including

Business Process Management

Published in association with the
Workflow Management Coalition

Edited by

Layna Fischer

Future Strategies Inc., Book Division
Lighthouse Point, Florida

Workflow Handbook 2006

Copyright © 2006 by Future Strategies Inc.

ISBN 0-9777527-0-4

06 05 04 03 3 4 5 6

Published by Future Strategies Inc., Book Division

2436 North Federal Highway #374
Lighthouse Point FL 33064 USA
954.782.3376 fax 954.782.6365
wfmc@wfmc.org

Cover design by Pearl & Associates

Publisher's Cataloging-in-Publication Data

Library of Congress Catalog Card No. 2006923396

Workflow Handbook 2006:
/Layna Fischer (editor)

p. cm.

Includes bibliographical references, glossary, appendices and index.

ISBN 0-9777527-0-4

1. Business Process Management. 2. Workflow Management.
3. Technological Innovation. 4. Information Technology. 5. Total Quality Management. 6. Organizational Change 7. Management Information Systems. 8. Office Practice_Automation. 9. Business Process Technology. 10. Electronic Commerce. 11. Process Analysis

Fischer, Layna

TABLE OF CONTENTS

TABLE OF CONTENTS

SECTION 2—STANDARDS

SECTION 3—DIRECTORIES AND APPENDICES

Foreword

Jon Pyke, WfMC Chair, United Kingdom

Welcome to the 2006 edition of the Workflow Management Coalition's official handbook.

Last year was a very exciting one for the Coalition. There were some significant changes in the standards arena, the most notable of which was the BPMI.org placing itself under the wing of The Object Management Group. This means that the Workflow Management Coalition (WfMC) is now the only standards group dedicated to the advancement of process related technologies. So I think it is worth recapping what we have done since our inception.

WfMC members established standards for software terminology, interoperability and connectivity between workflow products in 1993. The initial work of the Coalition focused on publishing the Workflow Reference Model and Glossary, defining a common architecture and terminology for the industry.

The Reference Model defines five components of workflow—the five interfaces to the workflow enactment services (what BPM calls the invocation engine). The standards associated with these interfaces are listed at www.wfmc.org. Understanding the five components helps distinguish between BPM and Workflow systems.

Working closely with other standards bodies in this space, WfMC has frequently demonstrated successful interoperability of its specifications with standards emanating from other bodies, most notably:

ASAP and Wf-XML 2.0

- OASIS' Asynchronous Service Access Protocol (ASAP) is a web services protocol that can be used to access a generic service that might take a long time to complete—for example services that last from minutes to months in duration. The service being invoked might be fully automated, a manual task that a person performs, or any mixture of the two. This capability to handle both automated and manual activities makes ASAP particularly suited for B2B and intra-organizational service request scenarios.
- WfMC's Wf-XML is a protocol for process engines that makes it easy to link engines together for interoperability. Wf-XML 2.0 is built on top of ASAP which is in turn built on Simple Object Access Protocol (SOAP) and extends this protocol to include BPM and workflow interchange capabilities. A business process engine is a special type of asynchronous service: it has the ability to be started, to involve people in that process, and to complete some time later. One BPM engine can be easily linked to another BPM engine using Wf-XML.

XPDL 2.0 and BPMN

- WfMC's XML Process Definition Language (XPDL) defines the technical representation of the process and to allow the interchange of a process description between different IT products and across different organizations. XPDL provides an XML file format that can be used to interchange process models between tools.
- The Business Process Modeling Notation (BPMN) from BPMI.org (now OMG) is used for the graphical modeling of a business process. In addition to the graphical notation, BPMN incorporated a number of

specific mechanisms for process modeling that had not yet been included in XPDL; among these, events and message passing between processes. XPDL 2.0 incorporates these mechanisms as well as the graphics and offers an extended meta-model that unifies XPDL and BPMN.

Standards are of no use unless they are adopted by industry and used on a regular basis. I mentioned in the 2005 edition of the Handbook that the United Kingdom National Workflow Project had adopted the Coalition's standards to support their project. This trend has continued, recently a significant "open source" consortium Sourceforge released the Open Business Engine which is a Java-based workflow engine that fully supports the WfMC XPDL standard. Furthermore, the Eclipse project has recently proposed a Java Workflow Tooling project that will provide graphical editing of XPDL process definitions, deployment and monitoring capabilities. The growing list of companies supporting XPDL is posted on the WfMC web site.

The WfMC continues to lead the industry in BPM and workflow process standards. Several articles on the importance of these standards have been published in the *Workflow Handbook* series, such as *ASAP/Wf-XML 2.0 Cookbook* by Keith D Swenson, Chair WfMC Technical Committee and Fujitsu VP of Research and Development and *XPDL 2.0: Integrating Process Interchange and BPMN* by Robert M. Shapiro, Chair WfMC XPDL Workgroup and VP Global 360 (available in the Workflow Standards section in this *Workflow Handbook*).

Of increasing importance is the growth in the WfMC's educational services. The recent XPDL tutorials have been so well received that we now intend to make them more widely available via a series of Webinars—these are planned for mid-year. Allied to the expansion of the educational work is the establishment of BPM-Focus in collaboration with BPM-WARIA (formerly the Workflow And Reengineering International Association). This initiative was started during the Seoul meeting last fall. The BPMF is tasked with establishing and coordinating localized BPM Forum Chapters to handle awareness campaigns and training/lecture seminars. There are already several BPM Forums in the Pacific Rim with keen interest shown by other regions in South America and Europe.

The members of the Workflow Management Coalition hope you enjoy our *Workflow Handbook 2006* and find it useful as you explore workflow and Business Process Management and their many diverse benefits.

Last, but by no means least, our thanks go to everybody who helped in the publication and to Layna Fischer, WfMC Executive Director, in particular, for her tireless efforts in marshalling the contributors, editing and publishing this important body of work.

Jon Pyke, Chair WfMC 2006
United Kingdom

Introduction

Layna Fischer, Executive Director
Workflow Management Coalition

The WfMC provides an important forum for the adoption of standards throughout the industry. Standards provide an infrastructure for inter-organizational business process automation and management. In this book, industry experts and thought leaders present significant new ideas and concepts to help you plan a successful future for your organization.

- **SECTION 1: World of Workflow and BPM** covers a wide spectrum of viewpoints and discussions by experts in their respective fields. Papers range putting Business Process Management in context for non-technical readers, case studies on manufacturing and healthcare through to Web Services workflow architectures with special spotlight on BPM and workflow in Greater China.
- **SECTION 2: Standards** deals with the importance of interoperability of standards, including technical instructions on Integrating Process Interchange (XPDL) and BPMN, and a chapter on Programming in XPDL.
- **SECTION 3: Directory and Appendices**—an explanation of the structure of the Workflow Management Coalition and references comprise the last section including a membership directory.

Section 1—World of Workflow and BPM

PUTTING BPM IN CONTEXT: NOW AND IN THE FUTURE 17
Jon Pyke, WfMC Chair, United Kingdom

This paper looks at the various technologies that make up the burgeoning Business Process Management (BPM) market and explores the impact that new methods of deployment and design will have on products and how those changes could affect end users. The paper also provides non-technical readers with a better understanding of what the all-encompassing term "Business Process Management" means by explaining several BPM-related terms in detail.

PRACTICAL LESSONS IN MANAGING REAL BPM INNOVATION 29
Fred van Leeuwen, DCE Consultants, Netherlands

Companies are paying lip service to the most essential prerequisites for innovation of work. After 15 years of process engineering, many of them are still not ready to cut across their functional silos. And they rarely initiate the innovation process from within the hearts of their process workers, without whom it will not happen. The author responds to the question, "Why has the idea of real-time steering information, placed in the hands of process workers, not materialized as quickly and fully as it could have, and what can we do to make it more successful?"

WORKFLOW—THE COMPLIANCE PROJECT ENGINE 33
Arnaud Bezancon, Advantys, France

Businesses today are required by law to comply with a vast range of regulations and standards. They have to implement new procedures to ensure full accountability, maintain records of all decisions taken and analyze any deviation through the use of audits. An organization's ability to manage compliance and governance projects efficiently has become key issue which impacts directly on their business performance. This chapter highlights a number of processes required by legislation such as Sarbanes Oxley, HIPAA & BALE 2, IT governance standards such as COBIT, ITIL & ISO 17799, as well as corporate project management.

BUSINESS PROCESS MANAGEMENT FOR SIX SIGMA PROJECTS 41

Dr. Setrag Khoshafian, Pegasystems Inc., USA

Often Business Process Management (BPM) and Six Sigma are positioned as competing alternatives for process optimization. Some analysts have proposed that companies don't need both but can choose one depending upon individual objectives. However, this premise is false. A modern Business Process Management Suite (BPMS) can provide an ideal platform for implementing successful Six Sigma projects. BPMS and Six Sigma are complementary approaches, interwoven in the continuous improvement cycle of digitized and automated processes.

EMPLOYING WORKFLOW TO DRIVE A COMPREHENSIVE AUDIT OF ENTERPRISE IDENTITY MANAGEMENT 51

Rami Elron, BMC Software, Israel

Workflow plays a key role in the implementation of a comprehensive approach to auditing required to accommodate regulatory compliance requirements. Workflow offers powerful methods that enable enterprises to effectively reduce potential threats to the business, and to facilitate attestation. This chapter illuminates key aspects pertaining to the role of workflow within a comprehensive auditing approach. This chapter highlights key business conditions and requirements that drive the need for auditing, explains how identity management auditing addresses these requirements, and examines how workflow contributes to the effectiveness of an identity-management audit process.

USING BPM TO MANAGE RISKS IN FINANCIAL SERVICES FIRMS 67

Sheila Donohue, CRIF Decision Solutions, Italy

The consequences of uncontrolled risk can result in large monetary losses, negative impact on share price, loss of jobs, closure of companies and even court prosecution, as seen in current events especially over the past five years. Spurring on the use of modern risk management techniques are regulatory bodies, and even investors, that now require companies to demonstrate solid risk management practices. This paper will focus on two types of risks which financial firms manage and how Business Process Management, BPM, can be applied to manage these risks.

EXCEPTION-BASED DYNAMIC SERVICE COORDINATION FRAMEWORK FOR WEB SERVICES 81

Dr Dongsoo Han and Sungjoon Park, Information and Communications University, Korea

Web services on the Internet are not always reliable in terms of service availability and performance. Dynamic service coordination capability of a system or application which invokes Web services is an essential feature to cope with such unreliable situations. In dynamic service coordination, if a Web service does not respond within a specific time constraint, it is replaced with another Web service at run time. For that, we develop a dynamic service coordination framework for Web services. In the framework, all necessary information for dynamic service coordination is explicitly specified and summarized as a set of attributes. Classes and workflows supporting dynamic service coordination and invoking Web services are then automatically created based on these attributes. Developers of Web service client programs can make the invocations of Web services reliable by calling the methods of the classes. Some performance loss has been observed in the indirect invocation of a Web service. However, when we consider the flexibility and reliability gained from the method, the performance loss would be acceptable in many cases.

Juan J. Moreno, Lithium Software/ Universidad Católica Uruguay; Luis Joyanes, Universidad Pontificia de Salamanca, Spain

An important part of the organizational knowledge needed to operate and grow is embedded in business processes automated via Workflow Management Systems (WMS) and BPMS. Organizations own this knowledge, but they are often unable to use it in the best way, mainly because it is extremely difficult to retrieve and interpret that information. This paper proposes a model that allows extraction and modelling of generated knowledge, stored in a Business Process Management System. With this knowledge available, we can make recommendations to human participants about good and bad decisions, to improve performance, reduce mistakes and shorten learning times. These recommendations are based on successful and unsuccessful cases in the past. We also can recommend the most suitable participant for each process instance, based on its characteristics and the participant's expertise and experience.

Tadeu Cruz, TRCR Knowledge, Brazil

This chapter discusses the implementation and use of Workflow systems to automate business processes in organizations of all types and economic sectors and how/why some of these organizations give up to use the software, even after hefty investments in such implementation projects. Use and Discard were the words chosen to characterize the adoption and abandonment of Workflow systems by part of the various organizations that after implementing it had stopped its use; as well as explaining the behavior of those that never installed it in any machine. The author's intention was to discover the causes of such situations, to understand and to explain, for those interested in Workflow systems, the reasons that drive the organizations to have these types of behaviors.

Ole Christian Astrup and Espen Wøien, DNV Software, Korea

The marine and offshore industry is faced with the same fierce competition as the rest of the business world and must also continually improve performance. But, best practices from other industry verticals are not readily adapted to this industry segment. The workforce of the marine and offshore industries consists of highly qualified knowledge workers undertaking complex design work spanning a long time frame. Their business processes are typically concurrent, multidiscipline, iterative and highly complex. Such organizations pose severe challenges to process management and workflow implementation supporting their best practices.

Steve Rotter, Adobe Systems Inc. USA

Although streamlining of system-to-system interactions is beneficial, it overlooks a major opportunity: one that comes from effectively bridging paper and digital workflows to encompass people and documents more fully in the BMP equation. Most humans are still accustomed to working with paper documents at certain points during a business process, yet computer systems require information in digital form. This has necessitated a flood of data entry and re-entry—an activity that is costly, time-consuming, and error-prone. The key to increased efficiency is to integrate both paper- and digital-based workflows into BPM. By doing so, enterprises can take full advantage of the potential of BPM systems in the enterprise.

THE POSSIBILITY AND REALITY OF MASSIVELY PARALLEL WORKFLOW IMPLEMENTATIONS 139

Kevin Erickson, Noridian Administrative Services, LLC and Michael Hurley, Green Square, Inc. USA

This case study will describe the enterprise-wide, massively parallel implementation approach used by Noridian Administrative Services, LLC. (NAS), showing the implications of the approach, the challenges that the NAS team faced, and the benefits gained by the approach. The reader will also see first hand how workflow automation addresses key issues in the healthcare and insurance industries.

GROWTH IN BUSINESS PROCESS MANAGEMENT SUITES IN GREATER CHINA 145

Linus K. Chow; Charles Choy Wing-Chiu and Carrine Wong

China continues to play an increasingly larger role in the world's economy. Companies in China, including local Small Medium Enterprises (SMEs) as well as Multi-Nationals are increasingly interested in modernizing their Information Systems. The drive to move up the global value chain, and build quality and compliance credibility has taken heightened priority due to political as well as market forces. This chapter describes the Chinese government's drive to modernize and open the financial markets places increasing focus on the transparency and compliance of processes that BPM suites provide.

THE KEYS TO BPM PROJECT SUCCESS 157

Derek Miers, Enix Consulting Ltd., United Kingdom

This paper focuses on the best practices associated with Business Process Management (BPM) project success. It describes a recipe for success, from the creation of a governance-oriented Steering Group, Project Selection, through Business Case Development and on to gaining Executive Sponsorship. With business commitment to the project, the approach focuses on gaining a deep understanding of business processes, before identifying improvement opportunities and eventual implementation on a BPM Suite. Along the way, the paper highlights a wide range of best practice approaches and pitfalls to avoid.

Section 2—Standards

XPDL 2.0: INTEGRATING PROCESS INTERCHANGE AND BPMN 183

Robert M. Shapiro, Global 360, USA

The Business Process Management Notation (BPMN) was developed by individuals working together in the Business Process Management Initiative to take the techniques employed in flowcharting tools, unify and extend the graphics to express the semantics required in workflow and EAI processes. BPMN 1.0 was released in May 2004. In addition to the graphical notation, BPMN incorporated a number of specific mechanisms for process modeling that had not yet been included in XPDL; among these in particular events and message passing between processes. XPDL 2.0 incorporates these mechanisms as well as the graphics and offers an extended meta-model that unifies XPDL and BPMN.

PROGRAMMING IN XPDL 195

Saša Bojanić, Vladimir Puškaš, Zoran Milaković, Together Teamlösungen, Austria

The authors elaborate the possibility of using XPDL (XML Process Definition Language defined by WfMC) to completely define event driven applications, that we call XPDL Applications. XPDL application is a normal XPDL process definition that complies only with few additional rules and restrictions. This definition, when being interpreted by an XPDL engine, and from an engine's point of view, results in an execution of a normal workflow process. The framework we will describe makes a difference. It also interprets XPDL in its own way and presents to the user an interface based on process definition and current state of the process instance.

FROM BPMN DIRECTLY TO IMPLEMENTATION-THE GRAPHICAL WAY 205

Heinz Lienhard and Bruno Bütler, ivyTeam-SORECOGroup, Switzerland

The authors state that BPMN process description must become what the name (Business Process Modeling Notation) actually implies: a true model that can be simulated, validated and immediately turned into a real-time application. Hence, the truly important step is implementing the process just as transparently and comprehensively as modeling of the process in the first place. This means using graphical objects as much as possible, right up to implementation. It will be shown how this can be done.

WORKFLOW MINING: DEFINITIONS, TECHNIQUES, AND FUTURE DIRECTIONS 213

Clarence A. Ellis, University of Colorado, Boulder, USA; Kwang-Hoon Kim, Kyonggi University, Korea; Aubrey J. Rembert, University of Colorado, Boulder, USA

Workflow Management Systems help to execute, monitor and manage work process flow and execution. These systems, as they are executing, keep a record of who does what and when (e.g. log of events). The activity of using computer software to examine these records, and deriving various structural data results is called workflow mining. This chapter defines, illustrates, and extends the concepts of workflow mining. The authors also present typical techniques for mining.

BUSINESS INTEGRATION USING STATE BASED ASYNCHRONOUS SERVICES 229

Alan McNamara, Badja Consulting and Dr. M. Ali Chishti, Defence Housing Authority, Australia

Architectural principles promote the use of interfaces—a facade behind which the implementation can be hidden. Current Service Oriented Service (SOA) analysis methods are based on providing synchronous services to expose transactional processes. However, this analysis method does not give a robust model for services implemented through workflow. The service model presented in the OASIS ASAP [1] standard provides a good basis for the business integration interface, but the state based service model is not fully defined. This paper provides an analysis of the requirements for business integration services for long running processes, and proposes how the service model presented in the ASAP standard can be extended to satisfy these requirements. Practical examples from industry are used to illustrate these points.

TOWARD WORKFLOW BLOCK ACTIVITY PATTERNS FOR REUSE IN WORKFLOW DESIGN 249

Lucinéia Heloisa Thom, Cirano Iochpe; Federal University of Rio Grande do Sul, Brazil; Vinícius Amaral, Daniel Viero, iProcess, Brazil

Research on workflow patterns has attracted increasing attention mainly because of the advantages of reusing patterns. The most extensively studied are in the field of control/data flow patterns as well as resource and application–oriented patterns. Such patterns are being used not only in business/workflow process modeling but also in critical evaluations of workflow languages and workflow tools. However, a lot less research can be found relating workflow design to a set of recurrent business process "pieces" or "parts" that must be atomically executed by the workflow process (e.g., an activity request execution and a notification activity). Although one can precisely characterize the semantics of such business process "pieces" and they have to be recurrently re-designed in practically every workflow modeling process, there is no known research relating these business process structures to workflow patterns.

Using Process Execution Data in Application Support   261
Udhai Reddy, Infosys Technologies, India

This paper is based on research and prototyping on using process execution data for assessing the priority and impact of system or application incidents (Trouble Tickets) to strategic business goals in application support. The research has been aimed at identifying the impact of the incident on the strategic business objectives using the business process execution data and process definition. The research is still in progress with respect to refinement of the models. This paper is a reflection of the status at a point where the first pilot was conducted.

Constructing a Workflow Application System to Conduct CMMI Processes in Software Development Teams   269
Dr. Yang Chi-Tsai, Flowring, Taiwan

The paper describes the software architecture, supporting software components and the analysis methodology to map the processes in CMMI (Capability Maturity Model Integration) PAs (process areas) to WfMS (workflow management system) process definition. The work described in the article is motivated by the idea to automate the software processes and provide sufficient tool support for the operations of CMMI ML3 software organizations. It demonstrates the capability of WfMS to enhance the whole lifecycle quality of product development and project delivery in software development organizations. In terms of contribution to the information technology, it gives several workflow integration scenarios with external application systems such as document management system (DMS) for document revision control, CASE (computer-aided software engineering) tools for issue tracking, and configuration management.

Section 3—Directory and Appendices

- The **Authors' Appendix** provides the contact details and biographies of the valuable contributors to this book. Each is a recognized expert in his or her respective field. You may contact them if you wish to pursue a discussion on their particular topics.
- The chapters on the **WfMC Structure and Membership** describe the Coalition's background, achievements and membership structure and sets out the obligations between members and the Coalition
- **WfMC Membership Directory:** WfMC members in good standing as of January 2006 are listed here. Full Members have the membership benefit of optionally including details on their products or services.

Our thanks and acknowledgements extend to not only the authors whose works are published in this Handbook, but also to the many more excellent submissions that could not be published due to lack of space.

Layna Fischer, Editor and Publisher, Future Strategies Inc.
Executive Director, WfMC

Section 1

The World of Workflow

and

Business Process Management

BPM in Context:
Now and in the Future

Jon Pyke, WfMC Chair, United Kingdom

1. PROCESS TECHNOLOGY—PUT IN PERSPECTIVE

Introduction

This paper looks at the various technologies that make up the burgeoning Business Process Management (BPM) market and explores the impact new methods of deployment and design will have on products and how those changes could affect end users. The paper also provides non-technical readers with a better understanding of what the all encompassing term "Business Process Management" means by explaining the following terms in detail:

- Business Process Management (BPMA)[1]
- Business Process Modelling (BPMO)
- Business Activity Monitoring (BAM)
- Business Operations Management (BOM)

We then draw the common threads together to give a concise picture of what process technology is all about. For completeness we will also take a look at the BPM standards world and try and make sense of what's happening and what impact that may have.

There are certain other technologies considered to be a vital part of the BPM landscape for example:

- Enterprise Application Integration (EAI)
- Web Services (all aspects including orchestration)
- Business Intelligence
- Application Servers
- XML

But despite their importance from a technology perspective we are not going to explain them in this document and the reason is quite simple—they don't matter! They don't matter to the business user—or the people who need to use technology to get some other business related task done, they see BPM as a way of managing cases or tasks in a predefined sequence; getting the right information to the right place at the right time to meet a business need. To them BPM is something that reduces the risk of error, gets tasks completed sooner and more effectively and makes the whole business or running a business easier and more manageable. The integration needs don't matter to them, Web Services could be anything and as for XML; who knows? We are going to address only those aspects of Process Technologies that the end-user cares about—*getting the job done.*

---

[1] Abbreviations are those of the author—to try to differentiate one BPM from another

One other component that was considered for inclusion in this paper was Business Process Measurement. Process Measurement is a vital aspect of any organization wishing to improve its execution of business processes—the constant feed-back loop and process life cycles are essential if the project to address the process needs of the organization is to deliver measurable benefits, however, we decided not to go down the six sigma or TQM paths since that is outside the scope of this document. However, we do look at feedback mechanisms, simulation, instrumentation etc., later on in this paper as part of the future direction of the Process Technology world.

THE CONTEXT

A good deal of the technology that underpins Process Automation concepts stems from the early efforts of the workflow community. Many of the offerings then were little more than simple document routing and integration tools. Companies such as Staffware, FileNet, Fujitsu, Global 360 (eiStream) and IBM have since spent much time and effort turning their software into full-blown, robust, scalable, transactional BPM products. These incorporate all the features and functions that are generally considered necessary to design, execute and monitor a wide range of processes. They can deal with anything from simplistic procedures through to highly complex line of business applications. Just as you would expect, these products derive from a wide range of underlying methods and architectures.

But before we can try to unravel where all the pieces fit, we need to clarify what Process Based Technology is (we will look at a definition of the basic components below). Well, it is not new. Business software has long supported major business processes. What *has* changed is the realization that business managers need to understand and improve those processes. This is the easiest way for their organizations to be competitive, adaptable and responsive and for them to manage costs. Using process-based software is the key to achieving that.

So we are not trying to solve any new problems—just to solve them differently. The old way was to create isolated 'stove pipe' solutions. These were rigid, difficult to maintain, costly to set up and, worst of all, obsolete by the time they arrived. We want to solve problems cheaply, quickly and effectively. How? By seeing those problems as a set of well-defined and integrated processes. In May 2003, Nicholas Carr wrote a paper for the *Harvard Business Review*[2] in which he argued that it is a mistake to assume that as IT's potency and ubiquity have increased, so too has its strategic value. What makes a resource truly strategic—what gives it the capacity to be the basis for a sustained competitive advantage—is not ubiquity but scarcity. You gain an edge over rivals only by having or doing something that they can't have or do. By now, the core functions of IT—data storage, data processing and data transport—have become available and affordable to all.

---

[2] Harvard Business Review, Publication Date: May 1, 2003 Author(s): Nicholas G. Carr Type: Harvard Business Review Article

Carr's article spawned a "may-bug"[3] industry of counter argument and re-buke—books were written, behemoths were angered—so this paper is not going to enter the fray except to say that what if Carr is right? That buying more IT simply keeps you in that game? What that means, of course, is that if an organization is only going to get to a "me too" position by spending vast sums on IT infrastructure then they need to look at what it is that will give them the edge and apply technology to that aspect to gain the competitive advantage—the obvious candidate is *process*—the way you do things—the backbone of your organization.

Applying IT to process technology is going to give you that competitive advantage; it will show a return on the investment—it will keep you in front—and that is where the value will come from—and that is what I believe the Process Revolution is all about.

2. WHAT PROCESS TECHNOLOGY COMPRISES

The Components

What are the basic components that contribute the ability of manage, monitor and automate core business processes?

Business Process Management

Dave McCoy of the Gartner Group encapsulated the essence of what BPMA is back in March 2001 when he said: "...**a blending of process management/workflow with application integration technology ... to support rich human interaction and deep application connectivity**."

I would go a stage further and define the technology thus:

> "**Specialist Rapid Application Development Software for:**
> - **the automation of rules-based processes**
> - **routing of documents, information and tasks**
> - **within and between organizations**
> - **in a timely manner**
> - **fully integrated with complementary technologies and legacy systems**
>
> **for significant, measurable benefits**."

So BPMA is a piece of technology that allows us to create a process layer, which provides a level of process abstraction, and removes the business processes from the *control* of applications. So, instead of having each application being in charge of a set of processes, and trying to subjugate adjacent applications, to drive its processes, BPMA takes the control of the process away from the individual applications, and make them equal peers, subjugated to a BPMA layer that controls the execution of the processes, and delegates tasks or activities to individual people and applications as dictated by the design and needs of the underlying business process.

In order to do this well, BPMA needs to support all the attributes of a business process. For example, it needs to be able to:

---

[3] Driven purely by the instinct for self-preservation and thankfully short lived

- Manage applications in parallel as well as series
- It needs to manage people-intensive applications
- Inside and outside the organization
- Continuous and discrete, and allow processes to change over time.

BPM can be sub-divided into two sub categories:

- EBPM
- HBPM

EBPM:

eBPM is enterprise class Process Management—nowadays this is found in expensive and complex integration suites, such as TIBCO, and have become less of a business driven solution. However, there are certain vendors who are championing the standalone message of the independent process layer and in doing so addressing the needs of the end users—vendors in this space include Global 360 (formally eiStream), Metastorm and Savvion.

HBPM:

hBPM is the hosted model or Process-on-Demand. Process-on-Demand delivers a simple-to-use Process Automation technology, where, and when it is needed. Deploying BPM as a managed service along with all the other services that can be found in today's organizations. Instead of buying expensive software licenses and supporting infrastructure, the users subscribe to the processes and services they need when they need them—ensuring cost effective deployment and efficient project roll-out. The ideal solution to the small to mid sized organizations.

Business Process Modeling

Virtually all BPMA solutions have a Process Modeling Component. Its main purpose is to assist the end user in documenting processes. These processes can be defined "as is" or "as you would like". The basic idea behind tools supplied by BPMA vendors is that you can use these tools as an alternative to writing code—a sort of "picture writes a thousand lines of code" approach—if you can draw a flowchart, you can define and automate a Business Process.

There is a school of thought that suggests these tools should be outside of the BPMA product portfolios—this is the view promoted (with a high degree of success) by the Modeling Tools vendors.

The answer as to which is a better approach—BPMA approach or BPMO approach lies, as you would expect somewhere between the two extremes. Modeling tools supplied by the BPMA vendors will let you build process definitions that will work with the specific BPMA engine you are deploying and will extract the best from the product and its features. BPMO will let you model to a more sophisticated level, but will not be a straightforward to implement—if that's what you decide to do.

The worst possible scenario is to try and use two products—you will give up—either find another way of defining the process or be willing to accept a compromise.

Business Activity Monitoring

BAM is driven by the needs for organizations to find ways of overcoming transactional lag. This need appears to be driven by the general requirement to improve customer satisfaction, to comply with regulatory requirements, shorten time to market, get a 360-degree view of the company etc. BAM is closely aligned to BPMA since the general belief is that most activities are part of a process and by monitoring the activities you will, by default, monitor the processes to see where the bottlenecks are, see where service levels are being missed resulting in process feedback and performance improvement.

The focus of most BAM tools is improving the efficacy of business decisions and facilitating fast and well informed responses. The benefits derived are beneficial to all organizations regardless of industry. Despite offering myriad business benefits the majority of BAM solutions currently available do not go far enough.

BAM breaks down into two key options.

Option 1—When the process cannot be extracted.

In the following diagram the internal systems are part of a "business process" but they are silo-based applications. Ordinarily, BPM vendors would argue that these applications would be better served if they were controlled by an independent process layer—a good idea—but not always feasible. The answer to this problem is to let the BAM tool monitor and manage the interaction of these systems and trigger exceptions and pass the exception processing to the BPMS. Once the exception is "caught" it can be passed to BPM tool for processing.

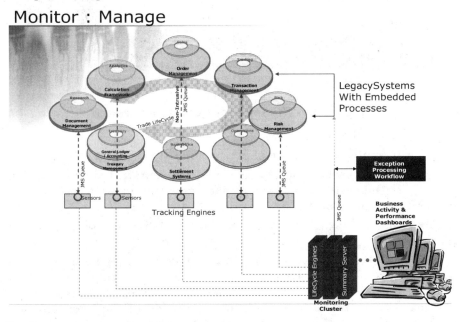

Monitor : Manage

Figure 1—Monitor/Manage

Option 2—When the process can be extracted.

In this particular scenario BPM users have recognized the need to re-engineer their systems and take a more process centric approach to implementation. This is the natural BPM vendor sweet spot and where a process suite solution fits best. Where the key differentiator comes in now is that this solution would offer a "real time" option rather than a "near" real time solution provided by reporting tools. The advantages of this are numerous and include:

- Real time process monitoring and managing—allowing for automated solutions and dynamic rerouting of work
- Easier integration into systems management systems such as Tivoli
- Extending the monitoring to sub flows (those triggered by EAI demands of process orchestration (web services))

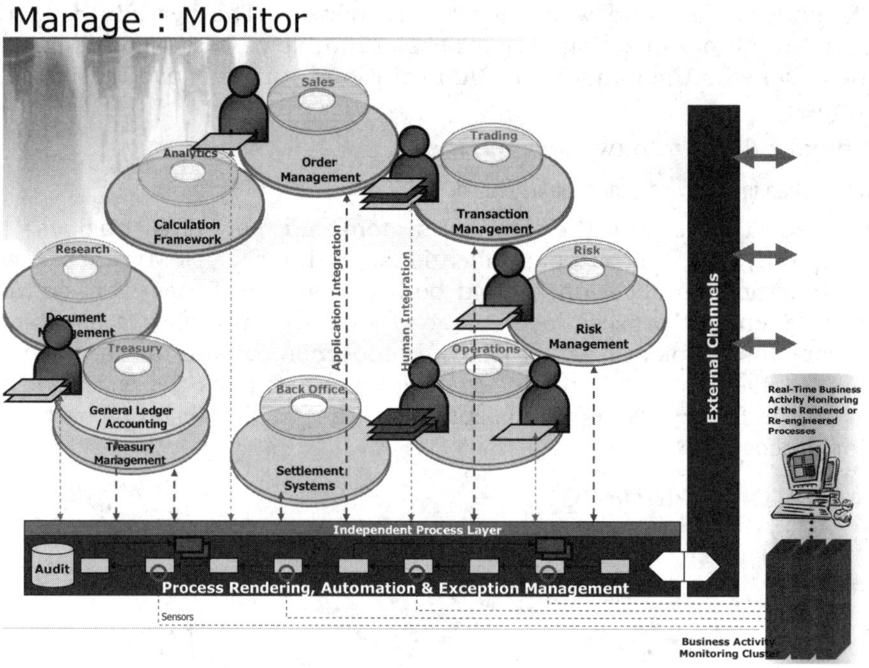

Manage : Monitor

Figure 2—The Process Centric approach

But there is a third option.

Option 3 is a combination of the above—composite processes.

There are situations where parts of an enterprise can be reengineered (option 2) and where there are certain silo applications that cannot be touched (option 1) but need to be part of an overall BPM strategy.

Complex Order Management in Telecommunications is probably as good a real life scenario as any to use by way of example.

In a COM situation, there are many back office stand-alone systems which are an important part of the provisioning process yet they cannot be fully integrated into the process for a whole host of reasons—complexity being one of the main ones. Yet despite them being outside of the managed process they do run "micro" (think of them as sub) processes which need to be monitored. If a delay occurs in one of these systems, the impact on the automated process could be very significant—so being able to monitor and manage the interactions between the "external" applications the main process can be modeled and controlled far more easily. I doubt this could be done in products as they exist today—yet the solution is relatively simple.

Composite Scenario

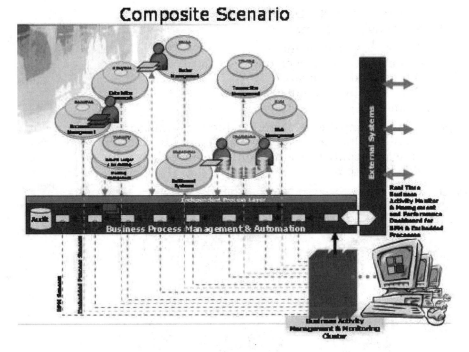

Figure 3—The Composite Approach

I believe this is what true BAM is all about—being able to manage and monitor processes of every shape and hue and adjust the operation of the business accordingly.

Business Operations Management

BOM concentrates on the needs of managers running teams of people. Basically, BOM accepts work from any third-party source, including major BPMA engines and applies a set of business rules on how that work is assigned to individuals, taking into account the available resources, their varying skill levels and efficiency, plus service level objectives. BOM also provides critical support for firms' compliance objectives, automatically supporting the enforcement of regulatory controls and gathering the evidence to prove that work was carried out in a compliant manner.

One critical aspect of BOM solutions is that it can be used as a stand-alone package, which means that if you do not have a full BPMA or BAM implementation you can link a BOM package to Line-of-Business systems so it provides effective management information for a wide range of audiences; from team leaders to senior executives. BOM provides a single view of all work, monitoring items from any source; paper, telephone calls, BPMA engine; e-mail and so on; to provide an integrated approach to work and resource management. As a result of this coordination, all work is managed, tracked and reported upon; enabling an optimal utilization of available resources.

BOM breaks down into three main subcomponents:

- Operational intelligence looks after:
  - Forecasting and prediction services
  - Consolidation and summaries
  - Reporting

- Performance KPIs, Dashboard integration etc.
- Work management handles:
  - Resource Management
  - Performance Management
  - Quality and Compliance
  - Customer Event Management
- Production Planning
  - Critical components of the Production Management component should include accurate capacity planning, short interval scheduling of resources against work, and load balancing of the available resources.

The Convergence Picture

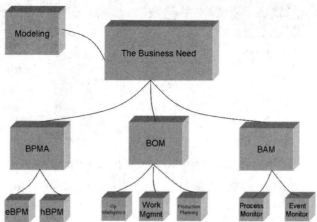

Figure 4—How the key components fit with the business need

Figure 4 drills down further into the key components so, on the face of it, it looks more complicated than ever but it really is quite simple:

Architecture of Deployment

This is a semi-technical bit. The following diagram shows what a typical IT architecture looks like with all the bits mentioned above included.

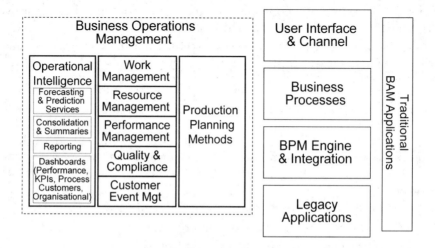

3. THE FUTURE

Two key factors will have an effect on the world of process technology.

Enterprise Process Analytics

At the high end, what we referred to as eBPM earlier, there will be less differentiation of large scale BPM engines. They will all:

- Be very scalable,
- Support key standards
- Have good integration capabilities
- Be infrastructure products

The key differentiators will be in the areas of simulation and statistics—in short Business Process Analytics. Organizations are beginning to realize that although they can implement BPMA and workflow solutions without analytics capabilities, they do not have a complete end-to-end solution. Their BPMA system does not help their strategic planning nor enable them to accurately develop contingency plans for opportunistic and threatening scenarios. They do not have real insight into their processes or the outcomes they produce let alone an automated way of addressing them.

Analytics give business managers and executives the ability to track and measure performance based on real-time feedback of their processes. This gives them real insight into how the organization operating. Once good and accurate analytics are in place, end users can make informed decisions because they are presented with issues that need to be addressed, as well as with the context so they can take the right action. They have the ability to "drill down" into an anomaly and to look at the information from different dimensions giving them greater understanding of the "information behind the information." Forecasting is made possible through ongoing statistical data capture, and reporting functions ensure real-time and predictive information is available.

The powerful combination of real-time process analytics and Business Operations Management means that users can:

- Adjust workflow to changing business dynamics
- Move from managing business processes to managing business process lifecycles
- Tie together Business objectives, strategic planning, process modeling, workflow, application/content management and analytics so that they interact
- Develop feedback loops for change management and incremental optimization of business processes
- Eliminate gap between strategy and business objectives
- Ensure workflow and processes support key business objectives
- Gain the control of operations to manage process lifecycles from end-to-end

Process-On-Demand

The lower end, referred to as hBPM, is where we will see a lot of innovation and rapid growth in the next three or four years. Process-on-demand is going to be a very interesting market segment. There is a general perception, especially amongst smaller organizations, that BPM is not for them; it's too expensive to buy, too difficult to implement, needs an expensive infrastructure and takes far too long to deliver real business benefits.

There are numerous examples of products being used as expensive alarm clocks or automating one or two steps of a process—the three-step process is not at all uncommon. Likewise, many implementations are over-engineered. This makes them unusable and unmanageable—hundreds of steps in a single process—not even broken down to sub-processes. There's one other problem that needs to be addressed—companies are no longer willing or indeed able to "roll their own" solutions. Building systems from the ground up is no longer an acceptable business practice and it certainly isn't cost effective.

So there is some confusion as to what BPM is best suited for, how it should be deployed and to what level. As a result there are many "enterprise deployments" that simply aren't!

Words and figures don't match when licenses sold are compared with licenses deployed. That's not to suggest any exaggeration on the part of vendors; just that the expectations and vision of the buyers is seldom met. The projects just don't roll out as planned—and this happens time and time again. So what can be done to address the problem?

Well, you could use what you need when you need it—sound simple enough and what makes it so is Process-on-Demand technology; making BPM a *business commodity* rather than infrastructure.

Process-on-Demand delivers a simple-to-use Process Automation technology, where, and when it is needed. Deploying BPM as a managed service along with all the other services that can be found in today's organizations. Instead of buying expensive software licenses and supporting infrastructure the users subscribe to the processes and services they need when they need them—ensuring cost effective deployment and efficient project roll-out. The IT departments get what they need and the end-users get what they need. The ideal solution to the small- to mid-sized organizations.

The idea behind process-on-demand is the concept of the schema-driven enterprise. All data is based on XML structures. XML is the basis for almost all development of new process-based and integration software tools. A schema (XSD) is essentially a way of formally describing the elements in an XML document. This description is then used to verify that each item of content in a document adheres to the description of the element in which the content is to be placed.

By defining all of the rules, inputs and interactions in an XSD, it is possible to dynamically define a business process—and then execute it—by defining the forms and documents used by an organization electronically—using simple drag and drop techniques. Rapid development, rapid deployment and rapid return on investment.

4. Standards

During the last couple of years there has been a significant rise in the amount of work being undertaken to define standards for process-based technology. You need only look at the number of bodies involved to get a feel for the scale of the problem—12 years ago there was only one body, now there are more than 10. The standards specifications have also grown. Those for the WfMC's reference models were, on average, 40 pages long. The average size of these new specifications is around 100 pages. I won't mention the complexity at this stage—it's too scary. Yet all we have done is to create confusion. There is confusion over which standards fit where and which apply to what situation. Unanswered are the questions such as—do they compete, are they complementary, will we have to pay for them?

There is no suggestion here that standards are a bad thing—on the contrary—no-one is questioning the needs for standards. There is significant value to be had from such standards as BPEL (Business Process Execution Language), BPMN (Business Process Modeling Notation), WfXML, XPDL and others; but unless those responsible for setting the standards start to work together to consolidate them there will be a substantial loss of interest in implementing them.

There will be a convergence of standards coalescing around:

- BPEL
- BPMN
- WfXML
- XPDL

However, unless standards are of clear benefit to use, they are at the least a distraction. At worst, they could lead you into a damaging technology lock-in. Dave Hollingsworth (Chair of the WfMC Technical Committee) summed it up very neatly when he said "the correct approach is to recognize what standards are needed where in the architecture, and for what purpose...Product vendors will adopt them if they add value—and this stems from having a thought through underlying architecture that clearly identifies the value and purpose of each standard."[4]

5 CONCLUSIONS

Most IT departments view BPM as part of the technical infrastructure. It is fair to say that many BPM solution vendors see it this way as well. The technology is seen, primarily, as a mechanism for integrating systems and a way of developing new applications. While this "positioning" or understanding may be true to a certain extent, it certainly isn't the full story. There's a business need to be addressed as well; the needs of the end-user.

The end-users, the people who need to use technology to get some other business-related task done, see BPM as a way of managing cases or tasks in a predefined sequence; getting the right information to the right place at the right time to meet a business need. To them it is something that reduces the risk of error, gets tasks completed sooner and more effectively and makes the whole business or running a business easier and more manageable.

As stated earlier, BPM is perceived to be expensive, complex to deploy and seldom used in the way the sponsor envisaged. There are numerous examples of products being used as expensive alarm clocks or automating one or two steps of a process—the three-step process is not at all uncommon. Likewise, many implementations are over-engineered. This makes them unusable and unmanageable—hundreds of steps in a single process—not even broken down to sub-processes. There's one other problem that needs to be

---

[4] "The Workflow Reference Model: 10 years On" by David Dave Hollingsworth, *Workflow Handbook 2004*, ed. Fischer, Layna

addressed—companies are no longer willing or indeed able to "roll their own" solutions. Building systems from the ground up is no longer an acceptable business practice and it certainly isn't cost effective.

So there is some confusion as to what BPM is best suited for, how it should be deployed and to what level. So what is the problem we are trying to solve? There are two:

- The needs of the Business Process Owner—the CEO—help in making the vision a reality
- But we must also address the needs of the Data Owner—the CIO

The CEO: in tough economic times, one thing moves to the top of the CEO's agenda—the need to improve business processes. Rapid payback and quick return on investment become crucial.

As well as reducing costs, the CEO needs to improve business controls, and provide quicker response to customers. And above all else, the CEO needs to deliver improved business processes by harmonizing with existing infrastructures and technologies, such as ERP and CRM. The only effective way of achieving these objectives is to improve the effectiveness and flexibility of end-to-end processes.

By implementing BPM, the business community will be able to build and execute processes that are designed with customers in mind, deliver better quality, faster and at lower costs, and retain competitive advantage by being able to execute processes that deliver the business strategy. The CEO doesn't care about systems integration or the concepts of straight through processing, however valid that may be. But the CEO does care about monitoring how the business is performing, being able to react to changes in the market, handling exceptions quickly and effectively and having a complete view of the organization.

The CIO has the task of making sure the needs of the CEO are fully met quickly, effectively and with zero disruption to the business. Systems implemented in today's rapidly changing technology world must show fast ROI and bring benefits to the bottom line, without having to discard what works.

Providing technology that enables users to define the business process in clear understandable notation is an important aspect of the technology, but it's only part of the solution. Being able to execute that process, facilitate simple integration with legacy systems and commercially available packages and monitor/manage how those processes are executing are also vital components. Furthermore, BPM as defined here, enables the CIO to implement new applications quickly and tie the front-office applications and the back-office systems. This reduces maintenance costs, time-to-deploy and makes the IT function far more responsive to the business needs.

The future for BPM technology is bright—arguably it will give the biggest return on investment of any technology deployed to date.

The advent of Process-on-demand technology and good analytics coupled with solid workforce management principles will enhance this capability still further.

There is not a single organization, large or small, that will be unaffected by the unstoppable deployment of ubiquitous process technology.

Practical Lessons in Managing Real BPM Innovation

Fred van Leeuwen, DCE Consultants, Netherlands

INTRODUCTION

Fred van Leeuwen, who has been involved with BPM for the past 15 years, poses the question[1]:

"How accurate are the assumptions around our BPM-projects?"

When introduced, Workflow technology was seen as a revolutionary approach, but the market for it grew steadily rather than explosively, and it did not take off when we started to call it Business Process Management.

"It is really an *evolution*," says Fred van Leeuwen, who, during his career at DCE Consultants, contributed to the fifteen-year long development of this expertise.

Why has the idea of real-time steering information, placed in the hands of process workers, not materialised as quickly and fully as it could have, and what can we do to make it more successful?

COMPETITIVE CHANGE

Prepare for competitive change, using the very real innovation of work that BPM can offer.

Real-time Process Managing—that was what it was all about, and that was the goal we all envisaged. According to Fred van Leeuwen, Managing Consultant with DCE Consultants, the rise of Workflow and Business Process Re-engineering (BPR) more or less coincided, and so we thought—Fred included—that an explosive growth in the use of Workflow technology would befall us. That sudden breakthrough never really transpired. Fred thought it must be the millennium bug taking up all the resources and—after that in major European countries—the introduction of the euro. But, by now we realise the change capacity that became available after these major undertakings still did not lead to a Workflow surge, and neither when Gartner relaunched it in new packaging as Business Process Management. We must reconcile ourselves to the fact that Workflow will continue as an evolution, and learn to take the advantages from that pace of growth.

Incorrect assumptions

The idea behind Business Process Management or Workflow is very relevant, but what are the reasons it did not break through in the manner we had expected? In the fullness of time Fred became aware that in many BPM-projects the real-time Process Management did not have much of a role to play. A lot of Workflow implementations did not advance much beyond the point of securing the process and integrating the traditional silo systems. Do

---

1 This interview by Robbert Hoeffnagel was originally published in Dutch in the *Business Process Magazine* by Array Publications, June 2005, Edition No. 22.

we absolutely need Business Process Management technology for that last challenge? The answer is that in many cases an EAI broker may be more appropriate. We have spent a lot of energy connecting the patchwork of existing systems and doing so-called 'Internal EDI projects'. Even with today's clear call for 'closing the business chain' one often does not really opt for much more than data interchange.

What happened? In the first instance we often worked on the basis of living in a rational and competitive world, but is that really true? To put that into perspective, was it really that vital for companies to start serving their customers better, or did they have plenty of room for serving their own internal interest? Consider the telecommunications and the utility sectors. Throughout the world large numbers of (semi-)state companies became deregulated and converted into commercial organisations. Did such companies really become customer-orientated? It does not seem to be the case. Their aim is seen as being to take up strong positions with regard to infrastructures and to control the customer channel. It revolved more around that than the interest of the consumer. We have seen something similar with most financial institutions. For most private consumers the products of these companies are simply too obscure. We assumed customers would make rational choices and have at their disposal information to do just that, but practice proves it does not work that way.

No doubt we must look at it from a different angle. The whole concept of putting customer service central was something of an illusion. Nowadays companies are strongly orientated towards short term shareholder values, and government institutions towards symptom-fighting in society. But for how long can one get away with that? Eventually perhaps you only build real value when your organisation adds value to the human way of life, and the word 'human' can be replaced by 'customer' as well as 'employee'. Possibly that is the most important factor for a company to be sustainably successful. That way the risk of blowing bubbles in stakeholder values will also diminish.

Two world wars

Let us once more look at the whole idea of real-time Process Management. This is only realisable when the silo walls existing within companies are broken down. By definition that can only be achieved by top management. Why? Because only at that level do the silos join. For years Fred was been puzzled as to why the silos are not tackled at that level. Does top management not want it to happen, or are these managers incapable? Fred has reached the conclusion that many top managers simply lack insight, particularly when taking into account the older generation of managers. The traditional top manager keeps viewing BPM as something technical that must be delegated rapidly and completely, while the real issue, of course, is managing interests; pre-eminently a management task. In practice silos are often institutionalised, misusing BPM-techniques. We have created all the management dashboards, often informing us on silo-bound performance. The sense of urgency to really manage process-wide is lacking in many cases.

Another observation is that many companies mainly react on incidents. As already stated, there is not a lot of company strategy focusing on sustainable improvement of the external position. Too rarely do we see a real pro-active approach. In this there is a strong relation with the learning abilities of an organisation. *Built to Last; Successful Habits of Visionary Companies*[2] by James Collins and Jerry Porras is a very interesting and recommended book. It is based on research as to why some companies are successful over the longer term, whilst others are not. It is remarkable that the authors' conclusions on organisational development can be mapped almost one-to-one against human development.

An important feature of strong organisations appears to be that they were not very successful from the start, but have grown through all sorts of crises. These crises have conditioned the survival instinct of these organisations in a way that is very similar to human-beings going through radical experiences. Apparently an organisation has a personality and learning abilities. That is an intrinsic power the authors found within organisations that had successfully endured both World Wars and the Big Recession. Adversity seems to be a requirement for developing a strong character.

On the other side of the spectrum we find young companies that have been striking a goldmine. They can be very successful but are often rather vulnerable on the longer term. Managers and employees of such young organisations have not closely experienced the various aspects of business life. They have limited life experience and when it comes down to it they are not too capable of handling real stress situations.

The real value of BPM?

Today in company strengths the difference is made by people. Too often, however, the human factor is primarily seen as a potential cause of mistakes and not as the carrier of creative ability. If we view man in the last light, we might find it easier to accept the possibility of human error, since it can be compensated by creative- and improvisation abilities. No doubt you can't have one without the other, but for many process architects this might be a hard thought to digest.

Perhaps that is the real role for BPM—to relieve people from unworthy repetitive actions in order to release their improvising talents on more worthy actions. We might well face a new challenge then—in many work processes there is a rather obscure line between the repetitive and the creative part. In other words—is the product or service defined in such a way that we are able to handle routine cases as such? The whole idea is to modularise products, service and processes in such a way as to give the customer the suggestion of custom-made goods, while in fact we are really mass-producing. In other words, to apply the tricks of the car industry. In a well-organised process, the employee can dedicate his attention to fulfilling the customer experience. Until now the mass custom-made practice has not been adopted too well in the service-industry.

Another factor to consider is the manager, or more precisely his capability to lead the required change. How did the manager get to his position? In many cases he was selected based on a close match to the rules of the game within his company. The problem is these rules are usually based on the rules of the past, while external circumstances are continually changing. Very often there will be a tension between today's change requirements and the qualities a manager has at his disposal. It is interesting to apply the same analy-

---

[2] HarperCollins Publishers; 1st edition (January 15, 1997)

sis to today's widespread misuse of so-called 'best practices'. In reality, companies often end up copying a practice they see through the rearview mirror—adopting a past practice fitting someone else's strength.

In *On Competition*[3] Michael Porter points out that such a dual mistake leads to 'verelendung' in the market sector—a development where companies simply keep cutting one another's margins. This type of operational improvement can be very harmful if not combined with simultaneous effort towards sustainable gains. Sustainable improvement requires insight into the unique strengths of the individual company. Managers must be able to see beyond the daily reality, looking through the external *and* the internal situation.

Measure by stories

Our companies are always busy improving and changing. The question is—shouldn't we establish a better balance in the ambition behind these changes? In the practice of BPM we run a very real risk of applying a rather one-sided instrumental approach. Quite often only clearly measurable values seem to be important, but what about the human factor? Is his sense of meaning being taken into account? Expressing an improvement in numbers is fine, but if we really want to achieve something it might be advisable to add a dimension to these figures. This might be a story about the type of experience we would like to give our customers, something about the way our employees will experience their work, or the behavior in which employees express their sense of meaning. Once we manage to achieve that, the targets are not just numbers; they will have meaningful appeal to our staff and this will determine the level of energy they contribute towards the change. Today's business climate seems to lead many companies in a direction where there is little room for human value. In our knowledge-based economy, sustainable results can only be achieved when this trend is reversed. One of the ways a manager can contribute to this is—measuring by listening to stories. Very interesting all these numbers, but what is their value to our customers, our company, our employees?

In the minds of Western managers, the idea of telling stories may seem woolly and inefficient. That is a misconception. The issue is—do we understand the true nature of process innovation? In spite of all the diagrams and instruments needed, people are the decisive factor in most of the work, and that is certainly the case for work innovation. Predicting whether innovation will fail or succeed is not too hard for an experienced manager. One prerequisite is that the manager will feel at ease with a situation where his influence is mainly indirect.

Now we have learned that the practice of Business Process Management is emerging gradually rather than radically, let us at least make sure we do it well. We should attempt to work in parallel on operational and strategic improvement, and in any case we should not simply follow the herd. Ideally we should reinforce the unique capability of our company, allowing ample space for the human component in that strength. In order to achieve this we might need more than process engineers. We might also need work architects and designers who know how to shape the work environment in such a way that it will trigger workers to fulfill maximum achievement.

---

[3] Harvard Business School Press Book; (September 30, 1998)

Workflow—the Compliance Project Engine

Arnaud Bezancon, Advantys, France

INTRODUCTION

Businesses today are required by law to comply with a vast range of regulations and standards. They have to implement new procedures to ensure full accountability, maintain records of all decisions taken and analyze any deviation through the use of audits.

An organization's ability to manage compliance and governance projects efficiently has become key issue which impacts directly on their business performance.

This chapter highlights a number of processes required by legislation such as Sarbanes Oxley, HIPAA & BASEL 2, IT governance standards such as COBIT, ITIL & ISO 17799, as well as corporate project management.

Automating this type of procedure with the help of a workflow solution is an essential part of any compliance project. Workflow must also be intrinsically linked to the existing IS, as well as a certain number of consultation and audit reports in order to cover all the requirements of the regulations and governance standards.

WORKFLOW – A COMPLIANCE PORTAL

Compliance is largely reliant upon the application and implementation of processes, meaning organizations concerned have to choose between:
- Finding manual hardcopy or electronic solutions,
- Investing in procedure-specific solutions,
- Implementing workflow software covering all the processes via a single Portal.

Manual solutions quickly reveal their limitations in terms of costs and resources.

Specific solutions for each procedure provide short-term answers, but are relatively costly in terms of initial investment, integration and maintenance. Furthermore, end users are regularly required to work with a large number of applications. Ten or more processes are often necessary in a particular IT compliance or governance project.

Using a workflow solution as a compliance portal provides not only financial gains in terms of procedural implementation, but also facilitates support for the changes involved in the project. Users all enter at the same point to initiate requests or perform actions within the compliance procedure, while statistics and other reports allow the various processes to be cross-referenced and compared. Finally, reduced training time means the new procedure will be simpler to deploy.

Speed is also of vital importance—laws and regulations change and so does the way a company is organized. A workflow solution allows for adjustments to be made in the definition of a procedure with far more flexibility than a singe, procedure-specific solution, and it provides the company's internal teams with the skills required to make the adjustments within a relatively short timeframe.

Accountability is also a key part of these laws, regulations and standards: auditors often want to know "who did what and when". Most workflow software provides a high degree of accountability allowing completed forms and actions implemented at each stage of the process to be traced back.

Using a workflow portal to generate the process part of a compliance project means many technical difficulties encountered when backtracking requests submitted and decisions taken.

SARBANES OXLEY ACT

Complying with SOX is an ongoing process for any business. It implies changes to internal organization and formal guidelines regarding the flow of information and, because the number of processes can rapidly escalate, developing specific measures for each individual process is not viable in terms of time and expense.

In addition, the process workflows need constant updating to integrate internal changes at both organization and IS levels. The SOX workflow is a constant preoccupation for any business.

Workflow means compliance with the Sarbanes Oxley Act is easier for two main reasons:

- rapid implementation of SOX-related processes,
- compatibility of the workflow solution with the technical constraints imposed by the application of the SOX standard.

Security

- authentication on the workflow portal is fully compliant with the company's security policy,
- access to information depends on the user's profile & access rights,
- forms can include certificate-based electronic signatures meaning information sent and user ID are secure,
- secure access to physical data storage on servers complies with the SOX standard.

Audit trail

- all actions performed during process execution are logged and stored,
- each version of all modified forms can be saved for maximum control,
- files and data circulating in the process can be exported at any point to third-party electronic data management systems.

Availability

- the workflow engine can be integrated into high-availability systems, including Web Farms.
- data and process replication also allows a failure recover plan to be implemented.

HIPAA

HIPAA compliance involves deploying a considerable number of processes and setting up technical safeguards.

The costs generated by HIPAA compliance projects can be dramatically reduced by implementing workflow. Instead of hiring new personnel to perform human-based processes or developing dozens of specific software applications, health care organizations can deploy fully compliant automated processes.

The workflow portal provides real time request follow-up, action tracking and audit trail functions as well as connectors to build gateways with legacy systems like HIS, databases, directories and ERPs.

Administrative safeguards require the implementation of several processes which can be automated using workflow. The administrative safeguards comprise over half the HIPAA processes and are grouped in the following standards:

- Security management process
- Assigned security responsibility
- Workforce security
- Information access management
- Security awareness and training
- Security incident processes
- Contingency plan
- Evaluation
- Business associates contracts and other arrangements

Security management process

This standard requires organizations concerned to "implement policies and processes to prevent, detect, contain and correct security violation".

The following processes defined in this standard can be successfully automated and optimized by using workflow software:
- Risk analysis
- Risk management
- Sanction policy
- Information system activity review

Each process can include the following features:
- e-Form for data entry and management
- Workflow to orchestrate requests and actions
- Connectors to populate e-Forms fields or import/export data during process execution
- If needed, an agent can monitor logs so as to trigger automatic audit processes, for example.

Workforce security

This standard requires organizations concerned to "implement policies and processes to ensure that all members of its workforce have appropriate access to electronic protected health information..."

This particular standard is one of the biggest challenges of the HIPAA in terms of change management.

IT departments are required to delegate access authorization responsibilities to departmental managers without compromising security.

Process examples:
- Authorization and/or supervision
- Workforce clearance processes
- Termination processes

By using workflow software to manage these processes, the costs involved in managing numerous requests every month can be dramatically reduced, while HIPAA traceability and audit requirements are fully complied with.

Workflow software's integration features allows data to be automatically imported from, or exported to your HIS, HR system or directory.

Information access management

This standard requires organizations concerned to "implement policies and processes for authorizing access to electronic health information..."

The following processes can be automated with Workflow:
- Access authorization
- Setting up & modifying access privileges

Security incident processes

This standard requires organizations concerned to "implement policies and processes to address security incidents."

Because implementing this standard is required for HIPAA compliance, healthcare organizations must have an effective solution to manage security incidents.

Workflow offers a fast and simple way of managing incident forms and associated workflows such as "response and reporting" processes.

BASEL 2

Published in 2004, the Basel 2 regulation is aimed at European financial institutions and involves implementing a business (credit, markets) and operational risk management system. Compliance involves a whole series of processes.

Workflow offers a fast and simple way of implementing these processes in full compliance with the regulation.

Incident management

This initially involves implementing procedures to collate incidents and providing a permanent log thereof.

Workflow provides an automated procedure facility with logging of requests and actions performed.

Other operations, such as importing or exporting data, can then be performed with the financial institution's other document or data bases and IS applications.

Risk management

Basel 2 also defines procedures for identifying and managing risks. In addition to automating procedures workflow means workflow data can be used with business intelligence software to generate reports and risk monitoring reports.

By optimizing and automating the procedures, workflow reduces the extra work associated with analyzing and monitoring risks generated by the financial institution's business units.

COBIT

COBIT is a standard managed by the IT Governance Institute (ITGI) defining a framework for the implementation of IT Governance.

COBIT defines both operational and control processes for IT departments. COBIT includes nearly 34 controls in four principal fields:
- Planning and Organizing
- Acquisition and Implementation
- Delivery and Support
- Monitoring

Hundreds of corresponding processes must be deployed to implement the various COBIT controls.

Planning and organizing

Who decided what, when and for whom?

Good IT governance relies on a clear definition of responsibilities and the traceability of decisions. Within the COBIT framework the processes to be implemented are particularly strategic. Workflow means the decision-making process can be modeled and implemented with a complete audit trial of actions and decisions taken.

Here are some examples of processes automated by workflow:
- IS strategic planning approval

- Investment management
- Compliance management
- Risk analysis and management
- Quality management
- Human resource management

Acquisition and Implementation

The analysis and implementation of a new IT solution is becoming an increasingly complex process for both purchasing approval and change management.

The large number of projects and people involved makes paper-based or email-based process management almost impossible. Workflow automates these processes and provides genuine productivity gains while integrating the increasingly heavy burden of compliance.

Here are some examples of processes automated by workflow:
- Solution analysis & approval
- Software acquisition and maintenance management
- IT procedure management
- System installation and accreditation management
- Change management

Delivery and support

This is one of the key issues in the new compliance standard, because it incorporates IS security management.

The IT department is required to delegate IT authorization management to the business units (e.g. a complete audit trail of access requests, personnel entry/exit needs to be implemented).

Workflow provides for effective management of these various processes by automating manual tasks that can be sources of errors and productivity losses.

Here are some examples of processes automated by workflow:
- SLA management
- Supplier management
- Performance management
- Authorization management
- Cost management
- Configuration management
- Problem and incident management
- Operation management

Monitoring

Monitoring within compliance projects is very time and resource consuming. Human-based monitoring is not practical because of the volume of data to analyze and the number of processes involved. Workflow software enables the automation of several monitoring processes and control and corrective action tracking.

Connection with the information system means the IT department can issue automatic alerts based on user-defined criteria.

Here are some examples of processes automated by workflow:
- Internal and independent audit management
- Corrective action management

IT INFRASTRUCTURE LIBRARY (ITIL)

The ITIL standard offers guidelines for IT department's governance that are being increasingly implemented by public and private organizations

Based on best practice, this process library comprises eight books:

- Software Asset management
- Service Support
- Service Delivery
- Security management
- Application management
- Infrastructure management
- Business outlook
- Management service implementation schedule

Several processes in each book have to be implemented. Workflow enables a quick and efficient automation of the ITIL processes, while providing compliance with the regulations of the organization's industry.

Workflow—the ITIL project accelerator

Thanks to fast deployment and powerful features, workflow dramatically reduces the implementation costs of the ITIL processes. The lack of time and resources often holds back ITIL project implementation. Yet ITIL processes do improve a company's agility by offering a better IT service to internal users, and provide a further step towards IT system governance and compliance with industry regulations.

Workflow provides a quick ROI while ensuring compliance with the regulations through the traceability and logging of actions and decisions. Workflow also integrates ITIL processes with existing applications (ERPs, databases, directories, etc).

Here are some examples of ITIL processes which can be incorporated into the workflow portal:

- Support management (Helpdesk)
- Incident management
- Configuration management
- Change management
- Update management
- Problem management
- SLA management
- Availability management
- Capacity management
- Service continuity management

ISO 17799

The ISO 17799 standard is a good example of today's laws and regulations on IS security and implementation is an excellent way of preparing for the compliance project.

ISO 17799 includes the following sets of standards:

- Risk appraisal & management
- Security Policy
- Information security organization
- Asset management
- Personnel Security
- Communications and Operations Management
- Access Control

- IS Acquisition, Development & Maintenance
- Information security related incident management
- Business Continuity Management
- Compliance

In addition to the technical actions, a large number of processes must be implemented. Using workflow facilitates ISO 17799 certification by automating the processes with the required level of audit trails.

Examples of ISO 17799 processes

ISO 17799 provides guidelines to implement IS security management in an enterprise, including risk management, definition of security policy, system access control, incident management and audit management.

Here are some examples of processes automated by the workflow portal:
- Analysis and risk management
- Definition of security policy

Personnel security:
- Definition of roles and responsibilities
- Clearance process at point of recruitment
- New employee
- Employee status change
- Employee termination
- Sanction management

Incident management:
- Incident report
- Analysis and management of an incident
- Corrective action management

PROJECT MANAGEMENT

In today's environment project management becomes a key activity for the enterprises. A product launch, the deployment of a new information system or aligning business activities with the market's demands are examples or complex projects that often have to be resolved simultaneously.

Project management is now standardized and structured in several processes ensuring a greater quality and traceability of operations. Compliance with new legislation also requires a greater rigor in project management. Automating processes via workflow is now a prerequisite to delivering projects on time and in line with the company's governance policy. Backers, project managers, project teams, task managers, clients, partners and vendors all play a role in project management workflows.

Defining the project

Good project definition and approval are the keys to successful corporate projects, and an increasing number of players are involved in this initial phase. The traceability of decisions and the use of check lists are examples of features offered by workflow for the automation of project management processes

Here are some examples of processes that can be automated by workflow:
- Project submission
- Project charter approval
- Statement of work approval
- Responsibility matrix approval
- Communication plan approval

Project scheduling

At this stage of the project the traceability of the decisions is critical especially regarding the risk management. Workflow provides a complete audit trail of the decisions made and can syndicate the risks identified in a knowledge base.

Here are some examples of processes that can be automated by workflow:
- Risk analysis and management
- Work Breakdown Structure (WBS) approval
- Schedule approval

Controlling the project

Project management now fully encompasses change management. Competition or new technologies can directly impact ongoing projects. Workflow enables the automation and improvement of change management and problem resolution, and decisions can be logged and stored in knowledge bases for later use.

Here are some examples:
- Problem analysis & management
- Task assignment
- Project status approval
- Change management
- Configuration management
- Closure report approval

Integration with the legacy IS

Automated project management processes can be seamlessly integrated with legacy databases, content bases or third-party project management applications. Project management process automation enables a quick and efficient automation of the project management processes while providing the compliance with the regulations of your organization's industry and significant productivity gains.

CONCLUSION

The new regulations on compliance and governance have forced businesses to speed up the changes in working methods and move to a more process-oriented organizational system.

As such, a huge quantity of messages currently sent via email are set to be turned into a workflow, structuring the continuity of actions and defining roles while providing full accountability and control.

The workflow portal will play a central role in any business's virtual office.

Workflow project management becomes particularly strategic where compliance and governance are concerned and there are many instances today where senior management and IT departments are involved in this type of project. The difficulty resides in the complexity of solutions based on separate business units (compliance with standard appraisal), organizational elements (change management modeling) and technical issues (implementation & integration with the legacy IS).

We have seen that workflow is the driving force behind these new projects and a tool which, once mastered, can generate a new source of added value for any company.

Business Process Management for Six Sigma Projects

Dr. Setrag Khoshafian, Pegasystems Inc., USA

SIX SIGMA AND BUSINESS PROCESS MANAGEMENT

Six Sigma has become a leading methodology by which companies manage and improve their business processes. Born out of work done by the Motorola Government Electronics Group in the 1980s, Six Sigma applies statistical methods and models to analyze and improve process defects. It applies a rigorous approach to identify key process characteristics and discover the process inputs or outputs that most influence process performance. The goal is to improve the process, especially through minimizing variances. Often Business Process Management (BPM) and Six Sigma are positioned as competing alternatives for process optimization. Some analysts have proposed that companies don't need both but can choose one depending upon individual objectives. However, this premise is false. A modern Business Process Management Suite (BPMS) can provide an ideal platform for implementing successful Six Sigma projects. BPMS and Six Sigma are complementary approaches, interwoven in the continuous improvement cycle of digitized and automated processes.

ARE SIX SIGMA AND BPM COMPETING METHODOLOGIES?

Some analysts and practitioners consider Six Sigma and BPMS as competing alternatives for process improvement. A BPMS is a software platform for automating, effecting and monitoring the execution of business processes. There is an implicit approach when one uses a BPMS. A common methodology, though not always noted explicitly, underlies a BPMS that includes modeling, deploying, executing, monitoring and improving business process solutions. In contrast, Six Sigma is a quantitative and statistical methodology for process improvement. Six Sigma does indeed involve the use of software but mainly for modeling and statistical analysis.

There are common improvement areas that are addressed by both Six Sigma and BPMS. This often leads to the belief that they are interchangeable or that one can be chosen over the other. The following lists some of the similarities.

Process Focus: The language, the approach, and the thinking in both are process focused. However, BPMSs have more rigorous definitions of process flows as sequence of steps or activities which can have human, system or trading partner participants executing activities. Six Sigma has a different connotation, which includes the BPMS definition but does not require automation or precise definition of a process meta-model. In Six Sigma the process focus is on the measurable data that is generated upon executing repeatable processes.

Measurement of repeatable processes: Six Sigma and BPMS each deal with measuring repeatable processes. These "process instances" pertain to the same process definitions in a BPMS. Measurement involves gathering detailed information on each of the steps or activities of the process: when was it executed, who executed it, what was the process data when it was executed, when was it completed, and so on. Reports or more detailed analysis can be developed from this process data. The process data in Six Sigma is gathered from a variety of sources, such as Enterprise Information Systems.

Continuous Improvement: While the core of Six Sigma is a continuous improvement methodology, BPMSs are also ideal for implementing continuous improvement. Implicit in continuous improvement is the notion of *change.* A current ("as-is") project yields measurable results which can lead to suggested improvements. The improvement will almost invariably involve changes to the process. For Six Sigma the attempt is to improve the sigma (reduce the variance)—to achieve a desired goal of 3.4 defects per million opportunities. For BPM improvements yield increased ROI measures and/or key performance measure that can be obtained through process data.

Iterative Methodology: While a BPMS is a software platform, it is associated with the basic methodology steps of "Model, Design, Implement, Monitor, Analyze, Control and Improve." Similarly, Six Sigma defines the cycle of each of its iterations through Define, Measure, Analyze, Improve and Control. Six Sigma and BPMS methodologies are iterative in nature. Iteration and change in processes go hand in hand with continuous improvements.

Project Portals: Six Sigma projects typically have project portals that can be used to monitor the current status of projects. These are sometimes homegrown project portals on an organization's Intranet or they may be a commercially available Six Sigma portal for managing and tracking Six Sigma projects. Regardless of the type, these portals primarily target Six Sigma practitioners such as Green Belts and Black Belts. BPMSs also provide out-of-the-box customizable portals for different communities of interest—Business Analysts, Process Architects or Business Managers. Increasingly BPMS platforms are making their portlets available through JSR-168 standards within enterprise portals.

The similarities of BPMSs and Six Sigma—each attempting to optimize processes through their own methodical approaches to continuously monitor, control, and improve processes—may foster the belief that they are competing approaches. However, that is only the surface. Core complementary differences between Six Sigma and BPMS make it apparent that *BPMS provides an ideal platform to implement Six Sigma projects.*

EVOLUTION OF BPMS TECHNOLOGY

It is not an accident that BPM is increasingly becoming an ideal platform for implementing successful Six Sigma projects. It has to do with maturity. BPMSs have evolved significantly over the past few decades. The core capabilities of a BPMS, including support for business rules, integration, reporting, simulation, piloting, and activity monitoring, are critical to Six Sigma.

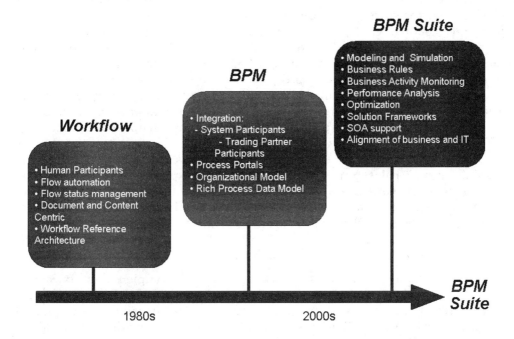

BPM Suite

- Modeling and Simulation
- Business Rules
- Business Activity Monitoring
- Performance Analysis
- Optimization
- Solution Frameworks
- SOA support
- Alignment of business and IT

BPM

- Integration:
  - System Participants
    - Trading Partner Participants
- Process Portals
- Organizational Model
- Rich Process Data Model

Workflow

- Human Participants
- Flow automation
- Flow status management
- Document and Content Centric
- Workflow Reference Architecture

1980s   2000s

BPM Suite

Evolution of BPM Suites

Since their inception, Business Process Management has evolved from human-centric workflow to more comprehensive business process management suites. Workflow products, at least in the earlier stages of their evolution, were document, form and content centric. In fact, some of the earliest implementations of workflows focused on converting and processing paper-based documents through digitized media. The main and significant difference between the workflow systems of the late 1980s or early to mid 1990s and the emergence of business process management in the mid 1990s was the incorporation of *system* participants. This meant in the same process flow that humans were performing some of the tasks, some of the steps were being performed by back-end Enterprise Information Systems such as Enterprise Resource Planning systems, Human Resources applications, or more generically Database Management Systems. BPM started to also include trading partners. One of the earliest definitions of BPM included *enterprise application integration (EAI)* as well as human-centric workflow and trading partners *business-to-business integration (B2Bi)*.

Another significant evolution towards business process management was the evolution of Business Rules Management technologies. In fact, initially business rules engines were deployed in isolation, often solving niche and complex business rules problems. As time passed and complexity, especially in developing and deploying business applications, started to increase exponentially, people soon realized that rules should not be executing in isolation. Business processes and business rules are now treated as two faces of the same coin. Organizations are recognized as aggregations of procedural flows: how things should be done; and policies: what are the guidelines that drive these procedures. Procedures and policies or guidelines must be specified and executed in the same context. As execution gets closer to exactly patterning the process and policy specifications, artificial boundaries in systems that concentrate on process automation and systems that execute business rules become counterproductive. This sometimes introduces additional complexities, especially in mapping or integrating disparate systems. The conclusion: The evolution of business process management suites has demonstrated that a single cohesive system that can digitize both procedural flows and declarative rules is the ideal solution. The declarative business rules *drive* and *streamline* the processes. Business rules are critical for Six Sigma. Through rules you can define declarative expressions for your critical performance measures. You also use rules to execute Service Level Agreements (SLAs), complex decisioning, event correlation, and agents. Each of these rules types provides significant advantages to Six Sigma projects.

BPMS + SIX SIGMA

There are numerous ways that BPMS supports and complements Six Sigma. BPM and Six Sigma practitioners can be seen as part of the same continuous improvement loop. BPMS roles (Process Architect, Business Analyst) and Six Sigma roles (Black Belt) can be incorporated in a continuous improvement project lifecycle involving both business processes and Six Sigma tools.

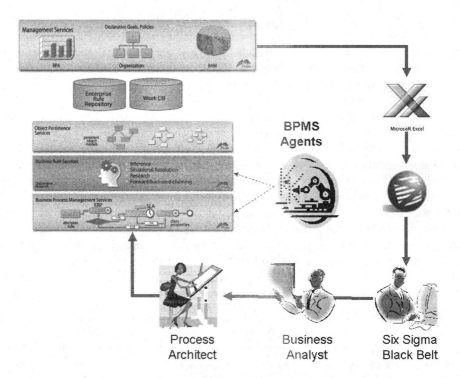

Process Architect	Business Analyst	Six Sigma Black Belt

Continuous Improvement with BPMS + Six Sigma

Process data can easily be exported from the BPMS to a Six Sigma tool. For instance, you can export to Excel or access it through relational database interfaces such as SQL/JDBC. The process data can then be analyzed through popular Six Sigma tools such as Minitab. Six Sigma Black Belts can conduct various hypothesis testing and analysis on the exported data. The process improvement changes, in collaboration with Process Architects, can then easily and immediately be propagated to the digitized processes. Interestingly, in some cases the Process Architect and Black Belt expert will be the same person or work closely in the same development group. In addition to the process data analysis cycle, you can also define business rules to continuously monitor process capabilities and make sure process measures are within the recommended upper and lower control limits.

DMAIC

The general methodologies recommended by BPMS vendors for identifying, improving, deploying and monitoring their processes are similar to the steps prescribed in the Six Sigma Define-Measure-Analyze-Improve-Control (DMAIC). However, even though the terms and connotations of the concepts sound similar, Six Sigma relies heavily on statistical analysis to quantify existing process capability and to prove the dependency between process inputs and outputs. Hence, each improvement idea can be defended using a rigorous approach and the results of implementing a change in the process. The goal is to accurately predict the net improvement in process performance.

Six Sigma defines variation as the enemy. Processes must perform in a predictable manner accurately and precisely around target performance metrics. Six Sigma practitioners argue that customers are impacted by process variance far worse than, for instance, the process mean (or average). In other words, predictability in product measures, financial measures, response times, or process duration is much more important than the average times of the measures. Six Sigma focuses on improving quality.

The DMAIC phases in the continuous improvement cycle of the Six Sigma methodology have several key steps. Each phase can be supported and enhanced by incorporating BPM as a platform for implementation.

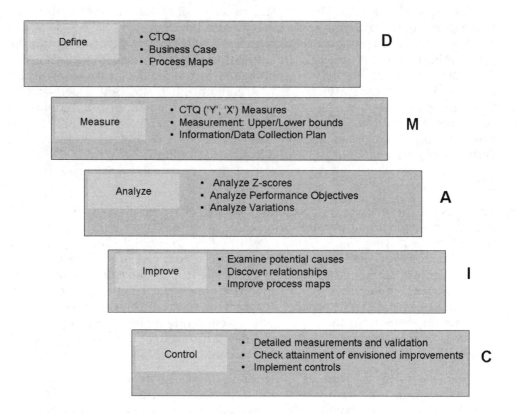

DMAIC Six Sigma Methodology

BPMS SUPPORTING THE DMAIC METHODOLOGY

Six Sigma is defined as *an enterprise or business performance improvement methodology,* which is different from BPMS solution development methodologies. However, in the measurement and improvement phases there are overwhelming similarities. In fact, BPMS can be used with other alternative methodologies for enterprise performance measurement, such as Balanced Scorecards. The focus of this analysis is BPM Suites—which means all the components of the suite including: Processes (modeling, simulation and execution), Business Rules, Integration, Information models, Business Activity Monitoring, and other core features are effectively used in supporting the Six Sigma project.

It is important to explore how a BPM Suite supports each of the phases of the DMAIC methodology in Six Sigma:

Define: In the Define phase, Critical To Quality (CTQ) business objectives must be defined. Typically these are defined in terms of "big" Ys. These Ys can depend on Xs, which in turn depend on "small" 'y's and 'x's. You can use BPMS business rules to support the 'D' phase:

Declarative expression support is essential functionality in BPM Suites that allows you to capture Ys ('y's) and X's('x's) as properties. Here are couple of examples:

Invoicing Application: Base properties include InvoiceIssueDate, InvoicePaidDate, InvoiceCity, CustomerID, etc.

Call Center Application: Base properties include CallDate, CallResponseDate, Severity, CustomerID, SupportCallType, etc,

So you can use expressions to capture $y=f(x_1, x_2, ..., x_n)$ dependencies.

DaysItTookToPay can be defined as:

InvoicePaidDate—InvoiceIssueDate

Amount can be defined as:

TotalAmount*DiscountRate + Tax

Each of the properties used in these expressions could also depend upon other properties: for example the Tax calculation could itself be a complex expression.

Another type of BPMS business rule that is essential is the notion of Service Level Agreements (SLAs). For instance if an agent is waiting for the delivery of the payment at a step, then a SLA is associated with this specific task and appropriate actions or escalations are enacted when the SLA is getting close to being violated. Ideally several levels: within goal, within deadline, pass deadline—with appropriate actions for each case.

You can use other types of rules such as triggering rules or rules that fire when values of properties change. It is important to note that these are the properties of executing processes and that their values are dynamically and continuously monitored while some of these values are evaluated through declarative expressions.

Measure: The performance specification limits (upper and lower) are constraints on the properties of processes. These constraints can also be expressed through predicate conditions on the properties, as declarative business rules.

Another important aspect of measurement is the data collection plan. For BPM Suites this should come almost free for automated or digitized processes. All relevant data can be extracted to easily generate reports or for export to other tools such as Excel or Minitab.

Constraint rules can be used to define Upper Limit or Lower Limit constraint. This means in an executing process when these constraints are violated immediate action is taken. The target performance limits are set declaratively. For instance, by stating that the Upper Spec Limit for a call response is 24 hours, this constraint can be expressed as a declarative rule and used and re-used in various contexts.

Analyze: In the Analyze phase, the target Sigma score is set and potential sources of variance are identified. The Analyze phase is principally concerned with establishing both the baseline and future state performance standards. This phase investigates the sources of the greatest process variations. The analysis might discover 'x's that are causing the variances. These could potentially be used to implement on the fly activation of business process artifacts (processes, rules, etc.), depending on the critical 'x' values.

Before giving an example of how this could be used in a business process management suite, it is important to emphasize that the BPMS is actually managing a repository of business processes and business rules in the context of applications that are typically organized in object-oriented class hierarchies. The "class" in a conventional object-oriented context includes only attributes and methods as meta-types. In BPM, these are present. In addition you have business rules of different categories, integration, user interface, and of course process flows. Similar to object-oriented modeling, you have generalization, aggregation, and association relationships between classes. You can have other types of specializations as well: based on time, geography, customer type, or version of the application. In other words, you have a rich and complex organization of process applications that can be used to support Six Sigma projects.

Assume the analysis shows variance due to the geographical location of the customer, the amount of the invoice, the frequency of the customer, or the size of the customer or any combinations of these. Corresponding to these variations you will need to create SLAs, business rules, decisioning, and even the entire process and have the underlying BPMS activate them conditionally. In other words, you need complex organization and specialization of the BPMS elements to achieve your Six Sigma goals. Variations that are discovered in the Six Sigma analysis phase are now used:

- To design and implement the situational alternatives.
- To dynamically activate any of the BPMS elements (business rules, integration, business processes, etc.) depending upon the current situation (customer type, amount, time, geography, etc.).

Therefore variations identified in the Analysis phase are supported directly and dynamically by the *classification* schemes of the BPMS.

Improve: The Measure and Analyze phases are concerned with finding problems. It is in this Improve phase that solutions are identified. Investigation, experimentation and piloting of new solutions all fall into this phase. The starting point of the Improve phase is the list of vital 'x's generated in the Analysis phase. Operating limits are placed on the 'x's or input variables so that the 'y' stays within specification.

The improve phase is supported through piloting different solutions. It is in this phase where the agility and flexibility features of BPMSs become apparent. BPMS allow for quick modification of processes and the ability to set rules/reminders on processes without impacting the process flow dramatically. Because these types of improvements are quick and simple in the BPMS, they can drive huge process improvements.

In the customer service example you can easily improve SLAs, introduce more complex business rules to capture causes/effects of customer complaint categories, or even have improvements in the overall customer service process flows.

In the invoicing example, you can easily introduce additional flows or steps to immediately start processing the invoice as well as contacting customer through reminder e-mails or service calls automatically. You can also notify managers early on, through SLA improvements in a cycle-time based projects.

The ability to simulate "to-be" processes and, perhaps even more importantly, to pilot alternative improvements are also important. The BPMS should allow you to try several alternative versions and roll-forward those improvements that provide the most promising improvements. It is important to be able to roll-back versions that do not appear to be contribute positively to the CTQ measures.

Control: The Control phase is designed to implement the necessary rigor and instrumentation to ensure that the process maintains performance standards over time and mitigates the risk of process degradation. The Control phase tries to keep the 'x's within tolerance by using appropriate controls, such as managing the risks or attempting to avoid mistakes. In this phase, plans must also be established to sustain the control of improved processes.

One of the big advantages of business process management suites is the ability to actively monitor processes and the CTQ values, sensing 'events' as they occur and quickly responding to the events automatically. The monitoring and the events will involve expressions on properties of processes and business rules that capture the control limits. BPMS can also use agent technologies to monitor and control either individual process instances or aggregate values across instances of a process. The combination of process automation, business rules for the control logic and expressions, and agent technologies implies BPMSs can dynamically and continuously control the potential risks and errors that could lead to out of control processes.

For example, in an invoicing application if there is a late payment risk score based on customer frequency, it is necessary to define SLAs that will be fired depending on the context of the late payment risk score. The SLA/Event manager could be used to prescribe responses to key risks identified in the running process, such as informing a collector, transmitting correspondence to the customer, or pushing the work object to a specialist.

Specification limits could be set on input parameters that restrict specific ranges of values for the property. Upon violation of the rule, the event correlation manager would fire an appropriate response.

Using agent technology, with agents executing in their own threads, rules could be setup that collect process data samples and calculate the mean and standard deviation of the CTQ properties. Rules could fire if the process appears to be moving out of an acceptable control range.

CONCLUSION

BPMS is a great enabler for Six Sigma. It is helpful to remember that the focus in BPMSs is on executing processes while Six Sigma on the other hand focuses on statistical analysis and continuous improvements of process data. BPMSs can have several executing instances of a process definition and each of these instances represents a particular execution instance case of the process. In Six Sigma, data is analyzed statistically to discover causes of variances to determine how the process can perform predictably. Because gathering of the process data in BPMS is automatic, this data can easily be exported to Six Sigma tools. Furthermore through the business rules (expressions, constraints, decision rules, triggers, SLAs, event rules, etc.) a BPMS can continuously monitor and control processes to make sure its CTQ values are within the prescribed limits. You control the process and avoid variations in process performances through dynamically monitoring the CTQ values continuously, avoiding variations in upper and lower process control limits.

Until recently Six Sigma practitioners (Green Belts, Black Belts, etc.) have been isolated from BPMS practitioners (Business Analysts, Process Architects). Each has evolved and developed its alternative way of looking at process analysis, continuous improvements, and continuous monitoring and measurement. With the emergence of BPM Suites that provide a cohesive platform combining business processes, business rules, and integration, we are witnessing the emergence of aggregated continuous improvement methodologies that leverage the best approaches from BPM and Six Sigma. The two communities can now become fully involved in automating processes and enacting business rules that can keep the processes under control. Six Sigma practitioners can use statistical tools to analyze and discover significant dependencies between process variables, and reflect the recommended changes in the BPMS solution. BPMS, thus, becomes the ideal platform to implement Six Sigma projects.

Employing Workflow to Drive a Comprehensive Audit of Enterprise Identity Management

Rami Elron, BMC Software, Israel

ABSTRACT

Workflow plays a key role in the implementation of a comprehensive approach to auditing required to accommodate regulatory compliance requirements. Workflow offers powerful methods that enable enterprises to effectively reduce potential threats to the business, and to facilitate attestation.

This chapter illuminates key aspects pertaining to the role of workflow within a comprehensive auditing approach. This chapter highlights key business conditions and requirements that drive the need for auditing, explains how identity management auditing addresses these requirements, and examines how workflow contributes to the effectiveness of an identity-management audit process.

REGULATORY COMPLIANCE CALLS FOR AUGMENTED MANAGEMENT OF IDENTITIES IN BUSINESSES

After many years at the back of most companies' IT priorities, auditing has finally moved into the business limelight, assuming a central role in the business' strategic regulatory compliance endeavor. Auditing has become a full-fledged practice encompassing a spectrum of duties from data aggregation and consolidation, to policy exception analysis, detailed reporting, and automated proactive mitigation procedures.

The dramatic rise in the importance of auditing did not happen overnight, but it was influenced and pronounced by an imminent need to comply with the requirements set forth by salient legislation, such as the U.S. Sarbanes-Oxley Act, which calls for controls over financial reporting, requires companies to establish and maintain a comprehensive approach to auditing that facilitates transparent financial reporting, and provides a reasonable assurance of control over the financial reporting process. IT, as it turns out, plays a significant role in attaining this objective.

A company's successful achievement of its business goals relies heavily on its deliverables, be they services, products, or both. As each deliverable is the product of a certain process, anything, and most significantly, anyone, capable of adversely affecting the process could pose a risk to attaining business objectives. Because people are the owners of company processes, their respective IT capabilities could expose the business to financial risk. Profiling the user's IT capabilities becomes an imperative objective, as is the need to verify that IT capabilities are granted and revoked appropriately, so that users possess only the capabilities defined by their required roles. Since identity-related data is scattered across various systems, being able to correlate between the pertinent identity's "pieces" is critical. Inability to do so may result in a false sense of security and a lacking audit report that fails to surface information that might indicate alarming risks.

Management of access rights is not a trivial process. Business agility warrants an approach to access management that supports quick, yet effective and secure, assignment of rights to users. Attaining this objective often calls for a process that may not be easy to implement using programmatic means alone. Furthermore, attaining regulatory compliance objectives warrants a process that *attests* to the validity of the control-based approach undertaken by the company.

A comprehensive approach to identity management auditing enables to correlate between processes and actions to personnel and enables to verify that access rights to critical business resources are defined, granted, and enforced pursuant to company policies. A critical success factor of this approach lies in the ability to effectively identify and manage exceptions to the company's access policy so that corrective actions can be taken appropriately and promptly.

Workflow plays a marked role in attaining the aforementioned goals. Processes are managed by people, and proper management and auditing of the procedure used to grant user access rights are imperative and key to a successful implementation of regulatory compliance practices.

ADDRESSING REGULATORY COMPLIANCE REQUIREMENTS VIA A COMPREHENSIVE AUDIT OF IDM: HIGHLIGHTING BUSINESS DRIVERS FOR IDENTITY MANAGEMENT AUDITING

Auditing is critical to enterprise IT management, and particularly to the management of resource access by users. Unsurprisingly, typical audit practices are quite effective at addressing questions such as: "who accessed what" or "when was resource x last accessed." A comprehensive approach to audit warrants examination of identity management-related records as well, in order to supplement the company's ability to review user access that occurred in the past, with an ability to assess user capabilities that can be exploited in the future.

Companies increasingly rely on IT to conduct daily business. IT and business operations have become inseparable in many respects and IT has been constantly expanding to include management of business services in addition to the management of the business' systems. The increasing deployment of new business systems in place of existing manual and less efficient processes has, in turn, demanded the creation and maintenance of new data records describing access permissions pertaining to the new applications. Over the past few years, companies have become aware that the effort involved in implementing multiple systems could be considerably reduced by centralizing and automating processes that entail creation and maintenance of user-related data (e.g., accounts, roles, etc.). As the scope of user activities expands, the company requires more control over the different identity-related records pertaining to a given person.

Identity management auditing helps address regulation compliance concerns by:

- **Aggregating and consolidating identity data**—being able to present a coherent and rich view of a given user's identity-related data, and consolidating information from every source where such data is kept, so that user actions captured in every system can be correlated to the right person.
- **Improving administrative/operational efficiency**—being able to reduce costs and operational overhead, via automation and business-oriented views, operations, reporting, and analysis tools. This enables the company to benefit from defined and mature provisioning processes, and facilitate easier identification of owners of business processes and authorizers.
- **Providing assurance and supporting attestation via technological means**—management of identities further empowers the

company with an ability to capture access-rights assignments; to investigate pertinent policies and handle exceptions; to provision to all business-critical systems; to collect and consolidate audit trail data; and to get proper behavior assurance from all business-critical systems.

THE CHALLENGES OF MANAGING THE IDENTITY LIFECYCLE

In order to better assess how identity management auditing accommodates regulatory compliance requirements, and how workflow facilitates an effective identity management audit, it is important to first understand the challenges of managing the identity lifecycle. Basically, identity management (IdM) is a practice governing the complete lifecycle of the identities of people and resources across pertinent systems, encompassing a myriad of aspects relating to such identities, including their creation, management, suspension/renewal, termination and more. IdM software offers organizations considerable operational benefits by automating this practice and supporting a variety of related tasks including password management, account provisioning, Web Single Sign-On (SSO), access management, and more. Over the years, many vendors have rushed to jump on the identity management bandwagon, often armed with merely a single application addressing a narrow, albeit important area of interest. Consequently, the term "identity management" has become something of an umbrella term, used primarily to group together disparate applications under a single toolset, sharing a single common denominator—a reference to user identity data.

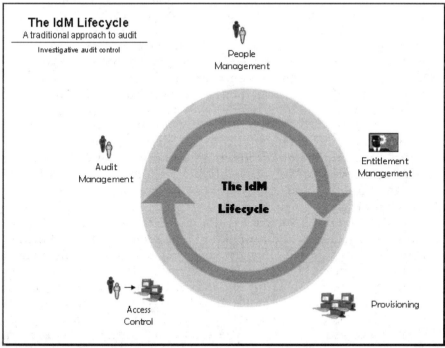

Figure 1. A traditional approach to auditing typically focuses on the examination of access records in pertinent enterprise systems. The auditing process follows the setup of access rights, and is typically applied on system access logs, thus serving to realize "who accessed what." This approach does not easily enable correlating log entries with their associated person, as each person might be represented differently in various enterprise systems. Furthermore, the approach does not address the question "who can access what" and lacks a mechanism to facilitate attestation to the validity of the process.

The boundaries of identity (and access) management are blurry and depend somewhat on how an identity is defined. Does an identity constitute a minimal set of attributes (required for identification of the pertinent principal) or does it virtually encompass all data relating to the principal (including data spanning companies)? This considerably affects the extent to which management of identities should reach. Nevertheless, identity management should not be considered an end in itself, but rather a supporting process for both management and execution of business processes. Following are select processes typically associated with common identity management implementations in organizations:

- **People management**—a process that governs the management of the data that constitutes the user's identity in the business (e.g., personal details, business properties, and more). This typically entails processes governing definition, creation, and management of user records in a dedicated HR system and in a designated directory. Many companies employ a central directory (or multiple directories) for storing user records that may serve various identity management applications.

- **Entitlement and access management**—a process that governs the management of user access rights to enterprise IT resources across the company's systems. This typically entails definition and management of user accounts on systems to which the pertinent user should possess access rights, as well as the definition and management of roles, rules, and procedures pertinent to the management of access rights in those systems. Access management encompasses applications that facilitate management of access rights, such as SSO, password management, and Web access management. SSO solutions enable a simplified login experience for users by enabling the user to authenticate once and subsequently gain access to password-protected applications without being required to re-authenticate. Password management solutions facilitate management of user passwords, while password synchronization solutions support synchronization of user passwords among managed systems. Web access management entails processes governing the definition and management of Web-based resources, as well as Web application roles and rules governing the assignment of user access rights to those resources.

- **Provisioning**—while differing widely among vendors, provisioning is at its core both a security and a management solution that facilitates centralized and automated management of user entitlements on multiple systems. Provisioning typically entails definition and management of a distinct enterprise-wide account for each managed user, along with the definition and management of policies and processes that define how the user gets provisioned access rights to enterprise systems. Significantly, provisioning solutions may feature a workflow service to facilitate human approval of provisioning-related actions, thereby addressing a critical business requirement.

- **Federated identity management**—part identity management, part access management, this relatively new field entails applications, specifications, and procedures that facilitate secure business interactions across domains via established trust relationships between business entities.

An enterprise approach to identity management should encompass the procedures and tools required to centrally administer any user's collective set of attributes distributed across enterprise systems, and to effectively manage the user's access to enterprise IT resources. Typically, each individual managed using such an identity management system has a corresponding identity record (a *person* account) specifying attributes identifying and characterizing the individual. These attributes enable the identity management system to determine which actions to apply with respect to the pertinent identity and help determine (if required) how to assign the individual appropriate access rights to enterprise resources. Attestation to the validity of this process is a salient requirement.

Attestation has a few facets. An *attestation audit* is an audit process required by certain regulations to attest to the effectiveness of implemented controls in providing reasonable assurance over financial reporting. Companies may elect to run an independent attestation process (see figure 2) to periodically review the company's implemented authorization process and to have managers attest to the validity of access rights assigned to their team members.

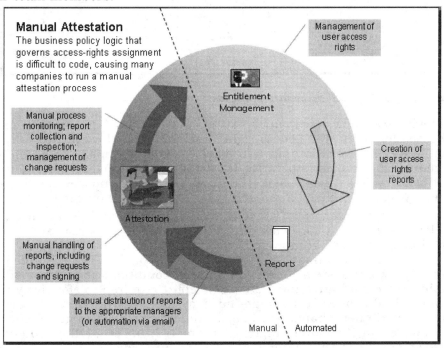

Figure 2. A manual attestation process

Workflow facilitates an attestation procedure by empowering the company with the ability to conduct a dynamic, flexible, policy-compliant, and auditable business process for approving access-rights assignments, which captures pertinent decisions and helps dealing with access rights that do not comply with company policies.

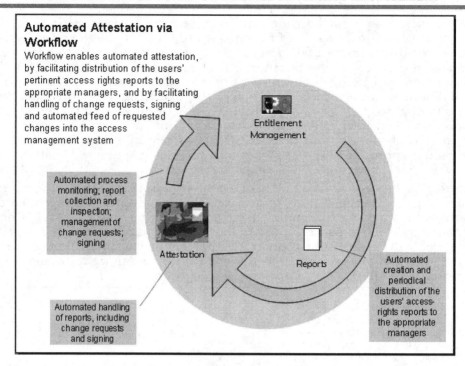

Automated Attestation via Workflow

Workflow enables automated attestation, by facilitating distribution of the users' pertinent access rights reports to the appropriate managers, and by facilitating handling of change requests, signing and automated feed of requested changes into the access management system

Entitlement Management

Automated process monitoring; report collection and inspection; management of change requests; signing

Attestation

Reports

Automated creation and periodical distribution of the users' access-rights reports to the appropriate managers

Automated handling of reports, including change requests and signing

Figure 3. An automated attestation process

Employing workflow, companies can effectively model business approval processes for requested access-rights assignments. However, to fully appreciate the role workflow plays in driving a comprehensive audit of identity management, it is imperative to further examine what the enterprise identity lifecycle generally looks like and to understand key implications of employing a role-based approach to access-rights management.

Access rights to enterprise IT resources are typically assigned to individuals either directly via corresponding user accounts (on a relevant system) or indirectly via user groups with which the users are associated. Moreover, assignments can be specified explicitly, or can be performed dynamically by the system, based on various conditions (e.g., time of day, certain user record attributes, etc.). The effort required to effectively manage individual identities is compounded by the fact that identities are not static — attributes change in time, to reflect business requirements. As an example, an individual might be promoted, an event that potentially implies a change in that individual's access permissions.

The decision and implementation of the appropriate security settings are typically done by the IT organization. Identities often are considered just another type of an IT resource and are correspondingly managed by IT personnel. It is thus perceived as the duty of IT people to determine and manage the appropriate composition of the identity record required to support the perceived IT security policies. This affects two critical management facets:

- **Risk management**—ability to assess any user's IT capabilities ("what can the user do?") as implied by their pertinent combined user rights. Typical auditing solutions concentrate on addressing "what did the user do?" and do not attempt to profile user capabilities based on analysis of the user entitlements.
- **Role management**—ability to conduct effective and efficient role modeling that facilitates assignment of business-related responsi-

bilities. Role-based access control (RBAC) is not a new concept, but is still far from being implemented throughout typical enterprises in an effective manner. Many organizations do not employ a policy mechanism to enforce separation of duties, nor do they have the means (or will) to undertake the effort of mining their role/rights assignments.

Select identity management tasks that benefit from a workflow approval process

- Change personal details
- Create a new user account
- Suspend a user account
- Restore a suspended user account
- Add new permissions to a user
- Remove certain user permissions
- Approve user entitlements
- Create a new group
- Associate a group with users

Table 1. Select identity management tasks that benefit from workflow-based approval

A comprehensive approach to identity management auditing requires tools that enable definition and enforcement of policies on identity management data. The ability to intelligently consolidate IdM-related data, filter it based on various criteria, automatically generate pertinent reports and *ultimately launch a business process* based on the findings is a boon to companies and should be the essence of a bona fide IdM audit service. Such ability empowers the company with information on the user activity profile. This information could be used to reveal and highlight user entitlements that are noncompliant with company policies, or that imply a certain risk factor according to those policies, and to identify job patterns and facilitate role design.

Let's examine select audit-related challenges facing a company that has not employed a comprehensive approach to identity management audit.

- Local system logging facilities record user access under a name that identifies the pertinent user to that system, but which is not necessarily identical across all systems. Auditing multiple system logs may, therefore, become a complicated process. In order to determine who accessed what, there is a need to correlate between the multiple "identities" and the relevant person.
- Local system access logs only reveal what users did in the past and do not show what IT capabilities users have. Inability to audit the user capabilities and verify their compliance with company policies reduces the effectiveness of the audit procedure and fails to surface potential risks. The model highlights the limitation of an *investigative* approach to auditing — failing to alert on risks implied by access rights that are noncompliant with company policies.

- In the absence of workflow, it is challenging to apply (i.e., code) the equivalent business process that typically would be required to accommodate the entitlement procedure. Attestation and attestation audit become much more challenging, as there is an increased effort to verify that a coded procedure reasonably addresses compliance requirements. Moreover, as the identity-management modeling process typically relies on an IT-oriented view of roles, it does not necessarily mirror any business logic and it is difficult to capture the reasoning behind any given association of access rights to a person—for auditing purposes. (This issue is discussed in detail in the following section "Introducing RAIL—a workflow-enabled, business-oriented approach to identity lifecycle management.")

Next, we shall review how an identity management auditing approach leveraging workflow helps realize the benefits associated with a comprehensive approach to identity management audit.

EMPLOYING A WORKFLOW-ENABLED IDENTITY MANAGEMENT AUDIT TO EFFECTIVELY ADDRESS REGULATORY COMPLIANCE CONCERNS

An identity management approach that only employs an investigative form of auditing and lacks a workflow process is ill equipped to effectively address the requirements implied by regulatory compliance. Figure 4 presents a model for an identity management lifecycle that is believed to better accommodate such requirements.

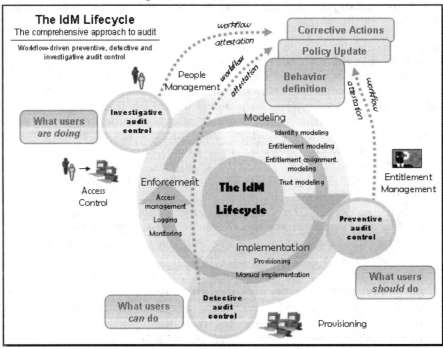

Figure 4. A comprehensive approach to identity management audit entails multiple audit controls that allow, among other things, to subject requested access-rights assignments to a reviewing and approval workflow process before the assignments are carried out, thus enabling to block requests for noncompliant access-rights assignments. The ability to detect noncompliant access rights by inspecting person records, in addition to system access logs, further enhances the effectiveness of the approach. By employing workflow, this approach also facilitates attestation to the validity of the entitlement management process.

Three key management processes characterize the depicted identity management lifecycle:

- **Modeling**—the objective of this process is to specify the characteristics determining the behavior of the identity management process. Modeling entails (1) Identity Modeling (definition and management of the key identity record (person, group) and related attributes); (2) Entitlement Modeling (definition and management of IT roles and rules governing accessibility to resources); (3) Entitlement Assignment Modeling (definition and management of the association of entitlement definitions with identities); and (4) Trust Modeling (definition and management of contracts with pertinent parties that affect the identity's scope). *Employment of workflow processes to facilitate the management of various identity-related processes, which are challenging to implement in code alone, facilitates audit attestation and represents a major argument in favor of using workflow within an identity-management lifecycle process.*

- **Implementation**—the objective of this process is to set up the user's access rights pursuant to the models specified in the previous step. Implementation is effectively divided into two steps: (1) setup of the access profile (at the end of this step it is possible to determine what the user is tentatively capable of doing); and (2) implementation of the access profile on the pertinent system/application, which entails automated (provisioning) or manual setup of pertinent applications on managed systems (at the end of this step it is possible to determine what the user is capable of doing in practice).

- **Enforcement**—entails (1) access control on local systems and applications; (2) federated access management; and (3) logging and monitoring of access (at this step it is possible to determine what users are actually doing).

Note that, in the context of identity management, a prime objective of auditing is to verify that assignment of access rights conforms to company policies. In various cases, it proves difficult to capture the logic required to grant access rights, and a workflow process is implemented instead, for submission of access-rights requests and their approval or rejection. Company policies are commonly defined to streamline processes by establishing standards for various operations. Notable examples of identity-management audit policies include *detection of excessive rights* (a policy that looks for access rights that are assigned to a user directly, and not indirectly via roles), and *separation of duties* (a policy that verifies that a person is not assigned apparently conflicting rights—such as rights to submit and approve the same request). Access rights that do not comply with company policies are labeled *exceptions*. The process of dealing with exceptions is called *exception management* and represents a key facet of a comprehensive auditing approach. Whether exceptions are approved by a business manager that is entitled to make such decisions, or removed altogether, *exceptions should be handled nevertheless*. Possible outcomes of exception management are policy updates or corrective actions. Significantly, given the importance associated with exception management, it warrants an appropriate approval process.

The common approach to auditing is frequently labeled *investigative* audit, as it deals with actions that occurred in the past. This explains why it is applied on the system's access logs, thus providing an ability to review who did what. The audit process is started either manually by an approved application user (e.g., auditor), or can be triggered automatically, either by a scheduling application, or perhaps more appropriately following a designated event.

If assignment of access rights were possible only from a single application, auditing could have been centered on that application. In reality, however, companies deploy numerous applications and systems with their own security application; thereby assignments can be carried out from many places. As a result, auditing at one point in time may prove to be limited. A comprehensive approach to auditing concordantly suggests multiple points where the application of auditing is beneficial, thus complementing the ability to review what was done with an ability to detect access-rights assignments before users exploit them:

- **Preventive control**—at the setup step of the implementation process. At this point, it is possible to prevent assignment of user access rights that do not comply with business policies.
- **Detective control**—immediately after the implementation process. At this point, it is possible to detect existing access-rights assignments that do not comply with business policies.
- **Investigative control**—at the enforcement process. At this point, it is possible to investigate which users accessed which resources.

Figure 5 illustrates how workflow drives a business process intended to approve or reject an exception, and to subsequently trigger pertinent corrective actions.

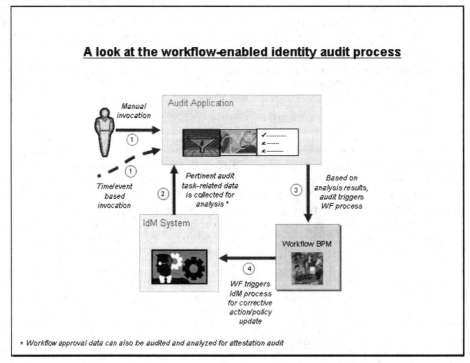

A look at the workflow-enabled identity audit process

Figure 5. The identity audit process can be initiated by a user or by an event (e.g., user access rights are modified on a system monitored by identity management). The audit function determines what data should be collected based on the requested or designated audit objective (e.g., get user entitlements from the identity management system), and runs a corresponding analysis process on that data (e.g., whether the new assignment complies with the company's separation-of-duties policy). The audit application may be configured to analyze the results (e.g., the assignment is noncompliant with company policies) and suggest recommended ac-

tions (e.g., suspend the pertinent user account). It also potentially could trigger a workflow process based on the audit results (e.g., submit a request to approve the recommended actions). The workflow process enables reviewing the recommended actions and approving or rejecting them. Records of this approval process can be audited and analyzed for attestation audit.

As noted above, exception management warrants an approval process. *This is another significant area for workflow processes.* Workflow software helps to streamline effective and efficient business decision-making by offering tools for modeling, automation, and monitoring of pertinent business processes. *By employing workflow to model business processes, companies capture decisions and actions concerning a given request, thus facilitating analysis of the rationale behind the approval or rejection of a request.* In the context of identity management, this potentially can be used to trace the actions leading to assignment of certain access rights. Regarding exceptions, workflow facilitates effective exception management, by implementing the business process required to approve decisions related to exceptions.

Using auditing to automatically trigger workflow processes under certain conditions is an example of employing workflow for enhanced auditing, which represents a fresh take on the traditional concept of auditing. Using auditing as a trigger for workflow processes enriches the identity management practice, and helps bridge the gap between IT and business, particularly in the area of role management.

Figure 6 illustrates a detailed view of the workflow-enabled identity audit process.

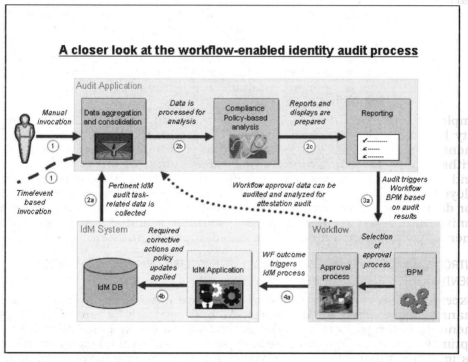

Figure 6. This is a more detailed view of the identity audit process. The process is initiated either manually or automatically based on a schedule/event trigger. The process selects an audit procedure appropriate for the particular situation, and data pertaining to the audit function is collected for analysis (e.g., identity management records, access log records, etc.). The analysis compares the data against pertinent company policies. Analysis results are captured, published within perti-

nent reports, and input to procedures responsible for suggesting recommended actions. Employing workflow, it is possible to facilitate appropriate handling of the recommendations by running a business process in response to these results. Designated approvers can thus review the recommended actions and approve or reject them. Records of this approval process can be audited and analyzed for attestation audit.

Following is a summary of select benefits that workflow brings to an effective identity-management audit process:

- Workflow enables to implement another layer of control over the assignment of access rights, by answering a burgeoning requirement to implement a business-oriented approach to access-rights assignment. Moreover, workflow enables association of a well-used and familiar business process with tasks that are unlikely to automatically be handled by IT or by the system.
- By incorporating business decision-making within the process governing access-rights assignment, workflow:
  - Facilitates *attestation*, by implementing a process that enables the capture of the business rationale behind assignment of access rights, thus enriching the database for audit analysis
  - Helps verify appropriateness of access-rights assignments
  - Facilitates practical handling of exceptions by obviating formalization of automatic exception handling

Workflow contributes to a more valuable identity management process, particularly for:

  - Risk management, by facilitating an optimized preventive control, and by supporting better detective and investigative control
  - Role management and analysis, by enriching the identity management metadata, providing better understanding of the assignment rationale and leading to better role modeling ability

Implementing a workflow decision process, as an integral part of the identity lifecycle, helps IT administrators to accommodate regulatory requirements and the ever-growing number of user accounts. These benefits notwithstanding, the effectiveness of key identity management audit aspects and workflow among them may suffer if the authorization process employed to assign access rights to users lacks a company-approved policy for defining, implementing, and managing user roles. The next section examines this issue and assesses how workflow's added value can be further augmented, via a business-oriented approach to roles.

INTRODUCING RAIL — A WORKFLOW-ENABLED, BUSINESS-ORIENTED APPROACH TO IDENTITY LIFECYCLE MANAGEMENT

Excessive rights and separation of duties are notable examples of identity management audit-related policies. As both typically rely on some implementation of roles, such implementation becomes a prerequisite for an optimal identity-management audit process. This raises some concerns, as implementation of roles is a staggering undertaking for most mid-sized to large organizations. The following paragraphs highlight various concerns regarding the dependency of certain auditing aspects on roles, and examine one possible approach to relieve these concerns.

Many IdM solutions were designed before the recent surge in regulatory compliance, and may not possess rich auditing capabilities. This is typically reflected in an inability to present a complete view of user capabilities *in a business context.* While individual capabilities are commonly requested by the business organization (e.g., by a manager or by the user via a workflow mechanism) in an orderly fashion, the procedure may suffer from a number of drawbacks. (1) The business organization typically expresses such requests for IT permissions as coarse-grained "*capabilities*" rather than in a finer-grained "*access permissions*" terminology utilized by IT (e.g., "Please grant Sarah the permissions to approve employee vacation requests"). (2) Commonly, the capabilities specified in requests are presented as a single "*request package*" that lacks any business meaning — it merely describes a collection of requested permissions. For example, a request to access a particular system does not imply whether it answers a particular business duty. It is thus upon the IT owner to dissect, analyze, and translate the business request to an IT-appropriate set of security assignments that need to be implemented. The issue is compounded by tracking access-rights changes at the IT level—with virtually zero accountability from the business side. *The bottom line is that the business context of the action typically gets lost in translation.*

Roles seemingly present a sound approach to address this issue. Roles are entities describing IT capabilities that are associated with a user (or a group of users). With roles, IT-related permissions required to support the user's daily work can be described as a composition of generic "access-rights permission sets"—or "roles"—each implying the access rights associated with a particular business function. A key objective of roles is to facilitate identity lifecycle management and expedite access-rights assignment to users by managing permissions in groups rather than individually. By enabling hierarchical relationships between roles, powerful modeling of role relationships is possible—supporting the definition of a wide spectrum of role structures.

This approach theoretically offers significant benefits. First, job changes and user lifecycle management are potentially easier to accommodate, security-wise. Second, changing a role definition applies to all users assigned the role, which is very helpful to administrators. Third, role-based management facilitates flexible auditing capabilities.

However, despite these notable benefits, implementation of roles has arguably become a nightmare for many organizations. As roles attempt to reflect business requirements pertinent to a company, classification of roles differs greatly among companies. In large companies with thousands of employees, the process of identifying, classifying, and defining roles may likely become a challenging undertaking. User access requirements are not as easily described using generic roles, resulting in a situation where each user could be represented only by using a unique role for that user. Implementation of roles also requires some considerable role-mining effort, in search for "hidden" roles implied by existing permission assignments.

Being essentially IT-created objects, roles typically lack any business context and are IT-only entities for the following reasons:

- Roles might originally have been conceived to address a business need but have frequently ended up becoming IT-oriented tools that unfortunately bear no meaningful business context. While some roles may imply a business-related function (e.g., manager), such roles are (as others) defined in terms of IT vernacular (access rights) that is practically incomprehensible by most non-IT people.
- Roles are typically created and assigned by IT personnel only. IT is concerned by assignment of improper rights to people (either di-

rectly or indirectly via groups) rather than being concerned of assigning rights to true business functions.

- Ultimately, from a business context, there is only one role: to fulfill the business responsibilities expected by the pertinent job title definition. Interestingly, business-title job types and business responsibilities associated with such job types are arguably well understood and share some considerable resemblance across companies.

The preceding sections emphasized the significance of *business context* within the identity lifecycle. IT roles lack the business context that is crucial for reviewing user access rights from a business perspective; moreover, employing only IT roles makes it challenging to capture the reasoning behind user entitlements. A responsibility-based approach to identity lifecycle management (RAIL) could better accommodate such requirements by introducing a business-oriented approach to role definition; coupled with workflow, RAIL presents a compelling approach to identity management in general, and identity management audit in particular.

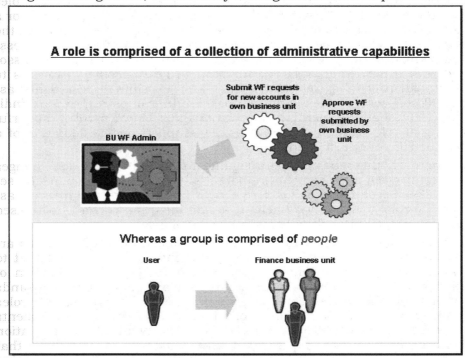

Figure 7. A role is a collection of administrative capabilities, whereas a group is a collection of people.

A *responsibility* is a business-oriented description of a duty (or duties) associated with a job *title*. Responsibilities are similar to roles — but possess some notable differences:

- The user's responsibilities represent the business permissions granted by the company to the individual by virtue of their title or job description. In contrast with roles, responsibilities are created and managed by business users. Within the business, any given user's title implies an appropriate assortment of responsibilities, many of which are explicitly defined, and well understood by business users (e.g., "report on expenses," etc.).

- Association of users or groups to IT roles directly results in a mapping that is not clearly understood by ordinary business users. IT roles are irrelevant to business users because they convey user permissions in IT terms. For example, a responsibility to submit expense reports is not expressed as a business-related operation, but as an IT access right on a probable vague resource. Because the role is described in non-business terms, it is rather difficult for IT, which typically lacks a good appreciation of the business requirements, to maintain and reuse roles in a business-efficient manner.

In a responsibility-oriented model, no access rights are assigned to users or groups directly. Instead, access rights (or groupings of such rights as IT roles) are assigned to responsibilities, which are in turn associated with appropriate users or groups. The onus for creating and maintaining the business-side aspect of user capabilities should be on *business users*—not on the IT personnel.

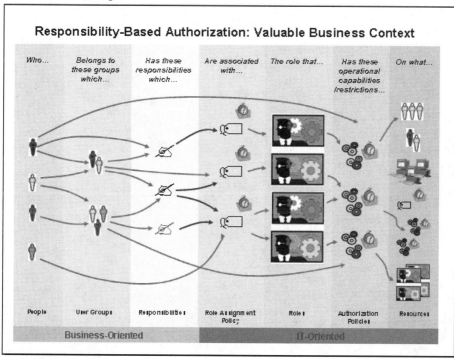

Responsibility-Based Authorization: Valuable Business Context

Figure 8. Responsibilities provide business with an abstraction of the IT model that facilitates better management of user entitlements. Responsibilities also improve the effectiveness of workflow in identity management audit, as business approval is now concerned with business-oriented entities (responsibilities), rather than with IT-oriented entities (roles).

The implication of this approach on a workflow-enabled audit process is substantial. As the effectiveness of an identity management audit is dependent on the roles, the significance of a responsibility-based approach or any alternative approach that improves role coherence and business context is incontrovertible. A workflow process supporting exception management is more effective if it entails an exception that could be better assessed by reviewers, as it is an exception to a *business definition* rather than an exception to an IT object.

CONCLUSION

Audit is increasingly being recognized as a critical component of the business strategy to comply with regulatory compliance requirements. IT and business have become inseparable in recent years and given the powerful IT capabilities possessed by users, being able to profile user capabilities has become a key business objective, as has the need to verify that user capabilities are granted and revoked pursuant to company policies. Attainment of these objectives calls for a more comprehensive approach to the management of identities. This approach entails a business-oriented model for user roles and responsibilities, implementation of preventive, detective, and investigative identity management auditing. It also requires a workflow service that drives the business process supporting the IT process. Such an approach enables an organization to assemble a comprehensive view of the IT capabilities granted to users, to reveal policy exceptions promptly, to deal with exceptions effectively, and to facilitate attestation processes by employing a business-oriented approval process that minimizes risk and maximizes value.

Using BPM to Manage Risks in Financial Services Firms

Sheila Donohue, CRIF Decision Solutions, Italy

INTRODUCTION TO RISK MANAGEMENT

Risk management, which used to be an activity concentrated in just certain departments of financial services companies, is now a widespread, integrated part of the operations of the entire firm. This is because the introduction of risk occurs during the day-to-day transactions among employees, customers and third parties and the lesson learned is to control each point at which the risk is most prevalent. The consequences of uncontrolled risk can result in large monetary losses, negative impact on share price, loss of jobs, closure of companies and even court prosecution, as seen in current events especially over the past five years. Spurring on the use of modern risk management techniques are regulatory bodies, and even investors, that now require companies to demonstrate solid risk management practices. This paper will focus on two types of risks which financial firms manage and how Business Process Management, BPM, can be applied to manage these risks.

Credit risk is the exposure resulting from the chance that a customer does not pay a financial obligation. The goal of credit risk management, which covers the entire financial firm's customer lifecycle from acquisition through portfolio management, is to minimize the risk exposure that a customer may not pay.

Operational risk is the "risk of losses resulting from inadequate or failed internal processes, people and systems or from external events."[1] Like credit risk, operational risk management requires the identification, assessment, monitoring and mitigation of the causes of such risk using methodologies, tools and systems. Manifestations of operational risk vary widely; some examples are: an employee applying special pricing without proper authorization, a customer falsifying data presented on their credit application, a user skipping a control activity that they are supposed to perform.

Credit risk management is a more mature practice while operational risk management is a newer development. However in both cases they involve identifying, monitoring and controlling potential exposures with proper systems, tools and procedures.

The basis for all risk management is defining a methodology. The methodology typically consists of these steps:

Identify → Model → Implement → Monitor

Once a significant risk is identified, an effort to model the behaviour of the risk begins so a way to prevent the risk is formulated. The formulation is implemented in the financial services organization and then it is monitored for effectiveness. Upon monitoring, changes are noted and the cycle begins again to keep tweak the formulation to it highest potential.

---

[1] Definition per Basel Committee.

IDENTIFY

Risk management starts with identifying the risk which involves recognizing a specific "bad event". That bad event occurs within a business process so the business process(s) impacted needs to be identified as well. Some examples of bad events are:

    a. When a customer defaults on a loan

This would be a type of credit risk impacting the credit application process which is the business process encompassing the evaluation and approval of an applicant wanting a financial services firm's credit product.

    b. When a customer is late on paying their bills

Once a firm takes on a customer, the firm takes on a risk that the customer will pay their bills and pay them on time. Since bills are often due monthly, the potential for this risk is ongoing. Financial services firms establish a business process called collections to monitor and manage this type of credit risk whose aim is to collect late payments from customers.

    c. When a bank teller employee, having ulterior motives, enters and manually approves a credit application for a friend in need of a loan, without forced involvement of another bank employee.

This would be a type of operational risk occurring within the credit application process.

Model

Once the risk is identified, there needs to be measures put in place to prevent and manage the risk. This is done in two steps:

    1. First there is a simulation activity performed to find a way to replicate or at least provide warning to the "bad event" risk. Results of this activity could be a calculation, business rule, new or changed manual activities, new databases or systems to access or a combination therein, all with the common goal to prevent the bad event from happening.

    2. Next, the impact to the business process is identified, specifying exactly where and how this new control will be retrofitted into the existing business process or perhaps necessitating a new business process.

Following along with the three bad events previously identified, this is what would happen within the modelling phase:

Bad Event A: Customer defaulting on a loan:

In the case of the customer defaulting on his loan, a statistical model can be created, or perhaps an existing "generic" one could be applied, to calculate the probability that this bad event will happen. Then an historical analysis, called a retro score, is done by running the model on previous loan applications belonging to the financial services firm to see what the model would have predicted in actual cases. The model is then adjusted to make it as predictive as possible. Once this is done, a calculation (known as a credit score) would need to be executed each time a potential customer applies for financing. Upon calculation of the credit score, a risk level is assigned. Then based on the risk level a decision to accept, reject or review the application is made and communicated to the potential customer.

With a credit score, a financial firm relies on the score to make decisions on applications. A firm can achieve significant benefits in terms of cost and increased revenue if they were to use the score to automate the credit application process. This process would retrieve all information needed by the score, perform calculation(s) and handle decision communication. The following business process flow is a start-up application process with this type of automation. This process flow shows a sequence of activities which can be manual (Web User Interface or UI) activities or automatic (e.g., connectors to other systems/databases, business rules, calls to a business rule engine, creation of documents) which together provide a complete credit application process from initiation of the request, retrieval of data from internal and external systems, calculation of credit score and determination of system decision, automatic contract document, credit decision notification to booking in

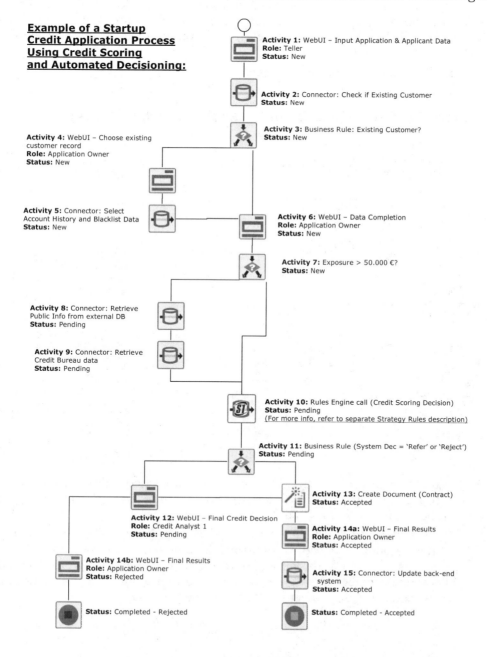

Example of a Startup Credit Application Process Using Credit Scoring and Automated Decisioning:

Activity 1: WebUI – Input Application & Applicant Data
Role: Teller
Status: New

Activity 2: Connector: Check if Existing Customer
Status: New

Activity 3: Business Rule: Existing Customer?
Status: New

Activity 4: WebUI – Choose existing customer record
Role: Application Owner
Status: New

Activity 5: Connector: Select Account History and Blacklist Data
Status: New

Activity 6: WebUI – Data Completion
Role: Application Owner
Status: New

Activity 7: Exposure > 50.000 €?
Status: New

Activity 8: Connector: Retrieve Public Info from external DB
Status: Pending

Activity 9: Connector: Retrieve Credit Bureau data
Status: Pending

Activity 10: Rules Engine call (Credit Scoring Decision)
Status: Pending
(For more info, refer to separate Strategy Rules description)

Activity 11: Business Rule (System Dec = 'Refer' or 'Reject')
Status: Pending

Activity 13: Create Document (Contract)
Status: Accepted

Activity 12: WebUI – Final Credit Decision
Role: Credit Analyst 1
Status: Pending

Activity 14a: WebUI – Final Results
Role: Application Owner
Status: Accepted

Activity 14b: WebUI – Final Results
Role: Application Owner
Status: Rejected

Activity 15: Connector: Update back-end system
Status: Accepted

Status: Completed - Rejected

Status: Completed - Accepted

a back-end system.

Note that the manual Web UI activities are assigned to a Role which defines the responsibility of a user of the process. After a user starts an application, they become the "Application Owner" which the person who has direct contact with the customer, needing to input required data and communicate decision / deliver contract to the customer.

You will notice that the rules engine in Activity 10 in the flow has an important role in driving the application to an accept or reject decision. First, all data needed by the rules engine is passed to it by the process. Implemented in the rules engine is a strategy designed for this application process. A strategy consists of a path of decision rules and calculations which results in a decision output. This strategy incorporates a credit score calculation to determine the risk level and ultimately the recommended system decision of Accept, Reject or Refer.

Here is the description of the strategy:

Strategy: Path of Decision Rules Resulting in a Decision

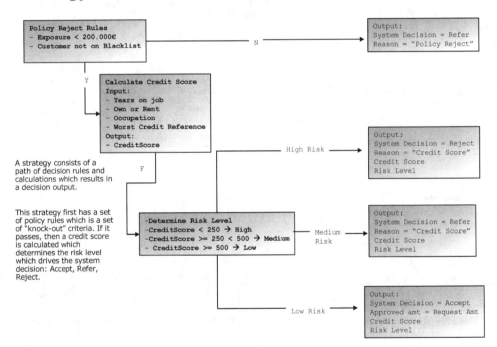

After execution of the strategy, the decision is returned back to the process which treats an Accept system decision as the final decision, providing an automatic approval. Meanwhile, Reject or Refer decision requires manual intervention to determine the final credit decision of Accept or Reject.

If the final decision is accept, a contract document is automatically created by the process, notifying the application owner who obtains signatures from the client after which the new contract is automatically booked into the back-end system via a connector activity in the process.

Bad Event B: Customer late on a bill:

1. In the case of the customer being late on a bill, a study on what actions are most effective in getting a late customer to pay could be taken. One "lesson learned" in the industry is to contact the customer at the moment in which they start to become late, doing so with a "soft" reminder such as a politely worded email reminding the customer to pay the bill. In order to fulfill this business requirement, a system solution is needed which would monitor the accounts history database for customers that are one day late with a payment. When this occurs, the system would send the client an email reminding them of the payment due.
2. A collections business process that could be designed to implement this activity is as follows:

Example of a Collections Process treating a customer 1 day in delay:

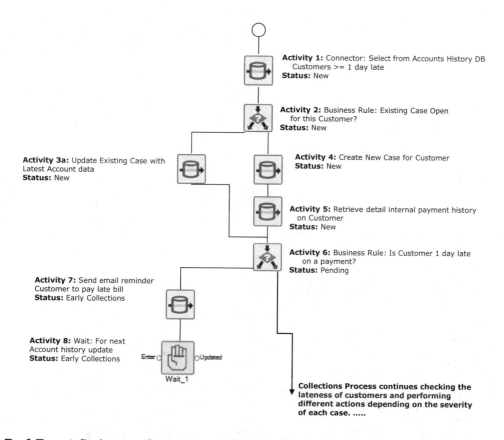

Activity 1: Connector: Select from Accounts History DB Customers >= 1 day late
Status: New

Activity 2: Business Rule: Existing Case Open for this Customer?
Status: New

Activity 3a: Update Existing Case with Latest Account data
Status: New

Activity 4: Create New Case for Customer
Status: New

Activity 5: Retrieve detail internal payment history on Customer
Status: New

Activity 6: Business Rule: Is Customer 1 day late on a payment?
Status: Pending

Activity 7: Send email reminder Customer to pay late bill
Status: Early Collections

Activity 8: Wait: For next Account history update
Status: Early Collections

Enter ○─ Wait_1 ─○ Updated

Collections Process continues checking the lateness of customers and performing different actions depending on the severity of each case. .....

Bad Event C: An employee single-handedly enters and approves a credit application:

1. The activity to provide final credit decision on an application is very sensitive as noted by the possible occurrence of an unattended person granting credit without the forced involvement of a second person. To prevent this from happening, the final credit approval activity needs to have a special control in place to ensure that the person performing this activity is not the same as the one who initiated the application. To be extra certain with ap-

plications of higher exposure, a second manual final credit decision activity may be inserted being sure that neither the application initiator (i.e., application owner) nor the person providing the first level credit approval performs this second and final decision activity.

2. Referring to the same credit application process flow above, the Final Credit Decision activity would have the described control checks implemented. Activity 12: "Final Credit Decision 1" ensures that that Application Owner does not perform this activity. Then if the result of Activity 12 is an accept decision, there is a business rule (Activity 12a) which uses the System Decision and Exposure to determine the necessity for a second level review. If

Example of the Startup Credit Application Process With 2 Level Credit Review:

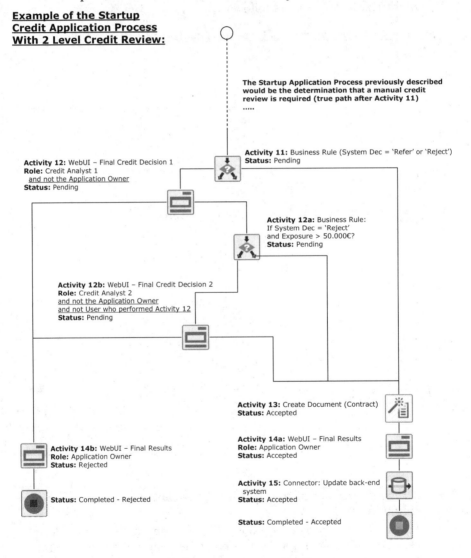

The Startup Application Process previously described would be the determination that a manual credit review is required (true path after Activity 11)
.....

Activity 11: Business Rule (System Dec = 'Refer' or 'Reject')
Status: Pending

Activity 12: WebUI – Final Credit Decision 1
Role: Credit Analyst 1
and not the Application Owner
Status: Pending

Activity 12a: Business Rule:
If System Dec = 'Reject'
and Exposure > 50.000€?
Status: Pending

Activity 12b: WebUI – Final Credit Decision 2
Role: Credit Analyst 2
and not the Application Owner
and not User who performed Activity 12
Status: Pending

Activity 13: Create Document (Contract)
Status: Accepted

Activity 14a: WebUI – Final Results
Role: Application Owner
Status: Accepted

Activity 14b: WebUI – Final Results
Role: Application Owner
Status: Rejected

Activity 15: Connector: Update back-end system
Status: Accepted

Status: Completed - Rejected

Status: Completed - Accepted

necessary, the process follows onto Activity 12b which passes onto a more senior role in which neither the Application Owner nor the user who performed the first level review can provide the Final Credit Decision.

IMPLEMENT

The business requirements coming out of the modelling step consist of the identification of specific business processes with integration of business rules and calculations. The business process has a mixture of manual and automatic activities. The manual activities are assigned to a specific person or to a group of persons who are assigned a role. This is so the person who is assigned the next step in the process is immediately notified, via a system which manages the activities of the process. The automatic activities of the process consist of:

- Call to a rules engine which executes a strategy, being a series of calculation and rules, coming out with a decision for the process to follow,
- Retrieval of data from a database or external system,
- Call to an external system which needs to perform an activity,
- Wait activity to allow for an external event to happen, such as receiving updates from external systems.

In determining the approach to implement, one should keep in mind the cyclical nature of the methodology. After implementation, the results are monitored and ways to improve risk identification are discovered. After which the cycle of identify, model, implementation is begun a-new. Therefore, financial services firms are encouraged to seek tools in which their business process and rules can be easily changed in the implementation phase.

Also, to make the easiest transition from modelling to implementation and also to ensure that the implementation meets the business requirements, there should be a one-to-one correlation between that which is modelled and afterwards implemented. In this way the risk of the implementation not meeting the business needs is minimized. It also allows the business users, who define the process and rules, to understand what has been implemented and therefore have more control over their processes and rules. To go one step further, firms seek tools in which non-technical people can actually perform the implementation, providing even more assurance that the business needs are met by the implementation and allowing to make the jump from modelling to implementation faster, providing the flexibility that financial firms seek.

Business Process Management software provides for such flexibility. Following along with the 3 scenarios presented, here is how the implementation could be done using BPM software:

Bad Event A: Customer defaulting on a loan:

The modelled solution consists of a business process, the Credit Application Process, and a strategy which determines the credit decision via credit scoring. The credit application process would be implemented using a Business Process Designer software in which a non technical person could:

- Define the data that is used by the process
- Define the process flow
- Define the individual activities

The business process as it would appear in the Process Designer software could be as follows, demonstrating using CreditFlow software, CRIF Decision Solutions BPM software:

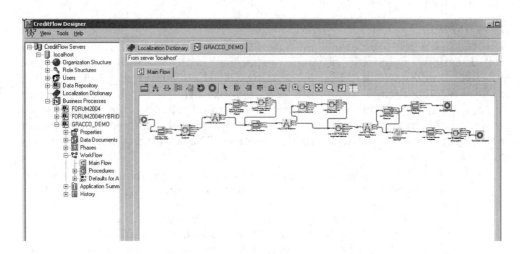

The left side of the screen are the parts of the tool to define process data, process flow, organization roles, users, all used by the workflow, or BPM, engine to execute the business process. The right side of the screen showing the activities and sequential flow as depicted in the credit application process shown early. Here is a focus on the activities involving the rules engine call and activities driven following the rules engine's decision leading to a completed accepted or rejected decision:

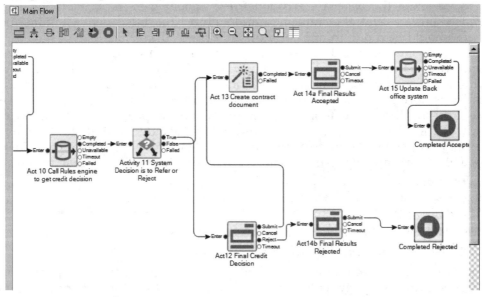

In activity 10, which is a connector activity to CRIF Decision Solutions rules engine StrategyOne, all data pertinent to calculate the credit score and make a credit decision is sent to StrategyOne. The strategy is designed using a designer tool similar to that for the process but instead to specify the strategy as described in the modelling section:

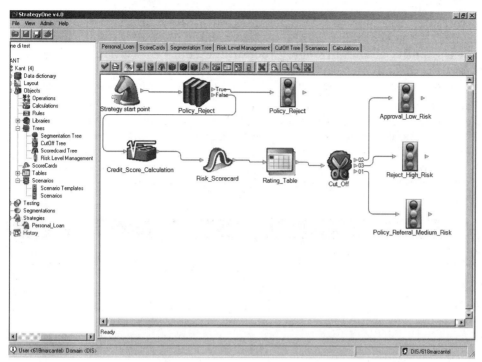

Associated with each object of the strategy is a UI editor such as this one to specify the scorecard variables and their weights which add up to the credit score:

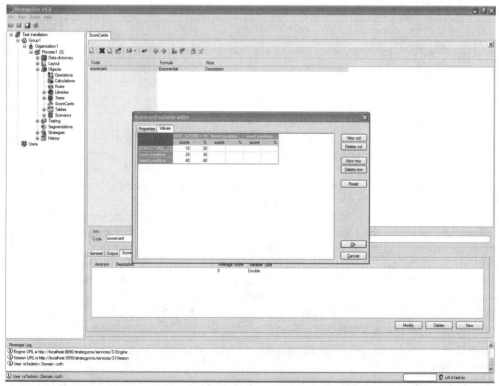

This is just one example of many types of editors that are in process and strategy/business rule designer tools which allow a non technical person to perform tasks necessary to set-up a working process or strategy with business rules. Some examples of other objects and activities to specify are business rules, paths of the strategy, process flow, data to view in the process' manual web UI activities, look and feel and function of the manual UI, and data to send to/from connectors which go to external databases/systems.

The end result after the process and strategy/business rules are implemented using the designer tools and loaded into the executable modules, the BPM and rules engines, is a process accessible to end users via a web browser where the user can start a new application process instance, view / work with applications assigned to them by the engine on their worklist and perform search, monitoring and worklist management functions via a web application looking like this:

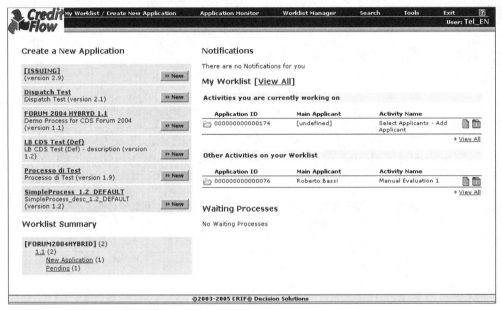

Bad Event B: Customer late on a bill:

Also in this case, the solution which the business will look for is one with flexibility allowing for the process to be modified for lessons learned on it collection activities. As such, a process designer tool, like the one previously shown, to specify the process flow is also used, especially to handle the changes in business rules and different type of actions which could be manual activities assigned to different types of collectors, administrative and legal personnel and outsourced collection agencies. Also automatic activities such sending emails, creating documents to send, connector to a back-end system to automatically suspend an accounts, play an important part and are also configurable using the process designer tool. Furthermore, a credit score which looks at the payment behavior of customers to predict for example the likelihood to collect could be created and implemented thus involving a strategy and rules engine as in previously described example.

Bad Event C: An employee single-handedly enters and approves a credit application:

In process designer tools, such as in CreditFlow, you define dispatch rules which tell the engine not only to whom an manual activity should be assigned but also to whom NOT to assign. In the example for Bad Event C, two of the most sensitive activities in terms of operational risk are the final credit decision activities, 12 and 12b. To prevent the person submitting the application from performing this activity you would indicate in the design for the activity that the process owner is excluded, selecting the first option in the User to Exclude in the screen shown below. Also, since the requirement in some cases is to force a second level of review which is yet a different person, you would also select the second option below which is to exclude the current worker, that is the person that performed Activity 12, the first level credit review. In this way, when the BPM engine is executing, it makes sure to exclude these two users from seeing the application on their worklist, thus enforcing the operational risk control.

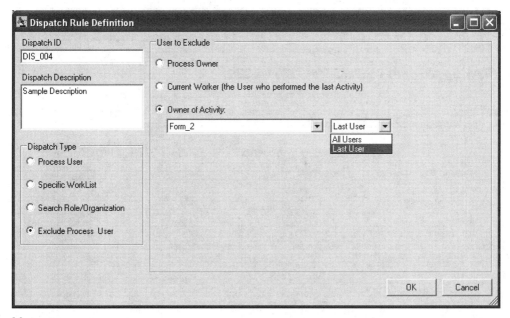

MONITOR

Monitor is a key step because you need to confirm that what you modelled is in fact producing the results that you expected. Also during the monitoring you look for other bad events which are occurring, which perhaps may be evident only when summarized information is analyzed. Then feedback from the monitoring phase leads back to re-visit the process of Identifying, Modelling, etc.

Bad Event A: Customer defaulting on a loan: Is the credit decision made in the application process accurately predicting the right risk level based on actual performance results?

Bad Event B: Customer late on a bill: Is the collections action implemented really getting late customers to pay their bills?

Bad Event C: An employee single-handedly enters and approves a credit application: Operational checking to know at any time "who did what when".

To respond to these questions, a business intelligence solution is recommended which gathers the necessary data to analyze the business results, calculating key business measurements and then providing results in a flexible reporting tool.

To take the first case, *customer defaulting on a loan*, the credit score for each application, in addition to other data gathered in the application process and calculated in the rules engine needs to be merged with account history data. After which, it is analyzed by users, ideally using a flexible reporting technology like OLAP which allows users to slice and dice data to best see the predictability of the original model as well as it weaknesses. An example of such a tool to perform this is StrategyMiner by CRIF Decision Solutions. Here is a sample online report in which the user can select a scorecard and by risk level you see the number and percentage of write-offs. This could then be compared to what the expected write-off was for the risk level which is determined by the scorecard, providing a starting point for the review of a model's effectiveness.

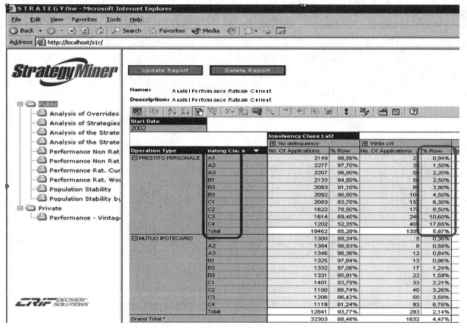

Meanwhile, in the third case involving operational risk prevention, *an employee single-handedly entering and approving a credit application*, access to real-time data is very important so to provide up-to-date details to business managers of the in-progress applications. Search tools are provided by the BPM system to get these details; since the BPM engine manages the individual process activities, it keeps track of "who did what when." Here is an example of such details accessible to CreditFlow web application end users showing for each activity the completion timestamp, elapsed time and user who performed the activity.

close window

Application ID:	000000000000132	Users that can work on the current Activity:
Main Applicant:	**Roberto Bassi**	🔍 **CreditAnalyst1**
Business Process:	**FORUM 2004 HYBRYD 1.1**	
Application Owner:	**Administrator (AdmOrganization)**	
Current User:	**CA1_EN (BranchEN)**	
Activity Status:	**Pending**	
Process Status:	**Freeze**	

Process started on Friday, December 02, 2005 at 12:27 PM, last step happened on Friday, December 02, 2005 at 12:27 PM, total elapsed time 28 sec, 390 ms

Process Activities (sorted by Leave Time):

Name	Exit	Enter Time	Elapsed	Activity Status	User
IE01_Input_Esterno	False	12/2/2005 12:27 PM	0 ms	NEW	Administrator
A01_Dati_Operazione	Submit	12/2/2005 12:27 PM	12 sec, 110 ms	NEW	Administrator
IE02_Input_Esterno	False	12/2/2005 12:27 PM	0 ms	Unknown	Administrator
Prepara_Richiedente		12/2/2005 12:27 PM	0 ms	NEW	Administrator
IE03_Input_Esterno	False	12/2/2005 12:27 PM	0 ms	NEW	Administrator
A02_Dati_Base_Anagrafica	Cerca	12/2/2005 12:27 PM	6 sec, 593 ms	NEW	Administrator
Cerca_Anagrafica		12/2/2005 12:27 PM	140 ms	NEW	Administrator
A04_Conferma_Anagrafica	Submit	12/2/2005 12:27 PM	4 sec, 983 ms	NEW	Administrator
Anagrafica_Cliente	True	12/2/2005 12:27 PM	17 ms	NEW	Administrator
Recupera_Account		12/2/2005 12:27 PM	46 ms	NEW	Administrator
Conferma_Dati_Anagrafica		12/2/2005 12:27 PM	14 ms	NEW	Administrator
A06_Riepilogo	Submit	12/2/2005 12:27 PM	3 sec, 953 ms	NEW	Administrator
Riepilogo_Anagrafiche		12/2/2005 12:27 PM	13 ms	NEW	Administrator
CutOff_1	False	12/2/2005 12:27 PM	267 ms	PENDING	Administrator
A09b_Valutazione_Manuale_1		12/2/2005 12:27 PM		PENDING	CA1_EN

APPLYING BPM FRAMEWORK TO RISK MANAGEMENT:

Risk management requires a suite of tools which measures the possible risk and brings efficiency and control to the underlying business processes. As these case studies show, it requires the ability to connect different organizations, people, data and systems together and along with methodologies and tools to model, implement, measure, modify and improve the underlying business process and procedures. All flavours of BPM, from process analysis and design, process and business rules implementation, application integration, through monitoring and process change improvement, contribute to fulfil the needs of risk management for a financial services firm.

These cases studies show the direct applicability of BPM to solving risk management issues bringing not only benefits to minimizes risks with automatic built-in controls and improved predictability of risk but also other quantitative business benefits can be realized such as lowered costs due to automation and higher revenue due to faster responsiveness to prospective clients. Some actual realized benefits from similar efforts have been:

- 50 percent reduction in the customer default rate
- 75 percent reduction in wait time for the client
- 70-80 percent increase in application booking rates.

Also many qualitative benefits can be realized due to a smoother overall process with direct routing to person(s) or system(s) which are responsible for the next step in the process and each user relying on a BPM system's worklist to know what is next for them to act on, becoming a paper-less work environment. These qualitative benefits bring with it also more ways to minimize operational risk such as errors due to mistyping because processes implemented using BPM software keep data gathered along the way and automatically send data to downstream systems, preventing users from having to re-key data and thus minimizing potential for manual errors.

While BPM cannot solve all risk issues, since much depends on organizational and external factors, it still provides the tools and framework for a financial services firm to follow through, in this ever changing and challenging world, with an effective risk management methodology: to model and implement rules and processes which minimize the occurrence of risk, and then to monitor and proactively improve.

Exception-Based Dynamic Service Coordination Framework for Web Services

Dr. Dongsoo Han and Sungjoon Park
Information and Communications University, Korea

ABSTRACT

Web services on the Internet are not always reliable in terms of service availability and performance. Dynamic service coordination capability of a system or application which invokes Web services is an essential feature to cope with such unreliable situations. In dynamic service coordination, if a Web service does not respond within a specific time constraint, it is replaced with another Web service at run time. For that, we develop a dynamic service coordination framework for Web services. In the framework, all necessary information for dynamic service coordination is explicitly specified and summarized as a set of attributes. Classes and workflows supporting dynamic service coordination and invoking Web services are then automatically created based on these attributes. Developers of Web service client programs can make the invocations of Web services reliable by calling the methods of the classes. Some performance loss has been observed in the indirect invocation of a Web service. However, when we consider the flexibility and reliability gained from the method, the performance loss would be acceptable in many cases.

1. INTRODUCTION

Web services are component services that are distributed, loosely coupled, standard-based, and process centric. These characteristics make Web-services-based applications more flexible than software systems that are built from traditional software components. In developing a business application, various Web services can be selected from distributed sources and easily connected and coordinated via their loosely coupled interfaces.

Moreover, Web services allow us to utilize business services across business boundaries via the Web through the use of standard languages and protocols such as SOAP (Simple Object Access Protocol), WSDL (Web Services Description Languages), UDDI (Universal Description Discovery and Integration) and HTTP (Hypertext Transfer Protocol). In addition, Web services provide us with a process-centric viewpoint of business applications such that we can regard them as parts in a complete business process.

However, Web services on the Internet are not always reliable in terms of service availability and performance. Some Web services may not be accessible and others may not respond within a reasonable period of time. As well, there are times when the service does not return the expected result.

Fortunately, in the Web services environment it is reasonable to assume that there exist other sites that provide similar or the same services. Based on this assumption, we can cope with the above situations by replacing the originally referred to Web services with those of other sites. The purpose of the dynamic service coordination of Web services is to replace one service with another at run time in the event the Web service is not accessible or does not respond within a pre-specified time limit.

There are several approaches that can be used to incorporate dynamic service coordination capability into applications or services. Even though the checking routines for conditions and situations may be hard coded in the applications, when we consider that some codes can be shared among applications, this approach is not efficient.

The second approach is to prepare an independent module that supports dynamic service coordination of Web services. Common condition and situation checking routines are prepared in the module with corresponding handling routines. Applications invoke a Web service indirectly by calling the routines in the module. This approach has an advantage in that applications can share a common code. Thus, we can relieve developers from developing all the dynamic service coordination routines for their applications.

Besides, we can consider a dynamic service coordination framework for Web services. In the framework, all necessary information for dynamic service coordination is explicitly specified and summarized as a set of attributes. Classes and workflows supporting dynamic service coordination and invoking Web services are generated based on these attributes. The exception handling mechanism of a workflow is mainly used in the specification of the workflow. Developers of Web service client programs can make the invocation reliable by calling the methods of the classes.

One drawback of the method is that it may bring some performance loss in calling a Web service. On average, 0.5 seconds latency is observed when invoking a Web service through a workflow. However, the flexibility and reliability gained from the method compensate for the performance loss in some situations. Note that the latency of invoking a Web service is not measured in an optimized situation. Thus, the added latency can be further reduced in the future.

The next section describes the notion of dynamic service coordination for Web services. Section 3 explains a dynamic service coordination framework to incorporate the dynamic service coordination capability into an application. Section 4 explains how the exception handling mechanism of a workflow system can be used for supporting the dynamic service coordination, its main purpose. We draw conclusion in Section 7.

2. DYNAMIC SERVICE COORDINATION FOR WEB SERVICES

2.1 Dynamic service coordination for Web services

For convenience, we use the term *dynamic service coordination* for the dynamic service coordination of Web Services. The notion of *dynamic service coordination* is not new. It originated from the concept of dynamic reconfiguration of workflow in which the predefined process itself and its associated attributes can be changed at run time. Similarly, in dynamic service coordination, a pre-specified Web service in an application or service program may be replaced with another at run time. When a Web service does not respond properly, using dynamic service coordination capability, we can allow other Web services to provide the service instead. Note that this replacement should be done at run time and within a reasonable time limitation. This capability is especially useful in a Web services environment which is, by nature, unreliable.

Though a Web services environment offers a diverse number of services and is ever-changing, there are two typical approaches for incorporation of dynamic service coordination capability into an application. In one approach, UDDI can play a major role in finding candidate Web services and changing access points for the dynamic service coordination at run time. In an ideal situation where UDDI is well equipped with registered services and can easily locate the best candidate services within a reasonable amount of time, this approach is appealing.

But in reality, we cannot assume such an ideal situation. UDDI is not at all complete, and many essential features are still missing in the standards of UDDI to support dynamic service coordination completely.

For example, in UDDI version 3.0.2, dynamic invocation service is included. UDDI registry holds bindingTemplate data for Web services of interest. The bindingTemplate contains the details about an instance of a given interface type, including the location at which a program starts interacting with the Web service. The dynamic invocation service is supported using that cached information. But UDDI version 3.0.2 is still missing many required features for the support of dynamic service coordination of Web services.

In the second approach, multiple candidates of Web services for a service are pre-specified and when a Web service does not respond properly, one of the pre-specified candidate services are selected and executed according to the situation and specification. This approach differs from the previous approach because UDDI does not play a major role in this case; rather, an exception handling mechanism of a workflow system is used in implementing this scenario. When a Web service does not respond properly, this situation is interpreted as an exception, which is handled by finding and invoking a replacement Web service.

2.2 Workflow and Web services

Workflow is a sequence of steps to achieve a certain business goal, where the business process usually lasts for a long time until it accomplishes its mission. Thus, it takes a certain amount of time for a workflow corresponding to the business process to finish its work. Workflow shares many common features with general program languages because it requires the specification of both control flow and data flow. The differences between workflow and programming language originate from the quantity of work specified in each step. As the steps of workflow should be specified at a level that makes them easily understood by general domain experts, the granularity of each step of a workflow must be sufficiently coarse. This situation matches well with that of Web services. The size of each Web service should be coarse enough to compensate for invoking the cost of remote Web services.

The coarseness of the steps in workflow allows for more flexibility in the handling of controls than does programming languages. In workflow, whenever the execution of a step is finished, the control of execution is handed over to a workflow system. The workflow system then decides the next step and hands control over to the step. This ping-pong control hand over between a workflow system and the steps in a workflow is repeated until the end of workflow execution. As a result, the workflow system can easily intervene in the steps during the execution of a process, taking appropriate actions when necessary. Note that this is not possible in the execution of a program. That is, the control remains in the program unless it explicitly specifies in the program to hand over control to external systems such as operating systems.

When we consider the above situations, it is reasonable to assign a Web service to a step of a workflow. Many standard activities and reports on Web services, like BPEL4WS, are built up based on this idea. What we suggest is to use a workflow for a Web service invocation in an application. For a Web service invocation, a workflow with a step of invoking the Web service is created, and the workflow is called in the application.

Several advantages can be expected from this approach. First of all, when we convert a direct invocation of a Web service into an indirect invocation of a Web service via workflow, many facilities of a workflow system can be used in handling the QoS related issues for the Web service invoking application. Transaction facilities, exception handling mechanisms, and other facilities that a workflow system can provide can be used to make an invocation of a Web service more reliable. Consequently, when there are changes in the Web services environment, they can be reflected in the invocation immediately, without affecting the surrounding systems.

However, such advantages are gained by sacrificing some performance loss in calling a Web service. This performance loss is either acceptable or unacceptable depending on the situation invoking the Web service. Thus, the extent of the performance loss of this approach should be understood precisely.

Dynamic service coordination capability can be incorporated at workflow or application level. That is, steps of a workflow may directly invoke a Web service or an application can invoke a Web service via dynamic service coordination. Here, we focus on the application level dynamic service coordination method, since once application level dynamic service coordination is possible, workflow level dynamic service coordination can be easily supported.

3. DYNAMIC SERVICE COORDINATION FRAMEWORK

3.1 Two Approaches to Support Dynamic Service Coordination

For an application to have dynamic service coordination capability, certain routines should be added in the application irrespective of the usage of UDDI. Condition or situation checking routines, replacement of Web service selecting and invoking routines, and other routines pertaining to the support of dynamic service coordination, should be appropriately called in the application. The exception handling mechanism of programming languages can be used for incorporating such routines. This approach is quite straightforward and easy to understand in some ways. But when we consider that the Web services environment is frequently changing, this approach is not proper. Numerous new Web services are continuously being launched and existing Web services sometimes disappear without any notification (see Figure 1); thus, we cannot expect such changes to be immediately reflected in an application. There are times when the code incorporating dynamic service coordination routines might be too intractably complex to understand.

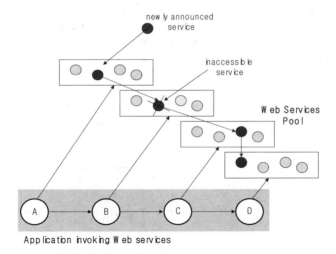

Fig. 1. Application invoking Web services.

Separating the dynamic service coordination part from the rest of the Web service invoking application can be a way of avoiding such deficiencies. In this approach, each reliable Web service invocation is designed beforehand for calling the Web service in an application. Necessary options for the Web service invocation are specified through a user interface, like a dialog box, and a class invoking the Web service with dynamic service coordination capability is then created using the information. An application can call the Web service by including the class in the application, creating an instance and invoking a method of the class. Since the dynamic service coordination capability is already implemented in the class, when the Web service invocation encounters a problem, the class instance will try another replacement Web service that has been prepared to cope with such a situation. This scenario is depicted in Figure 2.

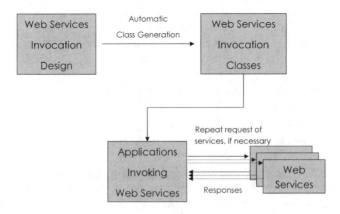

Fig. 2. Web services invoking class and dynamic service coordination.

The approach depicted above still has some limitations because in order to reflect newly available or disappearing Web services in the candidate list of Web services, the Web services invocation classes must be newly created and the application calling methods of the class should be recompiled.

If we can accept some performance loss in invoking Web services, much more flexible Web service invocation is possible. Figure 3 shows an application developing and running scenario when we use this method.

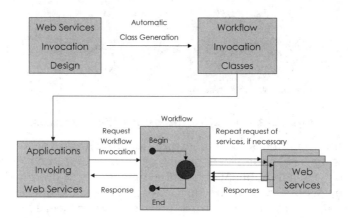

Fig. 3. Workflow invoking class and dynamic service coordination.

In this method, a workflow is created and it invokes a Web service on behalf of an application which invokes Web services. This method differs from the previous method because rather than creating a Web service invocation class, it creates a workflow invocation class, and a workflow instance is created and activated by the invocation of the workflow class instance.

There are several advantages of calling a Web service in this way. First of all, the facilities of the workflow system, such as exception handling and dynamic reconfiguration, can be used for the dynamic service coordination. For example, a change in the Web services environment such as the emergence of new Web services or the disappearance of those already in existence can be specified and handled easily through the exception handling mechanism of a workflow system. Whenever there is a change in the Web services environment, it can be immediately reflected impromptu without affecting the applications. Compilation of the application and workflow invocation class recreation is not necessary.

Moreover, when we use the exception handling mechanism of a workflow system, process level treatment of a Web service is possible. Since Web services advocate coarse grain service integration, process level treatment of Web service matches well with the nature of Web services. Lastly, when we use the exception handling mechanism of a workflow system, we can have much more flexibility for dynamic service coordination. Since the workflow system takes control whenever an exceptional situation is encountered, the exception handling mechanisms and facilities of the workflow system can be used, and any necessary steps can be easily inserted.

One problem of this method is that it inevitably incurs some performance loss in calling Web services. So when performance matters in invoking a Web service, using this method is not a proper approach.

3.2 Web Service Invocation Design

Several attributes should be decided and specified when a Web service is going to be called by an application. URL location, class name, method name, and the usage of the method are indispensable pieces of information for calling the Web service; at least such information should be specified in the design of the Web service invocation. To attach the dynamic service coordination function to the Web service invocation, additional information pertaining to the dynamic service coordination should be specified. The following table offers a list of attributes for the specification of dynamic service coordination.

Attributes	Descriptions
Replacing Web services	Specifies a list of candidate Web services when an invocation of a Web service fails.
Execution mode	Specifies the method of execution of Web services. Setting either parallel or sequential execution mode is possible through this option.
Latency	Specifies the time limitation until an application receives a response from a corresponding Web service. If an application does not receive any response from the Web service within this time limitation, a replacement Web service may be called instead.
UDDI update checking	Indicates whether a check on the update of the UDDI is needed when an application does not receive a response from a Web service.
Retrial	Indicates whether an application has to retry all the Web services in the candidate list again in the event it fails to receive a response from the Web service. The number of retrials can also be specified.
Pre/Post condition	Specifies the pre/post condition before or after the call of Web services. If those conditions are not satisfied, an exception is raised and notified.
Exception mode	Specifies the destination of control after handling an exception. *Resume, retry, ignore, break* and *terminate* are the five typical modes supported by a workflow system.
Class name	Specifies the name of class to be created.
Class type	Specifies the type of class to be created. Users can select either Web services invocation or workflow invocation classes.

Fig. 4. Design attributes of a Web service invocation.

Attributes in Figure 4 can be specified in textual form and a dialog box is more convenient to specify such information. Once all the attributes are set, a class can be created based on this information. The class includes dynamic service coordination functions as well as Web service invocation routines. As stated earlier, an application developer can easily incorporate dynamic service coordination capability in the application using this class. In the subsections that follow, we describe how to create a Web service invocation class and a workflow invocation class using attributes information set by users.

3.3 Generation of Web service invocation/Workflow invocation classes

Once all the attributes are set through the dialog box, the information is stored in the form of an XML document for later use. The primary usage of the XML document is to generate classes that satisfy the conditions and options specified in the XML document. Either Web service invocation or workflow invocation classes are created according to the specifications of class type attributes. Though the creation of classes is simple and straightforward, a module must be prepared to support this function. A class generation module has the role of creating classes. The class generation module parses the XML document and extracts essential information for the generation of a class and then creates a class.

```
import rwsc.*;

public class RWSC_Sample extends WebServicesInvoker {

        public RWSC_Sample() {
                super();

                setPreCondition("% pre-condition% ");
                setPostCondition("% post-condition% ");
                setRetrialCount(% retrial-count% );
                enableUDDIChecking();
        }

        protected Object invokeBasicCall() throws Exception {
                return % class-name% .% operation-name% .(% parameter-list% );
        }

        protected Object invokeCandidateCallsAll() throws Exception {
                try {
                        return % class-name% .% operation-name% .(% parameter-list% );
                }
                catch(Exception ignored) {}

                try {
                        return % class-name% .% operation-name% .(% parameter-list% );
                }
                catch(Exception ignored) {}

                return % class-name% .% operation-name% .(% parameter-list% );
        }

}
```

Fig. 5. Class template for the reliable invocation of a Web service.

Figure 5 shows one of the simplest class templates for automatic generation of Web service invocation classes. The final code is generated by replacing the strings in between % and % with attributes. Different class templates are used according to the attributes. All the class templates extend *WebServiceInvoker* class where routines for Web service invoking are implemented. So when an application calls a *public* method in the *WebServiceInvoker*, the method ensures an invocation of a Web service is reliable by calling the *protected* methods in *RWSC_Sample* class.

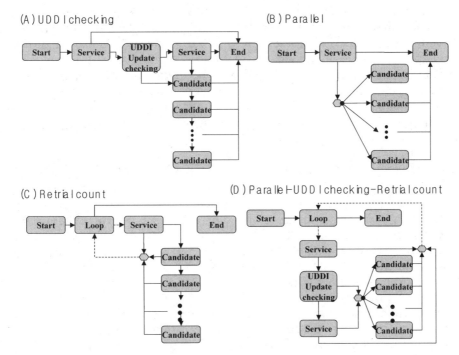

Fig. 6. Workflow patterns.

In the case of creating a workflow invocation class, we assume that a workflow and associated exception handling routines are already prepared to react to this invocation. Workflow and exception handling routines are created based on the attributes with the information of pre/post conditions and exception mode. Five exception modes, *resume, retry, ignore, break* and *terminate,* can be specified. In Section 4.1, we describe this in detail.

Eight kinds of workflow patterns are prepared and one of the workflow patterns is selected according to the options specified in the attributes. UDDI checking, retrial count and parallel mode are the options decided for the selection of patterns. Figure 6 shows four workflow patterns among eight. Workflow pattern (A) is chosen when only the UDDI checking option is selected. The UDDI checking step is inserted after the service step in which a Web service is invoked. In the UDDI checking step, any updates in the UDDI registry, such as a change of URL location or operation interface, are checked. Workflow pattern (B) is constructed as a parallel option. When the parallel option is chosen, all specified replacement Web services are requested simultaneously. If any of the Web services responds, it is considered that the request has been successfully conducted. Workflow pattern (C) is for the retrial count option. The retrial is repeated a specified number of times. If all three options are selected, workflow pattern (D) is chosen. Meanwhile, as the workflow takes most parts for the support of dynamic service coordination, the structure and contents of a workflow invocation class are relatively simple.

3.4 Web Services Invocation

If the classes in subsection 3.3 are successfully created, we can easily make reliable invocations for Web services in an application. As explained earlier, two kinds of classes can be created: one is a Web service invocation class and the other is a Web service calling workflow invocation class. The users of these classes should be careful in selecting the classes because the overhead for invoking a Web service of each class is very different. The details of this overhead problem are described in Section 5. At any rate, the decision of which class to use in an application should be made solely by developers.

Once the decision of which class is to be used in an application for an invocation of a Web service is made, all we need to do is include the created class in the application and call the methods in the class. Thus, incorporating the dynamic service capability into an application is simple.

4. DYNAMIC SERVICE COORDINATION IN EXCEPTION HANDLING OF WORKFLOW SYSTEM

When an application invokes a Web service via a workflow invocation class, the exception handling mechanism of a workflow system can be used to support dynamic service coordination. Figure 7 shows a typical sequence of steps when an application invokes a Web service via a workflow invocation class and encounters a time out exception. When a time out exception is raised during an invocation, the workflow system calls one of the handler routines, which then calls a replacement Web service. If the trial is successful, the result is delivered to the application via the workflow. If the trial is not successful, the handler may try the next replacement Web service. But since there are so many possible paths a handler can take, it should be guided by the set of attributes specified at the design of Web service invocation. That is, based on attribute information, handler routines are automatically generated and assigned to the workflow.

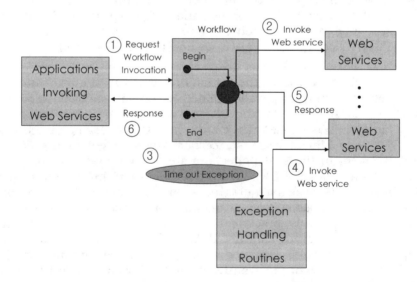

Fig. 7. Support of dynamic service coordination using the exception handling mechanism of a workflow system.

Since each workflow system has its own exception handling mechanism, each workflow system may have different mechanisms for handling the exceptions. In this case, we assume that user-defined exception handling routines can be attached to each activity of a workflow. In this section, we explain a sample exception handling mechanism of a workflow system.

The exception handling mechanism includes two main parts: exception specification and handling. In the exception specification part, *modes, models, triggering conditions* and *exception handlers* are specified. In the exception handling part, when an exception is raised at run time, the corresponding exception handler is invoked and it performs prescheduled exception handling steps. The following two subsections describe this, and their extensions for the support of dynamic services coordination, in more detail.

4.1 Dynamic Service Coordination in Exception Specification

In the exception specification part, various attributes are specified to define an exception. Triggering mode, conditions for raising an exception, exception handling mode and steps are defined in this part. User defined exception handling routines are also defined, and the dynamic service coordination is specified through the combination.

Handling Mode—This attribute specifies the degree of automation when triggering and terminating the exception handling process.

Automatic Mode denotes that the exception is fully controlled by the workflow system, and *Manual Mode* denotes that the exception is handled by user interactions. Since dynamic service coordination steps automatically select a compatible Web service to substitute an existing one, this attribute needs to be set to Automatic Mode.

Handling Model—As shown in Figure 8, there are five types of exception handling models. Since the dynamic service coordination makes the workflow continue its execution after replacing a service, "resume" needs to be selected for the model.

Exception Handler—An exception handler is defined as a set of activities to be executed when some exceptions are detected while executing a group of activities in a guarded block. The exception handler for the dynamic service coordination is composed of steps to find a compatible Web service, store intermediate results, substitute an existing service with a new Web service, and activate the new Web service with the intermediate results stored.

Timeout Condition—This attribute is newly added to accommodate the dynamic coordination capability in the exception handling mechanism. it checks the time duration of a step. If a step does not terminate within a specified time limit, a timeout exception occurs. This attribute is prepared to effectively cope with the situation in which a Web service is stalling for a request issued by a workflow step.

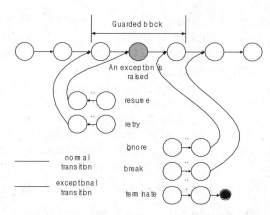

Fig. 8. Five exception handling models (resume, retry, ignore, break and terminate) supported by workflow system.

Once the attributes for the specification of dynamic service coordination are decided and associated exception handling routines are prepared, exceptions supporting dynamic service coordination are specified using the DTD (Document Type Definitions) in Figure 9. The DTD is a syntax to specify exception attributes in XPDL (XML Process Definition Language).

```
...
<!ELEMENT Package (PackageHeader,..., Exceptions?, ExtendedAttribu-
tes?)>
<!ELEMENT WorkflowProcess (ProcessHeader,...,Exceptions?,
          GuardedBlocks?, ExtendedAttributes?)>
<!ELEMENT Activity (Description?, ..., PreCondition,
          PostCondition, ExtendedAttributes?)>
<!ELEMENT PreCondition (#PCDATA | Xpression)*>
<!ELEMENT PostCondition (#PCDATA | Xpression)*>
<!ELEMENT Transitions (Transition*, ExceptionalTransition*)>
<!ELEMENT ExceptionalTransition (Condition?, Description?,
          ExtendedAttributes?)>
<!ATTLIST ExceptionalTransition
          Id NMTOKEN #REQUIRED
          From NMTOKEN #REQUIRED
          To NMTOKEN #REQUIRED
          Loop (NOLOOP | FROMLOOP | TOLOOP) #IMPLIED
          Name CDATA #IMPLIED>
<!ELEMENT Exceptions (Exception*)>
<!ELEMENT Exception (Description)?)>
<!ATTLIST Exception
          Id NMTOKEN #REQUIRED
          Name CDATA #IMPLIED>
```

```
<!ELEMENT GuardedBlocks(GuardedBlock*)>
<!ATTLIST GuardedBlock
          Id NMTOKEN #REQUIRED
          From NMTOKEN #REQUIRED
          To NMTOKEN #REQUIRED
          Name CDATA #IMPLIED>
<!ELEMENT OnExceptions (OnException*)>
<!ELEMENT OnException (RetryCount ?)>
<!ATTLIST OnException
          Id NMTOKEN #REQUIRED
          Name CDATA #IMPLIED>
<!ELEMENT RetryCount(#PCDATA)>
...
```

Fig. 9. DTD for representing exception attributes in XPDL.

The main elements necessary to represent dynamic service coordination in a workflow are summarized as follows:

Activity – Exceptions that activate the dynamic service coordination from an activity are specified in this part. The OnExceptions element can contain zero or more OnException attributes. Each OnException element contains attributes such as Id, Name, RetryCount.

Transitions – The ExceptionalTransition element specifies the path to reach the dynamic service coordination steps when an exception occurs.

Exceptions – A set of exceptions that trigger the dynamic service coordination can be defined in this element. Individual exceptions are described in the Exception element.

GuardedBlocks – The GuardedBlocks element specifies ranges of activities in which exceptions are caught and the dynamic service coordination steps are activated. An activity range is represented in From and To attributes in each GuardedBlock element.

Figure 10 shows an exception handling scenario that explains how the exception handling mechanism is used to support the dynamic service coordination. TimeoutException is attached in a guarded block and occurs during the execution of Activity 3, and the control follows along the path ExceptionalTransition1 designates, meaning Activity 5 is invoked as the exception handler (dynamic service coordinator). In this diagram, the circles denote the activities and the triangle denotes the exception. A guarded block represents a block in which exceptions are monitored and the dynamic service coordination is activated.

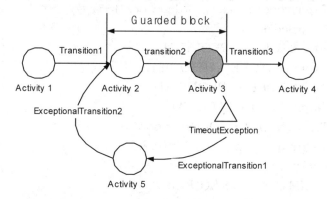

Fig. 10. Example scenario that shows how an exception is caught in a guarded block and the dynamic service coordination is performed.

Figure 11 shows the XPDL description of the above exception handling scenario.

```
<Package Id="1" Name="Sample Model">
<WorkflowProcesses>
  <WorkflowProcess Id="1" Name="Sample Process1">
  ...
  <Activities>
    <Activity Id="1" Name="Activity1">...</Activity>
    <Activity Id="2" Name="Activity2">...</Activity>
    <Activity Id="3" Name="Activity3">...</Activity>
    <Activity Id="4" Name="Activity4">...</Activity>
  </Activities>
  <Transitions>
    <Transition Id="1" From="1" To="2" Name="Transition1"/>
    <Transition Id="2" From="2" To="3" Name="Transition2"/>
    <Transition Id="3" From="3" To="4" Name="Transition2"/>
    <ExceptionalTransition Id="3" From="3"
    To="5" Name="ExceptionalTransition1"/>
    <ExceptionalTransition Id="5" From="2"
    To="4" Name="ExceptionalTransition2"/>
  </Transitions>
  <Exceptions>
    <Exception Id="1" Name="TimeoutException">
      <Description>Timeout occurred</Description>
    </Exception>
  </Exceptions>
  <GuardedBlocks>
   <GuardedBlock Id="1" From="2" To="3">
```

```
    <OnExceptions>
      <OnException Id="1" TransitionId="3"/>
    </OnExceptions>
    </GuardedBlock>
   </GuardedBlocks>
  </WorkflowProcess>
 ...
 </WorkflowProcesses>
 </Package>
```

Fig. 11. Example exception-handling specification written in XPDL.

4.2 Dynamic Service Coordination Specification and Invocation

As explained in 4.1, dynamic service coordination specification is simple and straightforward. After creating a workflow with an activity, mark guarded block for the activity invoking the Web service. All the attributes associated with dynamic service coordination are specified at the design of a Web service invocation. The attributes are used in the creation of a workflow. A workflow with an activity that invokes a Web service is then created and exceptions are specified according to the attributes.

Since dynamic service coordination specification is embedded into exception specification, the invocation of dynamic service coordination follows the mechanism of the exception handling mechanism. In the exception handling point of view, the only difference is associated handling routines for dynamic service coordination.

5. CONCLUSION

Component-based or service-oriented application integration will give us real power when there is a sufficient variety and quality of component services to reach the "critical mass." We believe that the widespread use of Web services will realize this critical mass and allow business users to quickly assemble applications from various Web services that are available inside and outside an enterprise.

Despite the bright future of Web services technology, there remain many hurdles to overcome before it achieves real success. For example, Web services on the Internet are not always reliable in terms of service availability and performance.

Exception-based dynamic service coordination method for Web services is discussed to resolve this problem. Web service invocation and workflow invocation classes are used to make an invocation of a Web service reliable by calling the Web service indirectly via such classes. Though an exception handling mechanism of a workflow system is used for the implementation, the method is not necessarily confined to the workflow system. Any workflow system with an exception handling mechanism can develop its own method by referring to the method.

We can expect some benefits by converting a direct invocation of a Web service into an indirect invocation. However, those benefits are the result of sacrificing performance in calling the Web service. If latency matters in invoking a Web service, direct or indirect invocation via a generated class are proper approaches. When we consider the nature of Web services, in which long-term business processes are the primary services to be implemented by connecting Web services, some performance losses in invoking a Web service could be endured to some extent.

The UDDI registry is well recognized as a useful means for dynamic access point management. The dynamic service coordination would be improved if the functions of the UDDI registry were merged with it.

Applying Knowledge Management to Exploit the Potential of Information Stored in a Business Process Management System

Juan J. Moreno, Lithium Software / Universidad Católica, Uruguay.
Luis Joyanes, Universidad Pontificia de Salamanca, Spain

ABSTRACT

An important part of the organizational knowledge needed to operate and grow is embedded in business processes automated via Workflow Management Systems (WMS) and Business Process Management Systems (BPMS). Organizations own this knowledge, but they are often unable to use it in the best way, mainly because it is extremely difficult to retrieve and interpret that information.

This paper proposes a model that allows extraction and modelling of generated knowledge, stored in a Business Process Management System. With this knowledge available, we can make recommendations to human participants about good and bad decisions, to improve performance, reduce mistakes and shorten learning times. These recommendations are based on successful and unsuccessful cases in the past. We also can recommend the most suitable participant for each process instance, based on its characteristics and the participant's expertise and experience.

The proposed model is based on a well-known Artificial Intelligence methodology, called Case Based Reasoning (CBR), applied on BPM and using BPEL (Business Process Execution Language) as the specification and execution language. Knowledge Maps are used to describe knowledge distribution in the organization. This model is extensible, so it can be adapted easily to the particularities of each business process.

Keywords: Knowledge Management (KM), Business Process Management (BPM), Workflow, BPEL, Case Based Reasoning (CBR), Knowledge Maps.

INTRODUCTION

Inside organizations, and mainly in their business processes, there is an important part of the knowledge needed by them to operate and grow.

But, what is knowledge? This question has been discussed since ancient Greek. The answer exceeds the scope of this work, so we use a simple definition: knowledge is a relationship between the knower (the person) and a proposition [BRA2004]. In the particular context of Business Process Management (BPM), we just say that knowledge is what allows a human to take a business decision. This knowledge is owned by organizations, but they are often unable to use it as they would like [MOR2003]. Lew Platt—CEO of Hewlett-Packard at this time—said that (repeating a retired HP Labs director words) "If HP knew what HP knows, it would be three times more profitable" [DAV2001]. This phrase resumes the shared conviction of many executives and company directors about the potential of the knowledge they own, and how extremely difficult it is to take advantage of it.

There is agreement in the management community that knowledge plays a vital role between successful and unsuccessful organizations. Luis Joyanes in [JOY2002] mentions that:

> ...the most valuable actives in an organization, are not tangible actives (machines, buildings, installations, stocks), but intangible actives, those with its origin in their own employees knowledge, abilities, values and attitudes. Those intangible actives are called intellectual capital, and connect implicit or explicit knowledge that generate economic value for the organization...

The economist Sidney Winter, in 1994 described enterprises as "organizations that know how to make things" [WIN1994]. An enterprise is, finally, a set of synchronized persons producing something, meaning goods, services or a combination of them. Its production capability depends on what they usually know and the knowledge acquired in their routines and production flows. An enterprise active material has limited value unless people know what to do with it. In this context, we use Marwick's definition [MAR2001] of knowledge management:

> The set of systematic and disciplined actions that an organization can take, to obtain the greatest value from the knowledge available to it.

Equivalent to this definition, and from a more practical point of view, knowledge management consists of:

> Giving people the data and information they need to be efficient and competent in their jobs.

Some organizations have tried to improve their performance using collaborative knowledge networks: peer to peer networks that connect persons with the required experience with peers needing it ([TIW2003], [TIW2005]). Unfortunately these solutions have not had the expected success ([BUS2005]).

As DeMichelis pointed out [DEM2004], information technologies can play an important role to strengthen knowledge-based communities in:

- Maintaining and enhancing community memory
- Enriching communication links among members
- Keeping communities open
  - Peripheral participation
  - Access to central participation
  - Bringing external knowledge to it.

Initially Workflow, and now Business Process Management, have helped organizations to reach their goals and compete in a rough market. They are largely adopted technologies and the majority of successful companies all around the world in every market segment, use them. **These systems execute most (or all) main business processes. In this context, the most important decisions and the most relevant information are stored in their databases. Important business knowledge exists in many Workflow and BPM related items**. We can distinguish three knowledge categories available in WMS and BPMS [MOR2003]:

- Business process modelling. When a formal or semi-formal representation of a business process is obtained, a great part of the knowledge related on how the business should work is encapsulated.
- Business process instance content. When a business process is executed, participants use and embed in the system part of their knowledge used to reach business goals.

- Process instances statistical information. A statistically valid number of process instances, could provide relevant information about the business, what is very useful for decisions makers.

In this work, we will explore the last two, exploiting the potential that this information has. In this context, we try to get the maximum benefit out of Business Process Management Systems available in the organization.

A tool that makes correct suggestions is aligned with a major objective all organizations: reduce the time it takes to make a decision [GEE2005]. Given the three knowledge management stages (knowledge acquisition, sharing and using) introduced by Nonaka and Takeuchi [NON1995], this work focuses in knowledge acquisition and sharing, to give people the data and information they need to be efficient and competent in their jobs.

To end this introductory stage, we present a very simple example that involves described concepts. Let's imagine a business process in a bank, in which credit card appliances are evaluated. After many executions, a pattern is found, that shows that the credit card is denied to people earning less than X and without immovable property. Probably, there is not a formal business rule that says that. However, expert evaluators use it daily. This knowledge resides in the process instances set stored in the BPMS database. If it is extracted and shown in an appropriated manner to new and inexpert evaluators, they would probably need shorter training times to do their job correctly.

Working Hypothesis

We use just a part of the knowledge stored in a BPMS, just necessary to prove the working hypothesis:

In a workflow application with human participants, automated with a WMS or a BPMS, due to the stored information, it is feasible to:

- **Recommend decisions in every step of the process, based on successful and unsuccessful decisions taken in the past for similar process instances.**
- **Suggest the most suitable participant for a stage of a process instance, based on the instance characteristics, the available participants and their abilities.**

Proposed solutions and models are applicable to BPMS and WMS, so from now we are using both of these terms.

PROPOSED SOLUTION

Every time an organization member participates in a process to realize a business objective, he uses its knowledge in accordance with the objective. In non-automated processes, the knowledge is used by a human, but it is not possible to extract it later from just the process instance.

When business processes are automated, it is feasible to extract part of the embedded knowledge in the process instance, because it is stored in the BPMS. Next step consists on extending this concept to all participations in the process instance life cycle. In this way, it is possible to store the major part of the knowledge used by expert participants.

Illustration 1 represents this concept, and compares it with a non-automated process. In the first one, after the expert acts, nothing is stored and the process instance simply advances in its life cycle. On the other hand, in the automated process, it is feasible to store part of the knowledge used to take decisions and execute tasks. In this way, at any stage of the life cycle of the process instance $n + 1$, there is relevant information available from the n previous instances.

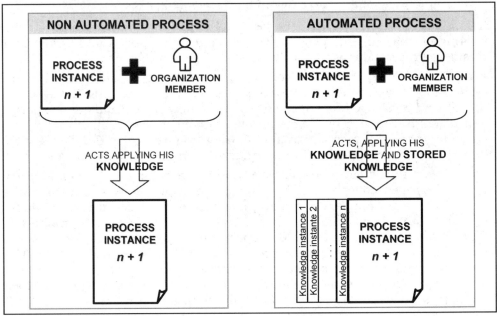

Illustration 1 Knowledge stored in process instances

Having stored part of the expert knowledge used during a process instance execution, now it is time to extract it, which will be described next.

RECOMMENDATION PROCESS

The process has 5 clearly defined steps, as shown in Illustration 2. Initially, the new case characteristics are obtained, corresponding to the process instance being evaluated. After that, the recommendation process occurs, using the available case database. The recommendation is returned (about the most suitable participant or the better decision). In any case, the user takes a decision that is later evaluated by an expert, feeding back the case database with the degree of success. The second step is the most interesting, shown in Illustration 3, and described in the next sections.

Illustration 2 Recommendation process

Using Patterns

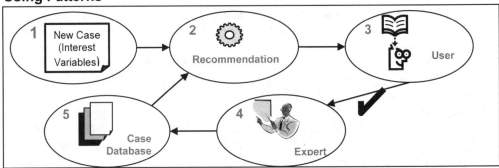

To retrieve information, Case Based Reasoning is used. A source case is evaluated through a similarity function and a destination case is recommended. To evaluate, interest variables are used, representing the most important values to characterize each process instance. Continuing with the credit card example, an interest variable should be the age of the applier, which is stored in the process instance, in the BPMS database.

A further analysis, demonstrates that it is impracticable to compare a process instance against all process instances stored in the database. There could be thousands, maybe millions. In this context, we are using **patterns**. We are proposing that from a base case, a destination case of different type will be returned. There are different types of cases since the base case is a process instances, and the destination case is a pattern. This is feasible due to the similarity function that compares instance process interest variables against pattern interest variables. We will say that a process instance is similar to a given pattern, when their interest variables values are similar.

Besides this, the information stored in these patterns is stored, balancing the patterns with the successfulness feedback (from the expert, another person or a system).

Case Based Reasoning

The CBR cycle has 4 steps, as shown in Illustration 3:

- **Retrieve** the most relevant cases considering the process instance being evaluated
- **Reuse** the solution from the chosen case
- **Revise or adapt** the solution if necessary.
- **Retain** the final solution when it has been validated.

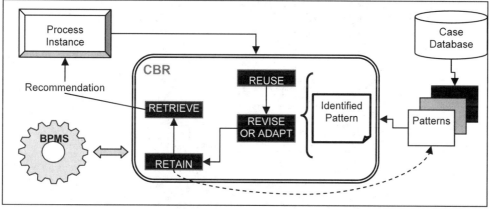

Illustration 3 Applying CBR to the problem

Given the process instance, it is compared against every available pattern, using the similarity function. Three scenarios could occur:

1. Just one pattern is enough similar to the process instance. The similarity function returns just one value higher than the defined threshold.
   a. This pattern is taken

2. Many patterns are similar to the process instance. The similarity function returns more than one value higher than the defined threshold.
   a. The pattern with the higher similarity function is taken. In case of a draw, the pattern is taken randomly.

3. No pattern is enough similar to the process instance. The similarity function does not return any value higher than the defined threshold.
   a. A new pattern is created, from the evaluated process instance. The pattern takes for its interest variables, the values from the process instance.

The most critical component when using CBR in this way is the similarity function, used to determine if a pattern is similar to a process instance or not. A very restrictive function would produce too many patterns, making it difficult to match patterns with process instances and the recommendation process. On the other hand, a very flexible function would generate too few patterns making recommendations valueless. The similarity function must be tuned with these points in mind. Manhattan and Euclidean similarity functions have demonstrated to perform well ([MAR2005]), but other type of functions should be considered too.

Knowledge generation in the proposed model attends a non linear structure ([KLA2003]), in which the old and new knowledge is integrated at any time, and both of them contribute to successful decisions. However, it could also be a problem, in case of tendencies, as described in Future Work.

Patterns Model

To represent the patterns, many structures are used (Illustration 4):

- *Pattern:* contains patterns with attribute values, the number of cases represented, and the number of successful and unsuccessful evaluations obtained after applying the pattern.
- *Activity:* represents available activities.
- *Attributes,* with a *weight* representing the importance of each one, used by the similarity function.
- *Activities_Patterns,* containing the number of successful and unsuccessful evaluations obtained after applying the pattern.
- *Attributes_Patterns*: containing the values of the attributes in the patterns.

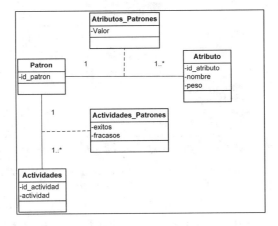

Illustration 4 Class diagram to support patterns [BUO2005]

Organizational Knowledge Maps

Organizational Knowledge Maps allows linking the knowledge with the people that own it. In this way, given a process instance that requires some abilities to be processed successfully, it is possible to know the most suitable participant to act.

Knowledge maps must be updated regularly in order to keep their validity. This is done in two ways. The first one is manual, and consists on updating each person abilities. The second is automatic, using inferences about the links between abilities. If a number of persons (over a threshold) have the abilities *A* and *B*, it could be inferred that these abilities are complementary or similar. In this context, if there is a process instance requiring ability B, a person with the ability A could act as a substitute of the ideal person (with the B ability) in a successful way.

The knowledge maps supporting model, should include persons, abilities, activities and the experience of each person in each activity. Patterns obviously, must be considered too, as shown in Illustration 5.

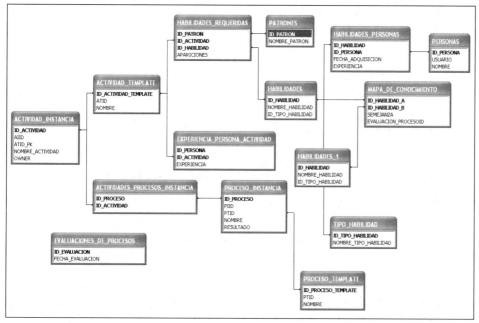

Illustration 5 Knowledge map entity diagram. [MRT2005]

Recommendation visualization

After obtaining a recommendation for a decision or a participant, the system must show this information to the user. Considering the decision example, there is a number of different ways to show it to the user. Illustration 6 shows two different ways of doing it. In the first one, the options are presented in a graphic process definition, highlighting the recommended. This could be useful for a person who knows the business and wants to see the process and decision consequences. In the second, the recommendation is integrated in the user application, and it is shown highlighting the button that corresponds to the recommended decision. This solution is much simpler, and the user does not need to know the process flow.

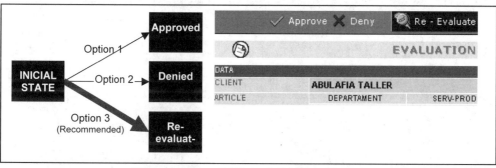

Illustration 6 Visual Suggestions

There are other visualization techniques that could be used (Parallel coordinates, Rule Viz, and so on), as described in [LOP2004]. The visualization technique to be used depends on the user type, the process complexity and the user application flexibility.

There is an important task that should not be forgotten, giving feedback to the user about the validity of the recommendation. Simple indicators could be used, as shown in Illustration 7 that shows the number of instances that support the recommendation, with the similarity of the pattern and the process instance. Another important tool is how many participants have taken the given recommendation.

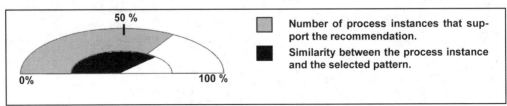

Illustration 7 User Feedback about recommendation validity

Social Issues.

Under-contribution is a typical problem for online communities, and of course, for a solution like the proposed. An important point of the collective effort model is that individuals contribute when they are reminded of their uniqueness and believe that their contribution is necessary to reach the group objective [BEE2004]. In this context, valuable participations are recognized and stored in the case database. Moreover, given that every participant takes his decision in a specific process stage, it affects directly the final result. Outstanding cases could be distributed to other participants.

Another important thing to consider is the communication between participants. Though recommendable, it could be so intensive that some participants could lose productivity. There are researches and automatic tools to detect if someone is interruptible or not by another community member, for example [HOR2004] y [BEG2004]. These tools must be considered in a scenario that presents interruption overload problems.

Validation and Verification

The proposed model was validated and verified through a credit card approval process prototype. BPEL was used as business process specification and execution language. IBM WebSphere Studio Application Developer Integration Edition V5.1 was used as modelling tool, and Java as programming language. Illustration 8 shows the implemented process in BPEL.

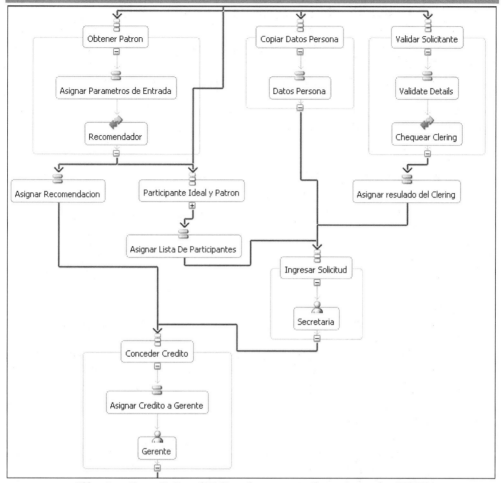

Illustration 8 Credit Card approval process in BPEL

The model has been successfully implemented in a commercial BPMS. BPEL has been used as specification and execution language. This prototype was also useful to refine some important aspects of the proposed solution.

CONCLUSIONS

Many technological and economical observers agree in the future of Information Technologies consists in the complete business process automation. The success of companies lies in the tools used to manage their processes. This made the Workflow and BPM technology grow rapidly in the last years, motivating the transfer of a great part of the organization knowledge from human brains to databases where process instances are stored. This knowledge used in every business process is absolutely necessary for organizations to operate, grow and reach their objectives. If these business processes are automated, they become a valuable knowledge library. The general objective of this work has been managing and taking the most out of this knowledge, optimizing organization performance.

The specific objective of this work has been to provide a framework, a model and a functionally complete prototype for building knowledge management systems over workflow and BPM applications.

The innovation of these systems is that they are able to **recommend the best decisions** to the process participants, given a process instance and a case database. The other non-less important innovation is the facility to

identify the most suitable participants to act in a process instance, based on their experience, abilities and process instance characteristics.

To reach the goal, the problem was fractionated in three clearly defined stages: knowledge extraction from process instances, its representation and storage in adequate mediums, and finally its visualization. The layer division approach allows the improvement of each one without affecting the whole system. This provides the flexibility—from the point of view of adaptability, updatability and extensibility—required for a solution that must support future requirements and extensions.

Having reached these objectives, it is possible to answer affirmatively to the working hypothesis:

- It is possible to suggest decisions in every step of the process, based on successful and unsuccessful decisions taken in the past for similar process instances.
- It is possible to suggest the most suitable participant for process instance stage, based on the instance characteristics and the available participants and their abilities.

FUTURE WORK

In automated business process, participants could write observations in natural language, supporting their decisions, for example in doubtful cases. Discussions between experts could have valuable information and knowledge. Natural Language Processing, available since decades ago, could provide useful tools in this context, as demonstrated in [KAO2005] , [MOO2005].

Detecting tendencies is a major issue to resolve. In a system like the proposed, already trained and with a big case database, tendencies could be detected too late. For example, given a process instance with a set of values in its interest variables X, in stage Z, decision Y has been always successfully taken. A market change makes this decision incorrect, and decision R must be taken for this kind of process instance. This will make that Y decisions receives unsuccessful evaluations and in the long term, the system will learn. But, if the tendency of n consecutives unsuccessful evaluations of Y decision is detected earlier, the lost produced by bad decisions could be minimized. There are many approaches for this. Log analysis as presented in [PEN2005], should not be overlooked.

ACKNOWLEDGEMENTS

The authors would like to thank the members of Lithium Software Research Team, and the Process Automation Working Group of the Universidad Católica del Uruguay, for rich discussions of concepts in this paper presented. We also would like to thank María Eugenia for her help.

REFERENCES

ALD2004   Aldaz, Guillermo; Moreno, Juan J and Novales, Rafael. **Knowledge Extraction Algorithms in Workflow.** (Algoritmos de extracción de conocimiento para procesos automatizados mediante Workflow). Research in IT Sciences Conference of the Universidad Católica del Uruguay. Montevideo, Uruguay. 2004.

BEE2004   Beenen, Gerard; Ling Kimberly; Wang, Xiaoqing; Chang, Klarissa; Frankowski, Dan; Resnick, Paul and Kraut, Robert. **Using Social Psychology to Motivate Contributions to Online Communities**. Proceedings of the Computer Supported Cooperative Work of the ACM. 2004.

BEG2004   Begole, James; Matsakis, Nicholas and Tang, John. **Lilsys: Sensing Unavailability**. Proceedings of the Computer Supported Cooperative Work of the ACM. 2004.

BRA2004   Brachman, Ronald and Levesque, Hector. **Knowledge Representation and Reasoning**. Elsevier. 2004.

BUO2005   Buonafina, Juan; Moreno, Juan J and Novales, Rafael. **Knowledge Extraction Algorithms in BPM**. (Algoritmos de extracción de conocimiento para procesos automatizados en un ambiente BPM.). Research in IT Sciences Conference of the Universidad Católica del Uruguay. Montevideo, Uruguay. 2005.

BUS2005   Bush, Ashley and Tiwana, Amrit. Designing Sticky Knowledge Networks. Communications of the ACM. May. 2005.

DAV2001   Davenport, Thomas and Prusak, Laurence. **Working Knowledge**. Prentice Hall. 2001.

DEM2004   DeMichelis, Giorgio. **Communities and Technologies: An approach to Foster Social Capital.** Proceedings of the Computer Supported Cooperative Work of the ACM. 2004.

GEE2005   Geer, David. **Developments Advance Web Conferencing**. IEEE Computer. February. 2005.

HOR2004   Horvitz, Eric; Koch, Paul and Apacible, Johnson. BusyBody: **Creating and Fielding Personalized Models of the Cost of Interruption**. Proceedings of the Computer Supported Cooperative Work of the ACM. 2004.

JOY2002   Joyanes, Luis. **La gestión del Conocimiento: El nuevo paradigma organizativo y empresarial (tendencias y portales)**. Revista Sociedad y Utopía. Nro. 18. Facultad de Informática, Universidad Pontificia de Salamanca, España. 2001.

KAO2005   Kao, Ane and Poteet, Steve. **Text Mining and Natural Language Processing.** SIGKDD Explorations of the ACM. 2005.

KLA2003   Klamma, Ralf and Spaniol, Marc. **Supporting Communication and Knowledge Creation in Digitally Networked Communities in the Humanities**. Bulletin of ACM Special Interest Group on Supporing Group Work (SIGGROUP). December. 2003.

LOP2004   López, Adrián; Moreno, Juan J and Novales, Rafael. **Visualization and Distribution Techniques for knowledge extracted from workflow applications**. (Técnicas de distribución y visualización de conocimiento extraído de aplicaciones de workflow.). Research in IT Sciences Conference of the Universidad Católica del Uruguay. Montevideo, Uruguay. 2004.

MAR2001   Marwick, A. D. **Knowledge management technology**. IBM Systems Journal, Vol 40, N° 4. 2001.

MAR2005   Martirena, Gastón; Novales, Rafael and Moreno, Juan J. **Similarity Functions for Knowledge Management in Business Process Management**. (Funciones de Similitud para la Gestión del Conocimiento en el Gerenciamiento de Procesos de Negocio). Research in IT Sciences Conference of the Universidad Católica del Uruguay. Montevideo, Uruguay. 2005.

MOO2005   Mooney, Raymond and Bunescu, Razvan. **Mining Knowledge from Text Using Information Extraction**. SIGKDD Explorations of the ACM. 2005.

MOR2002   Moreno, Juan J. and Ocampo, Ernesto. **Community of Practice in Business Process Automation at the Universidad Católica del Uruguay.** (Comunidad de Práctica en Automatización de Procesos de Negocios en la Universiada Católica del Uruguay).Proceedings of the 2nd International Congress of Information and Knowledge Society. (CISIC-2002). Madrid, Spain. 2002

MOR2003	Moreno, Juan J.; Aldaz, Guillermo and Joyanes, Luis. **Knowledge Management in business process automation.** (Gestión del Conocimiento en la automatización de procesos de negocios). Proceedings of the 2nd International Symposium of Information Systems and Software Engineering in the Knowledge Society. (SISOFT-2003). Lima, Peru. 2003.
MOR2005	Moreno, Juan J.; Aldaz, Guillermo and Joyanes, Luis. **Knowledge extraction in environments automated with Workflow Management Systems.** (Extracción de conocimiento en ambientes automatizados con Sistemas de Gestión de Workflow). Proceedings of the III International Symposium of Information Systems and Software Engineering in the Knowledge Society. (SISOFT-2005). Santo Domingo, República Dominicana. 2005.
MRT2005	Martínez, Valeria; Moreno, Juan J and Novales, Rafael. **Knowledge Maps in BPM**. (Mapas de Conocimiento Organizacionales en el Gerenciamiento de Procesos de Negocio). Research in IT Sciences Conference of the Universidad Católica del Uruguay. Montevideo, Uruguay. 2005.
NON1995	Nonaka, I. and Takeuchi, H. **The knowledge-creating company**. Oxford University Press. 1995.
PEN2005	Peng, Wei; Li, Tao and Ma, Sheng. **Mining Logs Files for Data-Driven System Management**. SIGKDD Explorations of the ACM. 2005.
TIW2005	Tiwana, Amrit and Bush, Ashley. **Continuance in expertise-sharing networks: A social perspective**. Communications of the ACM. February. 2005.
TIW203	Tiwana, Amrit. **Affinity to infinity in peer-to-peer knowledge platforms**. Communications of the ACM. May. 2003.
WIN1994	Winter, Sidney. **On Coase, Competence, and the Corporation**. Oxford University Press. 1994.

Use and Discard of Workflow Systems

Tadeu Cruz, TRCR Knowledge, Brazil

SUMMARY

This chapter discusses the implementation and use of Workflow systems to automate business processes in organizations of all types and economic sectors and how/why some of these organizations give up to use the software, even after hefty investments in such implementation projects.

Use and *Discard* were the words chosen to characterize the adoption and abandonment of Workflow systems by part of the various organizations that after implementing it had stopped its use; as well as explaining the behavior of those that never installed it in any machine.

The author's intention was to discover the causes of such situations, to understand and to explain, for those interested in Workflow systems, the reasons that drive the organizations to have these types of behaviors.

INTRODUCTION

The discoveries that we made, throughout ten years of participating in projects of implementation of Workflow systems, suggest that from the universe of organizations that could benefit from the functionalities of the Workflow model only a small number decided to try them, which means that there are a lot of organizations were it is possible to sell workflow systems. It seems they had still not massively adhered to the idea of automating business processes, even because the proper subject "business processes," their elements and its implementation, is something that is far of being consensus for great part of the executives. This, perhaps, occurs due to the taxonomy used to classify the existing elements in processes that, while not being an accurate science, allow each specialist to create their proper nomenclature, which makes it difficult for business processes to be universally understood and used in Workflow systems projects.

THE QUESTIONS THAT THIS WORK TRIED TO ANSWER

With the research we wanted to answer for some fidgets that afflict studious and specialists of Workflow systems, from academics to non-academics, such as:

- What does it take for organizations to develop Workflow implementation projects?
- What do the organizations expect from the implementation of Workflow systems?
- Why some organizations invest in Workflow systems implementation projects and they end up aborting and throwing away the software and all the investment made in it?
- Why the organizations cannot use the Workflow exploring its original characteristics and functionalities (3Rs)?
- How the organizations record, analyze and organize business processes in order to implement them in the Workflow systems?
- Is it possible to measure the return on the investment (ROI) made with the acquisition and the implementation of Workflow systems?

- How must Workflow systems be "sold" by the organization for the employees in order to make them to perceive the upcoming benefits to be gotten with the adoption of such softwares?
- Who, inside of the organizations, must assume the property (paternity of the solution) of the Workflow system?

The research like the one that we carried through asks many never formulated, or answered, questions before in other works dedicating itself to discover what fails in projects involving Workflow systems. The majority of the works, academic or not, presents cases of success or are written to guide the applicability of such and such product, such and such type of organization.

The result of this work must be understood as a small contribution for a new source of studies regarding the Workflow systems.

THE ORGANIZATIONS WITH WHICH WE HAD CONTACT

We studied 33 organizations; 15 Brazilian and 18 transnationals (10 of these are established in Brazil), private and government organizations, diverse economic sectors, from 2000 to 2004. Given the character of this work, we decided not to transcript the interviews that we made. However, analyzing them we concluded that there are certain patterns that make the answers quite similar. The main patterns are:

- Repeatability. The answers to the interviews follow a pattern of stable repeatability for certain questions. For example, all organizations, from any kind of economic sectors and origin of their capital, agree that for the success of any Workflow Project a business processes analysis and modeling methodology is indispensable. Another constant repetition is that high management must be permanently involved with the project, as a means to guaranteeing its implementation and consequent success. Almost all the organizations complain about the expensiveness of the softwares specialists.
- Scarcity of data and quantitative information. Consistently no organization wanted to disclose financial data about their projects, be they successful or not. One of the few times such information was given to us it was in a no-contextualized and unproven manner. The lack of financial data made it unable for us to calculate ROI and VOI, and if those values had or not been proven for the successful projects. In fact, we believe that the data existed in many organizations researched; they just weren't given to us.

Although the number of organizations researched were low, we can attest that many others, that didn't even receive us, have the same behavior, but we were unable to compute them at our present work because we did not establish any direct contact, even if informal, with any of their employees.

Here the kind of relationship we had with the studied organizations.

- In 55 percent of the organizations we had the direct participation in all the implementation phases of the Workflow project. Phases that went from the sale to the use of the software by its users.
- In 40 percent of the organizations we had the indirect participation and in some phases of the projects, for an example, we were involved only in the business process analysis and modeling
- In 5 percent of the organizations we only studied what had happened with the project for Workflow implementation.

HYPOTHESIS

We aimed to contextualize our conclusions in the subject of this paper: "Use and Discard of Workflow Systems," seeking to explain, in part, some of the causes for the behavior of organizations that were involved with Workflow systems.

When we set ourselves into investigating and studying why Workflow software is bought, why some are implemented while others end up inside a drawer or piled up on a shelf, why organizations stop using them, why they don't frequently update both the software and the processes that are executed on them, we didn't expect to find the difficulties that we had to overcome. We believe that the resistance presented by the interviewees was due to the fact of the explicit question that was made when we solicited an interview: we would like to know how the Workflow software is being used on your organization. Maybe, if we had given the research the approach of getting to know the causes and effects of project's *success*, the interviews would have been easier. Some of the refusals were extremely interesting:

For example: we had contact with a Brazilian bank that acquired an American Workflow software ten years ago and implemented on it a credit approval process and in these ten years never updated versions of the software nor the process. Which means: for ten years the software and process are the same. Obviously, no one in the bank wished to give us an interview, something that to a certain extent is comprehensible. The most interesting data was that we tried to retrieve information with one of the analysts that participated on the project. We asked him how a process could stay more then ten years without being updated, he replied: *So you can see how well made it was. We never needed to update it again. It has been working for ten years.*

The organizations studied by us, with rare exceptions, were in two extremes when they decided to implement Workflow. In one extreme were those that did not know the real use of the software and the changes required in the organization's culture for its implementation. In the other extreme were those that expected more that the software could actually deliver. We believe, that if we were to observe another group of companies from now on, it would be possible that this phenomenon would repeat itself, because the introduction of BPM software could have altered the referential already acquired with Workflow systems on the organizations that already knew it and introduced new doubts and worries on those that have not had any contact yet with Workflow. Through our studies we were able to conclude that when organizations interest themselves on implementing Workflow seldom they know what it is and what it is for.

Frequently, also, the responsible for Workflow implementation projects confuse it with Electronic Document Management Systems (EDMS). EDM is not part of the Workflow reference model, WfMC; therefore it is not Workflow, but both technologies can work integrated together. Some Workflow software brands include on their suites Electronic Document Management modules, which to us, confuses the users and makes it more difficult to understand that those technologies are unique, but complementary.

As a result we have seen that when two or more Workflow software are evaluated those that have an EDM module are at given an advantage over those which are purely Workflow systems; being that all buyers wish to "get more for less". However, what we detected is most unknown by the organizations is what are business processes and, consequently, the hard, but indispensable, work of mapping them, analyzing them, organizing them, and detailing them so that they can be "programmed" on the Workflow software. This indispensability puts the Workflow systems on a different platform of necessities then any other software.

In one of the companies we have been involved in a Workflow implementation project, during a meeting to discuss its development, five professionals of the business processes modeling and analysis area discussed among themselves for the better part of an hour over which event gave the start to a determined process without reaching any conclusion. We concluded, then, that in the case the project came to being the business processes modeling and analysis' team would have to be trained in the fundaments of business processes and in a methodology to work with them. That was effectively done.

There is also the problem of the initial un-operability of the Workflow software for the absolute lack of elements that allow it to run, in other words, the lack of legacy data obstruct Workflow systems from being implemented like other softwares. For example, when a company implements ERP software, it populates the databases with data from their legacy files, migrating them from existing systems. With Workflow software this is not possible because, except in rare exceptions, there are no legacy data of the processes if the analysis and modeling has not been done. Because of this the costs of implementation of Workflow software obligatorily involve elements that generally are not obligatorily present in the implementation of other kinds of software.

Another point of attention is: how to internally sell Workflow. We believe that those responsible for the implementation of Workflow system do not know how to "sell" to the organization the benefits generated by the implementation and utilization of this kind of software. The internal marketing has to be another worry for the team responsible for the Workflow implementation, because one of the greatest user's fear is that it becomes in a sort of technology from the "Ministry of Truth," depicted by George Orwell in the book *1984*[1] (where he depicts a scenario of *Big Brother is watching you*). We could verify with end users, that they are afraid that Workflow will contact their supervisors whenever an incident is late, any business rule is broken or that any other kind of "transgression" of the established order happens. Obviously, any Workflow software can go to the point of doing all that. However, the points that should be emphasized to the employees are: better control of the times needed to process each incident, better control over the execution of the business rules, and mainly, the liberation of people from bureaucratic, repetitive, and boring tasks such as, for example, seeking data and information in files of any kind, checking values, calculations and filling out forms.

In an organization, where Workflow software would be implemented, we faced an uncommon situation. The end-users didn't want, in any way, to cooperate with the project team because they said that "it was throwing money away" and that "for six months they were complaining to management for their installations to painted and new short walls to be installed to improve the conditions on their work-place, and while management wouldn't answer to their requisitions, they would spend all that money acquiring a Workflow software". It was necessary to handle the situation with a lot of care so they would collaborate with the project. In the end, we were able to implement the software in the planned deadline and to obtain success with the collaboration of the project's team, but the way we handled those that were boycotting the software was, in a way, more carefully then the rest of the group.

---

[1] 1984 by George Orwell, copyright Harcourt Brace Jovanovich 1949, and copyright renewed Sonia Brownell Orwell 1977.

However, in another organization, where the director used the Workflow implementation just to improve his personal status, nationally and internationally, the software had an extremely short life. Between the implementation and the abandonment, only eight months passed. As soon as the director got the post he wished for, he completely abandoned the Workflow. One important detail, the cost of this project was US$33,000. Conclusion: the director knew how to sell himself real well, but didn't know how to sell Workflow to his subordinates, or even to his replacement, who then discarded Workflow software, considering it unnecessary with expensive and difficult maintenance.

Another frequent problem is that the business processes analysis and modeling are rarely made with a methodology that details the processes in the way necessary so that this software can be properly implemented. We believe this was one of the primary problems that afflicted and/or afflict teams responsible for implementing Workflow systems, because without the data from business processes analysis and modeling there is no way to make the software work. Given certain characteristics from Workflow systems, between which is the indispensable necessity of changing the organizational culture, we verify that in the occasions the software was implemented on a incipient way, meaning, lacking data from the business processes, the results were problematic and, besides the wastage of what could be useful to the organization, we saw grow between the users a strong feeling of rejection to the software. Such behavior is explained by the disappointment that the users face while using Workflow almost as an e-mail program. However, with patience and hard work it was possible to avert many situations that seemed to lead to failure.

As an example, we cite the case of a company that needed to reduce the deadline given to their customers for the generation of proposals and product development. This process involved 140 users; and before the Workflow implementation the company wasn't even able to tell their customers the date that a proposal would be delivered. This means they weren't able to meet the deadlines agreed with their customers for the development and consequently the delivery of a product. At the risk of losing an important customer, responsible for a hefty sum of their revenue, the company decided on a Workflow implementation. It was dedicated for four months to the analysis and modeling of the business process: Customers Requisition. The results were very good, except for one detail: there was no agreement on what metrics should be assumed by each area for the control of times in accordance to their internal Service Level Agreement (SLA). This data was crucial so that Workflow could control bottlenecks and delays, especially in the system programming department. It is certain that all the times in the process were reduced, from proposal creation to product development, but the administration of times continued to be made, principally, by the account managers; responsible and the main connection with the customers of the company. Workflow, in this case, was under a great risk of transforming itself into a luxury e-mail service, being that the project had a total cost of US$133,000 in 2000.

When we state that the business processes analysis and modeling for the Workflow implementation must generate data so that the software can be "meticulously implemented" we are referring to the data necessary to automate the business rules, times, routes and roles (3Rs). Many responsible for projects of this kind state that ISO 9000 is enough to implement Workflow systems. We hear affirmations such as *we are ISO 9000 certificated, therefore our processes are ready to be automated.*

In a pulp and paper industry we had the following experience. When the project for Workflow implementation started, the industrial manager spent one morning telling us about the ISO certification of his area; of how the processes under his responsibility were documented and the level of detail they had.

When he ended his presentation we asked him:

- What are the intervals between the periodic audits for the recertification of these processes?
- From six weeks to six months, he answered.

We then asked:

- And in these periods how much time do you spend with the pre-audits, until the external audit team start their job of re-certification.
- From two to three weeks!

We conclude that, even thought the company was ISO certified, there was no process management culture sufficiently developed to make people stick to the rules of the business that set the standards for the operation.

We then analyzed the level of detail of each process and we found:

- Data and information about "the tasks" without separation into activities.
- Roles briefly detailed and documented.
- Inexistence of information about times.
- Business rules solely for detours.

Besides that, important connections were missing between processes of distinct areas such as, for example, between the process of chemical recipes update (we are talking of a chemical industry) and the process of industrial costs calculation, because every time a recipe was updated the new percentages were sent to the financial department, so they could update the industrial costs, on a piece of paper! Particularly in this project we had an additional difficulty to make people understand that the ISO norms delimitate, restrict and guide; but they were not made to detail who, when, how, in what time and where (the activity) the job must be made, fundamental information to any Workflow system.

Another point of attention was the ownership of the Workflow project. Without the involvement of someone with effective power to support the implementation and utilization of the Workflow system it tends to be put aside until discarded. To our understanding no other software has the need to be "sponsored" in a way as firmly and explicitly as Workflow. This is due not only for its cultural component, but also because the business processes analysis and modeling team frequently will need access to data and confidential information, or at least, of very restricted access and circulation, something that only someone with enough power will be able to authorize.

One time, in an important government organization, we had the need to access a certain record, crucial for calculating productivity of the installed capacity and estimate the resources necessary to operate the new process. When we solicited such data from the employee that was responsible for it, he told us: "Impossible. This data is confidential". However, since the data was indispensable for our work we appealed to a general manager who in front of us called the same employee that had denied our access and requested that he made available whatever we asked. In the same day all required data was sent to us.

However, even with strong sponsors, there are always exceptions.

In a project for implementation of Workflow all the information we needed were always provided for us. Until the day we needed to access the salaries and positions records, so that we could set the Workflow with the data that would enable it to calculate the cost of production of each incident; which was denied by the sponsor of the project, the CFO. She wouldn't back off this decision, objecting that we didn't need this level of detail to parameterize the Workflow system.

IN RESPECT OF USE AND DISCARD OF WORKFLOW SYSTEMS

There are people that consider it unimaginable to study the use and discard of Workflow systems instead of studying the benefits that the software that represents the Computer-Supported Cooperative Work (CSCW) concept better than anyone else, brings to the organizations. Some people ask us whether there are companies that would stop using Workflow. What kind of companies are these?

Here are the main questions of the research and their respective answers.

1. What does lead organizations to develop Workflow implementation projects?
   We concluded that, mainly, they expect:
   - To organize their processes;
   - To boost up the productivity of the processes automated by Workflow;
   - To organize and rationalize the volume of documents treated by the processes manually executed;
   - To diminish processing times.

2. What do the organizations expect from Workflow systems?
   We concluded that organizations expect more from Workflow systems then what they effectively offer, for factors such as:
   - Overselling by the representative of the Workflow software.
   - Not knowing its real benefits.
   - Not knowing the costs involved in a Workflow implementation project.
   - Not understanding the cultural transformations that will run through the entire organization as a result of the software implementation.

3. Why do some organizations invest in Workflow implementation projects and then abort them, shelving, purely and simply, the software?
   We have various answers for which we emphasize the following:
   - The Workflow's sponsor left the organization.
   - The Workflow's sponsor changed posts.
   - The Workflow's sponsor abandoned the project
   - The software became considered expensive for not being implemented correctly.
   - The software had difficult maintenance without hiring an expert on the product.
   - The expert on the product is very expensive.
   - The annual, obligatory, maintenance fee became prohibitive.

4. Why aren't the organizations able to continue on exploring the original characteristics and functionalities of Workflow?

5. How do organizations document, analyze and organize business processes to implement them on Workflow systems?

Both questions above have only one answer: Most of the time organizations cannot utilize Workflow, exploring its characteristics and original functionalities because they record, analyze, organize and detail business processes in an inconsistent manner, without proper methodology, and because of that cannot correctly utilize the software. The documentation of the processes, for Workflow automation, should not be long, because too much information will cause confusion on the software implementation team, keeping them from seeing the essential. It should also not be minimalist, because in this case the team would lack needed data for Workflow's correct implementation. The documentation generated by the business process analysis and modeling should be balanced to allow the implementation team to rapidly present results without, however, compromising the correct workings of the system. We know that this is a very difficult task, because it requires a process/Workflow analyst with practical experience and consequently knowledge that cannot be demanded from anyone.

6. Is it possible to measure the return on investment (ROI/VOI) made with the acquisition and implementation of Workflow systems?

We conclude that yes, it is possible. The calculation should be made taking into consideration the increase of productivity obtained in each process; that means, calculating the time spent on delays and re-works, or not, eliminated with the implementation of the software adding the processing time of each incident inside the process. There is a common known fact among general Workflow researchers that any process has a gain of 25 percent productivity when they are implemented on systems like these. Unfortunately, we could not localize the source of such figure. However, studies made by us, along the projects we have been involved show that this tendency is true, obtained by the elimination of re-work and delays of all kinds, including intentional errors or not.

In a certain project it was possible to calculate the increase in productivity and marginal gains obtained with the implementation of the Workflow system. It was an insurance company and this was its case:

The call center of this company received a request for quotation of products that totaled over US$500,000. However the insurance company missed the deadline to present their proposal because the CFO was traveling and nobody else could sign the proposal. In other words, there weren't business rules properly defined that would allow another employee to take the responsibility for signing a proposal of this size. There was also no control on the times nor formal routes. After Workflow was implemented the insurance company never missed deadlines again.

7. How can Workflow software be "sold" by the organization to the people that are part of it so that they can see the benefits that are possible to be obtained with its implementation?

We believe, from what we heard and experienced, that the main approach should be that the software will liberate people from repetitive, extremely mechanical tasks, transferring them over to Workflow and they will be able to use their productive time with the execution of nobler tasks, such as those that require decision making and creative thinking.

8. Who should assume the ownership of the Workflow system?

This is a question that generated polemic between those interviewed. And as such it was not possible to answer it with only one answer. However, the consensus seems to be attributing the responsibility for the Workflow system to levels higher-up on the organizational hierarchy. It doesn't seem appropriate to us attributing software such as Workflow on some employee on a middle hierarchy level that does not have the power to make it be implemented and used. In the organizations where the propriety of Workflow system was attributed to middle hierarchy level employees the software was unable to be used in its full-form, nor fulfill its potential, transforming itself rapidly into a luxury e-mail program.

There is an important point to be emphasized here:

Companies that develop and or sell Workflow software preach that their products are "user friendly," easy to install, parameterize and program, to the point of stating that any end user, with training, will be able to include, update and modify the descriptions, parameters, data and information of the processes automated by the software. Our perception is that this is nearly impossible. No end user, even trained on the software that was bought, will be able to assume such tasks because Workflow software products are complex, even the simpler ones, because they have a great variety of technological components; such as agents of various kinds, multiple language interfaces, telecommunication components, components of the operating system they are executed on and database integration modules, among many other things.

Another point to consider is that the logic to be employed on the creation of any process inside any Workflow software is not linear. For us to program and parameterize processes in a Workflow software we need to use various types of logic and business process analysis and modeling is not something that any end-user is ready to do, even because if he was he wouldn't have time for the other tasks and would be a process analyst and not an end-user.

When we asked to some of the executives why the software was "abandoned" we got answers such as:

"The software had a yearly maintenance too expensive, 20 percent its total value by year, tied to the dollar exchange rate at the time of payment. The software needed specialists to be updated or to have the process modified and that staff was also too expensive. We abandoned American software and changed to Lotus Notes, that while is not considered Workflow, suits well to our needs. Besides Lotus Notes programmers are plenty and cheap." Said the president of an American company settled in Brazil, emphasizing the cost versus benefit theme.

"The customers for whom we were working abandoned the project development for a new product. We believe that the software was too expensive to be used by solely us." Again the theme of cost versus benefit is present in the answer of the partner from a Brazilian company.

"First because we decided not to manufacture the new product anymore and because of that the software became too expensive for our size and needs." Quote extracted from the answer of the general manager of a French company settled in Brazil.

For many executives interviewed the software was abandoned for being too expensive. But what is expensive? If we wish to use the idea of cost versus benefit we could even calculate the return on investment, but people that made such statements were speaking in absolute terms. This means, they (and the organizations they work/worked for) were unable to perceive which were or would have been the benefits granted with the adoption of a workflow system as a solution to automating the business processes management (BPM). Being pragmatic, when people say it's expensive, they are explicitly recognizing that good or service is not worth what they are being asked for. It is different when people say it's expensive, but it's worth it! Then they are recognizing the intrinsic value of the product.

The costs involved with the implementation of a Workflow system are high, even with software "made in Brazil." Included in the project should be the costs of acquisition, maintenance and the consulting services for implementation, without forgetting the costs of the cultural change that Workflow imposes to the organizations, even harder to be measured.

In the root of the price of Workflow softwares it is what we call *cost of uselessness*. This type of cost factors in the composition of Workflow software because there is a vicious circle that imposes that who develops it to create, year after year, bigger and bigger features, adding to the product things that will never be used by the organizations, under the penalty of not being able to sell new versions to who already possesses the product; but at the same time imposing to the new customers the onus for functionalities that will never be utilized. This led us to conclude that customers will always be buying much more that they need or will come to need. Of all existing functionalities in any Workflow software the customers studied in this paper utilized, or utilize, 20 percent to 30 percent of them, but the software, each year, brings more and "better" functionalities, which will cost more and more; and will never be used.

It is in this context that we should understand the diverse organizations studied by us that opted for developing home-made solutions based on dynamic spreadsheets using Online Analytical Processing (OLAP), or preferred to use Lotus Notes, even knowing that both these solutions aren't essentially Workflow.

To conclude, we foresee that the evils that afflict the use and discard of Workflow systems will continue to exist, and with more intensity with the marketing actions that will be generated with the BPM acronym. This means that organizations are again beleaguered by specialists in all sectors, that now promise them a new software which will make all the business processes integrate customers, suppliers, partners, stakeholders, employees and all and any element that they can, may wish or have to interact, giving both the internal and external organization's ambient a complete view and essentially integrated from its operations. Things that Workflow systems already proposed to do and, if well planned and implemented, can do it very well!

CONCLUSION

The interviews gave us data and information to conclude that:

- Many organizations "bought" Workflow not knowing the real advantages and challenges that exist in the adoption of a technology that would make them organize and keep themselves organized.
- Various organizations expected more of the Workflow software bought which any of them could deliver. Expectations such as processes auto-organization, short implementation deadlines and easy maintenance to keep definitions updated are among the top unrealistic expectations, in great part created by the promises of the sellers.
- The major part of organizations studied that abandoned Workflow did it because they needed to permanently do business process analysis and modeling. This means, those responsible didn't expect the necessity of keeping a business process analysis and modeling team on their staff.
- It was also possible to conclude that the result of the business process analysis and modeling work, in a great number of the organizations interviewed, did not generate sufficient data and information so that the Workflow software could be programmed with fidelity to the environment and security by the process analysts in Workflow.
- Even though it seems routine, or at least it should be, software upgrading is always a high-risk activity. In the case of a Workflow upgrade the risk of stopping the entire organization is exponentially bigger. The following case illustrates with perfection the difficulties that organizations face to upgrade their Workflow systems.

One certain Workflow implementation project was developed by a company we will call "A" for a government organization. For problems that are not fit to describe here company "A" left the American software representation in Brazil and, obviously, ended its contact with the governmental customer after implementing with success a big and complex business process. One year later the manufacturer released a new software version and the process originally implemented (and working flawlessly for a year) by company "A" stopped working. Here we have the first problem that should be analyzed by the following question: how can an upgrade, of the same software, make the ambient that was working flawlessly for a year stop? Pressured by the customer, the manufacturer indicated another company, which we will call company "B" to make the ambient work as before. Suddenly, however, company "B" concluded that the problem was with the process originally implemented and working correctly for a year (we need to repeat it to make it clear that the solution worked for a year). In conversations with technicians of the customer we concluded that there was ignorance from the manufacturer, by his new representative in Brazil, to assume their functions and actions and even more so from company "B" to solve the situation caused by the newly-upgraded software version. The result was: company "B" blamed the problem on the business process analysis and modeling. According to people inside the governmental organization, company "B" said that the cause of interruption in the working of the process in the new version of the software was the very process.

We deduced that company "B" did not work hard enough to get to know the process, how it was programmed and even less knew the software in question. Beyond that, we recognize that it was a process with a high degree of complexity, being that not only was it running on low platform but it also accessed two mainframes located in different organizations situated on two distinct geographic places. On these occasions, consulting business process analysis and modeling companies think it is easier to remake the process then to understand the problem and correct it, even because, in theory, it is possible to (re)construct a process that works, even if less complex and sophisticated. The ignorance about the real functionalities of the software that is being acquired is another source of problems for all organizations that invariably end up abandoning the use of the software, for, consistently, expecting more then it can do. One of the episodes that marked us the most during the interviews was of a project that was being developed by a Brazilian consulting company that had aborted in the middle of the project by a customer when he found out that the manufacturer had made a promise of a solution that would not work ever in the way it had been sold/bought.

To illustrate the case is the following:

A consulting company had been hired just to develop the business process analysis and modeling project for its automation in Workflow software; and was developing the project normally when in a certain moment the customer wanted the software to make with six hundred licenses what could only be done with six thousand licenses. After a week arguing with the consulting experts ways that would not imply in having to buy six thousand licenses, the customer asked for the company that had sold the software so that those responsible could explain why they had promised something that the software would never do with the bought configuration. In the meeting, of which participated the three parts involved: the representative that had sold the software, by the way a branch office in Brazil of the American company that manufactured the same; the customer and the company hired to implement the solution, were discussed for more than two hours technical questions pertinent to the product and the process that should be implemented. The consulting company stated that there was no way to do what the customer wanted with the number of licenses acquired and the manufacturer's representatives ensured it was possible to do so.

One important detail to be noted here is that the consultants knew extremely well the software in question for they already had developed eight projects with the same product; while the representative had "specialists" that had been recently hired and, because of that, had no knowledge, or life-experience with the software. The customer, until then not knowing whom to believe, asked the two "specialists" of the Brazilian branch office to make a technical report on the problem with the following approaches:

- They should say if the solution that the consulting company had developed up to that point was technically accurate or not.
- If it was possible or not to develop the project with the characteristics that he, the customer, wanted and
- How, technically, should the solution be developed in case the same was possible to be implemented as they (the branch office representatives) had promised them with the store-bought solution.

Eight months after the meeting the report which the two specialists from the branch office in Brazil had committed into presenting in 72 hours was not neither made nor presented. Because of that the customer cancelled the project and returned the software.

We understand that the choice for any software should not be restricted to the analysis of the product's functionalities. It is also required to know the reputation of the manufacturer, of its representatives and even more so if the people who are in charge of support and technical assistance are fit for such tasks.

We finally conclude that organizations suffer the evils that repeat in a reoccurring form, because they can't break the vicious circle of "buying-technologies-to-solve-problems/solve-problems-because-bought-technologies" once they don't know or forget how important is the organizational culture (change management) and the business process analysis and modeling. Workflow continues to be a powerful instrument to automate processes and which sales, for various reasons, stood beyond what was expected by scholars, researchers and manufacturers of this kind of software.

Among the causes appointed by our research about the use and discard of Workflow two consistently repeated: lack of culture to work in the CSCW structure and the lack of methodologies fit for the business process analysis and modeling—AMOP, an acronym that we created to designate it.

It may seem that in these 10 years we were involved only with problematic projects or failed ones; however that is not true! The reason for this paper was to draw attention of those who may get involved with Workflow projects so that, in a kind of benchmarking, may be able to avoid the situations described here.

We hope that the research in this field has continuity and that Workflow systems may be implemented and used by any kind of organization with security and without stopping along the way in any problems it may face.

There is still much to learn about and with Workflow.

A Workflow Implementation Supporting the Commercial Ship Design Process

Ole Christian Astrup and Espen Wøien
DNV Software, Korea

INTRODUCTION

In the business world's race for companies to perform faster, better and cheaper, Business Process Management (BPM) and Workflow have been launched as the "Holy Grail" to success. Many of the BPM vendors are developing templates and frameworks (best practices) covering traditional industry verticals such as finance, manufacturing, telecom, and also government sectors. The marine and offshore industry is faced with the same fierce competition as the rest of the business world and must also continually improve performance. But, best practices from other industry verticals are not readily adapted to this industry segment. The workforce of the marine and offshore industries consists of highly qualified knowledge workers undertaking complex design work spanning a long time frame. Their business processes are typically concurrent, multi-discipline, iterative and highly complex. Such organisations pose severe challenges to process management and workflow implementation supporting their best practices.

PROCESS CATEGORIES AND WORKFLOW

What are processes? The question may sound trivial, but one would probably get a different answer each time the question is posed. The Delphi Group[1] categorises business processes into:

- System-to-system processes
- Person-to-system processes
- Person-to-person processes

Figure 1 depicts the above process categories around the axes of process complexity and process duration. Here, process complexity refers to how complex or simple a process is. A simple process may involve an application-to-application data transfer, such as an ERP transaction, while a complex process may involve several applications and people, such as a design process. Process duration refers to the length of the process from start to finish. An ERP transaction typically involves simple data transformation and as such, is a short duration process. The design process, on the other hand, can take months to complete.

The system-to-system category generally falls on the low end of process complexity and the short end of process duration.

---

[1] Delphi Group White Paper: BPM 2002 Market Milestone Report

At the other end of the scale we will generally find the person-to-person category of processes. In this type of process, a group of people collaborate and share knowledge and experience. In workflow terms we denote this as *horizontal* workflow.

In between these two categories, we find the person-to-system category. These are often defined by repeatable processes with few variations between instances. It is usually state-based, involving person-to-system intervention at specific steps, while the remaining steps may be automated through applications. In workflow terms person-to-system activities can be described as a *vertical* flow.

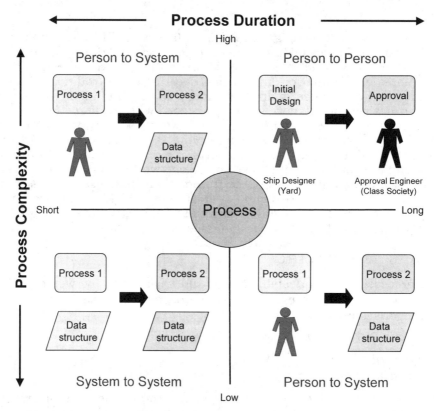

Figure 1: Process categories

CASE HANDLING AND KNOWLEDGE WORKERS

Depending on the business context, one usually finds that the majority of cases to be handled in a given business process follow an expected pattern. This is typically around 70-80 percent of cases (the 80-20 rule)[2], which, because of procedural efficiency, consume about 20 percent of the available resources (see Figure 2). The problem is that the other 20 percent of cases usually consume 80 percent of the available resource. Some of those cases

---

[2] Miers, D., Harmon, P. *The 2005 Business Suite Report.* Business Process Trends, October 2005

can be handled through well understood business rules, while others require a greater degree of collaboration.

Often an enterprise will find that a small percentage of the total cases (the two uppermost tiers in the pyramid) consume a larger share of resources and can have a huge impact on the profitability. Reducing these two tiers in the pyramid through, for example, process standardisation can have a big impact on the business bottom line.

However, reducing or eliminating the unique problems or the problems which require exception handling may not be achievable or even practical in the real world. This will generally be true for processes involving knowledge workers (the person-to-person process category). When knowledge workers interact with customers, they seldom follow a predicted pattern or behaviour. The real challenge for a business process framework will be to support these knowledge workers in an efficient and flexible manner.

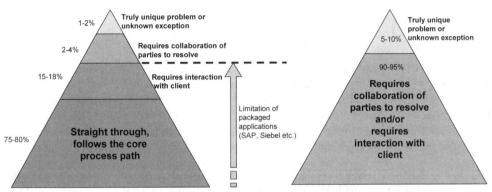

Figure 2: Comparison of case distribution between traditional industry verticals (left) and the marine industry (right)

The case distribution depicted to the left in Figure 2 may well be typical within the traditional industry verticals targeted by most BPM vendors. However for the part of the marine industry involving engineering and design (knowledge workers), this picture is not valid. Rather, the typical case distribution in a commercial ship design process would look more like the pyramid to the right in Figure 2. In a commercial ship design process, one may not have a core pattern to follow which does not require collaboration or interaction with the ship owner (client). Failure is to be expected if one embarks on a large process improvement and workflow integration project with the marine engineering and design industry without this picture in mind.

PROCESS CENTRIC VS DATA CENTRIC INTEGRATION

Most BPM vendors take a data or application centric approach to solve their client's process integration needs. This will be a suitable approach for the system-to-system and to some extent also the more complex person-to-system categories. These vendors usually offer a comprehensive toolbox for data and system integration[3]. However, the same data centric systems do not support person-to-person process integration very well. This process category is better supported by process-centric integration type of products[3].

Person-to-person processes require detailed knowledge about the business process. Because of the human involvement, a robust scheme for exception handling is required. It is also crucial that the exception handling can be managed *inside* the process framework.

COLLABORATION AND WORKFLOW

As outlined in the previous sections, the person-to-person processes involving knowledge workers pose a huge challenge for the process framework.

M. Ader has introduced the concept of *Collaboration-Enabled Processes Management*[4] (CPM) bringing together workflow and collaboration support systems within the same process framework. This concept is particularly suited for supporting the knowledge worker and person-to-person business processes.

CPM introduces advantages to the process framework in order to support the knowledge worker. The exception handling can be left to be resolved through collaboration. This again makes the task easier for the process analyst. The process activities need only include the main line of the process together with the routine exception situations, leaving the handling of the non-routine exceptions to be resolved through the process framework collaboration tool. This leads to simpler and clearer process templates and reduced process analysis time.

When the collaboration is part of the process framework, the process engine can keep an event log of all collaborations triggered by the users. Each collaboration event can be logged in detail with a reason, participants involved, start and end time. Additionally, the outcome (decision) of the collaboration can be recorded. Through that logging mechanism, the ad-hoc feature— added to the process engine through user initiated conversations—becomes an integral part of the history of the process. A systematic analysis of such exception traces can lead to enrichment of the process definition by analysing the most repetitive ones. The ability for an enterprise to learn from past performance and quickly improve the business process will constitute a competitive advantage in today's business environment.

Leaving the exceptions to be handled by the knowledge worker, and not by a business rule engine, will empower the worker. An empowered knowledge worker will feel much more comfortable and perform better in such an environment. People management and satisfaction is an important issue often

---

[3] Chang, J. *The Current State of BPM Technology*. Business Integration Journal, pp. 35-38, March 2004

[4] Ader. M. *Collaboration-enabled Process Management*. Workflow Handbook 2005, Workflow Management Coalition. Edited by Fischer, L.

neglected when integrating systems and people, and a key ingredient to corporate success[5].

BEST ENGINEERING PRACTICES AND KNOWLEDGE TRANSFER

Having recognized that knowledge assets are rapidly becoming their most precious source of competitive advantage, a large number of organisations are now attempting to transfer best practices. Yet best practices still remain stubbornly immobile[6]. Szulanski asks the question "Why don't best practices spread?" and then attempts to answer this question throughout his book[6]. He claims that stickiness applies not only to characteristics of the source of knowledge but also to the circumstances of the transfer itself. Szulanski also links stickiness (or knowledge transfer) to the organisation's performance.

In its simplest way, while still complicated, sharing best practice between two knowledge workers is: One person in the role of 'Donor' —the other one being 'Recipient'. Both of them act in their own working environment catering to what is on his or her personal agenda (context). The simple model is shown in Figure 3.

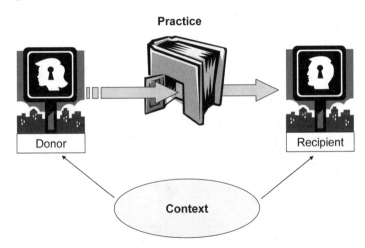

Figure 3: Model for sharing Best Engineering Practice in a knowledge intensive organisation, © Szulanski[6]

The reasons for not being able to transfer Best Engineering Practices are mainly caused by human nature. Szulanski offers a detailed discussion of the different barriers impeding knowledge transfer. These 'imaginary' barriers constraining effective knowledge sharing among knowledge workers are listed in Table 1. While we will find all the different barriers part of the knowledge sharing process between humans, ICT systems are not exposed to the same barriers.

---

[5] Miers, D. *BPM – Too Much BP, Not Enough of the M.* Workflow Handbook 2005, Workflow Management Coalition. Edited by Fischer, L.

[6] Szulanski , G.: *Sticky Knowledge : Barriers to Knowing in the Firm.* SAGE Publications (February 24, 2003)

Best Engineering Practice Model	Barriers	
	Human	ICT System
Best Engineering Practice	Low/Medium/High	Non existing
Causal ambiguity—practice is not well understood. Components and interaction not well identified. Limited ability to predict results. Limited ability to explain results		
Unproven—no evidence out there that proves that this is a good thing. No track record of transfers.		
Donor		
Lacks motivation—not willing to invest effort in the transfer.		
Lacks perceived reliability—perceived as unreliable source. Their results are not credible or inconsistent. They cannot teach how to do it.		
Recipient		
Lacks motivation—not willing to invest effort in absorbing the practice.		
Lacks absorptive capacity—can't recognize, understand or implement		
Lacks unlearning capacity—can't forget their old habits. Hard to teach "new tricks to an old dog".		
Context		
Barren context—no pressure to transfer, not easy to get support.		
Arduous relationship—donor and recipient relationship is not straight forward.		

Table 1: Framework and Comparison of important aspects transferring Best Engineering Practice, © Szulanski[6]

Consequently, by looking at Table 1, the formal and "dumb" nature of software could be of great interest to any organization looking for efficient knowledge sharing.

By introducing *Best Engineering Practice* as a concept, we have realised that integration of systems and people will only be successful if you are able to monitor and control the actual processes[7]. By its nature, software enforces structure on design organisations. Over time, technical software investments

---

[7] Rishoff, E.: *Best Engineering Practice in a Life Cycle Context.* DNV Software White paper, January 2005

often result in safeguarding engineering knowledge and should therefore be considered a very important part of a company's intellectual capital.

The challenge is to create frameworks that enable freedom of content while maintaining a well-defined structure. Such frameworks allow designers to focus their creativity on content – the design itself— rather than on infrastructure and technology related issues.

COMMERCIAL SHIPBUILDING & DESIGN

Over the past 30 years, the Republic of Korea has emerged as the world leading shipbuilding nation. In 2005, Korea produced 44 percent of the world's commercial ship tonnage, surpassing Japan for the third year in row. Over this time, South Korea has developed highly skilled engineers producing some of the world's most advanced ship designs in a very efficient manner.

However, competition from emerging low-cost shipbuilding nations like China and Vietnam will force the Korean ship yards to become even more efficient in the future to stay ahead of their competitors. ERP solutions are being introduced on a large scale including process improvement initiatives. These are only some of the practices that the Korean yards have implemented in order to improve their performance. Experience from some of the ERP implementations has revealed to the yards that these bundled solutions do not support their knowledge workers very well. One of the reasons is that these solutions typically take a data or application centric integration approach, offering little or no support for exception handling and collaboration.

The second largest yard in Korea, Daewoo Shipbuilding and Marine Engineering Ltd. (DSME), launched a project in 2005 with the objective of developing a workflow production system to support their engineers in their daily work. The initial scope of the project is to cover three different work processes:

- Vibration Analysis and Noise Free Design
- Basic Structural Design
- Marketing Design

The **Marketing Design** process is the most complex, involving some 150 engineers and more than 10 different engineering disciplines. The process covers the pre-contract engineering work at the yard. DSME has organised this as an *inquiry project*. An inquiry project is typically initiated by a ship-owner tendering for a ship to be built by the yard. The objective of the inquiry project is for the yard to establish a building cost and delivery date (schedule) for the ship. Each inquiry project has a responsible project manager, and is assigned engineering resources covering all major engineering disciplines. Inquiry projects are typically characterized by a short duration involving substantial collaboration and communication not only between the project participants, but also with the client (owner) and different suppliers. DSME typically carry out in excess of 200-300 inquiry projects every year. In order to conduct all of these projects in a timely manner and with quality, it is of crucial importance to utilise the DSME ship experience base. The DSME ship database consists of all ships delivered by the yard and holds vital information to quickly determine weight and cost estimates for the ship used as a basis for the final building cost. This working environment poses severe challenges to the solution framework. Not only must the process framework handle the process flow, but also allow for the participants to contribute and exchange information along the way in a flexible manner. All decisions should be monitored and logged for later reference and experience feedback (learning). A seamless integration with the DSME legacy systems for document management, project management and ship database is also required. The inquiry projects resulting in signing a contract with the owner (the yard will build the ship), are transferred into the contract-phase, and the inquiry project is terminated.

The **Basic Structural Design** process is involves 20-30 engineers working with the *ship hull* structural design. It is part of the contract work at the yard and the objective of this work process is to produce the information (drawings and calculations) required to obtain class approval by a *classification society*[8].

The process framework must provide management and sharing of documents and drawings that are produced during basic structural design. The system also provides management and integration with applications that are used by the engineers during the process. One of the main challenges is to support a seamless integration with the DSME legacy drafting system, providing easy access to all drawings as part of the process framework.

The **Vibration Analysis & Noise Free Design** process is also part of the contract work at the yard involving 10-15 specialists. This work process is characterised by spanning a long time frame, and the work is usually conducted by one or two engineers. The vibration analysis work starts during the ship design phase, continues throughout the building period and also covers the one-year warranty period of the ship starting from the delivery date. The total time span for a vibration project can be as long as 2-3 years. During the project period, all relevant documents and information must be maintained. In the course of the project, it is likely that the project resource(s) have to be exchanged. The process framework must support the re-assignment of the work and the knowledge transfer to the new engineer. The new engineer assigned to take over the project, must be able to easily see the progress and status of the project, find all relevant documents, and be able to track all previous decisions.

SUPPORTING BEST ENGINEERING PRACTICES AT THE YARD

When carrying out a project involving process improvements of any kind, the process owner's commitment and participation is vital in order to succeed. And even more true when person-to-person and person-to-system processes are involved. Realising this fact, DSME established a *Committee of Practice* (CoP) with members consisting of process owners, stakeholders and end-users. The CoP works closely with the project team assuring acceptance of

---

[8] Classification societies are organizations that establish and apply technical standards in relation to the design, construction and survey of marine related facilities including ships and offshore structures. These standards are issued by the classification society as published rules.

the solution during all phases of the implementation project (design, development/configuration and deployment). It is not unusual with two to three iterations to reach final consensus.

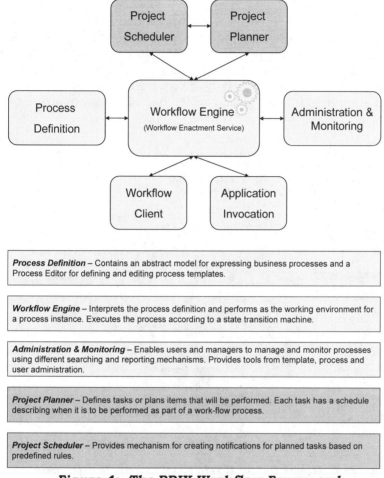

Figure 4: The BRIX Workflow Framework

The actual implementation of the engineering support system at DSME is based on a framework developed by DNV Software—BRIX Workflow Manager[9].

The framework is based on a Service Oriented Architecture (SOA) and consists of several parts. This article only focuses the workflow part of the framework used to support Best Engineering Practices and utilised in the implementation at DSME, see Figure 4.

The main design goals when developing the workflow functionality were to develop a system able to handle complex and interactive person-to-person work processes involving multiple applications and long-running transac-

---

[9] BRIX Development Framework,
http://www.dnv.com/software/developmentFramework/

tions. The initial workflow functionality was designed based on the concepts from the WfMC Reference Model[10] (easily recognised as the light grey boxes in Figure 4). The first workflow application to use these design concepts was released in 1999.

The workflow model has since been enhanced considerably with the objective of better support of engineering work processes; the latest additions being functionality supporting project planning and scheduling (blue boxes in Figure 4). Realising the rather simplistic information marshalling support by the Reference Model[11] the workflow model has also been modified by adding attributes identifying incoming and outgoing information flows associated with the activity.

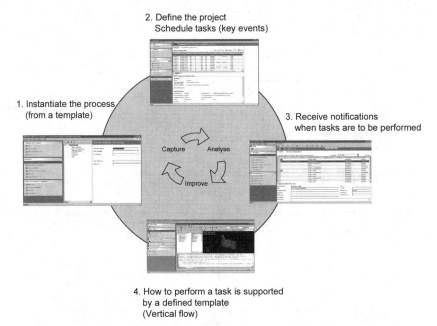

Figure 5: Steps in the Basic Structural Design process

All the three DSME processes described in the previous sections consist of both horizontal and vertical flows (person-to-system and person-to-person processes). In the Basic Structural Design process, the project manager (PM) instantiates the project based on a common business process template (best practice). The PM then carries out the activity scheduling (defining the key events or milestones) and assign resources to the different roles defined in the template. The assigned engineers are notified automatically about which tasks they have to carry out and when these tasks must be finished, see Figure 5.

[10] The Workflow Reference Model (WFMC-TC-1003, 19-Jan-95, 1.1)

[11] Hollingsworth, D. *The Workflow Reference Model 10 Years On.* Workflow Handbook 2004, Workflow Management Coalition. Edited by Fischer, L.

The engineer is provided with a pre-defined template for the activity to be carried out which can depend on the context (for example the role of the engineer or the state of the process).

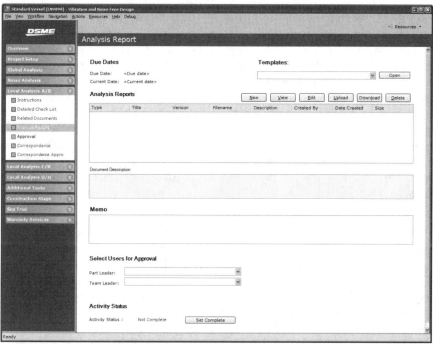

Figure 6: Workflow client displaying the Vibration Process

Figure 6 shows the workflow client displaying an activity part of the Vibration Process. The menu on the left side displays a list of all activities included in the process. A "*Service Centre*" is responsible for hosting applications. The application related to the chosen activity is shown to the right (hosted in the Service Centre). Information and operations of the application is based on the context, for example the chosen activity and its status. The role of the user is also used to introduce context switching thereby tailoring the information the user has available even more.

HTML pages, MS Office application or other third-party application can be hosted in the Service Centre using a standard integration controller while customized .NET (or COM) components are hosted by use of the Web Service API.

It is essential that the engineers have easy access to all important information based on their current context. In addition to data stored in databases, the engineer will also work with documents. The documents which are part of the process flow will appear as an integrated part of the application. This is made possible by interfacing directly with the DSME enterprise document management system (EDMS).

"Ad hoc" workflow is introduced as part of the solution in order to increase end user flexibility. As an example, the engineer which works on the Basic Structural Design process always has to carry out the *Rule Scantling* activity. For this purpose, he/she has a set of calculation tools (applications) provided by the classification societies at hand. For the main stream of projects (designs), these applications are sufficient. But from time to time, a design needs to be developed or studied in more detail. For this purpose, the engineer has to carry out a more detailed analysis using an application based on the Finite Element Method (FEM). During the process analysis phase we realised that this behaviour is an exception to the normal flow. Rather than modelling this activity into the standard flow of the Basic Structural Design process, we allow the user to dynamically add a sub-process to the activity of the running process when a more detailed analysis is required. The user can choose from a set of pre-defined templates covering the majority of expected exceptions. By this way, we keep the standard flow as clean as possible, and leaving the decision to the knowledge worker of when a detailed analysis is required. It is important to realise that the ad hoc changes only apply to the instantiated process template (running process). The changes are saved together with the process definition for later evaluation and experience feedback. If one encounters many similar changes to the same process, the process owner may choose to incorporate these as part of the global process *template*.

During the analysis phase of the Marketing Design Process at DSME, it was soon realised that it would be very difficult to represent the process with all exceptions in a workflow context. There were simply too many exceptions and roles involved. Rather than trying to fit all participants into one common template process, another approach was introduced. The Marketing Design process is characterised by being collaboration intensive. By introducing a collaboration mechanism as part of the framework, it is possible to define a much simpler process template. The deviations to the template flow are left to be resolved through the built-in collaboration mechanism instead of explicitly modelling it into the flow. The mechanism is simple but effective: by introducing a messaging scheme which is part of the framework, the engineer can request information at any time from any workflow participant. The messaging conversations are logged and kept as part of the process history for later analysis and learning. Other collaboration mechanisms like user notification in the workflow inbox, by email, or collaboration services like Microsoft Live Communication Server® are also utilised where appropriate.

A useful feature of the built in notification mechanism part of the framework is that messages are sent to the process role rather than the specific user. In this way, history (knowledge) is automatically communicated if for example one of the engineers responsible for some of the process activities is reassigned during the project life. The new engineer to take over the tasks of the role will automatically have access to all previous notifications.

CONCLUSION

When working with knowledge workers and knowledge intensive organisations, it is important that BPM implementation projects adopt a process centric approach. This will better support person-to-person processes commonly found in these types of organisations. The solution should cater for flexibility while maintaining the structure necessary for knowledge transfer and experience feedback. It is equally important to recognise knowledge stickiness and the human barriers constraining effective knowledge sharing. Introducing the concept of Best Engineering Practice may prove valuable to improve knowledge transfer and ultimately organisational performance.

Bridging Paper and Digital Workflows

(A Case Study)

Steve Rotter, Adobe Systems Inc. USA

DOCUMENTS: THE LINK BETWEEN PEOPLE AND BUSINESS PROCESSES

Since the dawn of modern commerce, people have driven business processes using documents—invoices, promissory notes, proposals, bills of lading, and contracts. The same remains true today. Documents continue to serve as the gateway for humans to participate in business processes. Surprisingly, however, most of today's business process management (BPM) systems do not adequately address the gaps between people, documents, systems, and business processes. Instead, they have traditionally focused on improving internal, system-to-system interactions.

Although streamlining of system-to-system interactions is beneficial, it overlooks a major opportunity: one that comes from effectively bridging paper and digital workflows to encompass people and documents more fully in the BPM equation. Most humans are still accustomed to working with paper documents at certain points during a business process, yet computer systems require information in digital form. This has necessitated a flood of data entry and re-entry—an activity that is costly, time-consuming, and error-prone. The key to increased efficiency is to integrate both paper- and digital-based workflows into BPM. By doing so, enterprises can take full advantage of the potential of BPM systems in the enterprise.

PAPER AND DIGITAL: AN UNEASY CO-EXISTENCE

BPM discussions and systems often overlook a main cause of delays and escalating costs: processing paper. In many ways, the oversight is understandable. Paper is so much a part of everyday transactions that it can be hard to imagine processes without it. Think about completing bank loan applications, submitting materials to government agencies, or working out details on sales contracts—the list of paper-dependent workflows is extensive. Even with continued automation of back-end processes and front-end web interfaces, paper remains a primary tool for many business transactions.

Whether interacting with an order-processing system or handling a medical claim, many workers find themselves spending hours each day keying data into a computer system. While some processes such as renewing an insurance policy might not have documentation attached to them, most processes do.

The reason for so much data entry is that documents continue to serve as the primary interface for humans participating in business processes. To date, people have acted as the interface to digital computer systems, and have taken on the task of integrating paper and digital workflows by rekeying data contained in documents. This has resulted in increased errors, high administrative outlays, and processing delays.

BRIDGING THE GAP WITH INTELLIGENT DOCUMENTS

Industry research typically estimates the expense of manually processing a single form, such as an employee time-off request, customer order form, and others, at over $50—and that assumes the form is completed correctly and does not require approval by multiple reviewers. In large companies where volumes of forms are completed and routed daily, the costs of these processes can quickly total tens of millions of dollars.

Today, continued reliance on manual document processes results from the fact that, until recently, viable technology alternatives were rare. Over the years, businesses have successfully automated back-end processes for data analysis, transaction processing, and the secure transfer of information from one application to another. The challenge now is to expand the focus to address how people interact with enterprise applications or how people rely on documents to collaborate inside and outside of an organization.

With advances in technology, there is a significant opportunity to move from conventional paper workflows to more automated processes using intelligent electronic documents. The more interactive, dynamic digital documents look like their paper counterparts and are easy to use. But unlike paper, intelligent documents can contain built-in features for automatic routing to one or multiple reviewers, for verifying that forms are filled out completely and properly, and for supporting document control and security.

The good news is that many organizations are working faster and more efficiently using BPM solutions that acknowledge the importance of documents at key points in their business workflows. These solutions automate processes using intelligent forms that enable organizations to leverage the advantages of the digital world, including enforcing policies, permissions, workflow management, compliance, and security.

IN PRACTICE: THE KANSAS DEPARTMENT OF TRANSPORTATION

The Kansas Department of Transportation (KDOT) is a good example of the effectiveness of using BPM to streamline paper-centric workflows and unite digital and paper-based processes. More than 3,000 employees at KDOT oversee the state's substantial network of roads and bridges. Employees are involved in maintaining the transportation system, collecting and evaluating data, scoping projects, overseeing design, and many other essential tasks.

These processes have traditionally been cumbersome and paper-centric. However, by adopting a solution that integrates paper and electronic processes, KDOT has seen time and accuracy improvements in its business workflows.

To automate its critical processes, KDOT embarked on a project to architect and implement an enterprise-wide Records and Workflow Management (RWM) solution. The RWM system had to provide a common and integrated framework for automating and managing workflows and reducing costs associated with converting and managing paper. Security and reliability concerns also had to be addressed. KDOT's information assets had to be protected while access to critical resources was expanded to authorized users.

BOTH ELECTRONIC AND PAPER DOCUMENTS REQUIRED AT KDOT

Many KDOT processes previously relied heavily on paper documents. For instance, responding to constituent requests required that staff route, review, and approve hundreds of pages of project information. Constituent documents include permit applications, drawings of proposed designs, and project schedules.

At the same time, the many construction projects managed by the agency require extensive collaboration among staff and with outside partners. For example, before roadwork can begin, staff must review thousands of documents outlining project details, designs, expenses, and public input. To accomplish this, KDOT had to integrate a variety of information systems and business processes with a solution that could interact with a document management system, computer-aided design (CAD) software, Microsoft tools, digital signature applications, e-mail, and electronic forms.

Clearly, both electronic and paper forms are vital to KDOT's operations. From submitting expense reports to handling constituent service requests, KDOT staff complete, approve, and process hundreds of forms monthly. For KDOT, the challenge was replacing manual workflows with efficient electronic document processing, so staff had more time to devote to higher value-added activities.

An Integrated System That Feels Like Paper, Acts Like Digital

Given the internal and external demands facing the agency, KDOT wanted to develop a fully integrated RWM that would enhance services, facilitate information sharing among staff, and streamline agency operations. To implement the system, the agency leveraged solutions from Adobe Systems Incorporated.

Two processes in particular that highlight the success of the RWM implementation involve issuing Highway Access Permits for building driveways and parking lots and for approving Project Authorizations. To speed processing of applications for Highway Access Permits, KDOT staff completes forms online, attaches related documents and plans, and then electronically routes materials for review. Upon approval, Highway Access Permits in Adobe Portable Document Format (PDF) are archived in the agency's document management system. Eventually, KDOT plans to enable citizens to submit applications over the web.

To eliminate routing paper for more than 3,000 construction Project Authorizations handled annually, KDOT used Adobe solutions to develop an eight-page online form that provides staff with a graphical interface for entering project information that is saved to back-end systems. The system then creates an authorization and a schedule for routing the form to managers for digital sign-off. Approved documents are saved instantly to the document management system, and staff is alerted by e-mail that project documents are available.

In addition to the Highway Access and Project Authorization workflows, KDOT is automating several other processes. For example, the agency converted 24 paper-based administrative workflows to fully electronic processes. Now, employees can use the agency intranet to complete leadership evaluations, procurement requests, and other internal business forms online. Once completed, the forms are automatically routed—based on an XML-driven rules process—to managers for review and electronic sign-off.

THE BOTTOM LINE FOR KDOT

KDOT is realizing impressive benefits from its RWM. Staff can efficiently handle administrative tasks and better manage project information. For instance, reports that previously took days to process can now be done in minutes. Handling access permit requests—a task that could take two months on paper—can now be completed in three weeks. Printing of purchase orders, which used to take up to 24 hours, can now be done on demand.

For KDOT, the efficiencies are evident agency-wide. By automating forms processes, the agency eliminated the wasted time and data errors that occurred as employees keyed data from paper forms into back-end systems. In addition, electronic forms are easier to process than paper forms because the agency doesn't have to deal with illegible handwriting. KDOT can also build controls into the forms to help ensure that information is entered into the proper fields and validated as needed.

Overall, the RWM has had a dramatic impact on the time and money the agency once devoted to managing documents on paper. Already, more than 60,000 digital documents have been added to the system, eliminating the need to print, copy, distribute and file materials. The estimated cost savings for this alone total more than $335,000.

BLENDING PAPER AND DIGITAL WORKFLOWS

Rather than trying to eliminate paper documents altogether, KDOT built a system that integrates document services to automate people-centric processes. This has made it easier for KDOT to create, capture, and integrate information across the organization.

The RWM leverages the advantages of paper. For instance, when paper documents such as purchase orders are required, they can be printed on demand. Employees have maintained high productivity because they are interacting with documents that look like familiar paper counterparts but have all of the advantages of intelligent digital forms. Because staff completes forms online and electronically routes materials for review, processes that took days to complete can now be done in minutes.

In recognition of its accomplishments, The Workflow Management Coalition (WfMC) and the Workflow And Reengineering International Association (WARIA) honored KDOT with the Global Excellence Award for Innovation and Excellence in Business Process Management (BPM) and workflow implementations. This award recognizes organizations that have demonstrated success in implementing innovative solutions to meet strategic business objectives.

KEYS TO SUCCESS: A CLOSER LOOK

Organizations such as KDOT that have succeeded at adopting automated, intelligent document processes frequently have addressed three key questions:

- How do people inside and outside the organization process documents?
- How do intelligent documents extend the value of enterprise systems such as ERP, Product Lifecycle Management (PLM), and CRM?
- What level of control and security needs to be built into electronic documents?

By answering these questions, most organizations can be well on their way toward a successful intelligent document strategy that unites digital and paper-based processes to automate people-centric processes.

INTEGRATING WITH ENTERPRISE SYSTEMS

Enterprise systems such as ERP or CRM systems can be difficult for employees to access—yet information in these systems is critical to their work. By developing secure, intelligent documents, companies are finding that they can enable more employees as well as customers and constituents to interact with core systems without jeopardizing critical data. The automated documents also present processes in ways that are easier for less technical users to understand.

 At KDOT, for instance, online forms provide staff with a graphical interface for entering project information that is automatically integrated into back-end systems. This not only eliminates the need to key information into systems, but also increases the value of data in back-end systems because information is entered into the proper fields and validated as needed. The benefits of KDOT's document management system are also enhanced, because final documents are reliably archived in PDF.

MAINTAINING DOCUMENT CONTROL AND SECURITY

Use of intelligent documents provides the opportunity to more rigorously control information. All types of organizations must keep a closer eye on information security. News stories abound about confidential corporate information—product development plans, sensitive financial data, and other details—making its way into the wrong hands. And, with increasing privacy regulations, medical, insurance, government, and other organizations are often responsible for safeguarding sensitive data.

Fortunately, technology advances have progressed to provide better control over digital documents. For instance, intelligent documents can have built-in controls to limit who can open materials, how long digital documents are available to recipients, and to track who opened or tried to open materials. Several companies and organizations also use digital signatures to streamline approvals and to ensure that approved materials are not altered by incorporating features that invalidate signatures if documents are changed.

SIMPLIFYING COLLABORATIVE PROCESSES

Business processes must be both secure and dynamic and enable organizations to extend process management beyond the firewall. Allowing users to participate in processes online or offline without compromising process control or data integrity illustrates how document-centric processes can be transformed through integrated, intelligent forms.

Most document-based business processes require review and collaboration. Documents can be as simple as an expense report that needs to be approved by a manager or as complicated as a product design drawing that requires extensive internal reviews, as well as review by outside manufacturing partners and approval from government regulators. In either case, certain protocols must be followed to move the business process and accompanying documents to completion.

Unfortunately, typical review and approval processes at many companies are anything but simple. Documents delivered on paper can sit for days or weeks in the inboxes of busy or traveling employees. At the same time, staff can wait days as materials travel via interoffice mail or courier to employees. Materials can also be lost, or, as KDOT experienced firsthand, it can be difficult to decipher handwritten reviewer comments on documents.

Processes for handling complex materials such as engineering drawings are even more problematic, often reverting fully to paper because reviewers lack the specialized software required to open materials. Intelligent document processes overcome this problem by enabling people to convert materials to platform-and application-independent electronic files readily available to reviewers anywhere and at any time.

In addition to being easy to view, digital documents can support automated routing, electronic commenting, and digital approvals, helping ensure that materials move consistently and reliably through review processes. If delays occur because people are out of the office, electronic documents can be forwarded automatically to the next reviewer, who can see comments and approvals from all previous reviewers. Once approved, original documents and comments can be archived for future reference.

At KDOT, collaboration has improved significantly due to the ability to complete forms online, attach related documents and plans, and then electronically route materials for review and digital sign-off. Upon approval, permits and other materials in PDF are archived reliably in the agency's document management system.

CONCLUSION

As technology evolves, businesses and organizations are taking a broader view of BPM. Where the focus was once on improving internal, system-to-system interactions, there is now a need to extend the reach of information and find better ways to connect employees with core systems, with each other, and with customers and constituents. The key is to bridge both paper and digital workflows using intelligent documents. With new technologies, organizations have an invaluable opportunity to rethink traditional approaches and use intelligent documents to enable people to engage in business processes in ways that are familiar, easy, and effective. For organizations like KDOT, the benefits are tremendous.

The Possibility and Reality of Massively Parallel Workflow Implementations

(A Case Study)

Kevin Erickson, Noridian Administrative Services, LLC. USA
Michael Hurley, Green Square, Inc. USA

INTRODUCTION

"But why, some say, the moon? Why choose this as our goal? ...We choose to go to the moon. We choose to go to the moon in this decade and do the other things, not because they are easy, but because they are hard, because that goal will serve to organize and measure the best of our energies and skills, ... and do all this, and do it right, and do it first before this decade is out—then we must be bold." – President John F. Kennedy September 12, 1962

It was hard not to think of Kennedy's ambitious goals when the vision was communicated to the team in April of 2005. The possibility of a massive expansion of the workflow environment by August 31 seemed... aggressive. It would require us to create some new technologies of our own. More importantly, this was an important project for the company and everyone in the room was clear about that. It was time for a bold vision. While we will not attempt to convince the reader that our "Cheetah" project, as it came to be known, is on par with man's first trip to the moon, at the time, the effort seemed equally Herculean.

This case study will describe the enterprise-wide, massively parallel implementation approach used by Noridian Administrative Services, LLC. (NAS), showing the implications of the approach, the challenges that the NAS team faced, and the benefits gained by the approach. The reader will also see first hand how workflow automation addresses key issues in the healthcare and insurance industries.

CHALLENGE: DELIVER COST-EFFECTIVE, QUALITY HEALTHCARE TO 42 MILLION AMERICANS

Healthcare cost and availability are a growing concern to everyone, especially to the country's growing population of senior citizens. The statistics are staggering. Approximately 42 million people get health care through Medicare. According to a report by the Centers for Medicare and Medicaid Services (CMS), national health expenditures are projected to reach $3.6 trillion by 2014, and health spending is projected to reach 18.7 percent of the gross domestic product (GDP). Medicare spending alone is projected to grow 8.5 percent in 2005.

These statistics are at the heart of NAS' growth from a small division of Noridian Mutual Insurance Company administering the federal Medicare program for one state, to a federal contractor for CMS serving 6.3 million Medicare beneficiaries and more than 130,000 providers in 14 states. NAS handles 6.3 million Medicare Part A claims and more than 69 million Part B claims.

Agility is a term rarely applied to a company handling this volume of transactions. And that's exactly why agility is the cornerstone of NAS' vision to be *the* benchmark by which all other Medicare/Medicaid contractors are measured. This is being accomplished through the aggressive and innovative application of technology to drive the following business objectives:

- **Performance** – Highest performance based on customer-oriented metrics
- **Quality** – Sustained, systematic quality in every NAS process
- **Cost** – Unparalleled technology-driven reduction in costs.
- **Agility** – Flexible, scalable, and radically adaptive processes that embrace change

"CMS is totally restructuring their Medicare contracting procedures over the next three years," stated Julie Paulson, Manager of Imaging Systems and Support at NAS, and one of the team leaders of the workflow initiative. "Agility is critical to our response to the upcoming changes in the Medicare delivery system. We are driving hard to expand and leverage our investments in process automation."

NAS manifested these objectives in the Cheetah project. The first phase of Cheetah was a massively parallel workflow automation project and was completed in August, 2005. The result was the automation of 20 key business processes in 13 departments in just 20 weeks.

A HISTORY OF WORKFLOW SUCCESS

In 1997, NAS Executive and Information Technology Management took a hard look at their paper bound processes. A forward-looking strategy was undertaken to explore alternatives that could move NAS towards a less-paper environment. A strategy was soon developed to introduce document management technologies to stop the paper "at the door" and provide digital access to the documents. Today, NAS digitizes and electronically stores over 15 million pieces of paper per year.

The success of this initiative spawned a move in 2001 to introduce process automation technologies in the form of workflow software. Workflow software involves digitizing paper bound business processes in order to deliver sustained, systematic results. Process, people, and systems are tightly integrated into a unified solution that delivers the right information, to the right person at the right time. Think of it as "just in time" business processes.

Convinced that workflow software had provided significant benefits to NAS and its customers, NAS engaged an independent consulting organization in 2004 to perform a detailed cost benefit analysis of a portion of the processes utilizing workflow. The study showed a savings of over $600,000 per year, for just a few of those processes. The study also illustrated the potential of enterprise deployment.

With this information, NAS Executive Management challenged the IT and business areas to devise a method to deploy document management and workflow technology as rapidly and as broadly as possible. In early 2005, the Cheetah Project was born.

CHEETAH IS BORN

NAS' success with imaging and workflow technologies was fairly prototypical. A methodical, department by department evaluation was done and workflow deployed in the areas with the greatest need first. We suggest that this approach is prototypical because most organizations we have worked with deploy workflow similarly. There are many benefits to this approach. Among them are lower risk, good value and incrementalist momentum building. The downside is that this method takes a very long time, rides the whims of ever changing budgets, resources and management support, and frequently costs more to implement. The question that confronted the NAS team was—is there an alternative to this snail-paced implementation? Can enterprise workflow be widely and rapidly deployed with high quality and value to the organization?

In April of 2005 a team was assembled to answer these questions. A combination of market conditions, competitive pressures and desire to pick up the pace of workflow implementation at NAS required an answer. Executive Management at NAS challenged the team to have a workflow solution deployed to every operational department by the end of August. To achieve this, the team would have to invent a new way of deploying workflow. We would need to move like a cheetah.

The Cheetah Project's goals were clear.

- Implement imaging and workflow for 20 processes in 13 departments affecting 350 employees in five different locations for production on September 1, 2005.
- Improve performance in each affected process without a negative impact on quality.
- Create a consistent, reusable and systematic workflow project process and methodology that NAS could leverage in future projects.

CHEETAH PHASES

The Cheetah goals called for a reinvention of the workflow project approach to meet the deadline. The reinvention created a living laboratory to question and reconsider previous workflow methods. The Cheetah process included the following phases:

- Scope Phase: Rapid business analysis of affected teams was performed and scope documents that outline current team functions and suggest imaging and workflow-enabled alternatives were drafted.
- Plan Phase: The Plan Phase began with the assembly of the project team including internal NAS resources and external resources from a consulting organization (Green Square) and On-Base Integrator (eDocument Resources). A tightly structured planning process ensured that the project was well-defined and understood by all and that the required resources were in place.
- Execute Phase: The Execute Phase encompassed all aspects of designing, creating, and deploying the solution into the target areas. Elements included design, test environment(s), programming, testing, installation and training.
- Conclude Phase: The Conclude Phase transitioned the project from implementation into a production lifecycle phase. Reviews with various stakeholders and user groups occurred. Project process and methodology documentation was completed in this phase.

The key to making the aggressive timeline was staggering the phases of execution within the targeted business units.

CHEETAH-LIKE RESULTS

Departments and teams that were part of the Cheetah project went into production beginning in early August. In all, 350 users went live over three weeks. They represented users in North Dakota, Colorado, Washington and other locations. Critical processes that were once paper-bound were now unleashed. The last workflow went live on August 26, three days ahead of the target. A great deal was achieved in a short timeframe.

PROJECT BENEFITS

In addition to being on time and on-budget, Cheetah needed to deliver real, measurable business value to NAS. Some of the key project benefits are as follows:

- Measurable improvements in process performance for every targeted process.
- Reduction in risk through improvements in privacy, security, and disaster recovery.
- Improved internal controls and auditability of critical paper-based processes.
- Improved organizational agility through a reusable project process and methodology for developing new workflows.

LESSONS OF A MASSIVELY PARALLEL WORKFLOW PROJECT

The Cheetah project created a new way of approaching workflow projects at NAS. What lasting learnings came from the project?

1. It starts with "Why?"

Plainly stated, without vision and mission there is no project. The purpose of many enterprise projects lack clarity and connection to the mission and values of the organization. Without this connection, team members are rudderless while making tough decisions. With Cheetah the "Why?" was crystal clear. World-Class processes are the future at NAS. Executive Management spoke with a single, unmistakable vision: Process Wins.

2. Who's on Second?

If "Why" is first, the second issue has to be the team. Jim Collins, Author of *Good to Great*, calls this getting the right people on the bus. An egoless, focused, motivated team on a mission is unstoppable. Cheetah succeeded because we assembled a cast of professionals that needed minimal direction or policing. Excellent teams are self-directed and self-policing.

3. To create an agile process, you must have an agile project process.

With "Why" and "Who" figured out, it is time to focus not on the project, but the process. We have all been on projects that create more paperwork than they hope to reduce. These projects tend to be choked with tons of methodology and reporting and very little meaningful communications. Cheetah required a nimble, streamlined project approach. What we found was that some sacred cows of doing enterprise projects can be left behind if you have the right people on the bus, and an expectation of honest communication.

4. Listening spells R.E.S.P.E.C.T.

The typical project is mostly talking with some occasional listening thrown in for good measure. That "communication of what we are doing to you" model had to go elsewhere for Cheetah to be successful. For Cheetah, we were able to flip that model. This is not to say that we nailed it. We made some mistakes. That said, the explicit intention of the team was respect for the business people that would be using the tools and absolute respect for the other team members.

5. Plan the work, work the Plan

Management Guru Tom Peters is right about project planning. He states that most projects are 10 percent planning and 90 percent execution. He argues for a Wow! Project that is 30 percent planning, 30 percent selling (communication), 30 percent execution and 10 percent celebration/hand-off. Cheetah's 20 weeks included a full eight weeks of planning, and it probably wasn't enough. While this made some team members uncomfortable at first, the results were impressive. Our list of fixes and defects on August 27th, the day after production was less than a dozen minor items. Planning pays big.

6. Yesterday would be better (Urgency)

There is nothing that can keep a team focused as well as a compelling, hard deadline. Period. Equally as clear as the project vision, executive management was profoundly clear on the deadline: Get it done. Cheetah was (and is) very important to the success of the organization. The department-by-department workflow crawl would not work for this effort. We all felt that this had to be done yesterday. It helped guide decisions, eliminate unnecessary steps and focus the team like a laser. To be clear, arbitrary deadlines will typically come back to bite you. Cheetah's deadline was clearly intertwined with corporate objectives. This was a real deadline.

7. Sell, Sell some more and then go out and Sell: The Secret Weapon —The Communication plan and its effects

Intentionality defines action, but requires rigor. You can intend to communicate well on projects, but if you do not have a well-considered, well-executed plan, the likelihood of realizing your intentions wane. From the initial meeting, communication was identified as strategic to the project. The team devised a concise written, communication plan early in the project. The plan defined the different stakeholders (audiences), communication methods tailored to the audiences and owners of the communication. The team deployed myriad tools to get the word out to all audiences. They included:

- Group and individual meetings
- Cheetah Logo
- Professionally designed posters and newsletters
- End User Presentations
- Executive communications

The result was a much anticipated "buzz" around the project and a desire to be a part of it. Cheetah landed softly on the users desktop. Communication became the secret weapon to provide a positive brand for the project. The communications clearly communicated what the users could expect and how it would affect their daily work.

8. WGMGD: What Gets Measured Gets Done.

Specifically referring to project approach, everything needs to get measured. How long, how much and how many. A project without measures is analogous to a blind cheetah running at top speed. The eyes for the Cheetah Project were clear measurements, project tracking, hours estimations and validation, and several other measures. While a blind cheetah may happen to run into dinner, it is more likely to run into a tree. Make sure that you identify and measure key project elements. With regard to the business processes, it is even more important to identify and build process measures/metrics into the solution that is delivered to business users.

THE MONDAY MORNING QUARTERBACK – WHAT WE MIGHT DO DIFFERENTLY

Many things went very well with the Cheetah project. All projects have room for improvement. What learnings came from the project?

- Communicate more information, sooner and more often. Our communications approach was a huge success. In spite of that, the key learning from the team was that we needed it earlier, with greater frequency with more end-user interaction.
- Make no assumptions about end-user technical literacy. NAS users are a fairly technology friendly group, but all of us need to wrap our minds around new technologies in a way that reduces fear of change. We needed to make fewer assumptions and confirm all assumptions, twice.
- Plan more. We saw significant angst from the designers and programmers when we said that we would not start programming until Mid-June. In retrospect, our planning was close to the right amount, but more would have definitely made the project deliverables richer and the user experience ever smoother.
- Plan for resource changes. Every project loses resources due to any number of good reasons. Even our short project was not immune to this phenomenon. We learned that we need to identify back-ups for key spots and have contingency plans for replacing key team members.
- Don't take infrastructure for granted. New software and hardware can stress even the healthiest of systems. Serious planning should be done with regard to computer systems and the impact of new systems.

THE FUTURE – THE HEALTHCARE MATRIX

As of this writing, Cheetah 2.0 is in full swing, upping the ante further, driving hard into the future. Team members joke about what Cheetah 12.0 might look like. While we have no crystal ball I think some things are clear. The definitions of "the department" and "the company" may be completely altered. After all, a process can be defined in many ways. Often it is trapped within a single department or organization only because we have allowed it to be so.

Workflow has made incredible inroads. Business Process Management (BPM) holds promise to take processes even further. The final frontier in healthcare may be a vastly wider definition of the healthcare processes. It may be a process that transparently spans from the patient to the doctor, hospital, clinic, pharmacy and the payer organization, such as NAS. This Healthcare Matrix would require inter-organizational connections that, for the most part, do not exist today. That said, as we look 10 years down the line and examine the learnings of projects like Cheetah, the question is not if, but when.

Considering the potential impact of workflow and BPM in healthcare, it is hard not to recall one of my favorite quotes from Michelangelo:

The greatest danger for most of us is not that our aim is too high and we miss it, but that it is too low and we reach it.

Growth in Business Process Management Suites in Greater China

Based on Practical Solutions Combining Legacy Systems with Technological Innovation

Linus K. Chow[1]; Charles Choy Wing-Chiu[2] and Carrine Wong[3]

INTRODUCTION

Companies in Greater China are highly competitive and are looking for an edge in our increasingly globalized marketplace. While they are looking to leap ahead of western companies by leveraging newer technologies, such as web services; they are also driven by a very competitive and dynamic local marketplace. A practical solution based value proposition for a BPM /workflow suite is required to leverage existing systems including ERP, CRM and e-commerce systems.

China continues to play an increasingly larger role in the world's economy. Companies in China, including local Small Medium Enterprises (SMEs) as well as Multi-Nationals are increasingly interested in modernizing their Information Systems. The drive to move up the global value chain, and build quality and compliance credibility has taken heightened priority due to political as well as market forces.

The adoption of technology is not new to Greater China, with many Enterprises already deployed or deploying CRM, ERP and financial systems. The current trend is to focus on the optimization of the workflow and business processes to derive additional levels of quality from existing or newly adopted systems. Additionally, political globalization pressure is mounting for Chinese industries to compete on the international level. The move into higher margin manufacturing as well as services industries is one catalyst for enhancing their information management systems with BPM and workflow, as its focus is not only on productivity, but also increased quality, consistency, and accountability. Additionally, the Chinese government's drive to modernize and open the financial markets places increasing focus on the transparency and compliance of processes that BPM suites provide.

THE UNIQUE MARKET OF GREATER CHINA

Greater China presents a very interesting marketplace driven by ready access to capital (via massive inflows of direct foreign investment and access to the public capital markets in Hong Kong) and strong government

---

[1] HandySoft, USA

[2] Hong Kong Small and Medium Enterprises Association, Hong Kong

[3] ISI-Dentsu (ISID), Hong Kong

involvement through state-owned enterprises, and government agency programs and policies. Government and the Private sector forces provide a complex set of economic strategies, government policies, market signals and entrepreneurial vision, which make for a very competitive business environment.[1]

A large segment of growth for China is Small Medium Enterprises (SMEs). SMEs in China are inherently face stiffer competition than counterparts in more developed nations. New foreign as well as domestic entrants increase the importance on processes that provide differentiation.

> "Stiff competition has put a lot of pressure on companies. Many of our members like to improve their operation efficiency and better manage their operations," said Charles Wing-Chiu Choy, Senior Vice President, Hong Kong Small and Medium Enterprises Association. "Especially those who have set up across the border in China, they have to improve their efficiency and reduce costs. Workflow/BPM and document management type solutions will provide significant benefits to them."

Current macro economic and political events has made 2005 and 2006 even more pivotal for businesses in China. There is increasing pressure for the Global economic community for China to make its currency markets more transparent and free market. In 2005 China made its first step, by loosening its peg to the US Dollar, and pressure is building for even larger readjustment of its valuation against major currencies, especially the US Dollar. This is having far reaching impact on the financial services industry in china.

Chinese regulators are encouraging foreign banks to take strategic stakes in the financial services industry, both as a source of funding and to upgrade local bank services with foreign managerial and technical expertise as the industry prepares for the opening of local financial markets to full foreign competition late this year.[2] Just at the end of January 2005, China's biggest lender, state-owned Industrial and Commercial Bank of China signed a $3.78 billion investment deal with Goldman Sachs Group Inc., American Express Co. and Germany's Allianz AG.

China's Insurance industry is also undergoing dramatic change as regulations have changed. China, which has been dominated exclusively by local insurers, just changed its regulations to allow startups and joint ventures in the country. Since then, ING Pacific has moved into the top 10 providers. As can be seen in the chart below Greater China's written premiums provide a lucrative "new" market, where the mainland alone is almost 3 times the value of India while the population is now about the same. [3] For example ING Insurance Taiwan is currently a customer of HandySoft, looking to leverage BizFlow, a leading BPMS in both their internal and external facing processes to better take advantage of the growing insurance market and regulatory changes taking place.

	Population (as of July 2004)	DPW Total (in millions USD)	DPW Nonlife (in millions USD)	DPW Life (in millions USD)
Singapore	4,353,893	8,898	3,337	5,561
Hong Kong	6,855,125	12,494	2,377	10,117
Australia	19,913,144	40,385	18.044	22,341
Taiwan	22,749,838	32,402	8,662	23,739
Thailand	64,865,523	4,932	1,711	3,222
Vietnam	82,689,518	550	218	331
Phillipines	86,241,697	1,192	489	702
Japan	127,333,002	478,865	97,530	381,335
Indonesia	238,452,932	3,107	1,733	1,373
India	1,065,070,607	17,302	3,712	13,590
China	1,298,847,624	46,911	14,468	32,442

Source: Population from U.S. Central Intelligence Agency; direct premium written (DPW) statistics from Swiss Re

Figure 1: Insurance Policy Statistics for APAC

China is in a pivotal period, where its markets are being opened to foreign competition. Local financial services institutions have to both gain best practices from global players as well as invest new technologies to protect their market share and differentiate themselves by emphasizing their local knowledge.

ATTRACTION OF BPM / WORKFLOW

There is increasing media attention on BPM Suites in China and vendors are aggressively promoting its value and use. But the real reason why interest in BPM / workflow is that there is increasing proof that implementations are providing value and return on Investment (ROI). The parallel maturation of BPM / workflow technologies in general along with the technological infrastructure of Chinese enterprises combine to provide a conducive environment for integrated solutions leveraging BPM / workflow. Of special interest to businesses is the capability of BPM / workflow to extend the lifetime of legacy systems, while upgrading the technological capability of advanced Web Services.(3)

"We have been deploying successful content management and workflow/BPM solutions in Greater China for years," said Stephen Lui, Director, Software & Professional Services, Sales Operation for Fuji Xerox Hong Kong, "The market is beginning to realize the potential of solutions using content management and BPM Suites. There are clearly increasing projects using BPM. I expect to see many more BPM projects being launched today compared to years past."

The level of interest of using BPM as a foundation for business best practices is making its way into China's education system, with leading institutions promoting BPM technologies as part of their curriculum. Obviously, demand for education in BPM supports the growing trend that BPM continues to mature and be in demand.

"BPM is clearly one of the hot topics in business today. Due to the increasing interest in using BPM Suites to improve business performance, we partner with industry leader like HandySoft and introduced BPM in our education curriculum, said Dr. F T Chan, Principal Programme Director and Head, Division of Information Technology of School of Professional and Continuing Education, The University Hong Kong. We see this will benefit our students in building up their capacity to tackle business challenges."

CASE STUDY #1

One of the largest printing companies in the world with over $10 Billion USD in sales a year and over 10,000 personnel world-wide needed to extend the capability of its existing legacy system. Anywhere that the increase in collaboration may help a manufacturer is a place that BPM as well as other automation solutions should be considered.

Nowadays, many manufacturers in China rely on ERP and possibly other software applications as well the run their business operations. Very often, there are gaps and overlaps between deployed applications. BPM plays an important role in integrating and synchronizing data among disparate systems through out an organization. Improving collaboration requires the ability to automate and integrate manual processes and system applications whenever possible, managing them explicitly and by leveraging additional information. Collaboration enables companies to understand the rationale behind inputs and outputs as well as how they may be adjusted to further improve their product and service quality as well as the overall efficiency.

Prior to the BPM implementation, existing legacy systems had these significant shortfalls:

- ERP and CRM systems do not allow easy communication between distinct data resources, both within and external to the enterprise. And, their machine-to-machine orientation leaves out the key decision-making component: people.
- Need to improved efficiency and allow quick response to changing requirements.
- Traditional workflow focus on document routing and approval and it's not easy and flexible enough to integrate with other systems and business processes

A BPM suite was selected to address the business challenges faced by the organization:

- Combine people and ERP, CRM, HR and document systems and cater for both manual processes and system applications
- Fast and flexible synchronization of data between applications, within the enterprise, and outward to partners and customers.
- A centralize and secure area for all documents with proper access control
- supply the right people with appropriate information at the time required
- Allow rapid development and deployment
- Easy to change
- Leverage existing IT investment

A combined BPM suite that included BPM / workflow, Document Management, and Portal Security was chosen to address these challenges:

- BPM / workflow
- Combine people and information systems via flexible and automated processes.
- Timeline control
- Real-time monitoring of business processes

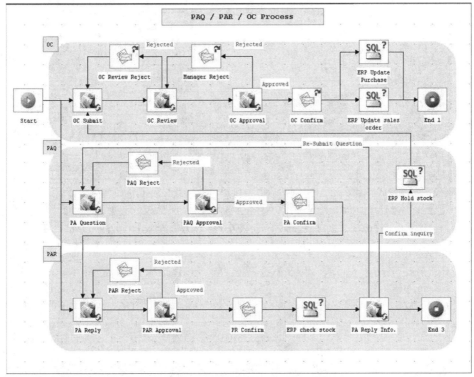

Figure 1-1: Example Process Flow

Document Management

- provide a centralize document repository
- incorporate user access control for various documents
- document versioning

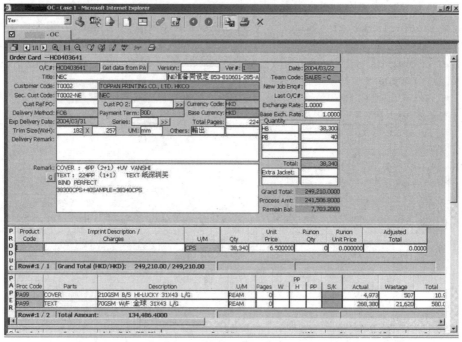

Figure 1-2: Example Work integrated with DM

Portal

- A secure interface to access system contents according to users' needs
- Bring together a collection of services and information in one single interface.
- A secure gateway to access required information and services by partners and customers

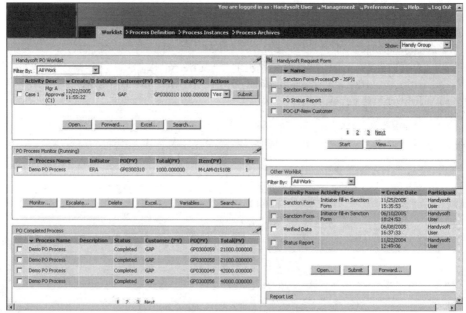

Figure 1-3: Portal Interface

Benefits of the BPM suite solution:

- Yield high levels of operational efficiency and improve customer services
- Eliminate unproductive costs
- No more missed deadlines
- Significantly shorten decision-making time
- Monitoring of business processes
- High return on investment through quick response to changing market and customer requirements
- Quick to see results and return on investment

One of the significant positive impacts the BPM solution had on their supply chain was the tightening up and automatic alert with the appropriate routing structure of the internal bidding process. This is both price booking as well as a healthy stock reservation. Both of these account for significant business improvement by both increasing sales margins as well as maintaining proper stock levels.

"Companies are striving to adapt to quickly-changing market forces. They need to optimize their operations, improve productivity and save costs so to stay competitive. BPM is the best solution to achieve their goals." Ir Charles Cheung, Ex-Chairman, British Computer Society (Hong Kong Section). "They can integrate with ERP, CRM and incorporate content management and management analysis to maximize its benefits. BPM solutions that can be deployed quickly can minimize risks and ensure the best return on investment."

CASE STUDY #2

One of China's largest property management groups with over 50 years of experience in property development in China implemented BPM to automate its internal business processes. It is considered one of the top three companies in the property development category for the region.

They are leveraging a BPM Suite approach to automate their internal processes to improve efficiency and costs.

Their current key objectives are:

1. To use Portal within their Intranet as internal information broadcast and also an entry gateway for key application.
2. To use BPM tools to automate as well as simplify their internal approval process, improve their operation collaboration.
3. To use DM tools to form/centralize their internal documentation library. In long run, a KM system is expected.
4. To use BI tools to form their corporate data warehouse and produce critical management reports at the end of thee date.
5. Through this exercise, they also make use of EAI technology to link up some of their legacy systems from many different industries (for example; (a) central purchase for assets over certain amount of value within the group, (b) consolidating some of accounting procedures within the group.

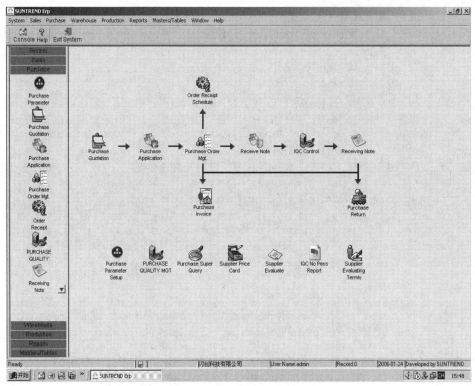

Fig 2-1: Purchase Order Process

They have already automated staff leave application, expenses claim and departmental purchase processes with good results.

They are now investigating projects to leverage their existing Property management system running on IBM AS 400 (large size); HR systems running on LAN and also AS400; Car Park management system running on UNIX box; Laundry retail and payroll system and many other small systems within their group of companies.

CASE STUDY #3

This garment manufacturer has been in production for over thirty years and is one of the world's largest manufacturers of gloves. It has production facilities in more than five countries across Asia, and is licensed to produce W.L. Gore-type products.

Even with the ERP system in place, they still found there are many areas they need to improve in order to provide better customer services and cater for further business growth. Most critical to their business are:

- Fast turnaround time for product development, procurement, order fulfillment processes, production management and on-time delivery to meet customers' expectations are all critical to their business.
- Product development, which covers order management and sampling preparation, is critical to customer service. They needed to improve these processes to cater for further growth of the business.

They faced specific challenges in their order management and sampling preparation processes:

- Involving various documents and different departments at different locations.
- Difficult to control the versions of documents.
- Difficult to maintain and locate of the requirement documents like customer order, change requests, product specifications and drawings etc.
- Lack of collaboration among different team members
- Getting necessary approval at the right time is critical.
- Tracking and monitoring the status of the processes is not easy.
- Following up frequent changes occur during the various stages of the processes is always a challenge.
- Most of the data was not available in their existing ERP

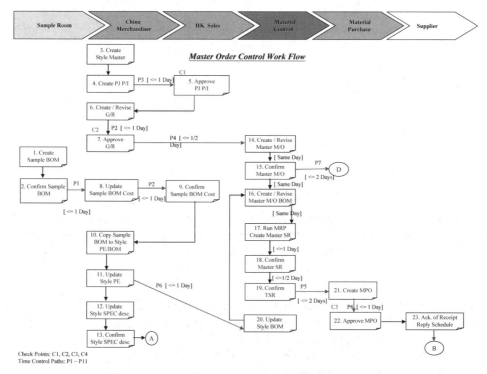

Figure 3-1: Master Control Work Flow

Their solution was to implement a combined Enterprise BPM and Document Management System.

BizFlow BPM

- A powerful BPM tool that can be easily adopted and fit different user requirements
- A proven tool used for different business processes
- Require short development time
- Can be deployed in short time frame.

Document Management

- A centralized repository for all documents for easy reference
- Ensure sharing of updated documents among team members and no more lost of documents
- Better access control for more secured documents

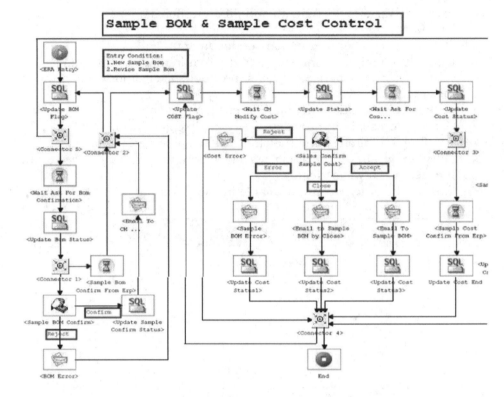

Figure 3-2: Example Process in BizFlow

After automating their processes with BPM, they saw significant benefits. They were able to see up to 50 percent reductions in processing time across their master order control process. Specifically, they had the following results and benefits.

Results

- A better organized document repository and it's easy to trace documents.
- Document security can be put in place.
- Customer PO processing time significantly reduced.
- Document flow is easy to follow.
- Document approval can be obtained at the right time.
- Goods dispatch process and notification time to customers significantly reduced.

Benefits

- No more lost of documents and everyone can refer to update versions of the documents.
- A time compressor used to simplify and improve efficiency.
- A planner that creates "Job To Do" list for each user.
- A reminder that constantly motivate user to do their job in time.
- A monitoring tool to report the status of the business processes.

CONCLUSION:

BPM is attracting enterprising companies in Greater China, such as AVON, Chipbond, Toppan Printing, ING Insurance, Olympus, A&W Food Services, Glory Moon Printing, HangLung Property, KingForce Paper Factory, Hitachi and Austin Marmon. This article examined how real life implementations of BPM suites in Greater China are impacted by the current market forces. The value proposition of BPM suites in the context of the complete solution is clear.

> "BPM/Workflow is one of the most discussed topics we hear from industry today," Jerry Hing-Fuk Sham, Vice President, Information and Software Industry Association, Hong Kong; and Executive Committee, Hong Kong Linux Industry Association, "Now that some BPM/Workflow implementations have reached maturity with proven ROI, there is an increased interest in new BPM/Workflow projects in this region."

Greater China is a rapidly changing dynamic marketplace facing pivotal years of technology adoption. With key market, economic and political forces currently acting on businesses in the region and BPM technologies showing more maturity in this market, there is increased interest in using BPM to remain competitive.

End Notes:

1. Gartner Hype Cycle for Emerging Technologies in China, 2005, Gartner 13 July 2005, Jamie Popkin,
2. China Bank Signs Deal With Goldman Group, Friday January 27, 9:50 am ET, By Elaine Kurtenbach, AP Business Writer
3. The APAC Insurance Industry is in the Midst of Change, Gartner 14 September 2005, Kimberly Harris-Ferrante

The Keys to BPM Project Success

Derek Miers, Enix Consulting Ltd., United Kingdom

Abstract

This paper focuses on the best practices associated with Business Process Management (BPM) project success. It describes a recipe for success, from the creation of a governance-oriented Steering Group, Project Selection, through Business Case Development and on to gaining Executive Sponsorship. With business commitment to the project, the approach focuses on gaining a deep understanding of business processes, before identifying improvement opportunities and eventual implementation on a BPM Suite. Along the way, the paper highlights a wide range of best practice approaches and pitfalls to avoid.

INTRODUCTION

The core driver of Business Process Management (BPM) projects is the delivery of enhanced business performance through cost reduction, increased productivity and the ability to turn the business on a dime (agility). It is primarily a business philosophy about *people*, the way they work *together* (their business processes), the *technology* they use and the *performance* objectives that these processes underpin. At the same time, BPM technology delivers the ability to make this vision a reality. With BPM projects springing up in most firms, a robust BPM project capability is now a competitive imperative. For those still standing on the sidelines, it is not a question of *if* they will engage in BPM oriented projects; just a question of *when*.

However, as people hear of the potential for substantial productivity improvements and the opportunities for more nimble and adaptable business operations, they are reminded of the hype that once surrounded ERP projects. Only later, to see a negative press highlighting failed projects. It was not just ERP projects—CRM, SCM, Six Sigma, TQM—all of these techniques have a strong association with business processes, but have attained patchy success rates. With experiences such as these, some question whether the benefits of BPM are real.

Regardless of the amount of hype around BPM, the vast majority of BPM technology projects **are** successful. According to Gartner who recently surveyed BPM projects, 95 percent said their BPM projects had been successful. Yet many firms are not choosing to promote their successes in order to avoid tipping off the competition—preferring instead to keep the results a closely guarded secret. Moreover, where project failure has occurred, it has usually been self-inflicted due to misguided or poor management practices. The reality is that this potential outcome is entirely avoidable if you pay attention to the details.

This paper provides a set of best practices for Business Process Management (BPM) projects. It assumes that the reader is setting up their first BPM project—laying out the ingredients for successful projects, and offering insights on what lies ahead. While the prospect may appear daunting at first, applying the techniques provided here and employing a bit of rigor, successful BPM projects are entirely manageable and achievable.

THE CORE APPROACH

To ensure success, it is vitally important that the organization develop a repeatable BPM delivery methodology. At its heart, a methodology is a series of steps that, if followed, will dramatically improve the chances of a successful outcome. Think of a methodology as a recipe for success.

A part of this overall BPM delivery methodology is the "BPM Project Delivery Framework." This component of the BPM delivery methodology establishes the guidelines for those tasked with managing and delivering individual BPM projects. It focuses on ensuring projects are tackled in the right order; that they are linked to defined business objectives; that they are scoped and resourced appropriately; and that they make effective use of available BPM technology.

The BPM Project Delivery Framework should first focus on targeting a relatively simple, achievable project with a clear business benefit. Concentrating on a short, tightly scoped project allows the team to prove the viability of the BPM approach while building skills and experience. For example, the "onboarding" process when new hires join the firm targets the needs of the Human Resources department. It allows them to ensure better traceability and clarity in their instructions to others in the business as they ensure that a desk is available, a PC provided and that appropriate personnel records are established.

These aspects of the BPM Project Delivery Framework are important as they enable the BPM program to demonstrate success and establish credibility within the organization before moving on to more demanding initiatives.

In order to understand the BPM Project Delivery Framework outlined in Figure 1, it is important to take a closer look at each step. To ensure proper governance principles, a high-level, cross-functional "Steering Group" oversees the framework and the individual projects undertaken. The benefit of the Steering Group is that it establishes a respected, business-centric body that can take an objective view and set priorities appropriately. It also guarantees business ownership and an effective partnership with IT, while creating a clear organizational context for change. In the short term, the Steering Group will validate the selection of the initial project.

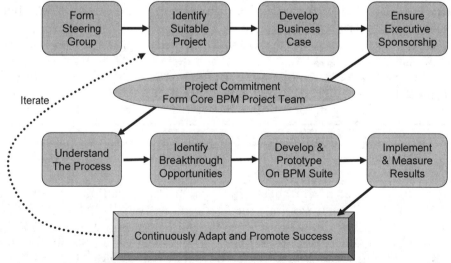

Figure 1 – A BPM Project Delivery Framework is itself a series of steps

Once the scope of the project is agreed, it is necessary to develop a pragmatic business case with supporting measures and benchmarks. A business case is necessary to gain executive sponsorship and to prove the value of the approach. Pinpoint the expected benefits and factor in the capabilities delivered by of modern BPM technology. Executive sponsorship is an absolute necessity as there will always be political hurdles to overcome. When executives have committed to the project, form the core of the BPM project team. Before leaping into implementation, take time to really *understand* the process and look for improvement opportunities. This is important since some are tempted to automate the existing approach, complete with its existing workarounds and inefficiencies. Having understood the process, prototype the solution on the chosen BPM Suite and seek user feedback to ensure the solution is delivering what people really want. Pay close attention to the related organizational change as failure to do so will affect acceptance of the solution. Having implemented, continuously measure results and optimize to encourage a culture of iteration and controlled adaptation. Finally, promote the success across the firm, demonstrating the benefits achieved.

STEP 1 – ESTABLISH THE STEERING GROUP

In order for the BPM project to move forward successfully, it is important that it be set on the right foundations. A neutral, business-oriented governance body should set the priorities, settle arguments and establish effective project principles. The Steering Group acts as that foundation. It also acts as an ongoing repository of knowledge for future BPM projects, carrying over the lessons learned. This knowledge and experience can later form the foundation of BPM Center of Excellence (CoE) for the organization.

A range of different people—forward looking IT people, visionary Line of Business managers, or high-level Executives, can initiate BPM programs. They see the power of an agile, process-oriented business structure as well as the performance, efficiency and flexibility benefits that direct process support technology support will bring. These individuals will probably form the nucleus of the Steering Group, leading and recruiting others to the cause.

As a foundation, the Steering Group needs to include:

- The Executive head of the affected business area involved. This individual will provide the sponsorship of initial project. Inevitably, he or she will need to overcome political obstacles and to push through the associated organizational change.
- The CIO or lead IT Executive is necessary to provide continuity into other technology programs, to represent the IT interests, and to ensure support for the high-level strategy of the firm.
- The overall BPM Program Manager (or the head of the BPM Center of Excellence if one exists) will act as individual responsible for day-to-day management of the initial BPM project. He or she will be responsible for implementing the decisions of the Steering Group.
- Senior LOB Managers from the functions directly affected. It is important to engage with the business units directly. With the senior LOB Managers as members of the Steering Group, any conflicting priorities are quickly resolved.

The Steering Group is the primary mechanism to engage the business in a specific project. Failure to have the business involved is a sure way of ensuring that the project will not succeed. This is because the business needs to own both the long-term change program, and the solutions that come out the other end. Otherwise, through a lack of buy in, people will not fully engage in delivering success and they will not give their full support to the project. One method to address this common change management issue is to setup a reward system that incentivizes the right behaviors and discourages the wrong ones.

To help get the process and project off to the right start, the first step is to hold a workshop for the Steering Group. This workshop provides an opportunity to get the key stakeholders together to agree the scope of the effort and establish overall goals. Participants will want to hear about the experiences of other firms to assure themselves that they are not at the bleeding edge of organizational innovation and taking an undue risk. In support of this, it is beneficial to have an external BPM expert lead and facilitate this session, providing case study material and anecdotal evidence where necessary.

The core deliverables of the initial Steering Group workshop are:
- Formal commitment from the business. This involves a stated promise to dedicate suitable resources to the initiative.
- Clarity around how the program directly supports the strategy of the firm and assists it in achieving its Key Business Objectives (KBOs) and the specific requirements of the targeted applications.
- Tactical agreement on the choice of project and consensus on scope. In support of this, the group should map out a realistic roadmap and delivery timeframe. This will help ensure that the project is not derailed later, or the team diverted toward supporting other goals.

By the time the Steering Group meets to agree on the macro issues, those driving the initiative will probably have an initial tactical project in mind. However, it is useful to take this opportunity to step back and validate that selection against the needs of the wider business based on its longer-term goals and objectives. These may be better efficiency, enhanced customer service, or reduced cycle time. To identify the right tactical project correctly, it is first necessary to step back and understand the larger context of the firm. Having selected a tactical project, the Steering Group must then ensure that the project team maintains a laser-like focus on successful execution against the stated goals.

STEP 2—IDENTIFY A SUITABLE TARGET

One of the most important factors that will influence the likelihood of success is the choice of the initial project. The aim is to identify a quick hit opportunity with a clear business benefit. With opportunities everywhere, the challenge is to find a process that balances the following dimensions:

Relatively low level of maturity—look for those processes where the tasks are poorly defined, or the flow of work is highly variable. It is much easier to improve a poorly understood process than one that is already carefully managed and measured.

High Impact—look at the KBOs of the firm and assess whether an effective solution will produce a high return. This is a question of orientation, Processes that touch customers or suppliers are usually good candidates as they are often full of workarounds and inefficiency. Other clues are lack of management visibility or traceability of the work, where small errors can dramatically affect sales or profitability.

Low complexity—identify situations where the complexity can be managed and bounded easily. Avoid sophisticated "end-to-end" processes. While a multi-faceted, inter-departmental scenario might create a bigger impact, these types of projects do not allow for quick iteration, extension and ongoing improvement. These types of processes normally involve too many touch points and provide opportunities for political infighting, delays and increased project risk. As a result, it is best to develop skills, expertise and other BPM capabilities before focusing on the "big-bang" projects.

A good rule of thumb is to ensure that the selected initial project can completed within 3-6 months. Otherwise, the opportunity for scope creep increases. Along with that goes increased complexity and a higher risk of failure. But the project should be important enough to avoid being seen as irrelevant. Typically, departmental targets are best as they provide an enclosed business environment (reducing complexity) while also enabling a significant and measurable impact. Remember that the key objective of the first project is to develop skills and expertise, while demonstrating to the organization that projects are entirely manageable.

There are a great many approaches to identifying the most appropriate process to start working upon. One useful technique is to consider the range of potential processes and then create a matrix to compare and contrast them using the three dimensions outlined above—maturity, impact and complexity.

For the maturity dimension agree on five definitions of maturity that range from the worst (1) to the very best (5). Lower maturity is characterized by higher error rates and widely distributed cycle times. High process maturity tends to imply careful management and ongoing optimization of processes. This enables the team to force differentiation between the maturity levels of the various processes (sometimes called the quality of the process). It may be useful to refer to the five levels of the Capability Maturity Model to help participants understand process maturity.

For impact it is necessary to find a neutral mechanism that does not necessarily favor one area over another. One approach is to develop a list of Critical Success Factors (CSFs) for the organization and consider how many CSFs are supported or impacted by the process. CSFs are those things which must go right for the organization to achieve its Key Business Objectives (KBOs). Given that an organization may have several KBOs, choose the one that is most important and then develop a list of CSFs that support that objective. If that is money, then decide what factors will deliver the lowest cost or generate the greatest revenue. If the core objective is better customer satisfaction, then compose the list of CSFs to focus on cycle time and other things that customers care about. Against each process, decide how many CSFs it impacts. Contrast this on the matrix with the perceived level of process maturity.

Next apply a 'big-small' indicator to the process to indicate the perceived level of complexity. Translate the results onto a grid like that shown in Figure 2. Individual processes are numbered here 1-8, positioning each process at its perceived level of process maturity, with the size of circle capturing the level of complexity (big-small) indicator. Those processes on the top left with a small circle will probably be the easiest to manage and have the greatest impact. Relative to the other processes, they are at the lowest level of maturity, yet will have the greatest impact on the over-arching objectives of the firm.

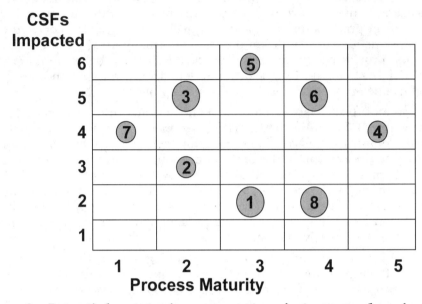

Figure 2 – Potential process improvement projects mapped against the quality levels and the numbers of CSFs

In our fictitious example (see Figure 2), Process 3 is deemed to be more complex than Process 7, which is also at the lowest level of process maturity. Any improvement in Process 7 will probably deliver a significant benefit, while also being more manageable.

Clearly, most organizations will have multiple goals and objectives, some of which may naturally compete with each other. For example, a firm might look to increase operating efficiency by 20 percent and at the same time drive up customer service scores. Using the big-small indicator, it is easy to adapt the technique to focus on other areas: costs and/or top line revenue growth; customer service and/or cycle time; how long ago the process was improved; how well it operates compared to the competition; or even how it impacts overall market share. The important point is that this approach provides a framework to prioritize and explore competing desired goals and objectives.

This technique is based on a facilitated conversation with the affected business unit managers, key change agents and IT. It does not require an extensive consulting assignment beforehand (although some neutral facilitation will probably help).

While the exercise might sound overly simplistic, the point is that it provides a relatively neutral way for all participants to discuss the issues and later arrive at an agreement. Another advantage of this particular exercise is that it helps managers look past the initial project, prioritizing a roadmap for the journey ahead. The key objective is to get business managers to establish and agree to priorities—which processes will be dealt with first and which parts of the business will be impacted. Otherwise, there will always be a tendency to fall into the common trap of scope creep.

But even more importantly, it is the *discussion* that is most valuable. It forces the business managers to sit down and consider the real state of their respective organizations. Moreover, it provides a method to ensure that the actions of the project team are aligned with business strategy (or at least allows them to understand how their work will impact the CSFs and their relative priority).

STEP 3 —DEVELOP THE BUSINESS CASE

By the time the Steering Group meets, it is likely that those sponsoring the workshop will probably have prepared an outline 'conceptual' business case, setting out the problems, issues and likely outcomes for the pilot project. Assuming that the validation exercise supports the identified pilot, the outline will probably form the basis for a more detailed and extensive business case that is needed before a project commitment is made. On the other hand, the benefit may be so obvious and the risk relatively slight (say a very clear departmental ROI) that the go ahead is readily provided. As a best practice, it is a good idea to develop the business case properly and document the expected benefits. This will provide a valuable reference point later on—a compass that will promote continued focus and avoid scope creep.

The detailed business case will need to present a rational and pragmatic explanation of the current way of doing things and the benefits of an alternative approach. It will need to capture the essence of the opportunity and/or how that current structure is under threat from loss of market share and lower profits, as more nimble and agile competitors take control of the opportunity space.

In order to win the hearts and minds of the decision makers, the business case will need to help them understand the reality of the current business situation. That means providing comparisons with competitors' value propositions and costs, where possible. Remarkably, much of that external information is available in the form of annual reports on the Web and other publicly available information sources.

It is important that the business case ties back to the KBOs of the organization, focusing on measurements and benchmarks that underpin those objectives. The business case will need to identify improvement opportunities up front and any areas where the organization can out-perform its competitors. For each of those improvement opportunities, show how that change is achievable, along with an identification of any associated risk factors. Where possible, demonstrate articulate the steps taken to mitigate those risks.

Measurement

Most successful firms already have a clear idea of their long-term objectives (their KBOs). What is sometimes less clear is the relationship between the measurement practices of the organization tied to the achievement of those objectives. As part of the business case development, it is a good idea to review the current approaches to measurement in the target area and develop a set of Key Performance Indicators (KPIs) that support the KBOs of the firm.

Many organizations have far too many metrics. Often, there is a lack of proper alignment with the KBOs or strategy of the company. Too many metrics creates a situation where people quickly loose sight of what is important, as there are simply too many goals to manage against. They lead to unnecessary confusion and complexity, increasing project risk. The key is to ensure that any metrics collected explicitly link back to KPIs that are in-turn aligned with key business objectives.

For example, a major retail bank in the UK found that they had literally hundreds of subtly different metrics (not to mention 130 different change programs that were leading to total confusion in the workforce). Breaking apart the overall set of metrics led to the identification of a relatively small set of metrics and benchmarks, allowing a rationalization of performance right across the firm. Most major organizations could tell a similar story— hundreds of different approaches to measurement, driven by a plethora of change initiatives (that may or may not still be in use) with the vast majority of them overlapping and largely irrelevant.

A review of performance metrics/benchmarks used will usually simplify the goals of the targeted BPM application considerably. If the overall objective of the pilot project is improved customer service, then focus on those measures that the customer really cares about, since they will make the most difference to overall performance. Once the project is complete, it is a good idea to review the measures used and develop a guide on the use of metrics within BPM projects generally.

The Goal Question Metric (GQM) technique developed by Victor Basili and his colleagues provide a useful way of ensuring alignment. The result is the specification of a measurement system targeting a particular set of issues and a set of rules for the interpretation of the measurement data. Each goal is refined into several questions that usually break down the issue into its major components. Each question is then refined into metrics, some of them objective, some of them subjective. Further information on the approach is readily available on the web.

Some useful questions to validate the effectiveness of a measure:
- What purpose will the measure serve? Who uses the measure? Does it tie back to the Key Business Objectives (KBOs)
- How will data be gathered and used? How costly are the measures? What other measures should be eliminated or modified?
- Reward systems and behavior—does it reinforce the right behaviors? How much feedback goes to the employee?

For each measure, capture the reality of what is happening in the business at this point. Where possible, compare and contrast with the competitors. Establish realistic stretch targets for each of those metrics based on the reality of the current situation.

The importance of measurement and associated benchmarks cannot be stressed enough. When it comes to proving the benefits to the business later, base-line figures are essential to convince anyone doubting the merits of the project. The key point is to focus on the metrics that directly support the firm's KBOs.

Expand the Benefits

Be sure to highlight the potential for both hard and soft benefits. Given a definition of productivity based on the value delivered divided by resources employed, hard benefits are easy to identify. Reducing the number of resources required to deliver a given value will drive up productivity. On the other hand, softer benefits are usually oriented around agility and the value side of the equation. They are far more difficult to quantify but equally important.

On the softer side of the equation, it is useful to survey and interview employees, customers and suppliers. Do not limit this to the three biggest and most friendly customers. The objective is to uncover the authentic experience of the majority, rather than highlighting the tributes of a few. Translate any soft benefits to show how they support and enable the achievement of hard dollar objectives (usually framed around the KBOs of the organization).

The Role of BPM Technology

It is vitally important to leverage the capabilities of Business Process Management (BPM) technology in developing options and executing the business case. BPM technology is enabling innovative new ways of more rapidly developing and deploying business applications. It provides a fundamentally new capability that was previously unavailable (at least in a fully integrated application development environment). It allows the complete decoupling of business processes and application systems, permitting the consolidation and independent upgrade of back-end systems.

BPM technology provides the ability to model the business processes of the firm and then use those models to drive work through the business. A process engine keeps track of the state of individual cases of work, integrating relevant third party applications and ensuring traceability afterwards. As the needs of the business change, so do the process models. The firm adjusts these models to achieve the desired performance goals. The point is that through the effective use of BPM technology, the organization can continuously improve its processes through rapid iteration and adaptation..

There are two predominant "domains" of BPM technology—modeling and execution. It is worth touching on the endless fascination that IT departments seem to have around *selecting* the right process modeling tool (as though the tool itself will make all the difference on success and failure). However, the time and money is better spent elsewhere. The reality is that firms need to also focus on developing skill sets and capabilities around process architecture and the implementation.

There are significant benefits associated with modeling, but they pail in comparison with those that derive from an effective BPM Suite. Modeling on its own is not enough. It is a good start but represents just one part of the wider picture. While many organizations have existing modeling repositories, their original purpose was normally to support other initiatives in other areas (i.e. they seldom relate directly to the BPM project focus). However, where effective models are available, make use of them, but do not set out to first populate a modeling repository. This sort of effort is usually time and resource intensive, consuming several man-years of effort building up a great deal of unnecessary detail that is often out of date before the modeling exercise is completed. Standalone modeling environments are generally a diversion on the path to achieving a successful BPM implementation. It is only when undertaking enterprise-wide initiatives that they deliver some degree of benefit. In the short term, the best practice is to look for a BPM Suite that provides a fully integrated modeling repository.

Simulation techniques can help extrapolate into the future when quantifying and predicting the potential benefits. Simulation models can help uncover counter-intuitive tendencies in the envisaged process and act as a confidence-builder, providing the peace of mind to decision-makers. However, be aware that simulation models can consume a vast amount of resource in their development and testing. In addition, they are only as good as the assumptions and abstractions made within them. Use simulation models to test assumptions rather than hide them.

The core components of a BPM Suite are a scalable process engine, a built-in modeling environment, a way of handling business data and content, a set of integration components (integrate existing applications), and an effective process monitoring/analytics capability to drive continuous process improvement. One company that combines all of these attributes in a single BPM suite is FileNet. FileNet provides an effective BPM Suite that incorporates all of these features. Their business event-aware environment tightly integrates with the processes, content and analytics capabilities—providing a continuous process improvement system to optimize business and operational performance.

Just focusing on the productivity and efficiency aspect for a moment, the BPM Suite is a critical enabler in this area. Through the electronic management of work items, hand-offs between roles are automated while delays and errors are virtually eliminated. For example, at Woori Bank (Korea's 2nd largest financial institution), they found that over 70 percent of the time of branch employees was spent on tedious back-end processes, limiting direct customer sales and marketing activities, and affecting employee morale. By automating the back end processes, the company was able to increase the time focused on value-added customer services to 70 percent. Indeed, their program aimed to deliver competitive advantage through service differentiation. They refocused how employees spent their time, generating new business and building stronger relationships with existing customers, while minimizing investments in non-revenue generating staff. Additionally, by improving the process and reducing document retrieval time from several hours or days to 1-2 seconds, loan-processing time halved—from six days down to three days. The result was a dramatic increase in customer satisfaction. They also saved over $21m dollars and increased top line growth by an estimated $115m.

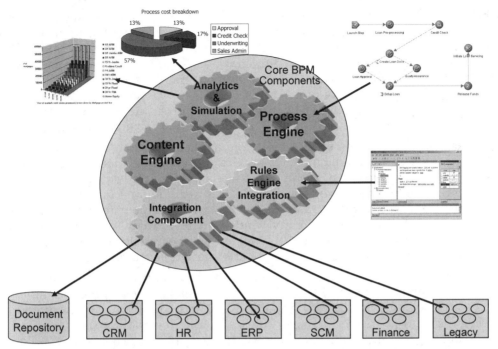

Figure 3 - Typical components in a BPM Suite

Recent advances in technology integration have really changed the landscape for BPM projects. The workflow management tools of the 90s soaked up as much as 70 percent of the project budget in integration work. Developers had to create individual scripts at each point where information from a third party system was required. Potentially, a complex application like an ERP system would have required thousands of such scripts. As a result, the complexity and cost was astronomical. Moreover, if the back end application or the process changed, then all of the relevant scripts needed redevelopment.

Now, modern BPM Suites incorporate sophisticated mechanisms that support the clean integration of third party applications. One of the key best practices is to employ a "service-oriented" approach using Web Services. Web Services provide a framework that enable easier connectivity and greater flexibility. They allow organizations to be more nimble and adaptable by enabling them to more rapidly create and deploy applications by easily assembling services for component applications.

As a result, the organization can now wrap and reclaim those "best of breed" package and legacy applications. They can ring fence them within reusable "service-oriented" business capabilities that quickly combine into new process models, which can then drive the business via the integrated process engine. When application systems are integrated around the needs of the process, the costs and difficulty of training staff can be reduced significantly. For instance, the California State University implemented an environment that allows employees to undertake all of their work without having to access any other systems. In addition to establishing the framework for future expansion and improving employee morale, they estimate that they have saved millions of dollars in training expenses alone.

There is also the critical need to manage the substance of those applications (the LOB data in all of its guises – transactions, structured content, documents, etc.). This is the data and information that describes the context of cases of work, supporting better decision making and more comprehensive audit and compliance. The key requirement is that events relating to changes in state of the content (i.e. as objects are created, modified or deleted, etc.), should automatically trigger the appropriate processes to deal with the change. Otherwise, it is back to humans to remember to respond.

For example, once a customer's mortgage application is created in the system, the process for managing that application instance should be immediately created and executed. If the mortgage is subsequently modified (say by raising the amount to be borrowed), then this *event* should *automatically* invoke the appropriate review process for that case. Supporting this requirement is a real challenge for many vendors. The content management and process engines need to be tightly welded to the integration components such that all process relevant data and information is accessible.

Most BPM environments have also included some form of business rules to support complex decisions. But the use of business rules can also simplify process development, allowing apparently different problems to share common processes (with the business rules component handling the variation). For example, a combined BPM Business Rules implementation within a Fortune 10 level company enabled the firm to simplify its core accounting process. The business rules component allowed one generic process to support interfaces to 60 different sales processes, each handling hundreds of products across 30 different operating companies. By extracting sophisticated rules into a responsive business rules component, the system can then more effectively support business change, straight through processing and compliance.

While all process engines imply support for business rules to a certain extent (conditional routing at a decision point in the process is one form of business rule), certain applications may need the capability to execute more sophisticated rules criteria and evaluate business policies. To do this, BPM Suites normally either integrate with third party rules engines or incorporate some capability internally. Often, those firms with a need for more sophisticated business rules already have an existing business rules engine in place (or already imbedded in a specialized application) and therefore, the BPM engine should snap in to the current environment re-using this functionality. Again the use of Web Services will continue to make this type of integration much more straightforward and standardized.

BPM Suites should also feature built-in process analytics, real-time Business Activity Monitoring (BAM) and simulation capabilities. This enables the ongoing optimization of the process, supporting evolutionary change as the organization adjusts its processes in bite sized chunks post implementation. If the business need changes (as it *will* do), then it is now trivial to reorient the process to deliver the desired results. Once the infrastructure is in place, the technology can deliver continuous process improvement, through incremental releases relieving the pressure in a controlled manner (versus an all at once approach). One of the best practices points to keep in mind is that there is no such thing as a perfect process. Processes will require iterative improvement over time.

To support this, firms should look for an integrated suite that brings together all of the necessary components. Ensure that a shared process model underpins the suite, ensuring their fidelity and accuracy, as they are developed, deployed, monitored, analyzed and optimized. This is in stark contrast with the alternative; where a mix and match set of software products handle each distinct challenge. With this latter tactic, it is often difficult to maintain the fidelity and accuracy of models. As a result, project risk is increased.

This is especially true where a standalone process-modeling environment is used. Rather than a standalone add-on, process modeling is an integral part of the BPM Suite. Where an external modeling environment is used, experience shows that the import and translation is generally a problem. A lot of semantic information is missing or is not fully described (well enough for execution). The harsh reality is that these models do not translate easily and will always require significant embellishment for them to take advantage of the features of the BPM Suite. Furthermore, changes to the executed model in the process engine are then difficult to synchronize with the third party modeling tool. On the other hand, with an integrated suite based on a shared process model, the modeling environment is capable of fully describing the process. It normally incorporates mechanisms to validate the model and ensure its fidelity as changes occur over time.

Moreover, with an integrated suite supported by a shared model, firms can develop proactive responses to key business events such as—a jump in interest rates, a hurricane in Florida, etc. This allows firms to create sets of well thought out actions in order to respond more quickly to changes in market conditions. Should that situation actually arise, then the firm is much better prepared to redeploy their resources and processes.

There are other components that one could include, but the core set is based around the process engine along with its attendant content repository, integrated modeling tool, superior integration mechanisms for third party applications, advanced analytics and simulation. In addition, the process engine itself must be geared for high performance—in order to address the eventual enterprise application needs that will demand the BPM system to support millions of transactions and thousands of users. Together, these elements (i.e. a comprehensive BPM platform) give managers both the vehicle and the levers for effective business performance optimization, allowing them to adapt and evolve more adroitly than competitors using traditional approaches. So when developing the business case, factor in these different capabilities and consider how they can help the organization as it relentlessly focuses on improving its KPIs and achieving its KBOs.

STEP 4 - GAIN EXECUTIVE SPONSORSHIP

A common concern, amongst those involved in BPM projects, is the perceived difficulty associated with gaining commitment from senior executives in the business. Projects can originate from various areas and individuals within the organization. They can come from the executive boardroom where there is recognition of the need to drive the organization toward its KBOs. They can also originate from the LOB itself or even IT. However, no matter what direction the project comes from, it is essential to identify an executive sponsor and champion.

Without an executive sponsor, a range of problems can arise and project risk is increased. The BPM Project Manager (see Step 5 – Form the BPM Project

Team on page 171) may have trouble in engaging affected business managers. Without a clear mandate from the top, the business may simply lose interest or divert resources onto other initiatives during the project. In addition, when the project completes successfully, the executive sponsor will help broadcast the results at senior levels and act as a catalyst for innovation on future BPM projects.

Typically, these individuals have job titles such as COO, CEO, LOB Manager, Senior VP, Business Unit Manager or Director (collectively described here as Executives). While it is impossible to cover all possible scenarios, this section attempts to highlight and discuss some of the central issues.

To get the high-level commitment and sponsorship necessary for success, it is essential to get the executives "intellectual" buy-in. The core tactic is to point to the business impact, and how the approach helps them drive the organization toward its strategic objectives.

Executives usually have a particular style and set of issues that they deem very important (their "hot buttons"). Understanding and working with these is critical. Remember that people have a lot of energy invested in the current approach (the processes) and their natural tendency is to reject initiatives that challenge the status quo. So take care when talking about their department or division. Instead of describing a business wrought with duplication and inefficiency, point to the issues but frame them in terms of opportunity. Rather than a negative, confrontational stance, help the Executive see the opportunity, engaging them into a collaborative effort that focuses on realizing the new vision.

When it comes to understanding how Executives make decisions, one has to keep in mind the typically frenetic lives they lead. Each Executive normally has a cadre of trusted employees from within their business unit or functional group who helps them make decisions. To get the project on the agenda and accepted, it is important to reach and continuously engage these "influencers."

Even getting the attention of the Executive can be a challenge—the BPM project is probably competing with a broad range of existing organizational initiatives. In most organizations, there are literally hundreds of disconnected projects and schemes. Indeed, this can act as a good starting point for the conversation. Integrating all of these disparate change programs under one umbrella can help reduce confusion in the business and rationalize the metrics that are used.

So what strategies are effective? It is always good to help them understand the trends in the industry and strategies employed by competitors. While relevant case studies and reference articles or books can be useful, the key objective is to bring in a bit of realism, helping them to understand deeply what is in fact happening in the organization. One approach is to walk them through "a day in the life of an order"—physically walking around the business tracing what happens. For example, at major insurance company, a health care claims process took an average of 7.6 days to complete. In an experiment, two senior managers hand carrying the same claim pushed it past the right parties in only 45 minutes.

To help build an understanding of customer perceptions of at one of the major US banks, senior Executives committed to sitting with Customer Service Representatives for 2 hours per month to listen to what customers were really saying about their firm. Others talk of holding regular "town-hall" meetings with employees. In other words, get the Executive to experience what is actually happening in the trenches and see the impact on the business. In the old days, it was known as "walking the job"—a senior manager would spend time to sit with employees to get a better picture of the issues being faced at the front line.

At Bank of America, the improvement team initially developed a series of 3-6 month education and awareness sessions for the executive team. These sessions were a sort of "Process 101" where the goal was to help them understand and focus on customers. The two key measures that the group focused upon were customer satisfaction and cycle time. The BPM team sought to highlight the fact that the firm's processes were the vehicles that deliver value and a common customer experience. The team was then able to demonstrate a causal relationship between well-designed processes, reduced cycle times and improved customer satisfaction scores. Improvements in these two key measures provided the momentum to get the initiative moving forward.

Focus on the monetary return in terms of how the project will help the organization achieve its KBOs. At the heart of the argument explain where savings and/or value innovations are going to come from; where opportunities exist to out-perform rivals and detail how this sort of change is achievable. Avoid blanket statements around cost reduction. Focus on specific examples and point to specific improvements. In that way, people will better understand the opportunity since it will be more tangible and concrete. Also highlight the risks but show what steps will help to minimize them. For longer-term BPM programs, set a series of stage gates and build a series of plans that get the business to those stages.

It is worth keeping in mind those Executives and LOB Managers have demanding performance objectives. BPM projects and the technology suites that support them will help them achieve those targets. So be aware of the challenges that they face. Help them understand how the BPM capability provides the mechanism that will deliver enhanced performance (doing more with less, more quickly), making the firm more agile and easier to do business with, and yet still ensuring compliance and reducing operational risk.

STEP 5 – FORM THE BPM PROJECT TEAM

The formation of an effective, cross-functional BPM Project Team is another critical step for the project. There are two general approaches. The first is to create a single team to develop and implement the Pilot project. This is an effective tactic as it allows the organization to focus on achieving a successful project—delivering a quick hit based on solving an immediate problem, proving the overall approach and delivering value in the short term. The BPM Project Team carries out the day-to-day work of the project, organizing and coordinating the work. Through the BPM Project Manager, the BPM Project Team is accountable to the Steering Group for the successful completion of the pilot project.

The other approach is to develop a BPM Center of Excellence (CoE). The idea is that a BPM CoE comprises a group of committed individuals who focus on the processes of the firm as they drive bottom-line profitability and performance. Such a group is usually responsible for supporting a number of BPM projects across the business, keeping momentum going across a broad front.

They provide a group of resources that are well versed in the best practices of process improvement. They are usually responsible for developing common principles, language, frameworks and methodologies for process development and process architecture management. In some companies, they have sought to develop an overall process architecture, clarifying how key processes interact and how they are used by the various business units.

However, in the early stages, the CoE can present an unnecessary overhead as it typically has a much wider scope than is necessary for the pilot. The increasing complexity that comes with too many interlocked variables can slow down the pilot and increase the risk of failure. The CoE concept comes into its own as the BPM program starts to address the needs of the wider organization. With more and more projects, the need increases for a coordinated and integrated approach. In a sense, the CoE becomes a direct descendant of the Steering Group. While still separate from the Steering Group, it provides a central repository for knowledge and best practices around BPM projects. So implementing a CoE is an evolutionary step as part of the BPM story and experience as it spreads across the entire organization —rather than a critical prerequisite for a successful pilot. Indeed, some firms prefer to remain fleet of foot, sticking with a series of quick-hit projects rather than undertake the transition to a BPM CoE. However, as you look at the opportunity more holistically, a COE provides a sound mechanism to maintain and ensure the momentum of process and business performance improvements.

For a successful pilot, avoid the CoE route and keep the BPM Project Team relatively small but effective. If the Project Team begins life with too many people it can easily become bogged down. In the short term, focus on what is achievable and then, having built the core skills, the group can grow as it attacks more complex and demanding processes. The necessary roles are:

The BPM Project Manager—this individual will have day-to-day responsibility for running the BPM project. He or she will report to the Steering Group and is tasked with ensuring that the project remains on schedule.

A Senior User from the area affected—effectively this person is the "Process Owner" for the affected business area. He or she will act as the primary project resource to handle political problems and maintain a focus on the business objective of the project.

One or more Subject Matter Experts (SME)—from the line-of-business (LOB) area, these individuals will have a consummate knowledge of the operational mechanics of the current way of doing things. They will also need a deep appreciation of the macro-level business objectives. An SME is needed for each of the major business areas affected (but not every role in the process).

Lead Business Analyst (or Process Architect)—this individual will provide the analytical rigor and techniques for the project. He or she will guide the SMEs and Senior User, helping them to identify improvement opportunities. Additional business analysts/process consultants may be necessary.

IT specialists—at least one or two are needed to advise on opportunities to leverage, and re-use, existing IT assets. These individuals will need a detailed understanding of the capabilities of the selected BPM technology and experience of integrating multiple systems.

One of the founding rules for a successful project is to ensure that Project Team positions go to suitably qualified individuals. In each of these roles, one is looking for experience and a deep level of understanding. When assembling people from the business, ensure that they have a profound appreciation of existing applications and work practices.

When looking for Business Analysts, one needs to find individuals that are business savvy, yet fluent in the capabilities of technology. They need a deep appreciation of the power of process and an intimate understanding of how change occurs inside organizations. The individual fulfilling the lead role will probably have experience of several major projects with process at their core. They will need to be well versed in either: Business Process Reengineering (BPR) principles and practices; and/or continuous process improvement (Six Sigma); and/or continuous quality improvement (TQM). Look for consummate diplomats who are capable of providing an effective bridge between IT and the business. This Business Analyst role is not suitable for a traditional IT systems analyst (who writes programming specifications). In some firms, the Business Analyst role has the title of Business Systems Manager where the individual acts as the primary interface between the IT department and the business unit or function.

Rather than allowing people to carry out roles for which they have little or no experience, it is probably better to take an external consultant. When selecting external consultants, be aware that virtually every consultant is trying to grow their expertise in this area. The key thing to look for is experience— experience in industry; experience in implementation; an understanding of best practices in change management and process improvement methodologies such as Six Sigma, TQM, BPR, etc. You want people who understand the implications of BPM for business and have already seen it in action. Discern between the sales representative and those who will undertake the work. Consulting firms will talk expansively about their expertise and skill sets (often of those experts who are in sales mode). Look for specific skills and resumes from individuals proposed to participate in the engagement. Ask for their individual credentials in BPM and assess their BPM project experience with customers. If you are bringing an individual in as a "process expert," look at the associated business results from the projects where their expertise was established. Checking customer references is also equally important when assessing expertise and credentials.

Step 6 – Understand the Process

The first challenge is to really *understand* the process; to step outside of it and see it for what it is. Automating a bad process just makes it go faster, exacerbating existing problems and potentially introducing new ones. Therefore, it is important to take a fresh look at how the process operates and the assumptions made about the underlying business need. Having deeply understood the process, it is much easier to see the opportunities for improvement before developing the improved process.

The temptation is to model to a high degree of detail. This is clearly difficult (if not impossible) and precisely the point where projects are stuck in analysis paralysis. The key argument to appreciate is that the detailed minutiae of the process are almost certainly a waste of time—the implemented solution will differ from the current way of doing things. The point is that what *most* people do is **not** the "best practice." After getting stuck in "analysis paralysis" for a while, they tend to implement what they have (something that is much the same as the original). After a year or two, they suddenly realize there is another way of looking at the process and end-up throwing out their first endeavor, re-implementing a radically improved process that reflects their newfound wisdom. However, along the way they have wasted several man-years of effort and untold lost opportunity space. They mistakenly believe that, by modeling the intricate detail of their end-to-end process (with flow diagrams), they have captured and understood the process.

Obviously, a starting point is needed. However, it is more important to look beyond the basic approaches and methods that enable improvement. Nevertheless, ensure that there is enough detail to provide a baseline for future measurements, reflecting the true nature of the current process. Technology can help—analysis of a detailed "as is" model (if available) using simulation tools can lead to improvements and a reduction in risk. But this sort of analysis will seldom reveal radical improvement ideas for the process itself. This is where a skilled Business Analyst and/or Process Architect will really add value. These people should be well trained and versed in alternative ways of looking at processes.

The best practice is to model the process several *times at a high level*—using complementary techniques that provide contrasting perspectives on the process. This is a critical point. Many organizations loose sight of the real objective and laboriously model the "as is" situation. Remember that whatever the implemented solution, the critical success factor for a successful application is to rapidly iterate and improve the process over time.

All models are, in the end, just one representation of reality (the old adage from Deming is "all models are wrong, some are useful"). With fresh perspectives of the process, the team can truly understand, seeing things that were just not visible when the only technique used was a flow diagram. Consider the use of Role Activity Diagrams (RADs) and Object State Transition Network (OSTN) techniques as complimentary to flow diagram based approaches.

RADs focus on how a "*Role* changes state as a result of the actions and interactions that occur." While looking superficially like some BPMN diagrams, the important point is that they allow people to focus on the behaviors and roles of the process, seeing who does what with whom. RADs also enable employees to see and understand the other roles in the process and more easily take the customer's point of view. The technique is extremely compact—for example, in a major mortgage business, a 24 page flow diagram was effectively represented on a single sheet. The best reference for RADs is Martyn Ould's book "Business Processes: A Rigorous Approach."

OSTN is part of a US DoD specification know as IDEF3 (Integrated Computer Aided Definition Language) and shows how things (the business objects) move through the process, changing state as different activities occur. The focus is on the object (not the order of activities). Effectively, the technique captures how the steps in the process modify and transform the state of the object. There are other modeling techniques that achieve the same sort of thing; but the key point is that these approaches focus the attention of the modeler on the steps in the process that *add value* (where the business object changes state).

When developing the initial set of flow diagrams (as for most that is the start point), ensure that the modeling team stick to the core process and the major exceptions rather than attempting to capture every potential route through the activities. But ensure that the team understands how much effort and time goes into managing exceptions.

To design appropriate process architectures—one that truly reflects the needs of both procedures and more fluid practices—is not a trivial exercise. This is not a technology problem but one of business design. First analysts need to understand the process fully— which is not the same as modeling every detail of the process. The very act of modeling a process usually changes the process itself (as people discover the inefficiencies of what they are doing). However, more importantly, trying to model everything about the process will inevitably lead to analysis paralysis (especially using drill-down functional decomposition techniques).

The key point to understand is that process optimization is a journey and not a one-time event. Understanding comes from contrasting different perspectives rather than trying to stick to one *true* approach. Moreover, a range of models can certainly help to understand processes better prior to attempting to implement a technological support environment (the expensive part). Having understood the process at a high level, iterative development is the core technique required to deal with the dynamic, ever-changing business environment.

STEP 7 – IDENTIFY BREAKTHROUGH OPPORTUNITIES

The primary opportunities for breakthrough improvements in business performance derive from the effective deployment of the BPM Suite. The BPM Suite enables a wide range of business benefits. With an understanding of the capabilities of the BPM Suite and the needs of the process, it is relatively straightforward to spot the opportunities for breakthrough improvement.

Some of the techniques introduced here are well known, but have an important function in analyzing the process. These ideas are introduced to help the team recognize areas of inefficiency. To some extent, they overlap with each other.

Potential for Faster Cycle Times

The core advantage of the BPM Suite is that it enables the organization to automate back-end processes, mixing them with manual steps in the front-office. This reduces cycle-time and removes opportunities for errors, improving customer service while allowing the organization to move staff to higher value-adding activities.

For example, Wells Fargo had grown dramatically through a series of key acquisitions. As a result, the Private Client Services group had to deal with a number of disparate information management systems. There was a lot of duplication in each of the 200 separate offices, time-and-labor intensive tasks that often had a negative impact on the company's most important commodity—customer service. Decision-making could take several days, with two-thirds of the time spent in simply tracking down relevant information. By focusing on the process and the real needs of the trust administrators, the bank was able to slash the time taken to make discretionary payments from weeks to days. At the same time, they improved efficiency by over 40 percent and achieved annual cost savings of 15 percent with no reduction in headcount.

Enhanced Customer Service

A good example of enhanced customer service is the Woori Bank example given earlier. By automating the back end processes, the company was able to increase the time focused on value-added customer services to 70 percent. They refocused how employees spent their time, generating new business and building stronger relationships with existing customers, while minimizing investments in non-revenue generating staff. As a result, loan processing times were cut in half – from six days down to three. This allowed to Woori to realize not only $20-million worth of savings but also realize up to $115-million in new business generation.

Channel Integration

Look for situations where the customer relationship is evolving across different digital channels such as mobile, the web self-service, call center and kiosk. In the past, firms generally developed distinct systems and processes that dealt with each channel. However, this approach is fatally flawed as it makes it virtually impossible to deliver a consistent experience to the customer. Look for ways to link and integrate those different channels into the overall process. Use RADs to breakdown the potential customer interactions and how they will be reflected in the overall solution.

Work Items Handled Multiple Times

In document intensive processes, it is quite normal to find that work items are handled many more times than is necessary. For instance, at Miami-Dade County Clerk of Courts (the fourth largest traffic court system in the US), it was found that a typical citation was handled a minimum of 37 times and half of all tasks consisted of moving paper from one desk to another. Because of streamlining the process (eliminating non-value adding manual tasks), installing a proactive process support system and managing the associated documents, they have achieved a 30 percent increase in the case load with 15 percent fewer staff members, leading to an annual saving of $1 million in personnel costs alone.

Role Rationalization

Where possible combine overlapping roles together to reduce the hand-offs and make better use of the resources available. The aim is to minimize the hand-offs. From a process point of view, that is where the risks often are—as work moves from one role to another, things can fall through the cracks and get forgotten or mislaid. All sorts of things can contribute to this risk factor from staff sickness and absenteeism, through to information leakage and miscommunication.

Use RADs to understand the process from the human perspective, facilitating the design of effective job roles that can take on greater responsibility (the once-and-done or one-stop shop). It also focuses on the behaviors that roles need to exhibit and the sorts of interactions expected. Remember that systems and other processes can take on a role. Using RAD based views of the process it is relatively easy to spot those roles that do not add much value (something that is quite hard with a flow diagram).

Manage and Monitor Personnel Performance

The management and review of workers is poorly handled in many BPM implementations. While the overall BPM program may target business performance, at the team level there is seldom an adequate understanding of what this really means. Having understood what their people are capable of and planned accordingly, team leaders need to track and monitor how well they actually perform against those targets. Through a focus on production management disciplines, some firms have derived as much as 40 percent additional productivity improvement, over and above that achieved through the introduction of process automation using a BPM engine.

At its heart, production management is about the supervision of the people who work within the process—what their collective efforts can achieve, where they are struggling, how much work they have coming down the pipe, and what they have to get out the door today, tomorrow, this week, or by the end of the month. First, look carefully at how management plans, communicates and allocates work to its employees. Then it is a case of monitoring, analyzing and of course, focusing on improvement over time. Focusing employees attention of how much they have to get done in a short period of time (say 3 hours), can make a big difference in the amount of work they get through in a week.

At Halifax plc (an internationally famous financial services based in the UK), first line managers are now driven to understand how much work they have in the system and what is likely to arrive. In turn, this has allowed them to think more deeply about the performance of the individual team members, assessing their skills and personal development in a more holistic way. Individuals are assigned work within their capabilities and monitored against performance—in terms of task completion and qualitatively. Managers are accountable against weekly plans. They must also predict productivity over the ensuing 12 weeks. As a result, the firm achieved a further 20 percent productivity improvement over the previous year alone. Week over week output is still rising and the costs of doing business are being driven ever lower. With over 2000 fulltime staff in the back office alone, that 20 percent improvement equated to 400 man-years—a big impact on the bottom line of the business. Moreover, the company achieved a real transformation in the overall management culture, building a virtuous circle of corporate performance, team working, and personal development.

Better Manage Exceptions

Very often, the management of exceptions is what differentiates an organization from its competitors. Further, given the backdrop of technology-based applications, the vast majority of the work and resources go into handling exceptions. A BPM Suite enables the automation of the core process with well-known exceptions managed in a standard and efficient fashion.

In the short term, stick to the core process and the obvious exceptions rather than attempting to cater for every possible scenario. In production, the process models used to drive the business are easily adapted to handle new exceptions, as they become an issue. It is worth building in a mechanism to route exceptional items to the process owner for resolution (if not provided in the BPM Suite). The process can then evolve rapidly over time in a controlled fashion.

Integrate Data and Documents

In these days of increasingly complex compliance regulations such as Basel II and Sarbanes Oxley, content has become even more critical to decision making processes. That means that the management of associated content is an essential aspect and therefore needs to be effectively incorporated into process descriptions. Indeed, firing processes of at critical points where content changes state is an effective way of ensuring the right information gets to the right people at the right time, allowing them to make the right decisions, faster. In this area, products such as FileNet's BPM Suite have a clear advantage over other so-called pure-play BPM products.

STEP 8 - DEVELOP AND PROTOTYPE ON THE BPM SUITE

Having gone through the various stages of understanding the process and identifying improvement opportunities, the next challenge is to develop and implement the application. This is not as difficult as it may sound. Once the team has understood the process and developed a clear idea of how it will work in the new environment, it is normally a straightforward exercise to build the process models on your selected BPM Suite.

To avoid an expectation gap, re-engage the business with a series of prototypes. Some projects achieve this part in just a few days or weeks. Demonstrate the prototypes to affected managers and workers in the business and actively seek their feedback. It is important to actively listen and incorporate any suggestions into the next prototype. Because of the iterative nature of the BPM applications, it is important to take all opportunities to optimize performance on a continuous basis.

Moreover, prototyping provides a mechanism to ensure the user buy-in and ownership of the solution. If the business people see their suggestions reflected in the initially delivered solution, they will have a greater tendency to drive the iterative adaptation of the system once in production. To support this it is important that the BPM Suite include integrated simulation capabilities to enable better analysis of the process prior to implementation and "in flight" when in production.

Where a separate stand-alone process modeling repository is used, it needs to be understood that it is typically not a simple exercise to export the set of process models and then import them into the BPM Suite. In such situations, it is quite normal for those process definitions (exported from the modeling repository) to require significant additional work to take advantage of the features of the BPM Suite. Generally, that involves integrating back end applications, and related content and implementing links to the organizational directory server (or equivalent mechanism within the BPM Suite). Moreover, any changes in the model in the execution environment are lost in the modeling repository, affecting process fidelity over time. As discussed earlier, a totally integrated (in-line) process model within a BPM Suite negates this problem.

STEP 9 – IMPLEMENT AND ALIGN ORGANIZATIONAL CHANGE

Changes to the organizational structure and associated roles and responsibilities go hand-in-hand with significant changes in process. As with all organizational change, there will be natural resistance that will need to be carefully planned and managed. Engaging specialist Organizational Development professionals into the project team will probably be useful.

To encourage the underlying cultural change required, focus on the generic roles and desired behaviors. Use RADs as a way of helping people understand the process, the new role that they have to play and those of others. RADs will also help them see the customers point of view, rather than limiting their scope to the activities they are directly involved in.

Training will play a big part in supporting that change and will require careful planning. In many firms, the training budget is not carried against the project itself as the functions are training their personnel anyway. A coherent communication plan is needed to ensure that the right message gets through to the right people.

Finally, it is important to establish regular monitoring and review practices, assessing performance against established benchmarks. This allows managers to identify issues before they become problems, further improving and enhancing performance. The business should also be encouraged to experiment with the underlying process models as they explore innovative ways to adapt to changing business needs.

Practical BPM Project Management

Process change initiatives often fail where management have attempted to set a path that is cast in stone, yet ignoring the changes going on around them. So be flexible in program and project management, otherwise the whole initiative could quickly get derailed.

Remember that this is a collaborative effort between all parties concerned. It is essential to engage the business early, and often throughout the project. Furthermore, a close partnership is needed between the business and IT to ensure success.

Given that, by definition, the BPM environment enables continuous adaptation of the solution, do not attempt to get everything perfectly mapped and running up front. Aim for an early implementation date, but plan on a period of rapid evolution to follow up the initial success. Work with the business to ensure that they take responsibility for this evolution, by developing their own capabilities to handle the environment going forward. This is a key objective of change management—developing a business methodology that encourages process oriented thinking and continuous performance improvement. Indeed, the goal of the BPM project is to provide a continuous improvement mechanism for the business.

As stated earlier, this framework underlines the need to develop a repeatable BPM project methodology. With a successful project implementation, the team should take time to review the lessons learnt and develop an inventory of skills developed. Overtime, it is these skills and experience that will form the underpinnings of a BPM Center of Excellence.

Pitfalls to Avoid

1. Excluding any of the affected business units from the Steering Group.
2. Spending too much time modeling the "As Is" process.
3. Failing to re-assess the metrics.
4. Failing to demonstrate benefits at a regular review points (to better focus benefit managers' minds). Indeed, reviewing the performance of processes should become a key management discipline.
5. Failing to ensure that Senior Executives and LOB Managers really understand the new, underlying capabilities of BPM technology and the implications this has on business strategy and management.

6. Focusing on a single modeling approach excluding others—even high level comparative approaches contribute to better understanding and better processes.

7. Assuming it is possible to develop the perfect system, first time. Process success comes from iteration and adaptation.

8. Assuming that the business is committed—typically, they are not initially.

9. Proceeding without executive level support.

10. "Selling" the project purely on staff reduction to the general workforce. This will impacts user acceptance substantially.

11. Ignoring the training and organizational change management aspects.

12. Automating a badly designed process.

13. Failing to ensure consensus on business strategy and project priorities.

14. Failing to identify a suitable BPM Engine that easily handles content, integrates with packaged back-end applications, or provide a forward-looking business process infrastructure that delivers appropriate analytics.

15. Allowing the scope of the project to creep due to the lack fo proper goal setting and associated agreements within the BPM Project Team and/or Steering Committee.

16. Failing to recruit the right team members with the proper skill-sets into the BPM project team.

CONCLUSION

BPM is a journey to increase business performance with out a definable destination. While the bumps on the road ahead may sound daunting, they are easy to overcome. The right tools (techniques, approaches, etc.), will help the project to avoid the common pitfalls.

Developing the expertise and capabilities in-house may sound expensive, but the benefits to the business, will certainly outweigh the perceived problems and cultural issues. Using the right techniques enables effective understanding at all levels of the organization. However, people need to see how the various procedures and practices combine and how they fit into the overall process. Once employees understand the overall process, they will begin to identify new ways of working which leads to performance and quality improvements.

Investments in process architecture are typically investments in operating assets for the firm (technology), and they can be significant. So ensure that an effective BPM Suite is selected—one that can act as an enabling platform for the ongoing monitoring, adaptation and improvement of processes. The whole point is that having got the basics right, the organization can adapt, improve and innovate as it drives to increase business performance and market leadership.

Section 2

Standards

XPDL 2.0: Integrating Process Interchange and BPMN

Robert M. Shapiro, Global 360, USA

HISTORY

The basic concepts that underlie XPDL[1] were formulated by individuals working together in the WfMC[2] who were from companies developing workflow and business process management (BPM) tools. These concepts were embodied in a meta-model and glossary which then guided the specification of interfaces for various aspects of the overall problem. The interchange of process definitions between different tools and also different vendors was regarded as an essential piece of this whole and the first version of a standard interchange language was the Workflow Process Definition Language (WPDL), published by the WfMC in November 1998.

The growing popularity of XML and its use for defining document formats for the Internet, combined with some years of accumulated experience using WPDL in workflow and BPM tools, led to the creation of XPDL 1.0, which was officially released in October 2002. XPDL retained the semantics of WPDL but defined a new syntax using an XML schema. Neither WPDL nor XPDL 1.0 proposed a specific graphical representation, although the underlying meta-model for a process was based on a directed graph structure consisting of activities as nodes and transitions as the edges or pathways between them.

The Business Process Management Notation (BPMN) was developed by individuals working together in the Business Process Management Initiative (BPMI.org[3]) to take the techniques employed in flowcharting tools, unify and extend the graphics to express the semantics required in workflow and EAI processes. BPMN 1.0 was released in May 2004.

In addition to the graphical notation, BPMN incorporated a number of specific mechanisms for process modeling that had not yet been included in XPDL; among these in particular events and message passing between processes. XPDL 2.0 incorporates these mechanisms as well as the graphics and offers an extended meta-model that unifies XPDL and BPMN. It was officially approved by the WfMC membership in October 2005.

BASICS

A Business Process Model consists of a collection of processes together with the applications and resources required to perform all the steps contained in the processes. We start with a discussion of the elements in a single process. To keep things simple we focus first on a minimal subset of elements.

- Activities (the steps in the process)
- Transitions (or sequence flow)

---

[1] XML Process Definition Language

[2] Workflow Management Coalition

[3] BPMI.org merged with the Object Management Group (OMG) in June 2005.

For a complete description of the graphics, syntax and semantics refer to the websites of BPMI.org[4] and WfMC.org. [5]

In the following picture the four round rectangles are activities and the four arrows are transitions which define possible paths between activities. The leftmost activity, Receive Payment, is the first activity to be performed in the process since it has no predecessor. Send Receipt is the last activity. Process Large Payment and Process Small Payment are alternatives: a payment is routed to one or the other according to the amount of the payment.

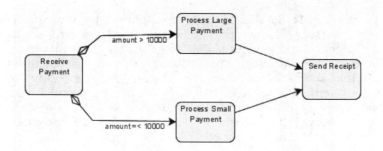

The Boolean expressions on the transitions determine which transition occurs, as determined by a piece of data, *amount*, associated with the payment. This notation is commonly employed in Petri Nets, a mathematical formalism that influenced the development of XPDL.

Flow charts often use specific graphical elements to indicate branching logic. To support this XPDL offers routing activities (gateways). The diagram could then be drawn as:

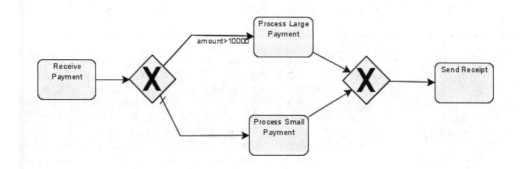

Here the diamond shaped nodes are routing activities and the X indicates exclusive-or logic. The XOR node on the left is a branch. Only one exit transition has a condition expression; the other path is marked as the default gate, to be taken only if the conditions on all other exit gates evaluate to **false**.

[4] BPMI.org; Business Process Modeling Notation (BPMN), version 1.0 – May 3, 2004

[5] WfMC.org: XPDL 2.0 WFMC-TC-1025 Version 1.0 October 3, 2005

There are a number of gateway types. For The most commonly used are:

 Exclusive (XOR)

 Parallel (AND)

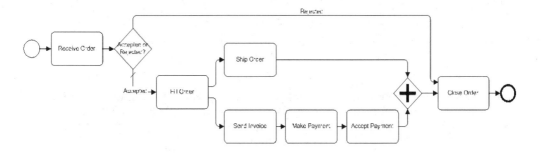

The nodes and transitions can form arbitrarily complex graphs with

- Sequential Activities
- Parallel Activities
- Loops / Cycles
- Conditional Paths

In the above flow we have introduced a third type of activity node, an Event. An event is something that "happens" during the course of a business process. These events affect the flow of the process and usually have a cause (trigger) or an impact (result). There are three types of Events, based on when they affect the flow: Start, Intermediate, and End. There a numerous trigger and result types. Some common combinations are:

 Start Event triggered by a message.

 Intermediate Event triggered by a Timer.

 End Event with Error Result

ACTIVITIES

We have said nothing about the details of a basic activity. It is a step in the process, but what happens at that step? Typically, to perform a step requires one or more resources: e.g. a person with a particular skill set or a system resource. A task or application may need to be executed to perform the step.

So basic activities have attributes which provide information about who can perform the activity, what application or web services should be invoked, what properties of the object being worked on are used and/or altered in this step, and so forth.

The participants (resources) and applications may be defined within a single process or for the entire collection of processes in the Business Process Model. The properties of work objects are likewise definable within a single process or for the entire model.

Activities have other attributes which further define their specific role or how they are implemented. Here we list a few:

- StartActivity   Indicates that process starts here.
- IsATransaction   Transaction-based semantics.

TASKS AND APPLICATIONS

There are seven standard Tasks that can be specified for a basic Activity and are used primarily for invoking Web Services and using WSDL[6] messaging. An eighth task type is used for invoking Applications whose signatures have been defined in the Business Process Model.

Applications that can be invoked by a process are defined at the Process or Package (See Package meta-model) level. There are multiple types of applications:

- Traditional applications
- Components
- Web Services
- Business Rules
- Form
- Script

COMPOUND ACTIVITIES

A compound activity refers to another process (independent or embedded). The graphics for a compound activity include a special marker to designate this.

Compound activities allow re-use of process definitions. If the reference is to an independent sub-process, a list of actual parameters can be passed to the sub-process at the time of invocation. An embedded sub-process shares the same data space so no parameters are passed. (As a technical detail not shown in the graphical representation, an embedded process is an XPDL activity set and the compound activity is referred to as a Block Activity). An independent sub-process may be invoked asynchronously, in which case the exit transitions from the compound activity immediately determine the routing of the work object to the successor of the compound activity. Synchro-

---

[6] Web Services Description Language

nous invocation requires that the sub-process complete before the compound activity can continue. Embedded sub-processes are always invoked synchronously.

PROCESS METAMODEL

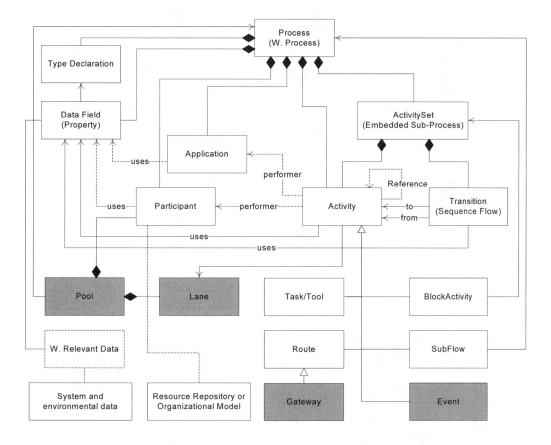

The meta-model depicts the relationships between all the elements in a Process. The shaded elements were not present in XPDL 1.0 and are now included in XPDL 2.0 to support BPMN constructs. Gateway and Event have already been described. Pool and Lane are elements that support the use of graphical Swimlanes which we discuss later in this chapter.

PACKAGE METAMODEL

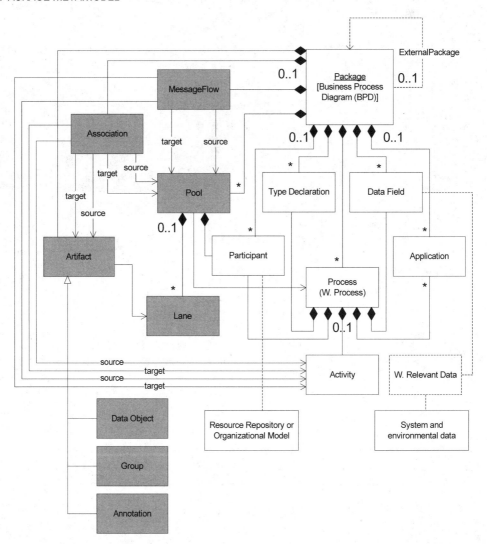

This meta-model describes the relationship between elements on the Package or Business Process Diagram level. The shaded elements were not present in XPDL 1.0 and are now included in XPDL 2.0 to support BPMN constructs.

SWIMLANES

In the following diagram we depict a single pool containing the process *Loan Application*. There are no lanes in the pool. The process can be either an independent sub-process or an embedded sub-process.

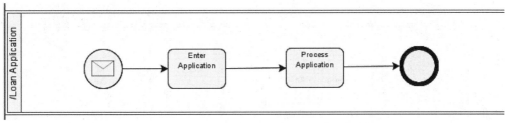

In the next diagram we depict a single pool containing the process *Loan Application*. This pool has two lanes. An activity in a lane requires as performer the resource designated by the name of the lane.

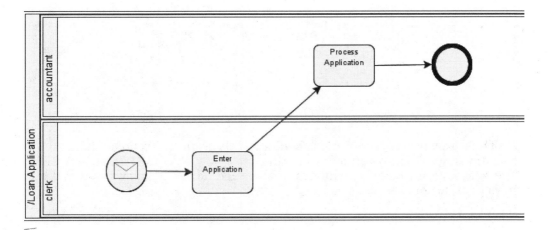

Notice that the transitions (sequence flow) may go across lanes in a pool. Transitions may not go across pools.

MESSAGE FLOW

Message Flow is normally implemented by Web Services and Message Queues.

In the example we illustrate how message flow may go between activities in different pools. This allows us to represent graphically aspects of the choreography between processes. It should be noted that message flow cannot occur between activities in the same pool. In other words, sequence flow is used to connect activities in the same pool whereas message flow is used to represent communication between activities in different pools.

In these examples pools have been drawn with a horizontal orientation and a width that extends across the entire page. However, the specification supports vertical pools as well, and also allows the width/height to be limited. This supports the use of pools in the specification of abstract processes and their choreography.

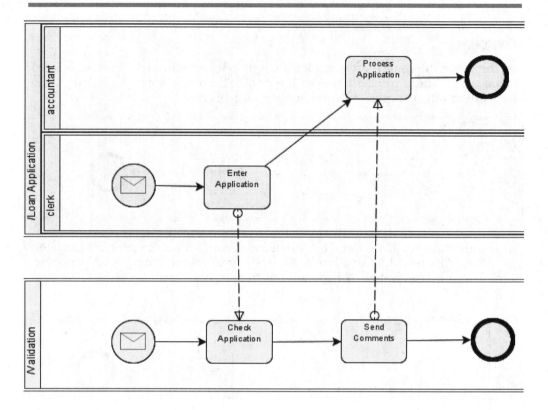

ARTIFACTS

Artifacts provide documentation facilities with graphical representation. Associations are used to connect the artifacts to flow objects such as activities. The association is like a sequence or message flow, but allows optional arrows at either or both ends of the pathway.

Data Object:

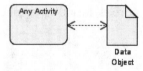

Text Annotation:

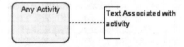

Group: Allows diverse objects to be labeled with the same name for reporting purposes.

PROCESS DEFINITION AND REPORTING

An XPDL 2.0 document contains the process definitions for a collection (Package) of processes. This XML document is used not only by modeling tools, simulation tools and execution (enactment) engines; it also provides the basic information for BAM[7] reporting tools and in particular provides the dimensions and members for OLAP[8] cube reporting technologies.

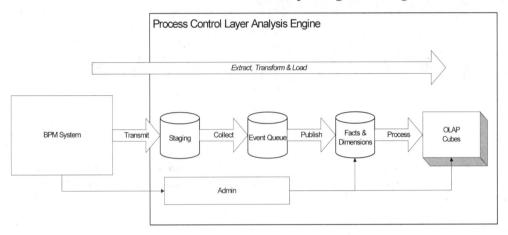

Here we depict a Business Process Management System which uses the Admin facility to send the XPDL process definitions to the analysis engine and transmits a stream of log events which capture the details of execution. The Analysis Engine structures the data base and OLAP cubes based on the process definitions, participant and queue information. The events are processed by the Analysis Engine to update the fact and dimension tables in the data base and cube processing completes the preparation for interactive slice and dice viewing of the data, using EXCEL and/or other proprietary Process and Business Intelligence tools. Below is an EXCEL chart based on historical data.

---

[7] Business Activity Monitoring

[8] OnLine Analytical Processing

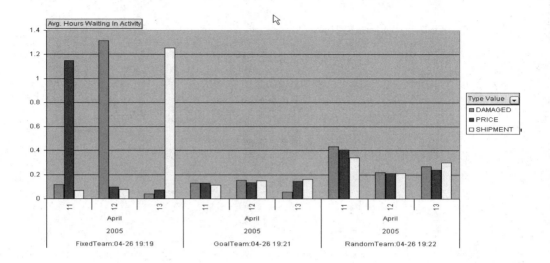

An alternate approach to data presentation shows selected data in the visual context of the process definition. This can be done for historical presentations as well as animations of the executing system or a simulation run.

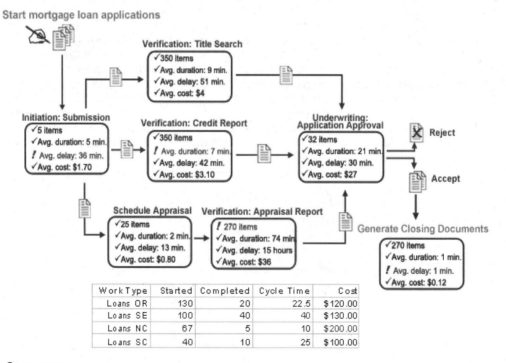

Work Type	Started	Completed	Cycle Time	Cost
Loans OR	130	20	22.5	$120.00
Loans SE	100	40	40	$130.00
Loans NC	67	5	10	$200.00
Loans SC	40	10	25	$100.00

SIMULATION

Simulation engines based on the WfMC meta-model and the XPDL file format have been available for a number of years. These engines are driven by XML scenario files. The XPDL package is supplemented by a number of additional schemata that provide information required for simulation, including details about the performance of the activities (e.g. duration information), schedules for the arrival of work, resource characteristics (skill sets, work schedules, cost etc.) and a variety of simulation options. Some of this data can be acquired automatically from historical information collected in the OLAP data base.

These simulators are able to generate log event streams identical to those produced by the BPM execution engine. Hence the same Analysis engine can be utilized to provide charts and reports that evaluate changes being tested using simulation.

The simulation technology needs to be extended to include new constructs incorporated in XPDL 2.0; in particular the BPMN **events** and **message flow**.

PROCESS INTERCHANGE

Common meta-model allows tools to exchange models.

Type of tools:

- Simulation tools
- Monitoring tools
- Execution tools
- Modeling tools
- Repository tools

The following diagram illustrates the use of process interchange in a BPM suite.

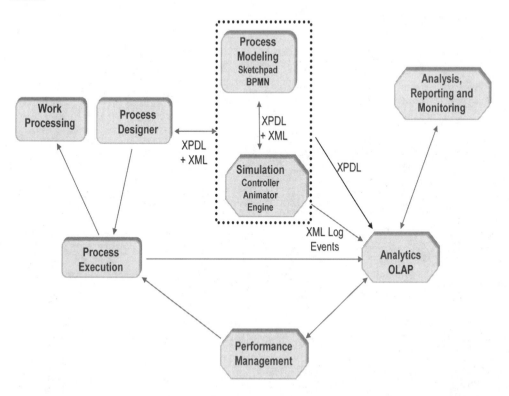

CONCLUSION

XPDL 2.0 provides a standard graphical approach to Business Process Definition based on BPMN graphics. XPDL 2.0 provides a standard file format for persisting BPMN diagrams and interchanging Process definitions. The file format is based on the WfMC meta-model which establishes a framework for defining, importing and exporting process definitions for numerous products including execution engines, simulators, BPA modeling tools, Business Activity Monitoring and reporting tools.

The schema defining the format is extensible and provides vendor and user extension capabilities as well as a natural path for future versions of the standard. Mappings to specific execution languages (e.g. BPEL) and other XML-based specifications (e.g. ebXML) are possible.

Programming in XPDL

Saša Bojanić, Vladimir Puškaš, Zoran Milaković,
Together Teamlösungen, Austria

ABSTRACT

In this article, we are elaborating the possibility of using XPDL (XML Process Definition Language defined by WfMC) to completely define event driven applications, that we call **XPDL Applications**.

XPDL application is a normal XPDL process definition that complies only with few additional rules and restrictions. This definition, when being interpreted by an XPDL engine, and from an engine's point of view, results in an execution of a normal workflow process. The framework we will describe makes a difference. It also interprets XPDL in its own way and presents to the user an interface based on process definition and current state of the process instance.

INTRODUCTION

XPDL with all of its powerful constructs can be considered as a special purpose fourth generation programming language. A graphical XPDL editor allows you to actually draw your programs, and having an XPDL based workflow engine, you have your programming language interpreter. Executing XPDL program means creation and execution of a new process instance based on XPDL definition.

Many applications nowadays follow the event driven pattern of execution: web-apps respond to discrete user requests; desktop applications receive mouse and keyboard events from operating system to act upon... Those external signals might appear in the order unknown at build time, so application typically maintains the state for their processing. In Workflow Management System, state is by a definition, basic property of any process instance. Event handling part, however, may be mapped into customized work list handling executable.

Typically, WMS provides work list handler application that manages your work list from all the process instances currently running on the engine.

Imagine that you have the following rules and restrictions for your XPDL definitions and WMS:

1. there should be always one user assigned to a task from a particular process instance (the user who started the process/application),

2. the process definitions should be written in a way that at a time there is only one active task for the user in a single process instance

Now, imagine that you have worklist handler that is always displaying the form representing one work item, enabling you to interact by updating process variables. Completing this item would result in next form displayed, based on next work item from the same process instance.

By putting it all together, raised the idea for the framework which would ease the development of afore mentioned XPDL applications. Principal parts of the proposed framework are:

a. *XPDL creation rules based on some restrictions and extended attributes interpretation:*

XPDL supports extended attributes element throughout the schema, hence extension of the language requires agreement only, on where to use what attributes. Purpose of the variable is ambiguous for activities with NO implementation (at least in XPDL 1.0), thus extended attributes may solve the problem there. Special rules for work item distribution – assignment allocation or details of tool agent/application are candidates to be extended attributes also.

b. *appropriate graphical XPDL editing tool based on the rules defined:*

In application design time, this framework will offer you a customized graphical XPDL editor, visually representing the application flow, with a custom validation based on the framework rules, custom property panels for defining application in details, ... for effectively creating XPDL applications.

c. *customized work-list handling executable, which parses the input data before feeding it through WAPI to the workflow management system, and transforms consequent WMS state into response fed back to the user (depending on a rules defined):*

In a runtime, this framework will provide UI based on XPDL definitions, rules and runtime information obtained from an engine. Framework will also push the information from a user input back to the engine and let engine drive the XPDL application flow.

d. *set of tool agents that execute application business logic:*

Predefined set of business functions are provided, and called through WfMC Interface 3 – tool agents.

XPDL As a (Visual) Programming Language

XPDL-based workflow engines are interpreting XPDL process definitions in the sense of distributing tasks to appropriate users at a certain point of time, depending on a certain rules and current context and state of a process instance.

In the case of XPDL applications, there will be only one user per the process instance, which will be sequentially performing all the tasks from the same process instance, just like if he is executing event driven application. So, the XPDL applications are special kinds of process definitions written only for one participant, and always for that one who instantiated the process. In these process definitions, there can't be more than one manual activity at a time.

The workflow engine will interpret such XPDLs in a standard way, but the framework will be a higher-level interpreter.

In a runtime, framework will communicate with an engine:

- It will read runtime information about currently active task, and data from XPDL (in order to display proper form to the user),
- It will pass the information user entered back to the engine, setting the context of process instance.

- It will conduct the engine based on the action user have chosen in order to give instructions how to drive XPDL application.

On the other side, as the process flow goes on, framework will communicate with the user:

- It will change the UI (based on the information retrieved from the engine about the current task),
- It will accept data entered by the user through UI (in order to pass it back to the engine),
- It will execute appropriate action depending on the user choice (i.e. to open a document, or to communicate back with the engine to conduct it to proceed with a process flow)

In such framework, a process definition itself can be considered as an application template or description of how will application look like and what will it do.

The XPDL programming language could help in user interface integration: activities that are by the definition "manually" handled by the entity outside Workflow Management System should be mapped to user interface entry points (i.e. dialog boxes or HTML forms). In a runtime, each manual activity instance will be represented as a new application form, containing buttons to press, links to click, and fields to enter or read data.

Parts or complete business procedures get implemented into applications, each day. Lots of problems occur during their reproduction in traditional programming languages. Many of those problems would be removed if business procedures would be drawn in XPDL instead. Hence, activities that are by the definition automatically executed by the engine could actually define the part of business logic of your application (i.e. reading/writing data from/to a DB, creating a document, performing some mathematical calculations, etc.), and will not be represented as an application forms.

The (conditional) transitions from a manual activity to other activities will be used for navigating through the application screens. Typically, transitions will be represented as buttons or links on the screen of manual activity being a transition's source. These buttons or links represent user option. By pressing a button or link, user navigates through the application flow.

The process definition variables will be typically displayed as fields for entering or reading data (text boxes, labels, combo boxes, lists, tables, check boxes, etc.), or a links handled by the framework to i.e. open a document.

The XPDL application definitions will represent a single business logic step/function definition. The application's formal parameters will define a signature of this function (function's parameter types and if they are IN, OUT or IN&OUT)

As already told, process definition entity can be considered as an application template. But also, it can be considered as a template for defining a segment of your business logic functionality if it contains only automated activities. We can use extended attributes, which will be read by the framework to distinct these two cases (i.e. framework will allow you only to start processes that represent application templates).

XPDL spec defines that process can be invoked from another one, through the usage of sub-flow concept. Using this concept, we can have something like application nesting (if calling one application template from another), or the means for defining re-usable business logic parts (if main application template calls process definition template that defines only business logic).

By modeling deadlines in your XPDL process definition, you are able to limit the time user is allowed to execute a certain part of the application.

Executing XPDL applications in WfMC standard-compliant WMS allows you to see who did what and when (through interface 5), without writing a single line of the code for tracking user inputs.

Considering what we explained so far, having a graphical XPDL editor, and a framework that interprets XPDLs as explained, you are able to define your entire application graphically.

The main thing to notice is that you can define application flow by (graphically) defining the network structure of activities and transitions of the process definition. Using the right tool you can **design** quite complex algorithms in XPDL completely, yet keeping them clear and easy to read.

XPDL APPLICATION FRAMEWORK

Graphical XPDL editor

To the majority of the people who come in contact with any program, the user interface is the program—XPDL editor is no exception. Raw, unmanaged power of XML Process Definition Language may intimidate some if served directly. XPDL is easier to consume when graphically appealing curtain hides the crude XML details.

Editor is customized with additional features and L&F based on framework rules. Beside features that any graphical XPDL editor should have, this one has some additional features:

- specialized property panels to edit extended attributes which are interpreted by the framework in a run-time,
- design-time validation of XPDL, based on framework defined rules (validation of special purpose extended attributes, special navigation variable, condition expressions, ...)

Editing tool might fill additional purpose by providing predefined activity types. Having "*DB query tool activity*" ("*XSLT transform activity*", "*Read-only manual activity*", "*Query overtime hours application*", etc.) ready to be inserted, greatly simplifies the process of creating XPDL application.

Using customized editor, changes in application can be done by non-programmers. This is very useful for persons responsible for modeling business processes who are typically not programmers. They can make changes in software without writing code, which makes maintenance of application much easier.

How to program with graphical XPDL editor?

After considering features and purpose of application, XPDL programmer starts to *draw* application in editor. Each activity is represented as one graphical node. Manual activities are used where user interface entry point is needed, and automatic activities are used to handle business logic.

For manual activities, programmer chooses which variables will be displayed on UI. Each variable type has predefined set of possible views. Optionally, it is possible to fine configure chosen view - for example to determine which attributes of complex variable to show.

To define the application flow, programmer connects inserted activities, and implicitly defines transition conditions. Framework will automatically determine which buttons has to be shown on the screen according to outgoing transitions of current manual activity. At a time of activity completion, user input handlers will collect information from user interface and update variables.

For each class of applications, framework needs to be configured differently. This basically means to have a predefined set of tool agents for application business logic, specific handlers for rendering user interface and processing user input. One class of applications can be for example document management applications. Here we need tool agents for creating document, retrieving documents from document management system, saving documents back to system, etc. Every tool agent represents a well-defined function of document management system, which can be called independently. If this is satisfied, *reusability* of functions is achieved. Combining these functions we can easily make changes in application by drawing automatic activities in editor and linking them in appropriate way.

Thus, programmer use variables of process and route these variables from activity to activity – manual or automatic – and builds application. Putting new manual activity in the graph actually means adding new application form. Editing its properties through a customized property panels means fine tuning the application UI. Putting an automatic activity, and using predefined set of tool agents, means implementing business logic.

Framework details

When representing framework through MVC paradigm, *model* is represented by XPDL variables, *view* is represented by rendering handlers, and *controller* is represented by the process definition interpreted through the framework.

Framework is built upon workflow engine as additional library. In architecture of framework there are four main parts that can be noticed:

- Part for communication with workflow engine:

  This part of the framework reads data from engine: extended attributes, navigation variable and all other relevant information. Also, it returns data back to workflow engine and updates process context.

- Part responsible for communication with user (rendering, handling user input and navigation handling):

  For each manual activity, information necessary for rendering is stored in a XPDL model. Framework uses the information from activity's extended attributes and activity's outgoing transitions. Interpreting these data, framework determines which variables to show and how to show them.

  When user clicks a button on UI, there is a handler for this event. It will read user input and transform input data back to process variables.

  Navigation handling is also very important part. Completing activity and automatic acceptance of next activity in process must follow user action on UI. Framework provides automatic recognition of possible routes after activity is completed. According to this, framework will render buttons on screen – one button for each possible route to next activity. A button action produces additional change of the process context that satisfies the condition of appropriate transition and completes the activity.

This allows making custom UI with programming only in XPDL.

- Predefined set of tool agents

Set of functions which are used to work with objects in system are developed as implementation of tool agents. This allows calling these functions from XPDL. These tool agents are used to model business logic of application.

- Graphical XPDL editor

Part of the framework used at a design time. This editor is customized according to the framework rules and restrictions.

Framework is build as extensible library. If new variable types and/or functions are needed, it is easy to extend current framework with new set of UI handlers and tool agents.

EXAMPLES

Having a framework and XPDL engine, let us show an example of defining a simple XPDL application.

Let say we are implementing a library's WEB site. One of the first things we will need is to build an application for searching the books based on some criteria.

The initial requirement is to have three sequential application screens:

- for entering search criteria,
- for displaying list of the books found based on the criteria,
- for displaying details about selected book

We also want to be able to *terminate* the application any time we like (from any screen), and to have a loop in order to be able to perform another search after viewing the book details. Termination does make sense if this is not the only XPDL application on your WEB site, so after terminating the application, you could be redirected to the site's home page.

Figure 1 shows how our initial XPDL process definition should look.

For each screen defined in spec, we have corresponding manual activity. We have two automated activities, representing business logic for getting a list of books based on the criteria user entered, and for getting the details for the selected book.

The first screen displays a form for entering search criteria, and contains two links, which correspond to the transitions going out of the activity. The links will be named after activities transitions are pointing to: '*Get list of books*' and '*End*'. Depending on the link selected by the user, the application either terminates, or proceeds to the next screen after executing business logic (retrieval of information about the books matching the criteria).

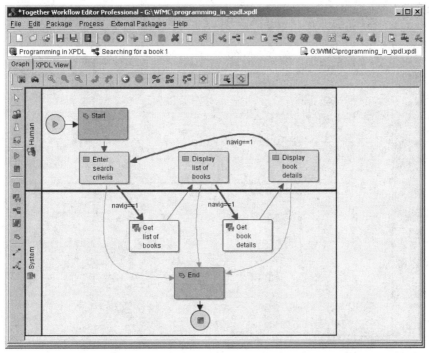

Figure 1: Initial process definition graph

The second screen displays the list of the books matching the criteria, and allows user to select one. This screen contains two links: *'Get book details'* and *'End'*. If user selects the former, business logic for retrieval of the selected book details is executed, and third screen will be shown.

The third screen displays the details about the selected book, and also shows two links: *'Enter search criteria'* and *'End'*. Depending on the user choice, application will either terminate, or will go back to the first screen, allowing user to enter a different criteria, and to continue the search.

Now let's say we got some new requirements:

- we want to have additional screen for viewing the free chapter of selected book
- we always want to be able to return back to the previous application screen

Changes to our process definition are shown in Figure 2.

As you can see, to satisfy *"go back"* requirement, we simply connected all the manual activities to the ones preceding in the flow. In a runtime, this change will result in having additional link on each screen. It is an option of going back.

To satisfy the requirement for additional application screen for viewing the free chapter, we introduced a business logic that retrieves this information, as well as the new manual activity for presenting it. Also, we connected activity *'Display book details'* to the automated activity *'Get free chapter'*. Connecting these two activities will result in a change of the screen for displaying book details. There will be another link with an option to get a free chapter of the book.

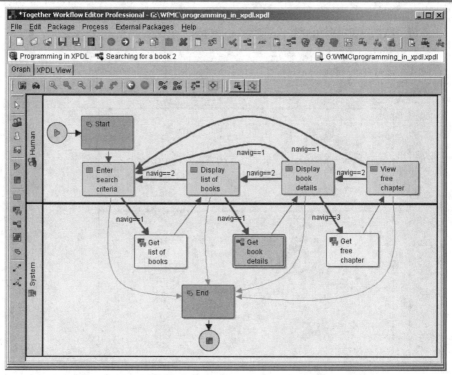

Figure 2: Changed process definition graph

You might have noticed that we also changed something that was not the part of the new specification. Hence, instead of the automated activity for getting book details, we introduced a sub-flow activity that calls newly defined fully automatic process. In this process, we refined the logic for getting the book details. Now, this new process represents our business logic in a detail.

Figure 3 shows our business logic for getting book details, represented as a separate fully automatic XPDL process.

We have several benefits of representing the logic in a separate process instead by a single automated activity:

1. this logic can be re-usable; it can be used from another XPDL application in the system (e.g. application for editing the book details),

2. we can maintain our business logic parts by maintaining appropriate XPDL process definitions; if the rules defining our business logic change, and we have split our logic into enough basic parts, modifying of application according to the new requirement could be possible just by graphically re-arranging activity and transition network,

3. when we change the XPDL definition representing the part of re-usable business logic, we automatically updated all the applications using it through the sub-flow concept

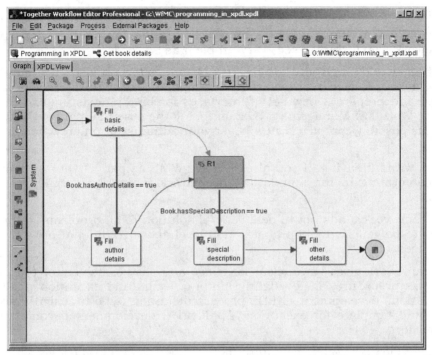

Figure 3: Graph of sub-process representing part of the business logic

Figure 4 shows activity seen from different angles: design time perspective representing activity within process definition graph and through the property panel, and runtime perspective representing HTML form generated out of this activity.

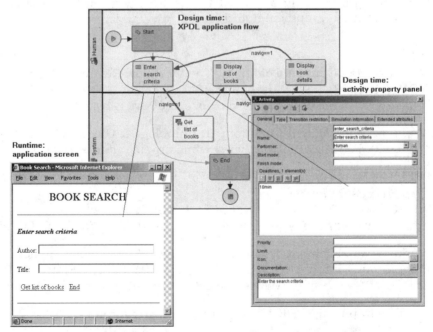

Figure 4: design-time – runtime relationship

SUMMARY

If the only tool you have is a process definition language and proposed framework, you'll start to see every problem as a process.

The framework's high level of abstraction and interpreted nature may hurt performance. It also requires your development team to learn a new language, and prepare a new set of interfaces for binding existing executables in. The Workflow Management System, being the essential part of the framework, is possibly completely new beast your administration crew has to master.

It goes without saying, if you already have WMS as part of your system (the one conforming to the standards), framework is simply a thin layer atop WMS.

This framework tends not to be a general solution to all problems; rather it's aimed to be generic tool on abstraction level above traditional programming languages.

The framework gives you a clear language and easy to use editor to express business procedures in, by tightly binding design and execution phases of applications development—XPDL process definition is both design time diagram and template for execution. Application development becomes faster and easier.

XPDL applications may easily interface to existing executables via WfMC interfaces 3 and 4, while interface 5 gives you a standard tool to administer the complete system. Additionally, embracing such applications into the existing WMS environment is a matter of design. WMS provides limit and deadline evaluation, which offers automatic signaling and /or removal of the stale XPDL applications.

XPDL version 2.0 recently approved by WfMC, adds new possibilities, and provides a standard graphical notation.

REFERENCES

1. Workflow Management Coalition: "The Workflow Reference Model",
    WfMC-TC-1003, 1.1, 19 Jan 1995.
    http://www.wfmc.org/standards/docs/tc003v11-16.pdf

2. Workflow Management Coalition: "Terminology & Glossary". WFMC-TC-1011, 3.0, Feb. 1999. http://www.wfmc.org/standards/docs/glossy3.pdf

3. Workflow Management Coalition: "*Workflow Process Definition Interface—XML Process Definition Language*".
    WFMC-TC-1025, 1.0 Final Draft, October 2002.
    http://www.wfmc.org/standards/docs/TC-1025_10_xpdl_102502.pdf

4. Workflow Management Coalition: "Workflow Management Application Programming Interface (Interface 2&3) Specification", WFMC TC-1009, 2.0, July 1998. http://www.wfmc.org/standards/docs/if2v20.pdf

5. JaWE - Graphical XPDL editor http://jawe.enhydra.org

6. Shark - XPDL workflow engine http://shark.enhydra.org

From BPMN Directly To Implementation: The Graphical Way

Heinz Lienhard and Bruno Bütler, ivyTeam-SORECOGroup, Switzerland

BPMN process description must become what the name (Business Process Modeling Notation) actually implies: a true model that can be simulated, validated and immediately turned into a real-time application.

TO MODEL—THAT'S IT?

With BPMN a lot has been accomplished towards a unified description of Business Processes readily understandable to all business users, included also—as stated in the introduction[1]—"to the technical developers responsible for implementing the technology that will perform those processes". But here the "understanding" is very likely to end.

Experience over the past 10 years has shown one thing: nice pictures of sophisticated business processes, per se, bring little value to the process. Although they may at first stimulate heated discussions, they are quickly forgotten to rot in some file cabinet. And giving those nice pictures to the IT department for implementation will more often then not lead to situations where business people (or "end users") who believe they understood the process, now find its implementation unintelligible.

Hence, the truly important step is *implementing* the process just as *transparently* and *comprehensively* as modeling of the process in the first place. This means using graphical objects as much as possible, right up to implementation. It will be shown how this can be done. First, starting from the upper level BPMN diagrams, the model is being refined and, by using an appropriate designer, the graphical symbols become true process building blocks (elements). With an integrated engine, the models built this way can be simulated and animated on any desired level. The final solution is obtained by the click of a button. Thus, process model and implemented workflow can be realized in one step:

"The BPMN model becomes the solution".

To go directly from model to solution has proven crucial to the success of real-life projects: when people can see how the solution will work—including on the level of implementation - they immediately become very involved and creative, and thereby participate constructively from the start.

Via example it can be shown how further development of BPMN might help to make process implementation much easier and, at the same time, more standardized.

---

[1] Working Draft BPMI.org

THE CASE FOR BPMN

According to the working draft (ref. 1) "the primary goal of BPMN is to provide a notation that is readily understandable by all business users, from the business analysts that create the initial drafts of the processes, to the technical developers responsible for implementing the technology that will perform those processes, and finally, to the business people who will manage and monitor those processes..." The intent is to create a standard visual language that all process modelers will recognize and understand. This also means conformance requirements for the appearance of the BPMN graphical elements are necessary. At the same time there is room for extensions, especially for new markers (e.g. to define a new event), or for additional artifacts (without, of course, interfering with any current object shape). So far so good—with one reservation: after a very promising start the whole standard seems to get out of hand. The proposed standard now has almost 300 pages, which is hardly compatible with the primary goal stated above. Nevertheless, the "core element set" is very useful for capturing the gist of a business process.

It is further claimed that "BPMN creates a standardized bridge for the gap between business process design and process implementation"—to a certain point; but the gap (or divide) between model and final implementation remains. Business people like visualizing business processes—but they are certainly lost when confronted with the mapping into a so-called execution language, which is in essence a programming language. They can only hope that what they originally agreed upon (the nice-looking BPMN diagram), will be realized by the implementation. And experience shows: the real problems usually start right here.

OBLITERATE THE DIVIDE

Smith and Fingar state in their book[2], "don't bridge the business-IT divide—obliterate it. That's the solution—only they fail to really show how to do it. A lot of hand wringing about Pi-Calculus won't do it. Besides, it is not even clear whether this mathematical underpinning is the best choice—see van der Aalst[3]. Certainly, a formal basis is necessary for the process elements, and tight integration of process modeling and workflow definition is a must to be able to go straight from model to executable solution[4].

Hence, why not present the implementation again in graphical form that can be simulated/animated, i.e. can be visualized to see how it works together with the necessary additions for a running workflow (e.g. the interactions with the users)? This way, transparency is obtained not only for the original process, but also for its realization. This is crucial, because very often hidden problems of a fine looking process model become only apparent during its execution. Now business people who do understand the process (and the implementation) can immediately help out to find the correct solution.

HOW TO DO IT

The process elements as graphical objects will have to become more than just that. They do please the eye as graphical elements, but underneath they

---

[2] H. Smith and P. Fingar: "Business Process Management—The Third Wave", 2003

[3] W.M.P. van der Aalst: "Pi calculus versus Petri nets...", 2005

[4] *Workflow Handbook 2002:* "Workflow as a Web Application – the Grand Unification"

are well-defined mathematical objects enabling the process model to control the workflow's behavior. It has been shown[5] that by providing an appropriate palette of such implementation process elements, process models can be composed that allow immediate simulation of their behavior and can readily be turned into a real-time application on a properly prepared Web server, i.e. with an appropriate workflow server package installed. The BPMN model is preferably designed in a modeling and simulation tool such as has been described before (ref. 5)—or it is imported into such a tool. Once the graphical model has been entered one way or the other, we proceed with implementation through the following main steps:

- With the help of a Process Data Editor, structure and type of all data used by the process are specified.
- Simple BPMN objects, like the start object, are directly parameterized, e.g. with the link address that will actually start the process. Thus the object becomes an implementation process element.
- Non-atomic BPMN objects, like the independent (reusable) sub-process, will require the proper name (identifier) of the BPMN process defining the sub-process.
- The non-atomic activity is then expanded for further refinement. In case of the sub-process mentioned above, it has to be decided whether a lower BPMN level is appropriate, i.e. other BPMN sub-processes down the hierarchy—or whether further refinement has to be done strictly for implementation reasons.
- In the latter case the atomic activities (tasks) will possibly become non-atomic in the implementation. But again graphical elements are used, like a special Data Base Element featuring an assistant to specify the particular DB operation (like reading or writing certain information), or a page element with an associated assistant to set up data exchanges (forms) with the workflow user—and all this without any programming.
- Tasks with message flow can be implemented in various ways using special process elements; e.g. an eMail Element might be dragged from the element palette and dropped into the task. It will automatically generate and send an email to an address either available from the process data or fetched from a data base. Other systems may be accessed via WebService Call Elements (see Ref. 5).
- Animate and test the obtained model within the design tool. The animation may be observed on any desired hierarchical level: a data object, represented by a red dot, moves through the model. Any forms for user interaction are displayed (preferably on one side of the screen) within the chosen Internet browser. This way interaction with the model and the actions of the model can be pursued simultaneously.
- Upload the model onto the Web server on which the server package has been installed.
- Run the implementation.

Evidently, the model design tool mentioned above has to offer a palette not only with BPMN graphical objects but also with process elements for implementation via model refinement (which is the case for Xpert.ivy from ivy-SORECOGroup). With such an approach neither BPEL nor anything like it is needed: the obtained workflow is perfectly capable of orchestrating any Web

---

[5] *Workflow Handbook 2003*: "Web Services and Workflow—a Unified Approach"

services (or choreographing them, to use this even more misplaced term—why can't IT people not stick to their turf?)

A PRACTICAL EXAMPLE

With a simple, yet practical, example from eGovernment (from the authors' country), the procedure expounded before makes it clear how elegantly processes specified in BPMN can be implemented as workflows. The Swiss government decided to model future eGovernment processes in BPMN (or rather in a useful subset of it) and to provide an exemplary process called "Entry with Working Permit". Through this process foreigners wishing to live and work in Switzerland are granted (or refused) an official permit. The process has been made public to help communities, cantons (states) and cities in modeling such government processes. Incidentally, it was this process that originally looked very different in various cantons until it was carefully re-modeled in BPMN. Only then it became apparent that it was much the same process everywhere (see Fig. 1).

The example contains two pools: the pool of applicants (usually the future employer of a foreigner), and the administration receiving and processing the application. The second pool contains three lanes specifying who is responsible for what activity. Since the actual communities may be organized in different ways—the norm in a federalist country—more or less abstract roles have been chosen which will be named differently depending on the concrete local administration. Without such a standard as BPMN, finding a common process would not have been possible.

The applicant is required to send certain documents with the application. When received by the administration, the Receiving Office will start the workflow (Fig. 2). Included in the expansion is an independent sub-process in which the documents are checked for completeness (Fig. 3). If incomplete, the flow is directed to the task "Ask for missing documents", where a message is sent, followed by the intermediate event (double circle), which will be triggered once the missing documents have been received and the case is resumed via work-list of the person having the proper role. The overall process should be easy to understand.

Two comments: RIPOL is a system where people wanted by police are registered; ZAR is a central register for foreigners. This year it will become accessible via Web Service Interface.

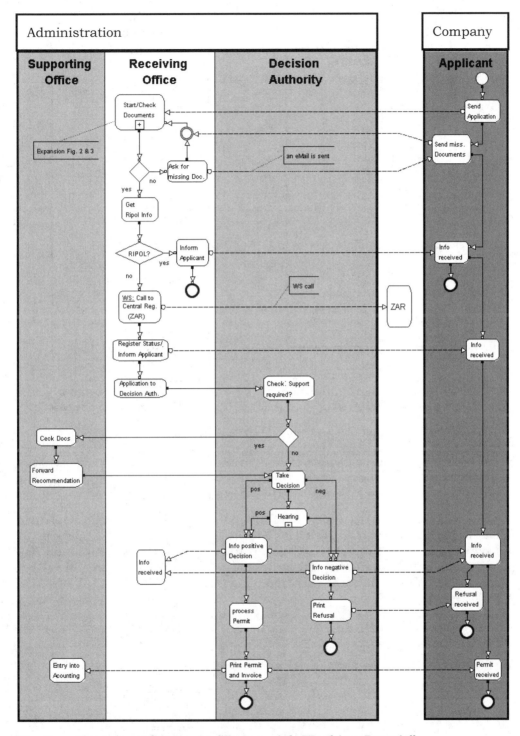

Fig. 1: eGovernment process "Entry with Working Permit"

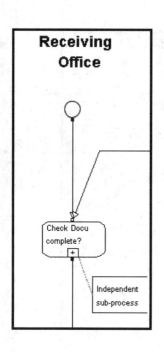

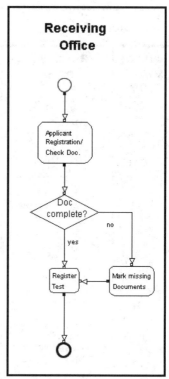

Fig. 2: Expansion of sub-process "Start/Check Documents".

Fig. 3: Independent sub-process "Check Docu complete?"

All three levels of BPMN diagrams in the first sub-process called "Start/Check Documents" are shown in Fig. 1-3. With further refinement of the independent sub-process (lowest BPMN level), a next level is necessary to implement its tasks. Here the BPMN description ends and implementation process elements from the tool's palette have to be used.

The task "Mark missing Documents" (Fig. 3) requires but a single implementation process element: a Dialog Element that will generate a form in the user's browser to enter data. This element comes with an assistant that helps to create such forms efficiently and without any programming. Fig. 4 shows the refinement of the corresponding task.

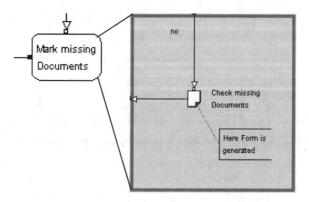

Fig 4: Task refinement

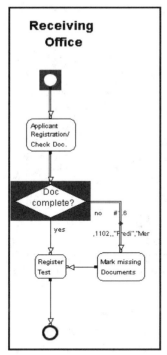

Now a sequence of snap shots should give an idea of what can be seen during simulation/animation. In Fig. 5 the independent sub-process (Fig 2) is being simulated; the data object (red dot) is about to enter the task having been refined in Fig. 4. Two data items are made visible: the number of the applicant and his name. An instant later this object can be seen within the refined task. This is shown in Fig. 6 together with the form on the right, generated by the Dialog Element. The process now waits until the form's "Submit" button is pressed after marking the corresponding documents. This information will be forwarded in the process for future use (e.g. by the eMail Element—see below).

Fig. 5: the independent sub-process during simulation.

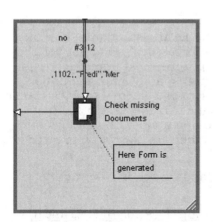

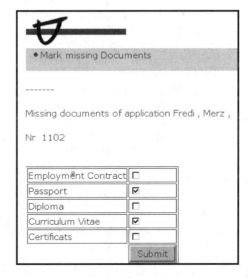

Fig. 6: Simulation after reaching the first implementation level. On the right side the form is displayed (with the logo from Canton Zug).

Going back to the top level (Fig. 1), we see how the data object is about to enter the task that will send a message to the applicant (partial view of top level in Fig. 7, left side). The object carries the result on the missing documents, which now will be used in the email. The task refinement is given on the right side of Fig. 7. Two special process elements are needed from the tool's palette: the Data Base Element to get the email address of the applicant and the Email Element to send an automatic mail to him. Once all required documents have been received from the applicant, the process moves on, down the lane "Receiving Office". The refinement of the task "Call to Central Reg." can again be done using a single process element: the WS Element (ref. 5), which can be readily configured to access the central register etc.

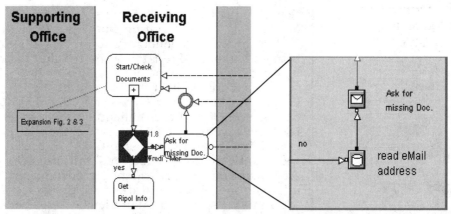

Fig. 7: Clipping of top level in simulation with task refinement.

The implementation of this eGovernment process example took roughly one day and was presented to the administration. Depending on further needs and requirements, another few days might be necessary to obtain a final solution.

WHAT ABOUT XPDL

When the (implemented) model has been validated, it can be uploaded onto the server, as described above. For this the model is currently encoded into XML format. This format will be changed in the next version of the tool, adapting it to XPDL. Hence, the approach presented here will also become an effective way to map BPMN to the XPDL process exchange format.

BENEFITS AND OUTLOOK

One group of people explicitly targeted by the BPMN standard—"the business people who will manage and monitor the processes"—has not yet been addressed here. But these people will likely profit the most from the possibility of rapid adaptation of processes *and* their transparent implementation. It has been explained elsewhere[6,7] how process management becomes much more efficient if processes are properly designed in the first place, e.g. by making judicious use of business rules in combination with catalogs of independent sub-processes, and implementing them in the way proposed in this chapter.

How to proceed with BPMN? Actually, the standard tends towards the verbose. A modest proposal follows:

For modeling, go back to the graphical core object set of BPMN, and then provide the possibility of an implementation layer, together with an expandable set of standard implementation blocks with well-defined semantics. Although the design tool mentioned above does this already, such an extension of the standard would bring transparency in the process implementations to the various users. It would help to achieve what has been claimed in the introduction:

"The BPMN model becomes the solution".

---

[6] Pallab Saha (Ed.) "Enterprise Systems Architecture Practice" to be published by IDEA GROUP, INC, Hershey, USA

[7] *Workflow Handbook 2005*, "Workflow and Business Rules—a Common Approach"

Workflow Mining: Definitions, Techniques, and Future Directions

Clarence A. Ellis, University of Colorado, Boulder, USA
Kwang-Hoon Kim, Kyonggi University, Korea
Aubrey J. Rembert, University of Colorado, Boulder, USA

ABSTRACT

Workflow Management Systems help to execute, monitor and manage work process flow and execution. These systems, as they are executing, keep a record of who does what and when (e.g. log of events). The activity of using computer software to examine these records, and deriving various structural data results is called workflow mining. This chapter defines, illustrates, and extends the concepts of workflow mining. The document also presents typical techniques for mining.

Workflow systems are "people systems" that must be designed, deployed, and understood within their social and organizational contexts. Thus, we argue in this chapter that there is a need to expand the concept of workflow mining to encompass social, organizational, and informational perspectives; as well as other perspectives. We introduce a general framework for workflow mining, and show how various perspectives can be effectively mined.

INTRODUCTION AND MOTIVATION

A Workflow Management System (WFMS) is defined as a system that (partially) automates the definition, creation, execution, and management of work processes through the use of software. That software is able to interpret the process definition, interact with workflow participants, and invoke the use of IT tools and applications where required [30]. Steps of a process are called tasks or *activities*, and jobs or transactions that flow through the system are called work cases or *process instances*.

When process execution and management is automated, it sometimes creates a mismatch of system-imposed behaviors versus organizational culture. Lucy Suchman [35] points out that much of the success within organizations is due to the social and opportunistic ways in which people work. There have been some spectacular success stories around workflow systems deployment and usage [5]. There have also been numerous stories of workflow systems failures; many of these failures stem from failure of some vendors and/or managers to understand and deal with the huge human/social component often present in work process enactment.

For example, if I find out over lunch conversation that you are traveling to New York tomorrow, I might act opportunistically, and convince you to deliver my package to my customer while you are there. You agree to this for social reasons, we are good friends; and the customer is delighted. This type of social networking within organizations is quite important, but not always immediately visible to the manager or outside consultant. Workflow management systems tend to decrease face-to-face interactions, and thereby, unfortunately, decrease the opportunities for social networking within organizations.

Traditionally, organizations first use a workflow modeling system to produce *workflow models* that formally define their processes. Then they use the workflow enactment technology to execute the specified workflow models. The definition phase is time consuming and error prone, requiring the collaboration of domain experts, workflow modeling experts, and managers. The result is frequently an inaccurate approximation to the actual ways of working within the organization. The authors have observed this phenomenon; especially in multinational organizations. For instance, the way of handling customers at headquarters in Korea is quite different from the way of handling customers at the branch in Brazil. However, the workers are required to use the identically same process specification enforced by the WFMS. Fortunately, people are frequently quite clever at performing "work-arounds" to somehow subvert the computer system.

This mismatch between the formal specification and the actual ways of working can sometimes be detected, measured, and corrected by the use of *workflow mining*. The concept of workflow mining is intuitive: rediscover the actual workflow model by analyzing information from the event log of a process in execution. The rediscovered workflow model can then be compared to the original workflow model to find the difference between how work is conceived to be done, and how work is actually done. In the workflow mining literature, this comparison is called *delta analysis* [40].

PRELIMINARIES

One of the potential advantages of this process automation is the automatic recording of event information by the WFMS. These recorded events are the basis for workflow mining. Typical events recorded are the start and completion of activity instances in particular process instances. For example, Mr. Jones' application for employment may be considered one work case, or one workflow, or one process instance within the class of processes collectively called the "employment application process." This employment process has many activities. When one of these activities commences, an instance of the activity is typically recorded as an event by the WFMS. The list of all the recorded events for Mr. Smith's application process is called a *workflow trace*. For any particular activity within the process, e.g. examination evaluation, we would distinguish the activity instance of Mr. Smith's evaluation from the activity instance of Mrs. Jones' evaluation. Thus, we have events from different people (e.g. from different process instances) that are interleaved in time. This information is stored in an archive called a *workflow event log*. This log is typically an interleaved list of events from multiple process instances. A workflow event log can contain many attributes; the mining focus of an organization determines what log information is used. A log entry typically records an event by capturing (at least) the following data:
1. Process instance identifier,
2. Activity instance identifier,
3. Event type (e.g. start or completion of activity),
4. Repository (data structure read from at the start, or written to at completion, of an activity),
5. Event handler (person, role, or subsystem performing the activity),
6. Date/time.

Clearly, this log information can be usefully searched to answer queries (e.g. where is case 39); to present statistical information (e.g. average number of work cases processed per day); or to deliver business intelligence information to managers [20].

Researchers and developers are combining ideas from the fields of machine learning, data mining, and workflow to explore and exploit the area of workflow mining. In this chapter, we present a framework for, and a general definition of, workflow mining, along with examples of mining techniques. Currently, most workflow mining algorithms have the goal of rediscovering a control flow model. We feel that this approach limits the scope and utility of workflow mining; it neglects the important point that workflow is much more than control flow. We consider control to be only one perspective from which to view a process. Therefore, in this document, we introduce the concept of *multidimensional workflow mining* to denote a suite of algorithms and tools aimed at the rediscovery, of multiple perspectives of an organizational process, as well as nontrivial information about the organizational process.

As previously defined, a workflow event log is an interleaved list of events from numerous process instances. By examining the log, we can detect the ordering of activity executions for each process instance, and then infer the general process structure. As a simple example, suppose we examine the log of a process that has four activities, a1, a2, a3, and a4. Suppose that all four activities are always executed in some order by each process instance. If we observe over a large number of process instances that a1 is always executed first and a4 is always executed last, then we can begin to piece together a process model that requires a1 to complete before the other activities, and a4 to execute after all others. If we find process instances in the log where a2 begins before a3, and others where a2 begins after a3, then we can infer that the process begins with a1; after it completes, a2 and a3 execute concurrently; and after they both complete, then a4 executes.

This is an extremely simplified example that ignores many interesting issues such as data dependencies and iteration. Our workflow mining algorithms ought to take into account that some process instances are exceptions that do not follow the standard process specification, and that organizations, including their processes, evolve significantly over time. Also an important question is "How do we take into account the all important social and organizational context issues?" In the remainder of this chapter, we present a multidimensional workflow mining framework and a general meta-model capable of addressing these issues. In later sections of the chapter, we present workflow mining techniques for several perspectives. Finally, we present a section on related work, and a section on summary and future directions.

THE WORKFLOW MINING FRAMEWORK

In general, a framework is a way of thinking; it is a way of conceptualizing an area of endeavor. It sometimes allows one to categorize, and to see the bigger picture within which studies, research, and development is being performed. A useful effect of a framework can be introduction of a means of communication, comparison, evaluation, and synthesis. In the fledgling area of workflow mining, different developers have different terminology and different methodologies. There is a need at this time for synthesis. The stage is set for productive communication, comparison, and combination. We hope this framework helps.

Most workflow mining research is narrowly aimed at the rediscovery of explicit control flow models. As mentioned in the introduction, we believe that this approach limits the scope and utility of workflow mining. It is indeed true that workflow technology is highly concerned with process execution, analysis, and improvement; but to address these process concerns adequately, it is frequently necessary to take into account the larger picture of organizational structures, goals, and resources. Thus, workflow mining needs to be concerned with gathering and discovering useful information about the organizational processes, and also the organizational structures that support these processes. We would like to extend the mining domain to give serious effort to mining of data-flow information, of organizational information, of human and social information, and of other perspectives. In this section, we introduce a framework that enables and facilitates workflow mining in this broader sense.

In general, we consider workflow mining to be a sub-area of Knowledge Discovery in Data (KDD). KDD is concerned with extracting knowledge from stored data. The KDD process consists of (1) understanding the domain, (2) data selection, (3) data cleaning, (4) data transformation, (5) data mining, and (6) result interpretation/evaluation [13].

Conceiving workflow mining in these broader terms opens up new vistas of possibility. In this chapter, we are only concerned with the data mining step in KDD. Data mining is the process of fitting models to, or discovering patterns from, stored data [13]. These models can be either statistical or logical. Statistical models are inherently nondeterministic, while logical models are purely deterministic. The selection of a model for data mining primarily depends on the *knowledge discovery goal*. In general, knowledge discovery goals are either descriptive or predictive. If the knowledge discovery goal is descriptive, the data mining step aims at finding a model that can describe the stored data in a human interpretable form. If the knowledge discovery goal is predictive, data mining aims at discovering a model that is used to predict some future behavior. Some useful techniques for discovering descriptive and predictive models are:
1. Classification: A function that maps data elements into predefined classes.
2. Clustering: A function that maps data elements into their natural classes.
3. Summarization: A function that summarizes the data elements (i.e. mean)
4. Dependency Modeling: A technique that attempts to define structural relationships between data elements.
5. Anomaly Detection: A technique that focuses on detecting patterns that deviate from normative behavior.

Data mining, in the context of workflow, is concerned with using the entire set of discovery techniques mentioned above to gain useful knowledge about an organizational process from a workflow event log. However, in this chapter we will focus on the discovery of a logical descriptive model via the dependency modeling technique.

In order to put the workflow mining step in KDD in its proper context, we must understand its interfaces. The interfaces to the workflow mining step are the output of the data transformation step, a workflow event log, and the input of the result interpretation/evaluation step, a workflow model. When given a workflow event log, *WL*, generated by a set of process instances *I*, and the knowledge discovery goal of finding a logical descriptive model of *WL*, a workflow mining algorithm attempts to discover a complete and consistent workflow model, *M*, with respect to *WL*. Completeness of a workflow model means that the discovered model can describe all of the workflow event sequences in *WL* without simply enumerating them. Consistency means that the discovered workflow model only describes the workflow event sequences in *WL* (or ones that are "consistent" with WL) and does not introduce superfluous or spurious event sequences. Stated more plainly, a workflow mining algorithm accepts as input a workflow event log and produces as output a complete and consistent workflow model.

The details of the log are dependent upon the details of the particular family of models. Thus, in the next section, we describe our workflow meta-model.

THE WORKFLOW META-MODEL

Different organizations have different goals, different resources, and thus different needs for automated assistance within their processes. Therefore, different organizations typically need different workflow products, different mining techniques, and different models to express different business perspectives. The concept of a meta-model provides a coherent, uniform notation and a set of conceptual tools for creating various models appropriate to various organizations.

A comprehensive workflow representation language is defined in [26] as a representation language that can be used to express the major organizational perspectives from which to examine a process. The Information Control Net (ICN) is an open-ended, graphical formalism conceived over 25 years ago (by one of the co-authors of this chapter) as a family of models for organizational process description, analyses, and implementation[11] [12]. In the Collaboration Technology Research Group (CTRG) at the University of Colorado, and the Collaboration Technology Research Lab (CTRL) at Kyonggi University in Korea, there has been ongoing research concerned with ICNs. In this section, we combine and extend ideas of comprehensive workflow representation languages with ICN concepts to present a meta-model suitable for *multidimensional workflow mining*.

The heart of the ICN meta-model is the observation that understanding of organizational processes begins with understanding of organizational goals, structures, and resources. Thus, in order to create a specific model of a specific enterprise, a modeler chooses certain objects of interest and structures from an organizational framework, from an organizational schema, and from an organizational net. The organizational framework is used to specify various classes of organizational objects (e.g. goals, constraints, resources, activities). The organizational schema is used to specify the set of mappings over the classes of organizational objects (e.g. who does what, which activities precede which). The organizational net is used to specify the dynamic behavior of an organization.

Within the ICN modeling methodology, basic workflow areas are organized as object sets called *dimensions*. Dimensions of interest might include the activities dimension (e.g. tasks done within an organization), the data dimension (e.g. descriptions of what information is used within the organization), the participants dimension (e.g. who are the human employees), and the roles dimension (e.g. job descriptions such as secretary and manager). More formally, a dimension is defined as a set of homogeneous objects (e.g. employees), a set of attributes associated with objects (e.g. employees' ages), a set of zero or more automorphisms (relationships, such as Abe reports to Bob) on the object set, and a set of constraints (rules that all employees must obey) associated with the automorphisms.

When we inter-relate the organizational objects of one or more dimensions, we form an organizational *perspective*. Organizational models are constructed by selecting workflow dimensions of interest, and relating them via mappings (multi-valued relationships) and constraints to form perspectives. A *multidimensional workflow model* for an enterprise is defined as an interrelated family of models, each depicting a perspective on the enterprise.

It is particularly interesting, from the standpoint of workflow, to relate the organizational objects of the activities dimension, activities, to the organizational objects of other dimensions. To the extent that an activity is actually captured in its processes, these types of relationships give insight into what an organization does. We conclude this section by briefly describing two typically useful organizational perspectives.

As an example, the *data flow perspective* is formed when we impose relationships between three dimensions: activities, data items, and repositories. The data dependence mapping is one of the most interesting in this perspective. It reveals the data dependencies of an activity. For example, the review university admissions application activity is data dependent on the repository that stores all of the university admissions applications, and the actual data within that repository.

Another example of interest is the *activity assignment perspective* formed by defining a set of relationships between three dimensions: employees, roles, and activities. Depending on the size and nature of an organization, the dimensions involved in the definition of this perspective can vary. For a small organization, with say 2 people and a relatively simple process, it is quite adequate and convenient to relate participants directly to the activities they perform. However, in organizations with Very Large Scale Workflow (VLSW)[29], this type of relationship is very impractical; it is more appropriate to relate activities to roles, then relate those roles to participants. Therefore, through one level on indirection, activities are related to participants. Mining this perspective in a small organization is typically easy and intuitive. Therefore, in our presentation, we will assume that the organizations have a VLSW such that mining of this perspective is nontrivial.

MULTIDIMENSIONAL WORKFLOW MINING ILLUSTRATION

In order to properly illustrate multidimensional workflow mining, we present a synthetic workflow event log in Table 1. Each row represents an event. The CASE column represents a process instance. Each process instance is represented by a unique integer. The ACTIVITY column identifies an activity instance for a particular process instance. The EVENT column specifies the event type of an activity instance (i.e. START or COMPLETE). The REPOSITORY column specifies the data repositories an activity instance writes to or reads from. The PARTICIPANT column specifies who performs an activity instance. The TIME column specifies the time an event occurred.

Now we will give some semantics to the activities of the log in Table 1. This is a workflow event log of the university admissions process of a fictitious university admissions office. Receiving a university application is represented by activity A. The decision to admit an applicant is represented by activity B. Activities C and D represent the mailing and emailing of an acceptance letter, respectively. The mailing of a rejection letter is represented by activity E. The processing of the application fee is represented by activity F.

Table 1 WORKFLOW EVENT LOG

CASE	ACTIVITY	EVENT	REPOSITORY	PARTICIPANT	TIME
1	A	START	CUST	T	12
2	A	START	CUST	M	23
1	A	COMPLETE	APF	T	24
2	A	COMPLETE	APF	M	30
1	B	START	APF	N,Z	45
1	B	COMPLETE	APF	N,Z	100
1	C	START	APF	T	120
1	D	START	APF	U	121
2	B	START	APF	U,Z	125
2	B	COMPLETE	RJF	U,Z	175
1	D	COMPLETE	MAF	U	200
1	C	COMPLETE	EAF	T	205
2	E	START	RJF	X	214
2	E	COMPLETE	MRF	X	221
1	F	START	APF	X	230
1	F	COMPLETE	PAF	X	234
2	F	START	APF	M	290
2	F	COMPLETE	PAF	M	299

MULTIDIMENSIONAL WORKFLOW MINING IN THE ACTIVITIES DIMENSION

Given the knowledge discovery goal of finding a logical descriptive model, mining of the activities dimension is aimed at the rediscovery of the precedence relationships amongst activity instances (a control flow model). This dimension is important to mine because it represents the main functionality of workflow technology.

Current workflow mining algorithms assume that a WFMS does not explicitly record AND-Split, AND-Join, OR-Split, and OR-Join instances in the workflow event log. We believe that this is a holdover from the traditional client/server implementation of workflow, where one server is responsible for controlling the entire workflow execution. For practical purposes, we believe that highly distributed workflow systems [4] [28] will be necessary to cope with organizations with VLSW; it will become increasingly important to explicitly include control activity instances along with their resource usage in the workflow event log. This type of log information can aid in understanding the nature of an executing process as well as provide assistance for load balancing decisions. In this section, however, we will continue the convention that only work activity instances are recorded in the workflow event log; therefore in the mining this dimension, the control constructs have to be deduced.

In the mining of the activities dimension, we are concerned with case numbers, activity instances, and event types. In a realistic situation, an organization may want to include other attributes. We will now describe a high level technique to rediscover an ICN activity model from a workflow event log.

The workflow event log of Table 1 contains two process instances, case 1 and case 2. We will now examine the workflow event sequence of case 1. First, we scan the workflow event log to discover the set of activity instances associated with case 1. The result of this scan is the activity instances A, B, C, D, and F. Next, we infer the precedence relationships between those activity instances. Since activity instance A occurs before activity instance B in the workflow trace of case 1, we say that A precedes B, thus inferring precedence relationship from A to B. Next, since activity instance B happens before activity instances C and D in case 1, we add a precedence relationship from B to C and from B to D. Then, we see that the events of activity instances C and D are interleaved. From this, we make the assumption that C and D are independent, which informally means that C does not precede D and vice versa. Finally, since activity instances C and D both occur before activity instance F; we add a precedence relationship from C to F, and from D to F.

Now, we will discover the precedence relationships that exist in case 2. First, we scan the workflow event log to discover the activity instances that make up the workflow trace of case 2. The result of this scan is the activity instances A, B, E, and F. Since activity instance A occurs before activity instance B, we add a precedence relationship from A to B. Next, since activity instance B happens before activity instance E, we add a precedence relationship from B to E. Finally, since activity instance E happens before activity instance F, we add a precedence relationship from E to F. Figure 1 depicts precedence graphs for case 1 and for case 2.

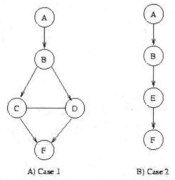

A) Case 1   B) Case 2

Figure 1 Precedence Graphs for the Workflow Traces of Cases 1 and 2 of the Workflow Event Log in Table 1

The next phase of this workflow mining technique takes these two precedence graphs and forms a dependency graph. A dependency graph models the precedence relationships across the entire workflow event log. To construct the dependency graph, we first let the precedence graph of case 1 be the preliminary dependency graph of the workflow event log. Then we add activity instance E from case 2 to the dependency graph; we also add edges (B,E) and (E,F) from the precedence graph of case 2 to the dependency graph. Figure 2 depicts the dependency graph of the workflow event log contained in Table 1.

The final phase of the workflow mining technique transforms the dependency graph into an ICN activity model. First, we create two sets for each activity instance; one containing sets of successors and the other containing sets of predecessors. The set of successors/predecessors of an activity instances is organized as follows: group activity instances that are independent of one another into the same set (an activity instance is independent of itself). Below is a representation of this. (SUCC = set of successor sets, PRED=set of predecessor sets)

PRED(A) = Ø, SUCC(A) = {{B}}.

PRED(B) = {{A}}, SUCC(B) = {{C,D}, {E}}

PRED(C) = {{B}}, SUCC(C) = {{F}}.

PRED(D) = {{B}}, SUCC(D) = {{F}}.

PRED(E) = {{B}}, SUCC(E) = {{F}},

PRED(F) = {{C,D}, {E}}, SUCC(F) = Ø.

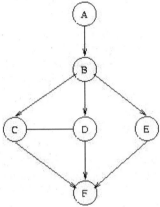

Figure 2. Dependency-Parallelism Graphs for the Workflow Event Log of Table 1

Using these sets of sets of activity instances, we form an ICN activity model. We do this by making the assumptions that, within a set of sets, activity instances within the same set are executed concurrently, and activity instances that are elements of different sets are executed mutually exclusive of one anther. From the above description, we can see that both of these assumptions occur in the SUCC set of sets of activity instance B and the PRED set of sets of activity instance F. If we look at activity instances B and F, we see that SUCC(B) = {{C,D}, {E}} and PRED(F) = {{C,D}, {E}}. We transform the dependency graph by inserting an AND-Split or AND-Join to connect activity instances that are to be executed concurrently. We transform the dependency graph by inserting an OR-Split or OR-Join to connect the activity instances that are in different sets. Figure 3 shows the ICN activity model that was transformed from dependency graph constructed above.

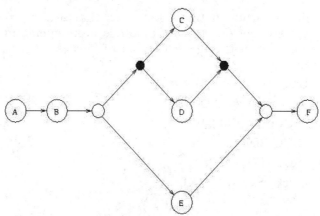

Figure 3. The Rediscovered ICN Activity Model of the Workflow Event Log of Table 1
(OR-Split/OR-Join is represented by an unlabeled hollow circle; AND-Split/AND-Join is represented by an unlabeled dark circle)

There are important issues in workflow mining in the activity dimension that this simple toy example does not expose. For instance, iteration is a complex issue that needs further investigation. At the present time, it is not quite clear how to handle iteration. In the workflow mining literature, it is assumed that iteration can be discovered; however, without conditions on the precedence relationships between activities instances, the discovered workflow models can produce an infinite amount of workflow events in a workflow trace, thereby making them inconsistent with the log. The occurrence of infinite looping constructs seems highly unlikely in real organizations.

Another subtle, but important problem in mining of the activities dimension is the notion of rediscovering human interpretable models. The present literature does not address this problem. A rediscovered model can be consistent and complete with respect to a workflow event log, but its presentation is "spaghetti-like" and therefore hard to interpret by humans. If the mined model can not be readily understood by people, the mining effort is less effective.

MULTIDIMENSIONAL WORKFLOW MINING IN THE ACTIVITY ASSIGNMENT PERSPECTIVE

Given participants and activity instances in a workflow event log, it is possible to discover mappings from participants to activities. The activity assignment perspective is important to mine because fundamentally workflow technology is a human/social centered technology. To our knowledge, this perspective has not been examined beyond a few toy examples [37]. In mining this perspective, a workflow analyst can discover what activities a participant can perform based on the roles they play.

The attributes in the event log that are needed to mine this perspective are the case numbers, the activity instances, the event types, and the participants. Other attributes might also be available in the log. Below we give a simple mining technique for this perspective.

First we will construct a participant dependency graph, which denotes who does what activity, for case 1. To do this, we scan the workflow event log to determine the set of participants that help execute case 1. The result of this scan is the participants T, N, Z, U, and X. Next, we discover the participant dependencies. Activity instance A is performed by participant T, therefore we add directed edge (T,A) to the participant dependency graph of case 1. Activity instance B is done by participants N and Z. So, we add directed edges (N,B) and (Z,B) to the participant dependency graph of case 1. Activity instance C is performed by participant T, so we add directed edge (T,C) to the dependency graph of case 1. Activity instance D is performed by participant U, therefore we add directed edge (U,D) to the participant dependency graph of case 1. Activity instance F is performed by participant X. So, we add directed edge (X,F) to participant dependency graph of case 1.

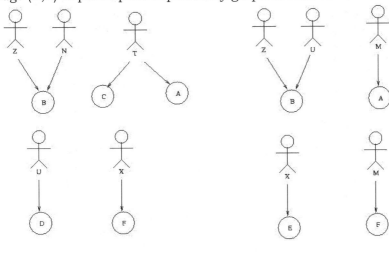

A) Case 1   B) Case 2

Figure 4. Participant Dependency Graphs for Cases 1 and 2 of Table 1

Now we construct a participant dependency graph for case 2. We once again scan the workflow event log to determine the set of participants needed to execute case 2. The result of this scan is the participants M, Z, U, and X. Next, we discover who performs each task. Activity instance A is done by participant M, so we add directed edge (M,A) to the participant dependency graph of case 2. Activity instance B is done by participants U and Z. Therefore, we add directed edges (U,B) and (Z,B) to the participant dependency graph of case 2. Activity instance E is performed by participant X. So, we add directed edge (X,E) to the participant dependency graph of case 2. Activity instance F is done by participant M. Therefore, we add directed edge (M,F) the participant dependency graph of case 2. Figure 4 represents the participant dependency graphs of case 1 and case 2.

We now combine the participant dependency graphs of case 1 and case 2 to form a participant dependency graph for the entire workflow event log. First we make the dependency graph of case 1 be a preliminary participant dependency graph for the entire workflow log. Then we add activity instance E, participant M, and directed edges (U,B), (M,F), and (X,E) from case 2 to case 1 to form the participant dependency graph for the entire workflow event log. Figure 5 represents the participant dependency graph for the workflow event log of Table 1.

Based on the participant dependency graph of the workflow event log, we can form some clusters. We let the connected components of the participant dependency graph form clusters. We then build the ICN activity assignment model from those clusters. We do this by associated to each cluster a role. We then relate the participants and activity instances of a cluster to the cluster's corresponding role. Figure 6 depicts the rediscovered ICN activity assignment model.

There are a number of significant challenges in mining this perspective, one being the development of clustering algorithms to form roles that fit naturally with the organization. For instance, if a sales clerk, Bob, is asked to fill in for a sales manager, James, while James is on vacation and Bob performs the activities of James for a couple of days, we do not want to infer that Bob is a manager. Another challenge is discovering "may" versus "must" assignments. For example, review of an employment application must be performed by someone, it may be performed by a human resources manager, but not necessarily; it could alternatively be reviewed by a manager in the department that the job vacancy exists in.

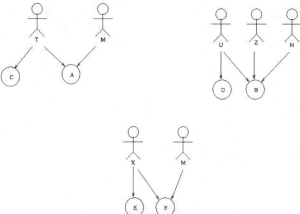

Figure 5. Participant Dependency Graph for the Workflow Event Log of Table 1

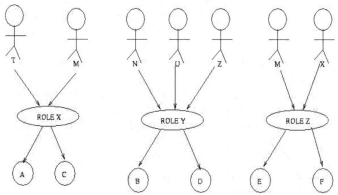

Figure 6. The Rediscovered ICN activity assignment model from the Workflow Event Log of Table 1.

RELATED WORK

The concept of mining a process from a log was first investigated within the context of software process discovery [6] [7]. Workflow mining is not new, it has been studied in [31], [9], [8] , [14], [15], [16], [18], [17], [19], [33], [32], [21], [23], [22], [25], [24], [42], [45], [3], [34], [10], [43], [44], [39], and [40]. It was first studied in [3] by Agrawal et al. In that paper, the authors describe workflow mining as a two step process: (1) discover a workflow graph that conforms to the workflow event log and (2) find the edge conditions of the workflow graph. The discovery of edge conditions is a necessary step in this workflow mining algorithm because workflow graphs can't explicitly represent AND-Control or OR-Control constructs. Agrawal et. al. also describe a method for dealing with iteration and noisy logs. In [32] and [33], Schimm describes a workflow mining algorithm that discovers properly nested workflow models via a model rewriting approach. Schimm's workflow mining algorithm is based on a workflow algebra. Similarly, Wainer, Kim, and Ellis in [42] describe a technique for inducing a properly nested workflow models using model rewriting rules. However, their work did not include a concrete workflow mining algorithm description. Herbst et. al. in [21], [22], [25], and [24] describe a machine learning approach to discover sequential workflow models in the ADONIS language.

Their work introduced a heuristic for discovering multiple instances of an activity (the duplicate activities problem). Their algorithm first constructs Stochastic Activity Graphs (SAG)s and transforms these graphs into sequential workflow models. Later, Herbst extended this machine learning approach in [23] to discover concurrent workflow models. Silva et. al.[34] investigated the idea of discovering probabilistic workflow models from workflow event log data. Their learning algorithm attempts to discover a probabilistic And/Or Graph. Greco et. al. in [14], [15], [16], [18], [17], and [19], provide some theoretical results about workflow mining. In [40], van der Aalst et. al. studied workflow mining with Petri Nets as the workflow representation language. He and his group developed the alpha-algorithm to discover a certain class of Petri Nets. In [9], they discuss some of the limitations of the alpha-algorithm, (mining short loops) and propose extensions. His group has also identified the non-free choice construct as problematic for current workflow mining algorithms to discover, especially ones that do a local search (i.e. model rewriting). In [36], van der Aalst et. al. proposed a genetic algorithm help solve the non-free choice problem. For a complete overview of workflow mining, the authors recommended the paper [38] [31].

SUMMARY AND FUTURE WORK

In this chapter, we have offered a general definition of workflow mining. We have couched this definition in the context of an extensible framework of organizational dimensions and perspectives. Currently, most workflow mining algorithms have the goal of rediscovering a control flow model. We feel that this approach limits the scope and utility of workflow mining; it neglects the important point that workflow is much more than control flow. We consider control to be only one dimension of workflow. Therefore, in this chapter, we introduced the concept of multidimensional workflow mining to denote a suite of algorithms and tools aimed at rediscovery of multiple perspectives of an organizational process. In the later sections we employed the ICN family of models to present techniques for mining in the activity dimension and in the activity assignment perspective. The stage is now set for productive communication, comparison, and combination of workflow mining algorithms and techniques.

Future work includes specification and mining of other perspectives (e.g: the security perspective, data flow perspective, and organizational perspective). We would like to investigate mining algorithms that address complex iteration constructs (i.e. concurrency within a loop), dynamic change, exceptions, and that operate upon logs that are noisy and incomplete. Workflow mining assumes that the some of the elements of the organizational framework are known in advance. As the field matures, we expect to remove this assumption, and do workflow discovery, not only workflow rediscovery.

ACKNOWLEDGEMENTS

The authors would like to thank the University of Colorado-Boulder and Kyonggi University for providing the resources to perform this work. We would also like to thank the members of the CTRG of the University of Colorado and the members of the CTRL of Kyonggi University for stimulating interactions and discussions. Finally, we would like to thank the workflow mining research community.

REFERENCES

1. Workflow Management Coalition Terminology & Glossary, 1999.
2. W.M.P. van der Aalst. The Application of Petri Nets to Workflow Management. The Journal of Circuits, Systems and Computers, 8(1):21–66, 1998.
3. R. Agrawal, D. Gunopulos, and F. Leymann. Mining Process Models from Workflow Logs. In Lecture Notes in Computer Science, EDBT 98 6th International Conference on Extending Database Technology, 1998.
4. G. Alonso, C. Mohan, R. Guenthoer, D. Agrawal, A. El Abbadi, and M. Kamath. Exotica/FMQM: A Persistent Message-Based Architecture for Distributed Workflow Management. Proc. IFIPWG8.1Working Conference on Information Systems for Decentralized Organizations, 1995.
5. D. Bartholomew. A Better Way to Work. InformationWeek, sep 1995.
6. J. E. Cook and A. L. Wolf. Event-Base Detection of Concurrency. In SIGSOFT FSE, SIGSOFT FSE 1998, page 35 45, 1998.
7. J.E. Cook and A.L. Wolf. Discovering Models of Software Processes from Event- Based Data. volume 3 of ACM Transactions Software Engineering Methodology, 1998.
8. A.K.A. de Medeiros, W.M.P. van der Aalst, and A. Weijters. Workflow Mining: Current Status and Future Directions. In Z. Tari R. Meersman and D.C. Schmidt, editors, On The Move to Meaningful Internet Systems, volume 2888 of LNCS, 2003.
9. A.K.A. de Medeiros, B.F. van Dongen, W.M.P. van der Aalst, and A.J.M.M. Weijter. Process Mining: Extending the alpha-algorithm to Mine Short Loops. BETA Working Paper Series, 2004.
10. S. Dustdar, T. Hoffmann, and W. van der Aalst. Mining of ad-hoc Business Processes with TeamLog. 2005.
11. C. Ellis. Information Control Nets: A Mathematical Model of Information Flow. Conference on Simulation, ACM Proc. Conf. Simulation, Modeling and Measurement of Computer Systems, pages 225–240. ACM, 1979.
12. C. Ellis. Formal and Informal Models of Office Activity. Information Processing 83, pages 11–22, 1983.
13. U. Fayyad, G. Piatetsky-Shapiro, and P. Smyth. From Data Mining to Knowledge Discovery in Databases. AAAI 97, 1997.
14. Greco G, A. Guzzo, and D. Sacca. Reasoning on Workflow Executions. 7th East-European Conference on Advances in Databases and Informations Systems, 2003.
15. G. Greco, A. Guzzo, G. Giuseppe, L. Pontieri, and D. Sacca. Mining Constrained Graphs: The Case of Workflow Systems. Constraint Based Mining and Inductive Databases. 2005.

16. G. Greco, A. Guzzo, G. Manco, and D. Sacca. Mining Frequent Instances on Workflows. The Seventh Pacific-Asia Conference on Knowledge Discovery and Data Mining, 2003.

17. G. Greco, A. Guzzo, G. Manco, and D. Sacca. Mining and Reasoning on-Workflows. IEEE Trans. on Knowledge and Data Engineering, 2005.

18. G. Greco, A. Guzzo, G. Manco, and D. Sacca. Mining Correlations in Workflows Executions. ADVANCED DATABASE SYSTEMS Sistemi Evoluti per Basi di Dati, 2005.

19. G. Greco, A. Guzzo, L. Pontieri, and D. Sacc`a. Mining Expressive Process Models by Clustering Workflow Traces. In PAKDD, PAKDD 2004, pages 52–62, 2004.

20. D. Grigori, F. Casati, M. Castellanos, U. Dayal, M. Sayal, and M. Shan. Business Process Intelligence. Computers in Industry, 53:321–343, 2004.

21. J. Herbst. Inducing Workflow Models from Workflow Instances. In Proc. Of the Concurrent Engineering Europe Conference. Society for Computer Simulation (SCS), 1999.

22. J. Herbst. A Machine Learning Approach to Workflow Management. In ECML 2000: 11th European Conference on Machine Learning, pages 183 – 194, 2000.

23. J. Herbst. Dealing with Concurrency inWorkflow Induction. European Concurrent Engineering Conference. SCS Europe, 2000., 2000.

24. J. Herbst and D. Karagiannis. An Inductive approach to the Acquisition and Adaptation of Workflow Models. Proceedings of the IJCAI'99 Workshop on Intelligent Workflow and Process Management: The New Frontier for AI in Business, 1999.

25. J. Herbst and D. Karagiannis. Workflow Mining with InWoLvE. Computers in Industry, 53(3), 2004.

26. S. Jablonski and C. Bussler. Workflow Management: Modeling Concepts, Architecture and Implementation. Thomson Computer Press, 1996.

27. K. Kim. A XML-Based Workflow Event Logging Mechanism for Workflow Mining. In APWeb Workshops, pages 132–136, 2006.

28. K. Kim. An Enterprise Workflow Grid/P2P Architecture for Massively Parallel and Very Large Scale Workflow Systems. In APWeb Workshops, pages 472–476, 2006.

29. K. Kim and H. Ahn. An EJB-Based Very Large Scale Workflow System and Its Performance Measurement. In Advances in Web-Age Information Management, 2005.

30. C. Plesums. Introduction to Workflow. Workflow Handbook 2002, 2002 ed. L Fischer, published by Future Strategies Inc.

31. A.J. Rembert. Comprehensive Workflow Mining. ACMSE 2006 44th ACM Southeast Conference, 2006.

32. G. Schimm. Process Miner - A Tool for Mining Process Schemes from Event-Based Data. JELIA 2002, 2002.

33. G. Schimm. Mining exact models of concurrent workflows. Computers in Industry, 53(3), 2004.

34. R. Silva, J. Zhang, and J.G. Shanahan. ProbabilisticWorkflow Mining. Proceedings of the eleventh ACM SIGKDD international conference on Knowledge Discovery in Data Mining, 2005.

35. L. Suchman. Plans and situated actions: the problem of human-machine communication. Cambridge University Press, Cambridge, 1987.

36. W. M. P. van der Aalst, A. K. A. de Medeiros, and A. J. M. M. Weijters. Genetic Process Mining. In ICATPN, pages 48–69, 2005.
37. W. M. P. van der Aalst and M. Song. Mining Social Networks: Uncovering Interaction Patterns in Business Processes. In Business Process Management, pages 244–260, 2004.
38. W. M. P. van der Aalst, B. F. van Dongena, J. Herbst, L. Marustera, G. Schimm, and A. J. M. M. Weijters. Workflow mining: A survey of issues and approaches. Data & Knowledge Engineering, Volume 47, Issue 2 , November 2003, pages 237–267, nov 2003.
39. W.M.P. van der Aalst and A.J.M.M.Weijters. Process Mining: A Research Agenda. Computers and Industry, 53(3):231–244, 2004.
40. W.M.P. van der Aalst, A.J.M.M. Weijters, and L. Maruster. Workflow Mining: Discovering process models from event logs. In Transactions on Knowledge and Data Engineering, 2004.
41. B.F. van Dongen and W.M.P. van der Aalst. A Meta Model for Process Mining Data. volume 2 of Proceedings of the CAiSE'05 WORKSHOPS, pages 309–320, 2005.
42. J. Wainer, K. Kim, and C. A. Ellis. A Workflow Mining Method Through Model Rewriting. CRIWG 2005: 184-191. 2005.
43. T. Weijters and W.M.P. van der Aalst. Process Mining: Discovering Workflow Models from EventBased Data. 2001.
44. T. Weijters and W.M.P. van der Aalst. Rediscovering Workflow Models from Event-Based Data. 2001.
45. L. Wen, J. Wang, W.M.P. van der Aalst, Z. Wang, and J. Sun. A Novel Approach for Process Mining Based on Event Types.

Business Integration Using State Based Asynchronous Services

Alan McNamara, Badja Consulting, Australia
Dr. M. Ali Chishti, Defence Housing Authority, Australia

ABSTRACT

Architectural principles promote the use of interfaces—a facade behind which the implementation can be hidden. Current Service Oriented Service (SOA) analysis methods are based on providing synchronous services to expose transactional processes. However, this analysis method does not give a robust model for services implemented through workflow.

A business integration interface (façade) will need to:
- hide process implementation
- allow long running processes
- allow tracking of process status
- allow additional data to be provided when required
- handle events, regarding supplier or requester of a service
- manage exceptions

The service model presented in the OASIS ASAP [1] standard provides a good basis for the business integration interface, but the state based service model is not fully defined. This paper provides an analysis of the requirements for business integration services for long running processes, and proposes how the service model presented in the ASAP standard can be extended to satisfy these requirements. Practical examples from industry are used to illustrate these points.

INTRODUCTION

The processes that provide business services necessarily look different from the outside than when viewed from the inside.

Consider the operations of a distributor. Their processes revolve around filling orders, maintaining stock levels, sending out bills (and ensuring they are paid) and paying their own bills. The processes to fulfill an order may involve checking the credit rating of the customer, checking stock levels, organizing transport, tracking delivery. In some cases, the goods can be supplied from current stock, in others they may need to be sourced from suppliers. A single order may have a combination of both. Some of the fulfillment processes may be internal, but some may be external—either outsourced or externally supplied.

But consider the same business function as viewed by the retailer who has ordered the goods. Many of the process steps do not concern them, only the outcomes. They are concerned about when the delivery will be made, being informed if delays occur, and being able to track their order—Is it still in the warehouse or in the hands of the carters? They are concerned about stock needing to be sourced from suppliers in terms of timeframes (especially if sourced from overseas or made to order), and ensuring the order has not been 'lost' or delayed somewhere in the process.

This paper takes the position that the customer's transaction and information requirements should be the basis of the interface between the parties. The complexity of the process which provides the asynchronous business service must be hidden behind a Façade [2]. Further, this paper describes how a state based model forms the best basis for that façade.

BUSINESS INTEGRATION

The unit of business interaction is a business service—for example, a purchase. This may appear to be stating the obvious, but it is important to note that the business interaction is a *purchase*, and not *processing a purchase order*.

The business interaction has at least two parties—a service provider and a service consumer. These roles are asymmetrical for each interaction (e.g. the roles of buyer and seller in the purchase business service), but a party may have different roles in different interactions. For example, the distributor or wholesaler may be a seller in one interaction and a buyer in another.

A business service is asynchronous. It takes time to fulfill the business service, and the activities of the service consumer do not stop while awaiting the delivery of the service outcome. Note that saying the service is asynchronous is not tied into the form of the messaging between the parties—this could be synchronous or asynchronous as required,

It is also important to consider the semantics of the service. In view of the customer, the 'Purchase' business service could be considered completed once the purchased goods or services have been delivered, while the supplier would only consider the interaction completed once both supply and payment have been completed. However, this may be better managed by the Purchase service spawning off the Payment process—as when payment may be through, for example, lease payments to a third party.

STATE BASED ASYNCHRONOUS BUSINESS SERVICE

The Asynchronous Service 'Process Façade' can be represented the set of services shown in Figure 1.

This model is based on ASAP/WfXML [1,3], and has the same purpose—to allow business processes to work together. A number of significant changes have been made however, most based on the philosophical change from Wf-XML's desire to *expose* workflow for integration, to this paper's proposal to *hide* the workflow behind a Façade.

Most notably, unlike the Wf-XML model, there are no activities accessible by the service consumer. These activities can exist in the implementation, but are hidden from the Service Consumer.

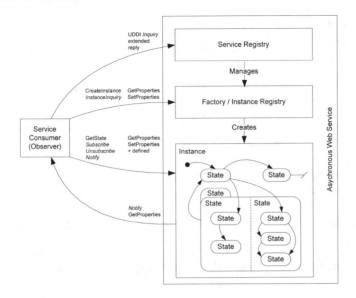

Figure 1. Service Model Overview
[Statechart shown is for illustrative purposes only.]

Service Registry

The service Registry for an asynchronous web services must describe the interfaces for both the Factory and Instances, and the state structure.

The model for the Instance is a UML Statechart [4]. The instanceDetails definition will therefore need to capable of describing the Statechart state-transition model. Further, each state has its own interface model:

- Events that the State recognizes;

- Properties (including type definitions), that can be set and un-set;

- Synchronous services which are valid if the Instance is in that state.

Utilising the registry enquiry function, the Service Consumer has access to the URI location of the Factory, and the description of the state model.

Factory

Instances are created by the Factory, and the URI of the Instance returned to the Service Consumer. The factory also has properties which can be viewed and set.

The Service Factory also acts as an Instance Repository. As a factory could have significant numbers of instances, an inquiry function needs to be available, at a minimum being able to filter on the instance status.

Instance

The Instance may act as either or both a NotificationConsumer and NotificationProducer [5].

Note that the service consumer cannot change state directly—only by changing properties or notifying the instance of an event. These may trigger a status change, depending on the transition rules.

Service Consumer (Observer)

The Service Consumer may act as either or both a NotificationConsumer and NotificationProducer.

SUPPLY CHAIN

Description

Consider the main actors in a simplified supply chain:

- **Stores**
- **Transport Services**
- **Warehouses**
- **Suppliers**

In our example situation, the Stores and Warehouses, and some (but not all) of the transport is managed by the same organization. Sometimes Suppliers deliver directly to the stores, however it is preferred to delivery to the warehouse to aggregate many smaller loads and so reduce congestion of the Store loading docks.

A Store stocks a number of **Items**. They maintain stock levels appropriate to the sale levels and expected delivery times, as part of the **Stock Management** process. To maintain this level, they need to order more stock items—but Stores do not care if this needs to be purchased and supplied by a Supplier, or supplied from the warehouse.

Supply Chain

One of the best principles for any architecture is separation of concerns—isolation between systems so that changes to one system have the minimum possible effect on any others. We therefore introduce an intermediate entity to hide the manner of how supply is achieved:

- **Supply Chain**

The Supply Chain accepts a store order from the Store, and then decides if this will result in a supply from a Supplier or from a Warehouse, or potentially, from another Store.

To correctly model this interaction as a process, rather than a document, we will use the verb **Supply**.

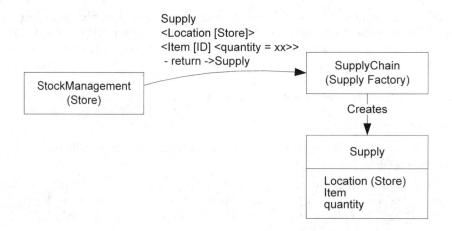

Figure 2. Creation of the Supply Process

The Stock Management process asks the Supply Chain to Supply a certain quantity of a Item. This interaction creates the Supply process, and the Stock Management requester is given a reference to this process.

Supply States

The supply process now needs to be monitored and supported. The Supply process is seen by the Stock Management process as a series of states, initially:

DetermingSource

Implied in creation of the Supply process is the subscription of the Stock Management process to the state changes in the Supply. The Supply service notifies the Stock Management when state changes occur.

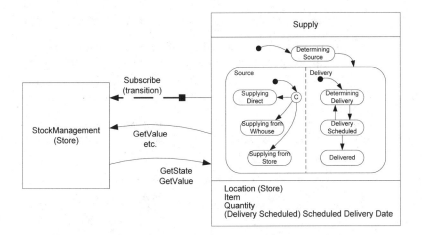

Figure 3. Monitoring and Servicing the Supply Process

The Supply process may need further information from the Stock Management process. This may be information or other functions.

Some Supply parameters are valid only for certain contexts—defined by the hierarchical states. For example, the Expected Delivery Date is only valid for Delivery Scheduled state.

Determining Method

The first state for the Supply process is determining the source of supply.

Looking now at a more specific example, the business rules in the Supply process may say that, for the selected product, the supply should first attempt to source from the local Warehouse.

The Supply process will attempt to start the dispatch process in the local warehouse. The Warehouse Management service will first check that either sufficient stock is on hand, or that stock can be sourced.

If the return to Supply service is OK, then the method of 'Supply from Warehouse" is selected, and the transition is made to:

SourceSupplyingFromWarehouse || Delivery.DeterminingDelivery.

Separate states for the supply source is used (rather than using a parameter) so that further sub-state modeling can be used.

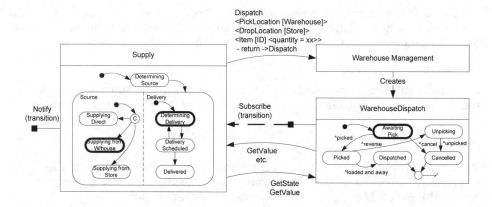

Figure 4. Obtaining Warehouse Dispatch

The Stock Management process is notified of this transition. Further, at any time, the Stock Management process can get the state of the Supply, and check on values of parameters that are valid for that state.

Determining Delivery

Once the Warehouse process is accepted as initiated, the transport can be arranged. A request for a Transport Dispatch is initiated, and scheduled.

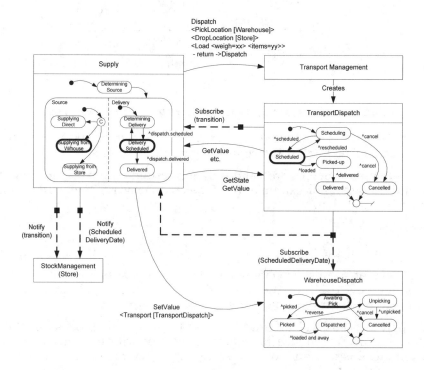

Figure 5. Obtaining Transport Dispatch

The Supply process receives the notification of the scheduling, which results in the transition of Delivery to Delivery Scheduled. The Warehouse Dispatch process is also notified of the Expected Delivery Date, so it can plan its picking process.

Re-scheduled Delivery

The discussion so far demonstrates how the various processes can be linked, but does not show how the state based models are superior to process step models.

If we now take the example where the Transport Dispatch fails—the scheduled pickup did not occur.

The Transport Dispatch process will be monitoring the dispatch against the schedule and notes the pickup did not occur. There is a choice between cancelation and rescheduling the Transport Dispatch—the operator decides to reschedule.

The state transition on Transport Dispatch triggers a notification to the Supply process. This triggers the Delivery state change from Delivery Scheduled back to Determining Delivery. In this case, the Supply operator decides not to override the reschedule with a cancel. The Stock Management is of course also notified that the state has dropped back to Determining Delivery.

In a slightly different case, consider if the Transport Dispatch Process has a policy that says it will only dispatch a truck for delivery if the items are already picked and waiting. In this case, Transport Dispatch Process may subscribe to the Warehouse Dispatch process, and reschedule if not Picked in time.

The Transport Dispatch process does its reschedule, and transitions to Scheduled. The both the Warehouse Dispatch and Supply processes will be notified of the new Scheduled Delivery Date, which is passed on by the latter to the Stock Management process.

Note how the Supply service acts as a façade for the Stock Management process—it only sees the Scheduled Delivery Date from the Supply service, and doesn't need to track or care about the transport or warehouses, only on the information it deems necessary to track.

HOUSING SERVICES

Description

Defence Housing Authority Australia [DHA] is a multi-billion dollar government business enterprise. It provides housing and relocation services to the members of other Australian public sector organizations. Since these members are the end-users of the services offered by DHA they are considered as **Customers** while their organizations are considered as **Clients**.

For this discussion DHA's Customer Service model is simplified into following business processes:

- Relocations Management—a process that involves point to point relocation of Customers as well as their family and dependents.
- Accommodation Management—a process that is mainly focused on provision of housing in the new location [**gaining location**].
- Property Management—Management of property stock that is controlled and managed by DHA.

In past three years DHA has reengineered its business processes to radically improve in the key process-performance measures such as cycle-time, cost, quality and customer-responsiveness. Reengineering effort was also aimed at overhauling the service delivery model and the information technology based business solutions. Before the overhaul DHA's business solutions were composed of numerous islands of automation that supported fragments of organizational functions. Integration between the solutions was limited and was devoid of important systemic qualities such as flexibility and extensibility. As a result staff had to rely on number of manual procedures and work-arounds to provide services to Customers.

While the entire application architecture was revisited during the reengineering exercise, this discussion is primarily focused on the redesign of the Accommodation (Management) Process.

ASAP model was used to design the underlying application services due to the fact that DHA's business processes often: have a longer life span; use complex rule-base and need to be flexible and responsive to the frequent changes in Customers' personal circumstances.

Some adjustments are made in the solution presented here for the purpose of theoretical generalization in-line with the model proposed in the earlier section however, the discussion is well grounded in the actual implementation. Also some elements of the workflow (including exception- and alternate-flows) have been either simplified or excluded in order to manage the scope of discussion.

Functional Overview

Following services were designed to perform specific functions within the Accommodation workflow:

1. **RelocationService**—to manage the lodgment-of, and processing of Application for Relocation [AFR]. This service primarliy supports Relocation Management and discussed here as a starting point of the occupancy and vacancy cycle of DHA's properties.
2. **OccupancyService**—to be used by RelocationService in determining a housing solution for a relocation.
3. **AllocationService**—to be used by OccupancyService for searching and selecting a house from DHA's property stock.
4. **VacancyService**—to be used by RelocationService to logically release a previously occupied property back into *available to occupy* housing stock.
5. **PropertyService**—to keep a record of current state of all properties managed by DHA in order to support Accommodation workflow as well as property life-cycle processes such as property maintenance and property portfolio management.

RelocationService is often initiated upon receiving a request for relocation from the Customer or Client. Once RelocationService establishes a valid case for relocation and determines the relocation and housing entitlements it initiates the OccupancyService and VacancyService in order to identify and hold an accommodation in the gaining location and to vacate a property in the current location [**losing location**] respectively.

Business rules built into OccupancyService determine the source of new accommodation e.g. property from DHA's housing stock [Service Residence or SR] or otherwise. If a Customer is entitled for a SR, OccupancyService creates an instance of the AllocationService to search for a SR (that is currently available or will be available in the right timeframe) in the gaining location according to Customer's entitlement.

If one or more properties are found, AllocationService allows Customer to choose a property of his / her liking from the list. This selection is termed as lockdown. Once a lockdown takes place all services directly involved in Accommodation workflow are directly or indirectly notified using a publish-subscribe arrangement. Upcoming and actual vacancies of properties are also managed and published using the similar arrangements. This design ensures that Customers' accommodation arrangements are made according to their entitlements and DHA's property stock is utilized to its full potential.

Logical Implementation

Webservices based notification [WS-Base Notification][5] and ASAP [1] concepts are used in this implementation. Change of internal state [state-transition] of NotificationProducer is the primary trigger (or situation) for a majority of notifications however, not all updates between the Notification-Producer [Instance] and NotificationConsumer [Observer] are attached to state-transition(s).

The model proposed in this document is largely followed although as stated earlier this discussion has made some adjustments in the hindsight.

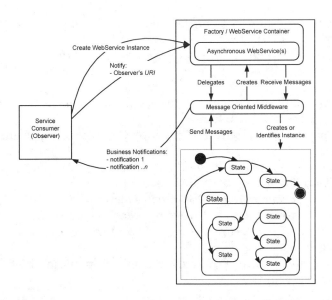

Figure 6: Logical implementation of Accommodation Workflow services

Right level of functional granularity is used while designing the relevant services this allowed separation of areas of concerns for each service and assisted in hiding the activities within a service behind a state-base façade.

A common interaction between observer and (service) instance is based on a HttpRequest for an asynchronous webservice that works as an instance factory and provides a reference of that instance to the subscriber.

A message oriented middleware [Message Queue or MQ] is used as a delegate for all incoming and outgoing notifications. As a result when a request for a service instance is received by the asynchronous webservice, Message Queue creates the instance with the parameters provided by the observer and sends a reference to the instance back to the observer via asynchronous webservice. When observer needs to update the instance a similar channel is followed. However when instance need to notify the observer, Message Queue directly invokes the observer's webservice on the behalf of instance. This implementation model did not require a UDDI since URIs of all webservices in the solution were already known. Figure 6 delineates the implementation model.

RelocationService

RelocationService supports the process of managing point to point relocation of DHA's Customers. An instance of RelocationService can have a life-span of a fortnight to six months. During that life-span it goes through number of transitions and states. There follows a simplified version of RelocationService' key states (that excludes the states in alternate and exception flows):

1. *Relocation Initiated*—A valid case for relocation has been established.
2. Application Data Entered—Information supplied by the Customer in the application for relocation has been captured including key dates such as: Expected Vacancy Date of the current residence and Expected Occupancy Date of the Future Residence.
3. *Housing Solution Confirmed*—Future housing has been arranged either from DHA's housing stock or otherwise.
4. *Movement Plan Confirmed*—Arrangements for pickup and delivery of household inventory and temporary accommodation has been finalized.
5. Financial Allowances Payment—Allowances relevant to the relocation are paid to the Customer.
6. *F&E Uplift*—Freight and inventory is picked up from the current address.
7. *Current Accommodation Vacated*—Current accommodation is either vacated or its vacancy date is confirmed.
8. *New Accommodation Occupied*—Occupancy of the future accommodation is confirmed i.e. future address becomes the current address.
9. *F&E Delivered*—Freight and Inventory is delivered to the new address.
10. *Relocation Confirmed & Closed*—Customer has been successfully relocated into the new location.

Occupancy Cycle

Since a housing is needed in the gaining location [step 3] with almost every relocation request RelocationService asks the OccupancyService to arrange for such housing regardless of its source i.e., either from—or outside of—DHA's housing stock. With this request RelocationService passes the necessary details about the Customer, gaining location, housing entitlements of the Customer and the Expected Future Occupancy Date. OccupancyService then creates a reference for this request and keep RelocationService upto-date about the progress made in arranging the housing for an AFR. Housing arrangement is referred to as '**housing solution**' in the Accommodation workflow.

OccupancyService

OccupancyService contains two subsets of states i.e., HousingSolution-Source and LockdownStatus. HousingSolutionSource represents the type of the housing solution (that is determined by the business rules) while Lockdownstatus represents the key states of progression in finding the housing solution.

HousingSolutionSource could have one of following states:

- *Own Means [OM]*—Customer will arrange his / her own accommodation and no assistance is required from DHA in either finding or paying for that accommodation.
- *Own Home [OH]*—Customer has a property in the gaining location that will be used as a housing solution.
- *Living In Accommodation [LIA]*—Customer will be accommodated on his / her actual posting site [e.g. Defence Base].
- *Service Residence [SR]*—Customer will be accommodated in one of DHA's property in the gaining location.
- *Rental Assistance [RA]*—Customer will find a rental property and DHA will contribute in the rent payments.

LockdownStatus states, on the other hand, translates into the following:

- Searching—This state represents the fact that OccupancyService has requested the relevant '*property search service*' (e.g. AllocationService in case of SR) to find a housing solution according to Customer's entitlements. This mainly applies to search for SR using AllocationService at this stage however this design allows for additional functionality to search for other types of housing solution.
- Unlocked—This state indicates that a property search service (AllocationService) is awaiting for the Customer to select [lock] a property from a subset of available to occupy properties in the gaining location. This state is also more meaningful in SR context.
- Locked—It is a generic state that suggest that a property has been selected as a housing solution. A property address is needed (among other information) before a transition is made to Locked state.
- Occupied—Also a generic state that is reached once Customer actually occupy the housing solution and RelocationService notifies the OccupancyService with the Actual Occupancy Date.

After initiation HousingSolutionSource and LockdownStatus together defines the current composite state of the OccupancyService. For example, in a prevalent business scenario, where RelocationService requests a housing solution for a Customer and business rules determines that the Customer is entitled for a SR, OccupancyService makes a transition from initial state of FindingAcommodation to the following state and notifies RelocationService:

HousingSolutionSource.SR || LockdownStatus.Searching

This state represents the fact that Customer's housing entitlement has been determined and OccupancyService has invoked the AllocationService to find a SR in the gaining location according to Customer's entitlement. Once AllocationService indicates that one or more SR exists in the gaining location (and a Customer login has been created) OccupancyService makes a transition to following state and notifies the RelocationService:

HousingSolutionSource.SR || LockdownStatus.Unlocked

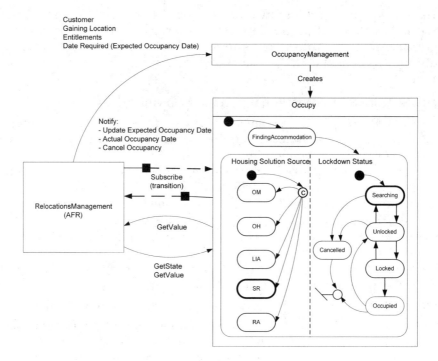

Figure 7: Obtaining a HousingSolution

In a situation where a property cannot be found according to entitlement DHA staff can intervene and allow OccupancyService to offer properties that are outside of Customer's entitlement by altering the search criteria. This also assist DHA staff to reserve / un-reserve a property as well as to offer a particular property to the Customer (these activities are still represented by Searching and Unlocked states and Customer still have to lock a reserved or specially offered property using the AllocationService).

Next, Customer selects the property using AllocationService which results in notification to OccupancyService with necessary details. This allows OccupancyService to make a transition to the following state:

HousingSolutionSource.SR || LockdownStatus.Locked

OccupancyService now notifies the new state to RelocationService, provide the details of HousingSolution and awaits for notification from RelcoationService for the Actual Occupancy of the housing solution. Once actual occupancy date becomes known transition to following state is made and both AllocationService and RelocationService are notified with the new state:

HousingSolutionSource.SR || LockdownStatus.Occupied

OccupancyService is also notified by the RelocationService about updates to expected and actual occupancy dates and cancellation of a Relocation. While changes in expected occupancy dates have little impact on OccupancyService, cancellation results in moving the LockdownStatus back to Unlocked state.

AllocationService

AllocationService is also a state based service that performs the following tasks:

- Search for SR in gaining location using the search criteria as notified by the OccupancyService.
- Create login credentials and notify the Customer if one or more properties are found.
- Let Customer login and lock a property.
- Unlock a property upon instructions from OccupancyService.
- Notify OccupancyService & PropertyService with key states and property information.

Following is the description of the key states in the AllocationService:

- Searching—DHA's property stock is being searched according to search criteria provided by the OccupancyService.
- Unlocked—A property has not been selected yet or the selection has been reverted.
- Locked—Customer has selected a property.
- Occupied—Selected property has been occupied.

As stated earlier AllocationService is an implementation of a 'property search service' and it only assist in searching, locking and unlocking SR. When OccupancyService request a search for a SR in gaining location an Allocate object is created with the search parameters provided by the OccupancyService.

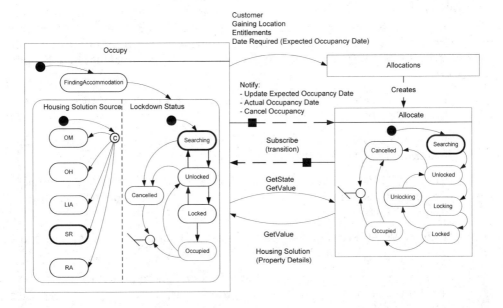

Figure 8: Allocating a Property

If one or more SR are found according to search criteria AllocationService makes a transition to the Unlocked state and notifies the OccupancyService. At this stage a Customer login is also created and he / she is notified.

Next Customer login into the AllocationService and selects a property. This results in transition to Locked state. At this point both PropertyService and OccupancyService are notified with the change in state and housing solution details.

Similarly when OccupancyService notifies about a cancellation, Allocation-Service makes a transition back to Unlocked state and subsequently to Canceled state.

Notification of Actual Occupancy Date results in transition to Occupied state which in turn triggers the similar notification to the PropertyService.

PropertyService

PropertyService performs following specific tasks:

- Storing and maintaining addresses of all properties that exists within Accommodation workflow regardless of their source i.e., owned by DHA or otherwise.
- Maintaining Occupancy / Vacancy Details of all properties that are managed by DHA including those that are on lease from external sources.
- Notifying other subscriber services whenever a property status is changed including those services that are relevant to other workflows such as maintenance, estate & portfolio management, and account-ing & financial management.

From Accommodation workflow viewpoint property status is represented by two logical states—available to occupy [VAV i.e. VOID Available] or unavail-able to occupy [VUN i.e. VOID Unavailable]. Sub-states are used to further explain the property status. For example a property which is Vacant but un-available could be in such state because it has been allocated to a Customer who is expected to occupy the property on a particular date. This informa-tion could easily allow the time window for periodic maintenance to be com-pleted. There follows a brief description of the composite states in Proper-tyService:

- LET || OCC (Let / Occupied)—Property is allocated and is occupied by the Customer.

- VAV || FUTV (Vacant Available / Future Vacant)—Property is either available now or its availability in future is known.

- VUN || FVA (Vacant Unavailable / Future Vacant Allocated)—Property is vacant and has been allocated and expected occupancy date is known.

- VAV || VCAP (Vacant Available / Vacant Property)—Property is avail-able for allocation and is currently vacant.

- VUN || VA (Vacant Unavailable / Vacant Allocated) Property is not available because it has been allocated.

AllocationService notifies PropertyService with all transitions.

Within accommodation workflow, PropertyService acts in both roles as an observer and as an instance. As an observer to AllocationService and VacancyService it receives notifications for all status changes as well as information about housing solution including dates for actual and expected future occupancy and vacancy.

Following table provides the mapping between the key states of OccupancyService, AllocationService and PropertyService.

OccupancyService	AllocationService	PropertyStatus || StatusReason
HousingSolutionSource.SR || LockdownStatus.Locked	Locked (Create Future Occupancy of a particular SR)	• If property status is VAV with property reason of FUTV then set property reason to FVA. • If property status is VUN then set property reason to FVA. • If property status is VAV with property reason of VACP then set reason to VA. • If property status is VUN then set property reason to VA.
HousingSolutionSource.SR || LockdownStatus.Occupied	Create Actual Occupancy	• Let / OCC
HousingSolutionSource.SR || LockdownStatus.Canceled	Canceled (if there was no actual occupancy date supplied by AllocationService it will be considered by PropertyService as a request for canceling a future occupancy)	• If property status was VUN and property reason is FA then set property reason to FUTV. • If property status was VUN and property reason is VA then set property reason to VACP.
HousingSolutionSource.SR || LockdownStatus.Canceled	Canceled (Cancel Actual Occupancy)	• VA • VACP • TUAV (Temporary Unavailable) • PUAV (Permanently Unavailable)

Table 1: Mapping between the key states of RelocationService, OccupancyService, AllocationService and PropertyService

Figure 9 shows the information flow for the occupancy cycle:

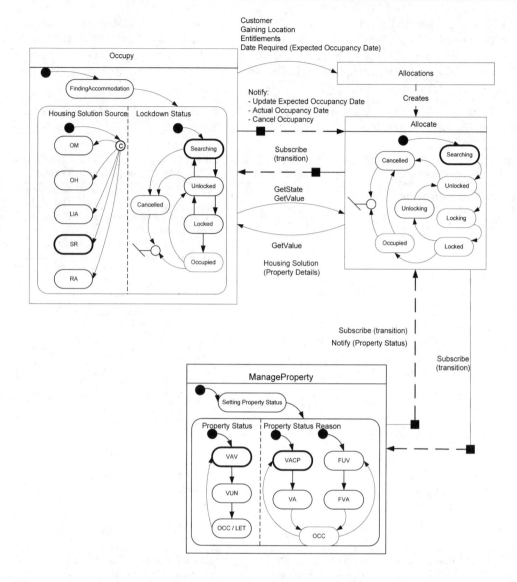

Figure 9: The Occupancy Cycle

VacancyService

VacancyService, as the name suggest is used by RelocationService to (logically) vacate a housing solution. When a Customer is expected to move out of a current residence a Future Vacancy needs to be created. RelocationService requests the VacancyService to vacate the housing solution. VacancyService creates a Vacate instance and provide a reference of that instance to RelocationService.

Again sub-states are used to fully represent the current state of VacancyService.

HousingSolutionSource sub-states are used to identify which type of housing solution is being vacated while VacancyStatus sub-states are used to represent the progress made.

For example when business rules within VacancyService identifies that RelocationService has requested a vacancy of SR and has provided the Expected (Future) Vacancy Date it makes a transition from its initial state to the following and notifies the RelocationService with the new state:

HousingSolutionSource.SR || VacancyStatus.Vacating

Since PropertyService has an interest in future vacancies and has a subscription to VacancyService it is also notified with the new state and the Expected Vacancy Date.

Similarly when RelocationService notifies the Actual Vacancy Date, VacancyService makes a transition to HousingSolutionSource.SR || VacancyStatus.Vacated and notifies both the RelocationService and the PropertyService.

Table 2 provides the mapping between the key states of VacancyService and PropertyService while Figure 10 provides the details of interactions between RelocationService, VacancyService and PropertyService.

VacancyService	Implications for PropertyService States	
	Property Status	Property Reason
HousingSolutionSource.SR || VacancyStatus.Vacating *(Create Future Vacancy)*	VAV	• FUTV—Future vacant
HousingSolutionSource.SR || VacancyStatus.Vacated *(Create Actual Vacancy)*	If a property was not locked down then set the status to VAV else set it to VUN.	• If property was not locked down set reason to VACP. • If property was locked down and future occupancy date does exist then set reason to VA.
HousingSolutionSource.SR || VacancyStatus.Canceled *(Cancel Future Vacancy)*	LET is set to previous status.	• OCC is set to previous reason.
Notification of new Future Vacancy Date (Update Future Vacancy)	No change to status.	No Change
Notification of change in Actual Vacancy Date (Update Actual Vacancy)	No change to status.	No Change

Table 2: Mapping between the key states of VacancyService and PropertyService

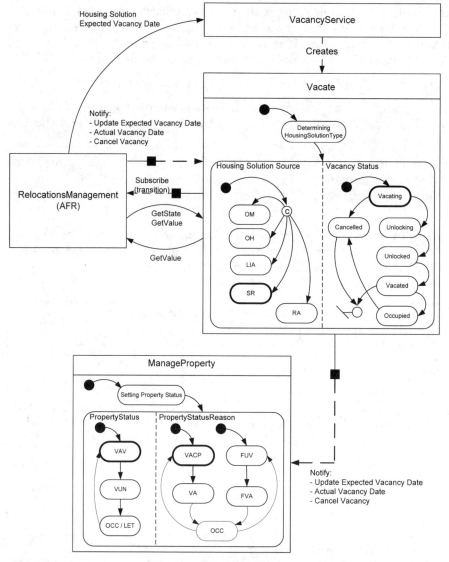

Figure 10: The Vacancy Cycle

RELATIONSHIPS TO EXISTING STANDARDS

ASAP / WfXML

The concept of the state-based, asynchronous model is primarily based on the OASIS ASAP / Workflow Coalition Wf-XML models [1,3]. The primary difference is that the interface is designed specifically as a façade to be presented to external parties, rather than managing the process itself.

In this role, the expressiveness of the state model becomes very important.

ASAP modeling [1] of the of the status focuses on the status of the work engine (state types):

open.notrunning.suspended: A resource is in this state when it has initiated its participation in the enactment of a work process, but has been suspended. At this point, no resources contained within it may be started.

open.running: A resource is in this state when it is performing its part in the normal execution of a work process.

closed.completed: A resource is in this state when it has finished its task in the overall work process. All resources contained within it are assumed complete at this point.

closed.abnormalCompleted: A resource is in this state when it has completed abnormally. At this point, the results for the completed tasks are returned.

closed.abnormalCompleted.terminated: A resource is in this state when it has been terminated by the requesting resource before it completed its work process. At this point, all resources contained within it are assumed to be completed or terminated.

closed.abnormalCompleted.aborted: A resource is in this state when the execution of its process has been abnormally ended before it completed its work process. At this point, no assumptions are made about the state of the resources contained within it.

The examples shown illustrate that these statuses are unimportant to the interface, and that the interface designer must be able to specify their own status models.

Further, these example shows that the interface status model must be as expressive as UML Statecharts [4]. In particular, the ability to express hierarchical and parallel states is very important

UDDI and UML

It is proposed that the service Registry for Asynchronous Web Services be an extended version of UDDI [6]. The UDDI entry should describe both the Factory and Instance interfaces.

The factory interface would be described in standard UDDI fashion—as these services are traditional synchronous web services. The instance interface, however, requires extension to the UDDI instanceDetails.

The UML 2.0 specification [7] supports the modeling of an Interface as a ProtocolStateMachine.

Package ProtocolStateMachines

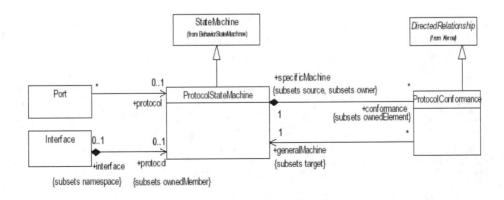

Figure 11: Protocol State Machines

Serialisation of this model using XMI [8] may be a suitable base for defining the StateChart and associated Interface as a ProtocolStateMachine.

CONCLUSION

This paper proposes a new approach in considering asynchronous web services. In particular, it is proposed that the model for asynchronous services should stress the state nature of the façade presented to consumers, and to hide the process supporting the service.

Further work is required to ensure the specification of ASAP and UDDI standards can be modified to properly support this new approach. Standards based on UML are preferred.

REFERENCES

[1]   OASIS (2005) Asynchronous Service Access Protocol (ASAP) Version 1.0 Proposed Committee Draft, May 18, 2005

[2]   Gamma, E et al (1994) "Design Patterns—Elements of Reusable Object-Oriented Software." Addison Wesley Longman: Reading Massachusetts).

[3]   Workflow Management Coalition (2004) Wf-XML 2.0—XML Based Protocol for Run-Time Integration of Process Engines, Draft October 8, 2004.

[4]   OMG (2003) UML 2.0 Infrastructure Specification OMG Adopted Specification ptc/03-09-15.

[5]   OASIS (2005) Web Services Base Notification 1.3—(WS-BaseNotification) Public Review Draft 01, 07 July 2005

[6]   OASIS (2004) UDDI Version 3.0.2 Spec Technical Committee Draft, Dated 20041019.

[7]   OMG (2005) Unified Modeling Language: Superstructure version 2.0 formal/05-07-04

[8]   OMG (2005) XML Metadata Interchange (XMI) Specification May 2005 Version 2.0 formal/05-05-01

Toward Workflow Block Activity Patterns for Reuse in Workflow Design

Lucinéia Heloisa Thom and Cirano Iochpe
Federal University of Rio Grande do Sul, Brazil;
Vinícius Amaral and Daniel Viero, iProcess, Brazil

1. Introduction

Research on both business process modeling and implementation issues related to workflow technology have quickly increased over the last years. The most significant initiatives are in the field of standardization [1], [2], [4], specification [5] and workflow definition languages [6], [7], [3]. However, since it is a relatively new and still evolving technology, workflow design presents some challenges, especially with respect to techniques that can enforce correctness as well as efficiency during both the requirements analysis and the modeling phase of the workflow project.

Within this context, research on workflow patterns has attracted increasing attention mainly because of the advantages of reusing patterns [8], [9]. The most extensively studied are in the field of control/data flow patterns [10], [11] as well as resource and application–oriented patterns (12). Such patterns are being used not only in business/workflow process modeling but also in critical evaluations of workflow languages and workflow tools (13).

However, a lot less research can be found relating workflow design to a set of recurrent business process "pieces" or "parts" that must be atomically executed by the workflow process (e.g., an activity request execution and a notification activity). Although one can precisely characterize the semantics of such business process "pieces" [14], [15], [16] and they have to be recurrently re-designed in practically every workflow modeling process, there is no known research relating these business process structures to workflow patterns.

1.1 Approach

Our approach applies the concept of block activity to well-known business processes. An activity set is a self-contained set of activities and transitions [7]. Transitions in the set should refer only to activities in the same set and there should be no transitions into or out of the set. Activity sets can be modeled as block activities. The block execution starts at the first activity in the set and executes the next activities by following the partial order imposed upon them by the transitions until an exit activity is reached. Workflow execution then returns to the next activity following the block.

In this paper, we apply the block activity concept in order to represent a set of business (sub-)process types (e.g., logistic, financial, information and decision) that we call "workflow block activity patterns". These patterns are related to a set of specific atomic structures that are frequently found in business processes and have already been identified in the literature [14], [15],

[16], [10], [6]. According to [17] a pattern is the abstraction from a concrete form which keeps recurring in specific non-arbitrary contexts.

The block activity concept is suitable for representing the business (sub-)process types because it can encapsulate their well-defined semantics as well as represent their atomic characteristic. This means that all activities defined inside the block activity pattern must completely execute before workflow continues execution.

Since our pattern representations may require input/output parameters and the block activity concept does not support parameters, we applied the transaction perspective of the serialization theory to overcome this limitation [18]. An input parameter is represented as a database read operation of "one-time-only" readable information. Similarly, an output parameter is represented in the block as a database write operation of "one-time-only" writeable information.

As part of our investigation, after integrating different pattern classifications found in the literature, we decided to describe the so-called workflow block activity patterns in a common language. UML 2.0[19] was chosen for this purpose[1]. In order to verify whether these workflow patterns are modeled as often as their counterparts in business processes, we conducted some case studies by analyzing both a set of workflow definition languages and a set of workflow processes.

1.2 Related Work

Wil van der Aalst proposed 21 workflow patterns for the description of business process behavior [10]. More recently, van der Aalst proposed a set of workflow data patterns [11] and a set of resource workflow patterns [12]. Our approach differs from van der Aalst's approach because each of our patterns has a well-defined goal (e.g., activity execution request and process status notification).

SAP created a cross-application tool called SAP Business Workflow. The tool makes feasible the integration of business tasks between applications including a workflow wizard with workflow templates [6]. Within this context, the Massachusetts Institute of Technology (MIT) started development in 1991 of the Process Handbook, an online knowledge base with entries for over 5000 business activities [15]. We consider some of our patterns more application independent than SAP and MIT patterns. The advantage of this is the different levels of abstraction that our patterns can provide when used to model both business processes and workflow processes. In our investigation we observed that some of our patterns are more application –oriented while other are more information sys –oriented.

The remainder of the paper is structured as follow. Section 2 presents an overview of different business process types. Section 3 describes some of these process types through UML 2.0. In order to investigate whether they are implemented in workflow components of different workflow tools as well as different applications, a matching exercise was performed. The results are summarized in Section 4. Finally, Section 5 concludes the paper and describes future directions.

---

[1] UML is being considered a flexible language that makes possible the mapping of an UML process to a BPEL4WS process. Such mapping can be useful when thinking about implementation issues [8].

2 BUSINESS (SUB-)PROCESS TYPES

Processes in organizations can be grouped into several categories, depending on the nature of the process object[2] [16]. According to [16], while *logistic processes* are performed with the goal of manipulating a physical object (also called material process [14], [20]) or provisioning a service (e.g., the manufacturing of a product and both selling and buying of goods), *financial processes* are performed when monetary value is exchanged between two parties. Each of these processes is accompanied by an *information process*, which represents the flow of data in the company's information systems that is set in motion by the relevant logistics and financial processes. Figure 1 illustrates the semantics of the concepts.

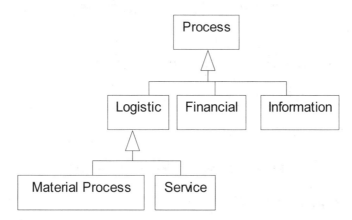

Figure 1 : Semantic of Concepts

Within this context, Michael zur Muehlen [16] explains that the participants of a process communicate by exchanging messages. A message exchange involves two players: a sender or producer (sends a message) and a receiver or consumer (receives a message). The author classifies messages as unidirectional or bi-directional. Unidirectional messages are used either by a sender to request the execution of an activity from a receiver (also called a *unidirectional performative message or communication*), or by a receiver to notify a sender (*notification message[3]*). Bi-directional messages form a request/respond pair, where a sender asks a receiver to perform an activity and the receiver answers the sender (also called (*bi-directional performative message or communication*), or they form a solicit/respond pair, where a receiver asks the sender for information which is supplied subsequently (*informative message*).

In our approach the activities of an information process are the *messages* that implement the organization's flow of data instigated by both logistic and financial processes. For example, in an "approval process" the activity concerning a "document review request" generates a bi-directional performative message (a sender requests a receiver to perform an activity). Figure 2 illustrates a simple workflow meta-model, defined as an aggregation of applica-

---

[2] A process object forms the object of work inside a process. The activities which are to be executed inside a process contribute to the change of the process object's state. This organization-focused understanding of objects has to be distinguished from the computer science term "object" (object as an encapsulation of data and function)[21].

[3] In a workflow process it can be used to inform the status of an activity execution.

tion processes (i.e., logistic and financial processes) and information processes (i.e. the kinds of message exchange).

We emphasize that either application processes or information processes can
be related to a *decision process* i.e., a cognitive process of selecting a course
of activities from among multiple alternatives [22], [15]. In the case of an application process it refers to a decision-making action such as the approving
or rejecting in an approval process. In an information process the decision
occurs in terms of workflow routing.

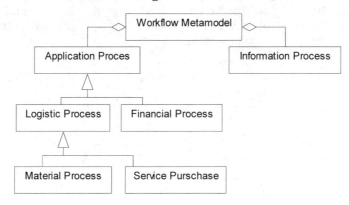

Figure 2 : Workflow metamodel

3 BLOCK ACTIVITY PATTERNS

Within the context of a business as well as a workflow process there are a
variety of different "parts," each of which is related either to the application
domain (e.g., logistic and financial activities) or to the organization's information process (e.g. decision or some kind of message exchange). These
parts can be understood as self-contained activity blocks with a specific and
well defined semantic. It is worth observing that the same "part" can be repeated within the same process. At execution time different copies of a same
"part" may be receiving either the same or different parameter values.

This section presents not only the basic logistic and financial activities but
also the types of message exchange in UML 2.0 notation. We mainly focus
on logistic, financial and information processes because these processes are
widely recognized among different authors [14], [16]. Nevertheless, we rely
on the block activity concept of the Workflow Management Coalition to
model structures which should be executed atomically. Figures 4 to 13 must
be read according to the legend presented in Figure 3. We used the Visual
Paradigm for the UML Community Edition based on UML 2.0 as an editing
tool to design the patterns.

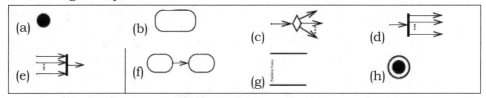

*Figure 3 : From right to left (a) InitialNode – a signal indicating a
start point in a process; (b) Action – refers to an atomic activity; (c) De-
cisionNode; (d) ForkNode or AND-Split; (e) JoinNode; (f) ControlFlow (g)
ActivityPartition or Swimlane; (h) ActivityF*

3.1 Logistic Pattern

A logistic process can refer to the manufacturing, buying and selling of products or it can also comprise the offering of a service. Our intention here is not to present a detailed pattern for each of these logistic activities but to illustrate the main general possible logistic activities related to it. We focus on the information data (in terms of message exchange) these logistic activities can generate. Accordingly, Figure 4 shows a conceptual view of the main logistic activities. Based on an order specification, for example, one of several kinds of activities will be chosen to start the execution.

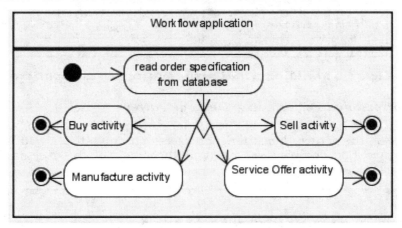

Figure 4 : Logistic pattern

3.2 Financial Pattern

This pattern represents a financial process. As shown in Figure 5, the financial activity manipulates and, eventually, generates a new monetary value.

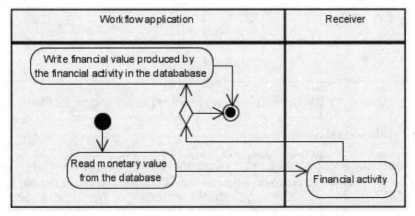

Figure 5 : Financial pattern

3.3 Unidirectional Performative Message Pattern

This pattern represents a unidirectional performative message. As shown in Figure 6, first there is an activity execution request. Based on the activity description, a work item is assigned to a receiver (a specific workflow participant responsible for the activity execution). After that, the process can continue execution without waiting for a response. Both the write and read activities would be modeled as parameters if allowed by a block activity.

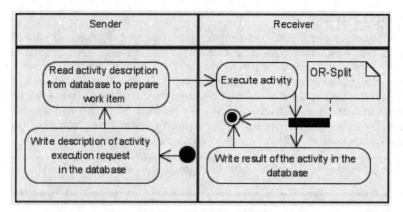

Figure 6 : Unidirectional performative message pattern

3.4 Bi-directional Performative Message Pattern

This pattern is based on the bi-directional performative message. As shown in Figure 7, the activity block finishes execution only after a notification of activity execution complete is sent and the result of the execution is recorded in the database (AND-Split).

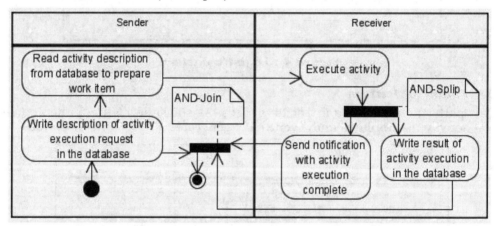

Figure 7 : Bi-directional performative message pattern

3.5 Informative Pattern

The informative pattern is based on the informative message. As illustrated in Figure 8, the activity block starts with an information request and finishes when the information required is received. This pattern differs from the bi-directional performative message mainly in terms of the type of activity result being requested, i.e., a piece of information.

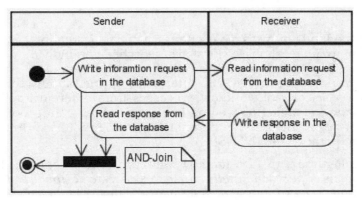

Figure 8 : Informative pattern

3.6 Notification Pattern

As shown Figure 9, this pattern is based on the notification message. It comprises a notification activity that can either inform the end of an activity execution or post news inherent to the workflow application. In the last case, the sender usually sends a notification. Since it informs the status of an activity execution, it can be understood as part of the bi-directional message. In our approach we are treating the notification activity as a self-contained activity because we assume that a notification activity status can eventually be sent after previously being requested to do so.

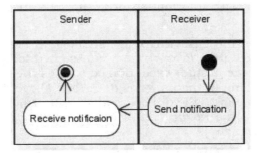

Figure 9 : Notification pattern

3.7 Decision Pattern

The decision pattern is similar to the decision control flow proposed in [19] (see Figure 10). In our approach this pattern is to be used in conjunction with other patterns. In this context, it can assume more significance such as in an approval process.

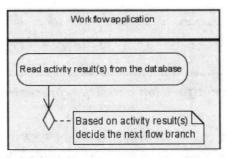

Figure 10 : Decision pattern

4 CASE STUDY

To identify the kinds of message exchange patterns in real processes we performed a "matching exercise". First we searched for individual as well as combinations of patterns in the workflow modeling language supported by the Oracle Workflow Cartridge [23]. After that, we tried to find the same patterns within a set of real workflow processes from different application domains that were modeled as well as implemented with that tool. In a third step we analyzed some of the main modeling elements of the Business Process Modeling Notation—BPMN [5].

Note that in Figures 9 to 12 a *dashed line* represents a *notification pattern*; a *filled line* means a *decision pattern*; a *circle* illustrates a *unidirectional performative message pattern* and a *dotted line* indicates a *bi-directional performative message pattern*.

4.1 Block Activity Patterns Represented by Oracle Cartridge Components

The Oracle Workflow Cartridge offers a set of components to be used in workflow process design (e.g., item types; lookup types; activities, attributes, roles). From these components we investigated mainly the activity types.

In Oracle an activity is defined as a unit of work that contributes toward the accomplishment of a process [22]. An activity can be a notification, a function, an event, or a process. Our investigation started with the notification activity, which sends a message to a workflow user. The message may simply provide the user with information or request the user to take some action.

Figure 11 illustrates the case when the notification activity comprises the request of a task execution (a work item is assigned for a workflow participant who must execute it. After execution completes the requester receives a notification). According to the patterns described above, the notification activity can be said to express two block activity patterns, a *bi-directional performative message* and a *notification* (because of the activity: "notify sender about execution complete").

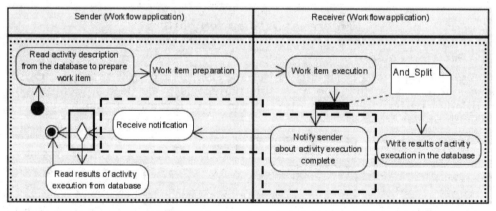

Figure 11 : Oracle notification activity represented as block activity pattern

4.2 Block Activity Patterns Represented by BPMN

The Business Process Management Initiative (BPMI) has developed a standard Business Process Modeling Notation (BPMN). The primary goal of BPMN is to provide a notation that is readily understandable by all business users, from the business analysts that create the initial drafts of the processes, to the technical developers responsible for implementing the technology that will perform those processes, and finally, to the business people who will manage and monitor those processes [5].

BPMN has created a set of modeling elements which are classified as Events, Activities, Gateways, Pool, Lane, Artifacts, Sequence Flow, Message Flow, Association, Exception Flow and Compensation Association. As we are still studying most of these modeling elements in this paper we only present the analyses we performed with the "End Event". According to [5] an Event is something that "happens" during the course of a business process. These Events affect the flow of the Process and usually have a cause or an impact. The main Events in BPMN are the *Start* and *End* Events, respectively. Figure 12 illustrates the logic of the *end event* represented as a block activity in UML.

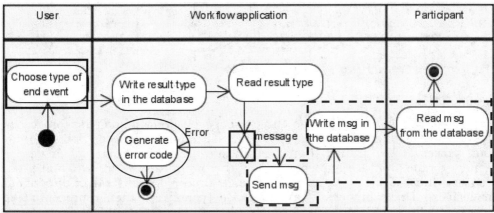

Figure 12 : BPM End event represented as block activity

End Events may define a "Result" that is a consequence of a Sequence Flow ending. There are multiple types of Results. Figure 12 illustrates two kinds of results: (a) generate error code and; (b) send message. The activity "choose type of end event" for example can be understood as an *application decision* because the user must choose one of several kinds of end events or results to be used in a specific process modeling. Based on this, either an error code must be supplied (Generate error code) or a message needs to be sent reporting the reason for the end event (Send msg).

In addition to the decision message, Figure 12 shows two examples of block activity patterns, the *unidirectional performative message* that is generated by the activity "Generate code" and the *notification message* which is generated by the activity "Send msg".

4.3 Block Activity Patterns Identified in Workflow Applications

We analyzed about 200 workflow (sub-)processes (such as the one presented in Figure 13) from different domain applications in order to identify the block activity patterns in the (sub)processes. To do so, we matched the content of one or more business activities (e.g., notify parties in charge about new launching – meaning that the workflow participant must perform an evaluation) with the pattern (e.g., unidirectional performative message).

Figure 13 illustrates the case where the launching of a new product is evaluated. Accordingly, the activities "Notify parties in charge about new launching" and "Notify financial department about approvals" generate notification messages that are implemented by the organization's information system. On the other hand, the activity "Evaluate launching" generates a *unidirectional performative message* because it is related to an activity execution request. Last but not least, the activity "Check whether there are new products to be evaluated" generates a *bi-directional performative message* because it concerns an activity execution request (the workflow system is the performer) that must return a value, i.e., there exist or do not exist new launchings to be evaluated.

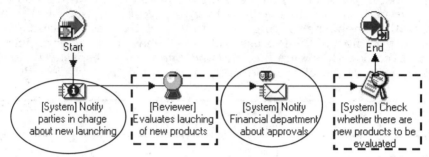

Figure 13 : Launching of new products

5 CONCLUSIONS

In this paper we reported the three most well-known business processes found in the literature, i.e., logistic process, financial process and information process. We argued that both logistic as well as financial processes generate data that are implemented by the organization's information process activities as message exchanges (e.g., unidirectional and bi-directional messages). These processes and message types were then represented as block activities via UML 2.0. Through case studies we identified these block activity patterns not only in workflow elements but also in workflow applications. The main results of the "matching exercise" were: (a) the patterns could be identified in most of the analyzed workflow elements, which suggests to us that the patterns are probably present in workflow applications developed on the basis of such workflow elements; (b) the patterns were also identified in specific "pieces" of a workflow application, which makes feasible their reuse in similar new applications.

By applying the WfMC concept of "block activity" to define patterns we provide the atomicity property, meaning that whole activities inherent to a specific pattern are completely executed from beginning to end before the flow (outside the activity block) can continue. The serializability theory approach was also suitable to cover the parameter expression limitation of the block activity. Finally, the representation of the patterns as well as the workflow elements and applications in a common language (UML 2.0) as an early step before the "matching exercise" proved to be an efficient method to avoid ambiguities during the process identification.

We observed that both logistic and financial patterns are application domain -oriented. On the other hand, the message exchange patterns are more related to the organization's information system. The decision pattern is an exception because it depends on the context, i.e., whether it is used for a control-flow purpose or for an application purpose such as an approval process. Our aim is to use the proposed patterns to improve both the quality and the performance of the design phase in a workflow project mainly because of the reuse advantages of pattern approaches. We believe our approach represents a useful way to separate the business process parts, which depend on the application domain, from the parts which depend on the information system. These different abstractions of the same process are useful to determine the designer profile as well as to focus the design in one specific dimension just as occurs with the UML diagrams, for example.

In the future we plan to follow two avenues of research. The first involves the search for new patterns through the investigation of both workflow elements of different tools/notations such as the BPMN elements and workflow applications of different domains. Second, we plan to investigate whether our patterns fit in the pattern classifications proposed by van der Aalst [10], [11], [12], SAP [6] and MIT [15]. The idea is to propose a new category when none of the existing ones match any of our patterns.

ACKNOWLEDGEMENTS

The authors would like to thank the German Academic Exchange Service—DAAD, the Coordination for the Improvement of Graduated students—CAPES, the Institute for Parallel and Distributed Systems—IPVS of University of Stuttgart (Stuttgart, Germany) in special Prof. Dr.-Ing. habil. Bernhard Mitschang and the Informatics Institute of Federal University of Rio Grande do Sul—UFRGS (Porto Alegre, Brazil).

REFERENCES

1. Workflow Management Coalition. Terminology & Glossary. Bruxelas, Feb. 1999. 65p. Available at: <http://www.wfmc.org>. Visited in Nov. 2005.

2. Workflow Management Coalition. Interface 1: process definition interchange organizational model. 1998. Available at: <http://www.wfmc.org>. Visited in Aug. 2005.

3. Eriksson H.-E., Penker, M. Business Modeling with UML. John Wiley & Sons, Inc., 2001. 459p.

4. Castano, S. et. Al. Workflow on Intelligent Distributed database Environment: workflow reference models. (ESPIRIT Project 20280). Politecnco di Milano.1997.

5. White, Stephen A. Introduction to BPMN. 2004. Available at: <www.bpmn.org>. Visited in May. 2004.

6. Andrews, T. et al.: Business Execution Language For Web Services, (Version 1.1). Available at: <www.ibm.org>, 2003.

7. Workflow Management Coalition Workflow Standard. Process Definition Interface: XML Process Definition Language. Doc. Number: WFMC-TC-1025. 2005.

8. Thom, L., Iochpe, C., Mitschang, B. 2005. Improving the Workflow Project Quality Via Business Process Patterns Based on Organizational Structure Aspects. In: *1st GI Workshop XML4BPM—XML for Business Process Management* at BTW, Karlsruhe Germany.

9. Hohpe, G.; Woolf, B. Enterprise integration patterns: Designing, Building, and Deploying Messaging Solutions. Boston: Addison-Wesley. c2004.

10. van der Aalst, W.M.P. et al. Workflow Patterns. In Distributed and Parallel Databases, 14(3), pages 5-51, July 2003.

11. Russell, N., Hofstede, A. H. M ter, Edmond, D.: Workflow Data Patterns. In: Informatik 2004—Informatik verbindet (Band 1), Lecture Notes in Informatics (LNI). Proceedings... Ulm. v. p-50, 2004a.

12. Russell, N. et. al. Workflow Resource Patterns. Technical report, FIT-TR-2004-01, Queensland University of Technology, Brisbane, 2004b.

13. van der Aalst, W.M.P. et al. Patterns and XPDL: A Critical Evaluation of the XML Process Definition Language. QUT Technical report, FIT-TR-2003-06, Queensland University of Technology, Brisbane, 2003.

14. Medina-Mora, R. et. Al. The action workflow approach to workflow management technology. 1992. Available in : www.acm.org. Visited in Jun/05.

15. Malone, T. W.; Crownston, K.; Herman, G. A. Organizing Business Knowledge: The MIT Process Handbook. ISBN 0-262-13429-2. 2004. Partes deste livro estão disponíveis no site: (http://ccs.mit.edu/ph/).

16. zur Muehlen, M. Workflow-based process controlling: foundations, design, and application of workflow-driven process information systems. Logos Verlang Berlin : Berlin. 299 p. 2002.

17. Gamma, E. et al. Design Ptterns. Addison-Wesley, 1995.

18. Bernstein, P. A.; Hadzilacos, V.; Goodman, N. Concurrency Control and Recovery in Database Systems. Reading: Addison-Wesley, c1987. 370 p. : il

19. Object Management Group. Unified Modeling Language: Superstructure. V.2.0.2005.

20. Geurts, G.; Geelhoed, A. Business process decomposition and service identification using communication patterns. 2002. Available in: http://msdn.microsoft.com/library/. Visited in Jun/05.

21. Rosemann, M.: Erstellung und Integration von Prozeßmodellen. Methodenspezifische Gestaltungsempfehlungen für die Informationsmodellierung. Diss., Universität Münster 1995.

22. Oracle Workflow Guide. Realise 2.6.2. v. 1. 2001. 1056p.

Using Process Execution Data in Application Support

Udhai Reddy, Infosys Technologies, India

ABSTRACT

This paper is based on research and prototyping on using process execution data for assessing the priority and impact of system or application incidents (Trouble Tickets) to strategic business goals in application support.

The research has been aimed at identifying the impact of the incident on the strategic business objectives using the business process execution data and process definition. The research is still in progress with respect to refinement of the models. This paper is a reflection of the status at a point where the first pilot was conducted.

The paper does not elaborate a method for defining a service level agreement based on strategic business goals.

1. INTRODUCTION

Organizations are constantly looking at improving maintenance and support of their applications. Simultaneously they are also looking to reduce cost and reduce their dependence on knowledge held by specific individuals. Frameworks like ITIL [4] are being adopted by organizations to improve their infrastructure and application support by implementing "best" practices. The ITIL framework has been created to help organizations achieve excellence in various aspects of their IT service management.

There are various methods being adopted by organizations to reduce cost of IT service management, the primary approach being offshoring or outsourcing. Organizations which are looking to reduce dependence of knowledge held by specific individuals are looking at various knowledge initiatives.

The approach which has been detailed in this paper looks at a more accurate assessment of relative impact of application incidents, based on actual process execution data within the application. In the ITIL framework this is referred to as *Incident Prioritization*. Refer to work by Turbitt [5],[6] on why the ITIL framework should be used.

This paper looks at the specific challenge with respect to assessing the impact of an incident in application support. This paper is limited to support for transaction processing applications and does not include reporting and business intelligence systems. This paper does not address the various methods available to service the incidents queues, allocation of resources to various queues nor does it address the skill requirements for support. The approach has been developed using a sample of system and data. The selection of samples and data was not done using statistical analysis and hence is not representative.

2. PRIORITIZATION AND SLA

There are various types of Service Level Agreements (SLA) definitions which are closely linked to the impact assessment method that has been followed. A method for prioritization of incidents is required by all companies which have (SLA) with priority levels in IT service management. Refer to [2] on why prioritization of systems incidents in required in IT service management. There is a lot of research and viewpoints on how to define an SLA, refer to [3] and [7] for some of the perspectives on how to define an SLA. Also refer to [1] which presents a view on aligning prioritization towards business goals.

The objective here is not to propose a method for defining an SLA. Elaborated here is the type of SLA definitions for which the proposed impact assessment mechanism is applicable.

In the first impact assessment approach, the business impact is assumed or calculated and the SLA for the application is defined on parameters such as availability. The impact of the application not being available is taken as a constant. This type of SLA works well for websites which have a constant high volume of traffic and there is little to no difference in importance of one user or one instance of the process with another. When an SLA is defined as 99.9 percent availability of the system, it already assumes a certain impact due to non-availability of the system on the application and in turn customer satisfaction, number of orders, lost customers or lost revenue. The method detailed in this paper is not applicable is this scenario.

In the second impact approach, broad guidelines are defined based on certain strategic objectives (in this case it is "customer first") and support resources are expected to use knowledge gained from experience or do a detailed analysis to assess the business impact of the incident. This approach is knowledge intensive. Below is an example of the priority criteria used in a bank which has adopted this approach.

Example of prioritization criteria used in a bank:

Highest Priority: Any problem directly affecting the customer.

High Priority: Any problem affecting a financial transaction.

Normal Priority: All other problems.

Here the SLAs are defined in terms of time taken for incident resolution within each priority level. The support resource uses the above guidelines and exercise discretion based on knowledge in prioritizing system incidents. Usually the prioritization is based on knowledge and assumed impact. The effort involved in manually assessing the impact of the incident is a major detriment to adopting the same.

The last type of SLA definition is relatively complex and defined in terms of acceptable impact on strategic organizational goals like loss of revenue and impact on customer satisfaction due to system or application related issues. The more strategic measures like customer satisfaction might also be broken into process goals like time taken for fulfilling an order. This approach will require support to determine the impact of any system or application on the defined goals before prioritizing the same. The specific problem taken up for research was linking the system incident to process, strategic and financial goals. Below are some examples of the SLA for an order management application.

Example 1:

Acceptable percentage of delay in order fulfilling process (180 Min) due to problems in system or application—2 percent per month.

Example 2:

Acceptable loss of revenue in orders due to problems in system or application—0.1 percent of revenue per month.

Refer to [2] for a perspective on factors which influence the priority of incidents. The focus of this research is only with respect to identifying the impact of the incident. Research was also extended to some initial work on prioritizing based on impact.

In this section we have defined the type of SLA for which an impact assessment mechanism which is based on calculating the actual impact of a system incident on process, financial and strategic goals. The next section details the method that was developed as part of the research.

3. IMPACT ASSESSMENT AND PRIORITY

The method proposed in this section is based on research for relating the system incident to a business impact. The research is still in progress. The method detailed is reflective of the state in which the pilot was conducted.

The method was broken into the following key stages:

STEP 1: Identify business process related to the incident.

STEP 2: Identify participant, customers and process parameters affected by the incident.

STEP 3: Identify relative importance of customer, participants and parameters of process.

STEP 4: Calculate impact of the incident.

STEP 5: Calculate priority of the incident.

STEP 1:

This step involves identifying the portion of the process that is linked the incident. The incident can be either at a system or application level.

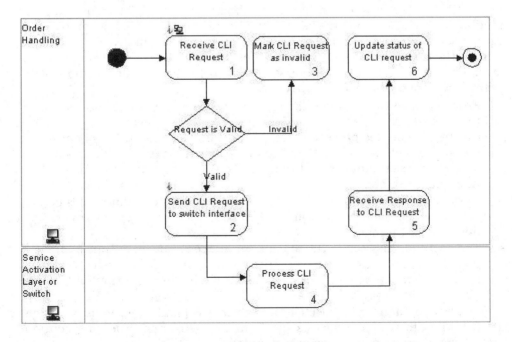

Figure 1: Process for handling CLI requests.

Here we use the process definition and system documentation to identify the process activities that the system or application component is linked to. The essential requirement for this step is that the process definition includes linkage to specific application and system components.

In an environment where BPM technology has been used for definition and orchestration, this information is available from the BPM definition, else the same will need to created. A sample process definition for handling Caller Line Initiation (CLI) requests is shown in figure 1.

Once the process definition is complete, the process and activities should be linked to the participant or customer who is involved in that particular process or activity. This repository of activities, process and systems should be available to users when they report an incident. All incidents should be reported against a process, system or activity. If an incident is raised against a process, the whole process is assumed to be affected. If an incident is raised against an activity, then all the processes in which the activity exists are assumed to be affected. If an incident is reported against a system, then all processes (either directly or through the activity) which are linked to the system are assumed to be affected. Refer to [9] for an approach to identify linkage between system and process.

- The input of this step is the incident and the output is the affected processes.
- The key requirement for this step is a process catalogue, process models (with link to systems) and ensuring that incidents are reported against the system, process, activity or component.

STEP 2:

This step involves identification of the actual process data against the incident. In this step the process execution information is critical. The process execution information is required in a form that is linked to the process model. It was found that a process warehouse had all of the required information in various components. Note: The process warehouse many other components which are not required for the purpose detailed in this paper, but all the components required for the purpose detailed in this paper are available in the process warehouse. Refer to [8] for the description of the process warehouse and its components.

- From a process warehouse the relevant process execution information relevant to the process and activity affected are retrieved. The processes execution includes process state, performance against process parameters (like time), participants in the process instances, specific customers in the process instances and the financial values (including type – revenue, purchase etc.
- In the case of time, the delay between expected time and actual time is calculated for each process and instance in its current state. This is defined as time impact.
- The input of this step is the affected processes and the output is the actual affected processes participants, instance information and customers along with the affected processes. Also included in the output is the time impact on each process instance.
- The key requirement for this step is a process catalogue, process models (with link to systems), process performance goals and process execution information (with link to process models).

STEP 3:

This step involves retrieving the relative importance of the affected participants and customers. Here we typically refer to a static rating of various participants or more sophisticated methods involving data warehouse and business intelligence to retrieve the rating of suppliers. If the rating is static then it is available on a scale of 1 to 10 with 10 being the most important (CEO). If the rating is available through a data warehouse and business intelligence systems then the method to convert the same to the scale is:

- Relative Importance = (1-number of specific customer/[total number of customers+1])*10
- So the topmost customer in a company having 100 customers will have a relative importance of 9.9. The relative rating is retrieved for all affected customers and participants.
- There is also a static rating of relative importance of each process on a scale of 1 to 10 with 10 being the most important. This information is also retrieved for each affected process.
- The input of this step the output of step2 and the output includes the input and the relative importance of each affected process, participants and customers.
- The key requirement for this step is a rating or ranking of each process, participant and customer either on a defined scale or relative to the total list.

STEP 4

This step involves calculation of impact of the incident on each parameter (or business measure), namely participant, customer and process. The parameters chosen here are limited and based on a sample four projects. It is recognized that the list is indicative. The parameters can change across scenarios. No attempt was made to create a consolidated master list of all parameters. The below list contains only those parameters which were used in two or more projects of the sample.

Impact of incident on

- Participant = Total for all affected participants (relative importance of participant)
- Customer = Total for all affected customers (relative importance of customer)
- Financial = Total value across all affected processes instances
- Time = Sum of time across all process instances.
- Process = Total for all related processes (relative importance of process * number of instances of the process]
- This is where the difference due to using process execution information becomes very distinct. An illustration; if process A and B are affected due to two separate systems incidents X and Y respectively. Process B is rated as being 1.5 times as important as A. There are two instances of process A and once instance of process B currently being executed.
- Traditional Method: Process B is rated as higher importance and hence impact of incident Y is higher.
- Proposed Method: Impact of incident Y on process = Impact of incident X on process * 1.5 (relative importance)/ 2 (number of instances). Therefore in this case impact of incident X is 4/3 of Y and hence impact of X is greater.
- The output of this stage is the impact of the incident along various parameters.

STEP 5

This stage is currently still under research and involves calculation of a relative priority based on the impact of the incident on the various parameters and other factors. The research at this stage is limited to using only the measure of impact to determine priority. The relationship of other factors like resolution time to priority of incidents has been identified as future research direction in later sections.

- This stage is dependent on the relative priority of each parameter. This has been referred to as impact weight. Proposed here is a method used for calculating the relative priority based on the impact weight and impact. The aspect of determining the impact weight is research in progress.
- Priority of incident = Total of (Impact Weight * Impact of incident on parameter or business measure).
- In the case of pilot the impact weight was determined using a team of business and technology participants from the organization who reviewed the relation of each parameter or business measure against the organization objectives. This approach will need to be reviewed where there is any change in organizational objectives. There is ongoing research to look at methods to determine the impact weight.
- In this section, we have defined the method for calculating the impact of the incident on various business measure or parameters using process execution information and definitions. Later we have gone on to define a method for calculation of relative priority from impact.

4. WHY PROCESS WAREHOUSE?

Let us review the key requirements for the approach that has been detailed. They are:

1. The process data would need to be stored outside the existing systems as it is required even when the system is not available.
2. The process needs to be modeled and stored in a format that is accessible.
3. The process data should be correlated to the process models.
4. The process models should contain information regarding the users, supplier and customers.
5. Process models should have compliance requirements and penalties.
6. Support resources should be able to model the prioritization "formulae" and maintain the same.
7. Rating mechanisms for supplier, customer, and users should be available.

When looking at these requirements it seems logical to look at a process warehouse as proposed by Kannan [8]. All the common for the proposed approach are available in the components of the process warehouse identified by Kannan[8].

5. WHY AUTOMATE PRIORITIZATION

This though a future research direction, warrants a separate section as we believe that automatic prioritization of incidents based on impact of the same on strategic objectives can revolutionize application support by laying the foundation for shared resources in support.

Let us consider a scenario where the same pool of resources is required to support multiple applications. The support resources will be required to prioritize incidents not just within an application, but across applications. This would require the support resources to have required knowledge of all applications and the business environment. This might not be feasible when dealing with complex applications.

Therefore an approach which does not depend on the knowledge of the support resources is the foundations for having a common pool of resources support multiple applications. The method proposed here for prioritization can be automated. The cost benefit analysis and applicability in various scenarios need to be studied.

6. FURTHER RESEARCH

Following are the key aspects which need further research:

- Impact of other criteria like "resolution time" which will need to be used along with impact for calculation of prioritization. Though it was recognized that various other factors influence prioritization of incidents, the current state of research has been focused on calculating impact and the role of impact on prioritization.
- Effort will have to be taken to identify additional business measures and parameters along which impact can be measured.
- Method for identification of "impact weight".
- Research is also required into grouping the incidents based on their relative priority and also address the impact of relative priority on the queuing of incidents.
- Research is also required into better definition of SLA on business performance measures and converting the same into process measures, relative priority of participants, relative priority of customers and relative priority of process.

7. CONCLUSION

This paper is based on research to create a model for calculating the business impact of incidents in IT service management. The research has been done to eliminate the need for knowledge resources in prioritization of incidents and to increase the accuracy of prioritization by basing the same on the calculation of actual impact versus assuming a certain impact.

- The method proposed in the paper is applicable only to support of applications which support business processes within an organizations and are not applicable to reporting and analysis systems.
- The method proposed in this paper using the process definitions and process execution information to determine the actual impact of any system or application incident on various business measures and use this impact to determine the relative priority of the incident.

Definitions

Detailed here are some definitions of terminologies used in the paper. Some of these definitions are viewpoints and have to be regarding as such.

[i] Impact: This refers to identifying the value of an incident along various identified business measures. The impact of any incident can be assessed along one or more unique business measures.

[ii) Priority: This refers to relative priority of incidents based on the weighted (using the impact weight of each measure) average of the impact along various measures.

[iii] Impact Weight: This refers to the multiplier for each business measure or parameter in the impact assessment to relate the same to the other impact measures.

[iv] Incident: This refers to a problem that is reported in an application. The incident can range from total system outage to data or logic problems.

[v] Process Catalog: This refers to a catalog of all the processes existing in the organization. The information includes the process name, description and owner. The information items mentioned here are those required for the purpose detailed in this paper, more information can be stored against the process in the catalog to suit other purposes.

[vi] Process Models - In order document and share understanding of the business process, a model of the process is required along and the different process steps (activities) involved. The granularity and standards for modeling are quite varied. For purposes detailed in this paper, the standards used were BPMN. Though no standard or approach has been detailed for granularity, suffice to say that the granularity of processes modeling will influence the granularity and accuracy of impact analysis and prioritization.

[vii] Process Execution Data: This refers to the actual data within the application which refers to the execution of the process. This includes financial information, customers and users of the executed process.

[viii] Legal and Regulatory Compliance: This refers to the activities or process which are related to legal or regulatory compliance and have a penalty associated with them. This information was to be linked to the relevant activity or process.

References

Claudio Bartolini, Mathias Salle, "Business Driven Prioritization of Service Incidents" 2004

Kathiresan Lakshmanan, "The Importance of Classifying Incidents, Service Calls" 2005

M. J. Buco, R. N. Chang, L. Z. Luan, C. Ward, J. L. Wolf, and P. S. Yu, "Utility computing SLA management based upon business objectives"

http://www.itil.org.uk

Ken Turbitt, "ITIL -The Business Perspective Approach", 2005

Ken Turbitt , "Why You Should Follow ITIL's Business Perspective Approach"

Edward Wustenhoff, "Service Level Agreement in the Data Center", 2002

Nari Kannan, "Process Warehouse: The Missing Link in Business Performance Management", 2005

Mayank Gupta, Udhai Reddy, "Assessing the Operational Impact of Changes in business", 2004

Constructing a Workflow Application System to Conduct CMMI Processes in Software Development Teams

Dr. Yang Chi-Tsai, Flowring, Taiwan

ABSTRACT

CMMI (Capability Maturity Model Integration) is a process-oriented reference model developed by SEI (Software Engineering Institute) of CMU (Carnegie-Mellon University) to define the maturity levels of software development organizations. It is widely adopted by numerous software firms in USA, India and Japan to ensure their capability to deliver quality software products/projects to the customers during whole project life cycle.

CMMI provides all the stakeholders in software projects with common languages through software development cycles in both development and management aspects. It defines several process areas (PAs) across maturity level (ML) 2 to 5. For example, in ML2 there are seven PAs guiding the processes for project planning (PP), requirement management (REQM), configuration management (CM), project monitoring control (PMC), product and product quality assurance (PPQA), measurement and analysis (MA), and supplier agreement management (SAM).

The article describes the software architecture, supporting software components and the analysis methodology to map the processes in CMMI PAs to WfMS (workflow management system) process definition. The work described in the article is motivated by the idea to automate the software processes and provide sufficient tool support for the operations of CMMI ML3 software organizations. It demonstrates the capability of WfMS to enhance the whole lifecycle quality of product development and project delivery in software development organizations. In terms of contribution to the information technology, it gives several workflow integration scenarios with external application systems such as document management system (DMS) for document revision control, CASE (computer-aided software engineering) tools for issue tracking, and configuration management.

1. INTRODUCTION

CMMI is a framework that contains key process elements to build software systems. It can be used as the guidelines for software teams to establish quality software processes. The process capability and the organizational maturity defined in CMMI can be used to assert the capability of an organization to perform some software engineering tasks defined in the process. In CMMI's *staged representation*, when we say that a software organization is at a particular CMMI maturity level, it implies that the organization is capable of performing some sets (i.e. process areas) of processes.

The core model of CMMI is CMMI/SE/SW (system engineering and software engineering). If the organization needs to focus on early and continuous stakeholder involvement, it can adopt the extended model CMMI/SE /SW/IPPD (integrated product and process development). If the activities about supplier and sourcing are considered, it can adopt the CMMI/SE/

SW/IPPD/SS (supplier and sourcing) model. CMMI also excerpts the CMMI-AM (CMMI Acquisition Module) from the CMMI model for beginning process improvement.

Maturity Levels		Process Category and Process Area			
		Process Management	Project Management	Engineering	Support
2	Managed (7 PAs)		PP PMC SAM	REQM	CM PPQA MA
3	Defined (11 PAs)	OPF OPD OT	IPM RSKM	RD VER TS VAL PI	DAR
4	Quantitative managed (2 PAs)	OPP	QPM		
5	Optimizing (2 PAs)	OID			CAR

Acronym List

CAR – Causal analysis and resolution

CM – Configuration management

DAR – Decision analysis and resolution

IPM – Integrated product management

MA – Measurement and analysis

OID – Organizational innovation and deployment

OPD – Organizational process Definition

OPF – Organizational process Focus

OPP – Organizational process performance

OT – Organizational training

PI – Product integration

PMC – Project monitoring and control

PP – Project planning

PPQA – Process and product quality assurance

QPM – Quantitative project management

RD – Requirement development

REQM – Requirement management

RSKM – Risk management

SAM – Supplier agreement management

TS – Technical solution

VAL – Validation

VER – Verification

Note: **ISM** – Integrated supplier management, **IT**—Integrated training, **OEI**—Organizational environment for integration are PAs that only appear in CMMI / SE / SW / IPPD / SS. They are not list in the table.

Table 1. CMMI maturity level, process categories, and process areas in the staged representation

CMMI categorizes the processes and activities in the software development teams into four groups in terms of the following aspects: organizational process management, project management, engineering, and supporting. In each process categories, CMMI defines several Process Areas (PAs) as the responsibility for the software development team to establish the customized process definitions, according to the software development teams, characteristic and the specific goals listed in each process area. It then requires the software development team to perform them. For example, in the 'Project Plan (PP) process area, CMMI lists Specific Practices (SP) in each Specific Goal (SG):

SG for PP	SP for PP
SG1: Establish estimates	SP 1.1-1 Estimate the Scope of the Project
	SP 1.2-1 Establish Estimates of Work Product and Task Attributes
	SP 1.3-1 Define Project Life Cycle
	SP 1.4-1 Determine Estimates of Effort and Cost
SG2: Develop a project plan	SP 2.1-1 Establish the Budget and Schedule
	SP 2.2-1 Identify Project Risks
	SP 2.3-1 Plan for Data Management
	SP 2.4-1 Plan for Project Resources
	SP 2.5-1 Plan for Needed Knowledge and Skills
	SP 2.6-1 Plan Stakeholder Involvement
	SP 2.7-1 Establish the Project Plan
SG3: Obtain commitment to the plan	SP 3.1-1 Review Plans that Affect the Project
	SP 3.2-1 Reconcile Work and Resource Levels
	SP 3.3-1 Obtain Plan Commitment

Table 2. CMMI specific goals and specific practices for project plan process area

To consider the *SG* and *SP* in the project plan process area, the software development team usually takes the following actions so that the practices in the PA can be proficient:

1. Review the team's existing PP-related activities and practices against the ones in the PA.
2. To refine and clarify the responsibility of team roles, the team should clearly define the roles and responsibility for the practices. For example, the *project manager* is assigned to SP1.3-1, SP2.1-1. The project manager, the domain expert, and the IT expert in the team work together to identify the project risk for SP2.2-1.
3. Set up the mechanism for the team to perform the practices that are not well performed or not performed. The senior team members or consultants may (1) Arrange the training courses for team members, (2) Write working instructions as the guidance for such practices, (3) Choose software tools to support the practices if the selected tools greatly reduce the human effort, or (4) Develop workflow applications to enforce or guide the practices if the practice is too complicated to follow by the team. For example, the practice may involve multiple stakeholders need sophisticated activities collaboration.
4. Establish the auditing mechanism to make sure the practices are regularly performed without exception.

Based on the actions taken by the software development teams, we can observe the opportunities that the WfMS (Workflow Management System) can help when the software development teams are conducting CMMI-based process improvements. The following are the WfMS' major contributions to CMMI-based process improvements:

1. For the process management category, WfMS directs the team with process-oriented viewpoint of software project development. Several practices in OPD can be supported by common workflow tools. For example, the 'Establish Standard Processes SP' can be supported by the process modeling tool in WfMS, and the 'Establish the Organization's Process Asset Library SP' can be achieved by using WfMS' processes definition repository features. The 'Establish Process Performance Measures SP' of OPP process area can be implemented by the process performance monitoring module in most workflow systems.

2. For software project monitoring and management, WfMS can model the major life-cycle processes and activities of the software development project, so that WfMS' process state monitor and process execution history can be provided as part of information for software project monitoring and management. During the process run-time, the process instance for some specific software project would transit among several process states and move through process nodes according to the process definition and the run-time activities of software development progress (e.g. to check-in the software test plan to the document management system to complete a workflow task named 'submit software test plan') and project management decisions (e.g. to decide by checking/reviewing the completeness of previous project execution artifacts). The iteration of software life-cycle stages/nodes, major project progress and milestones, and process execution history can be recorded and reflected directly in the WfMS' process execution monitor.

3. WfMS models and implements the supportive software processes and activities so that the major software development processes can invoke those supporting processes when necessary. These supportive processes can also be invoked by the periodical state-checking programs if they have detected that some pre-defined trigger conditions are satisfied. The concept of separating the possible workflow processes found in the CMMI-based processes into 'major life-cycle processes' and 'supportive software processes' helps to construct the processes structure in the WfMS. The concept is also helpful for further process tailoring if the software life-cycle stages or procedures in supportive processes change according to organizational policies.

4. To integrate software engineering tools in the CMMI-based processes, the WfMS can interact with software engineering tools through APIs or in other forms of tool interaction interface. With the help of the software engineering tool integration, the end-user interface in the WfMS can act as the more simple front-end of software engineering tools. Software development team members can interact with the software engineering tools more easily by means of process-controlled environments and simplified user interfaces.

   In addition, the WfMS can suggest and remind the team members through workflow's *worklist* to help and enforce them to use the associated software engineering tools at the right time. This enforces and improves the usage of software engineering tools during the software life-cycle. Without the support of WfMS, the team members usually fail to or forget to follow the correct procedures when the project artifact or information needs to be updated into the required software engineering tools. Therefore the information in the software project cannot be correctly reflected to the project managers and members.

2. DEFINE AND ESTABLISH SOFTWARE PROCESSES FOR CMMI-BASED PROCESS IMPROVEMENT

CMMI is a process-oriented model, which describes lots of best practices categorized by process areas for the software development teams to consider the space for improvement in their existing processes. According to CMMI's definition, a process area is *a cluster of related practices in an area that satisfy a set of goal considered important for making significant improvement in that area.* Therefore, there are no 'standard processes' defined in the CMMI for software development teams to follow.

For an enterprise to establish software processes for its software development teams based on CMMI process improvement, the first step is to establish and define its own basic software development processes according to the enterprise's business characteristics (i.e. the customer types, the product or project types, the business management policies). The process definitions for the enterprise must be checked against enterprise's daily business and software development needs, so they certainly contain some activities that are not in the scope of CMMI.

After the processes has been defined for enterprise's actual needs, the SGs and SPs (specific goals and specific practices) list in the related CMMI PA can be used to check the improvement possibility for current basic processes. For example, in the process definition for the software team to make project plans, if it lacks the *'identify project risks'* activity after check the process definition against the SGs/SPs in Table 2, the team can refine the current process definition by adding workflow activities to make sure the 'project risk identification' can be executed in every project plan process.

Define and Establish the Basic Software Process Environment

The procedures to define basic software processes for software development teams are the same as define business processes for the enterprise. Firstly the process modeling elements such as process nodes, roles, artifacts, and other supportive applications are identified for process analysis.

There are several business process modeling notations can be used to express the business processes. For example, we can choose from the activity diagram of UML, BPMN, or the vendor-specific notations for their own process modeling tools. As shown in Figure 1, different departments of one enterprise may describe the software development project from different viewpoints and detail levels. If the goal is to construct workflow-enabled applications to conduct the CMMI software processes, it is better to choose the viewpoint that is much closer to software-oriented domains. Figure 2 shows the analysis result prepared from software development viewpoint.

After the basic activities that are directly related to software development are defined, the software team can then step to the next stage to plan supportive processes such as configuration management activities.

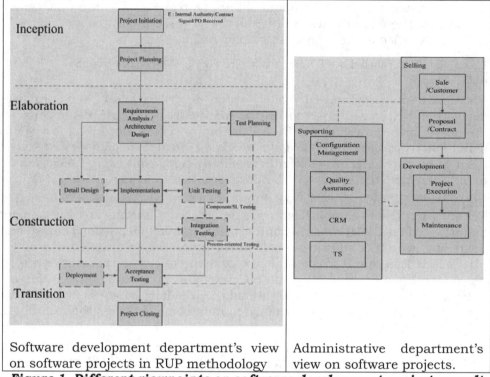

| Software development department's view on software projects in RUP methodology | Administrative department's view on software projects. |

Figure 1. Different viewpoints on software development projects result in different analysis output

In CMMI the SGs are usually categorized into two types of actions: **establish** and **invoke**. Therefore, in short, to define and establish the basic software processes, the members who are in charge of constructing the CMMI-based process improvement environment can follow the steps below:

1. Describe the current core software processes in some form of process modeling notation.
2. Identify and define supportive activities such as configuration management or decision analysis and resolution.
3. Assign senior members or software engineering tool mentors to plan the procedures and deploy the mechanism to **establish** the environment make sure the software-related activities can be executed.
4. Train and assign roles to practice and **invoke** the activities under the established environment.

Factors to Consider During Adaptation and Refinement

It is often that the enterprise already has established the software development environment based on some form of quality management system and software development methodology. Sometimes the enterprise has several kinds of software projects and development environments.

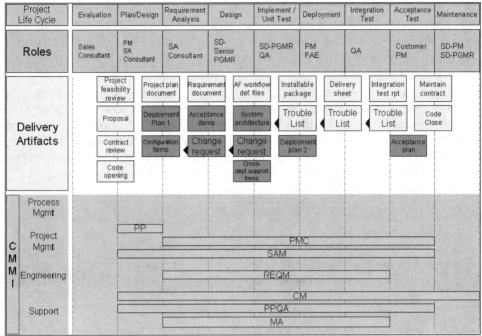

Figure 2. A sample analysis describing the relationship between development stages, roles, artifacts, and PAs

For example, in the real world the enterprise has to make the CMMI-based process improvement activities and processes to work with the ISO 9000:2000 QMS standards. In addition, it needs to consider and deal with the variances in different development teams, such as:

- Different life-cycle models: XP (eXtreme Programming), RUP (Rational Unified Process), waterfall model.
- Different analysis and design methods: Structured analysis and design, object-oriented analysis and design
- Different programming style: Traditional programming languages (i.e. C, C++, Java), RAD (Rapid Application Development) prototype tools.
- Different project types: Customization project, product project, porting project, maintenance project, etc.

Boris and Harvey have discussed in detail to explore the CMMI and ISO 9000:2000 synergy. They also provide a good transition guide between CMMI and ISO in both directions. Because the document control procedure is mandatory in ISO 9000, there are lots of off-the-shelf document control application packages to choose from. For software development teams that lack some form of document control, they can easily build the document control mechanism by applying the ISO 9000's document framework (i.e. use the document structure for quality manual, quality procedures, work instruction and checklist, forms and records.)

3. SOFTWARE ARCHITECTURES TO INTEGRATING CMMI-BASED PROCESS IMPROVEMENT ENVIRONMENTS

To support the CMMI-based process improvement environments, the software architecture depicted in Figure 3 adopts three main systems to build the application environment: (1) Workflow management system, (2) Document management system, and (3) Supporting tool for specific software engineering tasks.

Under the software architecture, stakeholders in the software development environment use the Web browser to operate the workflow application systems and the document management systems. These two systems are integrated into single Web-based process portal and share the same account system via the single sign-on feature.

The supporting tools are external to the workflow and document management systems. The software development team members may operate these tools through the native GUI provided by the supporting tools. Sometimes, in some situation, the team members may use the workflow application's GUI as the front-end, and let the workflow application to communicate with the external supporting tools through APIs or other forms of program interactions.

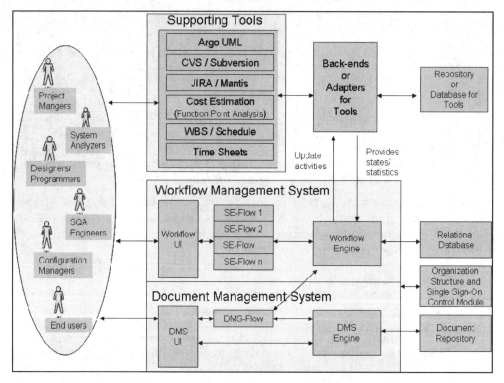

Figure 3. The software architecture for CMMI-based process improvement environment

WfMS and Workflow Applications

The workflow applications are developed on top of the WfMS platform. There are two types of workflow applications shown in the Figure 2. One is SE-Flow and the other is DMS-Flow. Some SE-Flows are major software life-cycle processes to control the progress and stages/state transition of a running software project. Other SE-Flows are supportive processes invoked by the major life-cycle processes or the periodically executed project-states detection programs.

The DMS-Flows are workflow processes that control the approval sequence when some artifacts of software developments (e.g. QMS procedures, project plan document, meeting minutes of project kick-off meetings, risk analysis report for projects) are moving in or out from the DMS repository.

The workflow UI is presented to the end-users by a Web-based enterprise process portal that provides the features such as worklist for workflow tasks, workflow process launcher, and other general web applications. In the process portal, the project dashboard can be implemented as a general web application that aggregates information from all workflow processes of the same software project to provide the project manager with necessary information to monitor the project states, progress, pending tasks and issues waiting for decision, etc.

Document Management System

The document management system is seamlessly integrated with the WfMS to deal with the part of the working artifacts in the software development process. For example, the document for the QMS process definition, the meeting minutes for the project kick-off meeting or review meeting. Generally speaking, in the CMMI-based process improving, the artifacts to be managed by the DMS can be categorized into the following artifact types:

- Processes definition and procedures
- Work instructions and guidelines
- Templates for Forms and check lists
- Records by filling or extending the templates

The DMS can optionally add the *text translation* module on top of the AEPP (Agentflow Enterprise Process Portal) to translate the display language. Currently the module provides only the translation between Traditional and Simplified Chinese. The *search engine* module in the DMS provides full-text search in the document repository. The *document security* module works with the access control module to protect the document in the DMS from unauthorized print out or duplication.

The DMS processes provides the DMS with more flexible process control over the document-related activities such as document check-in, check-out, creation, renewal, revision, expiration. The process to control such activities can be customized by the process definition tool in the WfMS.

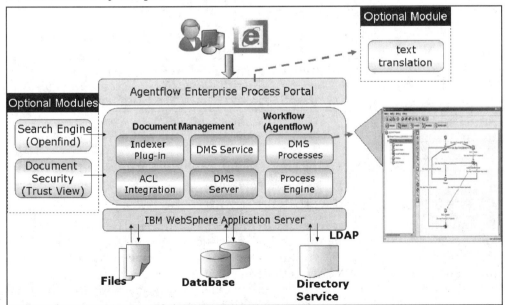

Figure 4. Typical document management system integration with WfMS

Supportive Software Engineering Tools

There are several supportive software engineering tools that work with CMMI-based process improvement. In this section, we introduce some of the tasks supported by the tools and the integration method in the system environment. As shown in the Table 4, several software engineering tasks can be supported by off-the-shelf open source tools or commercial products. Most of the tools provide standard and common methods for tool integration mechanism.

Task to perform	Tool name	Integration method	Mechanism
Requirements in UML use case	ARGO UML	XMI file format	Standard exchangeable file format in XML
Version control and configuration management	CVS, Subversion	Subversion client library for pure Java, C, and Perl	API for programming language
Effort and cost estimation in function point	FPA (Function Point Analyzer)	HTTP-based file upload for UML use-case. Web Services interaction	File exchange Standard Web-Services API
Change management and issue tracking	JIRA	Java API for JIRA	API for programming language
Effort measurement	Time Sheet	Open the database tables and schema	Shared database tables
Test supporting tools	JUnit	Java API	API for programming language
	STAF (Software Testing Automation Framework)	Through services written in C/C++, Java	API for programming language
Automatic build tools	Ant	Java API	API for programming language

Table 4: Possible software engineering tools in CMMI-based process improvements

4. WEAVE SGS/SPS IN CMMI PAS TOGETHER INTO EXECUTABLE WORKFLOW PROCESSES

To implement the CMMI processes in WfMS according to the analysis result and process definitions mentioned in the previous sections, it is not trivial to implement each PA or SG as an independent workflow processes. As we mentioned before, the PA only acts as key process elements. It is the duty of workflow designers to weave the separate SG/SP workflow activities together into a complete workflow process definition. For example, when we model a business process named *making plans for a new project*, we may include several SPs of *PP*, *SAM* and *PMC* as the process nodes inside the workflow process.

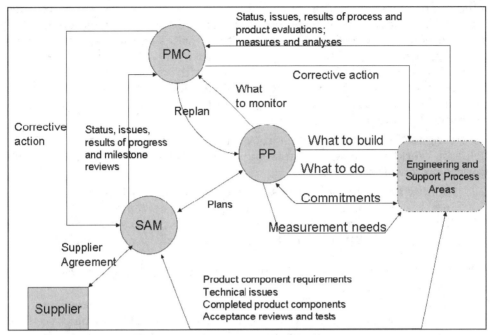

Figure 5. The basic interactions between PAs of the project management category

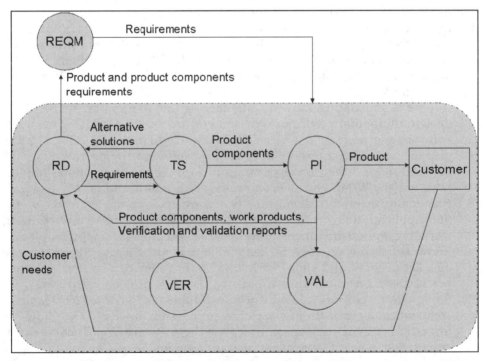

Figure 6. More example, the interactions between PAs of the engineering category

There are no mandatory rules in CMMI for grouping several SPs across different PAs inside one workflow process. The grouping philosophy may depend on how the software development team's management and development tasks are assigned to roles or departments. As shown in Figure 5, there are several interactions between PAs in the project management categories. For these interactions, the workflow designers should set the priority to implement them as the executable workflows. High priority activities or the tasks that should be enforced by the workflow can be arranged in the scope of early workflow application construction plans. Interactions with low priority or minor affect for the business can be practiced in the development team in the form of human executed procedures (with the guideline or work instruction as the reference documents).

According to the policy described above, the following hints can be applied to help the workflow designers to weave the CMMI practices into executable workflow processes:

1. Identify and define the core software development processes in terms of business needs, as described in the previous sections.
2. Review the SG from the PAs against the core process activities. If there are applicable SPs in some SG to improve the raw activities, pick up the SP, say *SP_ X*, for further consideration.
3. Decide how the *SP_X* can be practiced. The following are some possible decisions:
4. Make it an item in the checklist for some workflow activities. The stakeholders who participate in the workflow should manually confirm the *SP_X* is executed and then update the corresponding checklist item.
5. Make it one or more workflow activities. The workflow designer adds process nodes in the workflow and implements the related functions to guide the *SP_X* execution on the computer.
6. Make it a sub-process in the workflow. The workflow designer implements the sub-process in the WfMS and makes a call to the sub-process from the parent workflow. If one SP is applicable to several circumstances in the software development life-cycle, it is a good candidate for a sub-process.
7. If there is an existing software engineering tool to support the *SP_X*, design interaction scenarios between end-users, WfMS, and supportive software engineering tool. The usual action is to make *SP_X* a integrated process node that interacts with existing software engineering tools through API or other forms of program-to-program interaction. In addition, use the WfMS end-user interface as the front-end for the tools.
8. Practically, when a real-world software project is managed in the workflow application environment, it must have several concurrent running workflow process instances to control the activities for the project teams. For workflow designers, it is reasonable to model the workflow processes as a set of small and short workflows so that they can be flexibly composed and interlinked for complicated software project execution.
9. Some WfMSs can provide advanced mechanisms like *inter-workflow communication* for running workflow process instances to exchange information or synchronization. Because the software project can be represented as a set of loosely-coupled process instances, using the mechanism can significantly simplify the CMMI process modeling. It also makes the result process definition diagram more clear and readable.
10. Finally, we can find some SPs important to the software processes but not included in any main workflow processes. For these SPs, consider their external trigger condition in the project execution environment and then design an agent program to monitor these trigger conditions to invoke the SP's workflow process.

5. SOFTWARE ENGINEERING TOOLS THAT SUPPORT CMMI PROCESSES

In CMMI process areas, there are a lot of software engineering activities, such as project plan, requirement tracking, cost estimation, integration testing, can be supported by off-the-shelf commercial (e.g. Borland, IBM/Rational) or open source (e.g. TIGRIS.org) software packages. As mentioned in the previous section, the WfMS can integrate these software engineering tools into the application environment for CMMI through several mechanisms. By bringing the usage of software engineering tools under the control of WfMS, stakeholders in the software development teams can be reminded through their worklist to update/insert information to these tools. This solves the problem of (1) no *remind* mechanism for SE tools operation, and (2) no technical enforcement on all stakeholders.

By viewing the software engineering tool as a software service that provides several functions to the public through APIs or Web Services, the WfMS can orchestrate multiple tools to combine their functions to build higher-level software engineering tasks. Of course, the WfMS solves only the issues of *process orchestration* by means of workflow or Web Services orchestration mechanisms like ASAP/Wf-XML 2.0 or BPEL. The application environment designers should deal with the semantic of exchanged data among orchestrated software engineering tools.

Process Category	ML2 & ML3 PAs	Major Tools	Explanation
Process mgmt	OPD	WfMS process definition tool, e.g. Agentflow®	Use process definition tool to model executable process definition.
	OPF, OT	DMS	Use DMS to manage the process policy, guideline, work instruction, and course material. The team members access the material through DMS.
Project mgmt	PP	1. MS Project 2. Function point analyzer	1. Plan for resource and schedules. 2. Use function point analyzer to estimate cost.
	PMC	JIRA	Train the team members to update project progress and issue status in JIRA
	SAM	Flow Application	Implement "Software project outsourcing" workflow application to control to supplier agreement management PA.
	IPM, RSKM	DMS	Guide the team member to fill the risk analysis form with the template stored in DMS.

Engineering	REQM, RD	1. RTM tool 2. DMS	1. Use RTM tool to track the requirement mapping. 2. Requirement documents are managed by the DMS.
	VER, VAL	Test suites V&V tools	Follow QMS team's work procedures.
	TS, PI	DMS	Use the template in DMS to guide the process of TS and PI.
Support	CM	CVS, Subversion	Source code check-in and check-out.
	PPQA	Test tools	Use test tools to work with: test script, test suite, test configuration, test log, and test report.
	MA	Time sheets (home-brew)	Link with accounting system to calculate project effort and cost Calculate the effort distribution across software life-cycle stages.
	DAR	Template from DMS	Check out the template from the DMS to guide the DAR conducting steps.

Table 5. Tool adoption example in CMMI-based process improvements

6. CONCLUSION

In this article we explored the possibility of applying WfMSs in constructing an application environment for a CMMI-based process improvement. For a software team to increase the maturity level defined in the CMMI, it usually needs to adopt better software practices. As the number of practices increase, it appears that the WfMS' process-oriented modeling capability can help the workflow designer to weave these practices naturally to an organization's existing software development processes. The *weaved practices* in the workflow processes assure more unawareness of important software practices during the project execution.

In addition, the software architecture for the application environment allows the WfMS, software engineering tools and DMS to work together. The application integration (i.e. EAI–enterprise application integration) and process orchestration capability in WfMS bring together several software engineering tools to conduct higher level software engineering tasks. The WfMS and DMS work together to provide the document control procedures for procedures/instructions/guidelines used in CMMI processes, as well as the practical evidence such as documents, forms and records.

In the application system, stakeholders of the software project can collaborate on the WfMS-enabled work platform for software development, project control with supportive processes and tools.

Section 3

Appendices

WfMC Structure and Membership Information

WHAT IS THE WORKFLOW MANAGEMENT COALITION?

The Workflow Management Coalition, founded in August 1993, is a non-profit, international organization of workflow vendors, users, analysts and university/research groups. The Coalition's mission is to promote and develop the use of workflow through the establishment of standards for software terminology, interoperability and connectivity between workflow products. Comprising more than 250 members spread throughout the world, the Coalition is the primary standards body for this software market.

WORKFLOW STANDARDS FRAMEWORK

The Coalition has developed a framework for the establishment of workflow standards. This framework includes five categories of interoperability and communication standards that will allow multiple workflow products to co-exist and interoperate within a user's environment. Technical details are included in the white paper entitled, "The Work of the Coalition," available at www.wfmc.org.

ACHIEVEMENTS

The initial work of the Coalition focused on publishing the Reference Model and Glossary, defining a common architecture and terminology for the industry. A major milestone was achieved with the publication of the first versions of the Workflow API (WAPI) specification, covering the Workflow Client Application Interface, and the Workflow Interoperability specification. The Audit Data specification was added in 1997, being followed by the Process Definition Import/Export specification.

Achievements in 2005 included the release of XPDL 2.0 which has generated strong support throughout the industry. The Coalition has validated the use of its specifications through international demonstrations and prototype implementations. In direct response to growing user demand, live demonstrations of a workflow interoperability scenario have shown how business can successfully exchange and process work across multiple workflow products using the Coalition's specifications.

WORKFLOW MANAGEMENT COALITION STRUCTURE

The Coalition is divided into three major committees, the Technical Committee, the External Relations Committee, and the Steering Committee. Small working groups exist within each committee for the purpose of defining workflow terminology, interoperability and connectivity standards, conformance requirements, and for assisting in the communication of this information to the workflow user community.

The Coalition's major committees meet three times per calendar year for three days at a time, with meetings usually alternating between a North American and a European location. The working group meetings are held during these three days, and as necessary throughout the year.

Coalition membership is open to all interested parties involved in the creation, analysis or deployment of workflow software systems. Membership is governed by a Document of Understanding, which outlines meeting regulations, voting rights etc. Membership material is available at www.wfmc.org.

COALITION WORKING GROUPS

The Coalition has established a number of Working Groups, each working on a particular area of specification. The working groups are loosely structured around the "Workflow Reference Model" which provides the framework for the Coalition's standards program. The Reference Model identifies the common characteristics of workflow systems and defines five discrete functional interfaces through which a workflow management system interacts with its environment—users, computer tools and applications, other software services, etc. Working groups meet individually, and also under the umbrella of the Technical Committee, which is responsible for overall technical direction and co-ordination.

WORKFLOW REFERENCE MODEL DIAGRAM

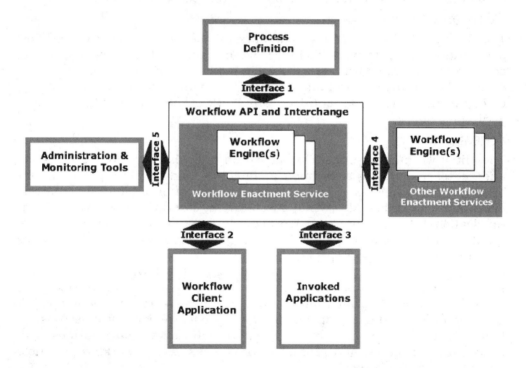

WHY YOU SHOULD JOIN

Being a member of the Workflow Management Coalition gives you the unique opportunity to participate in the creation of standards for the workflow industry as they are developing. Your contributions to our community ensure that progress continues in the adoption of royalty-free workflow and process standards.

MEMBERSHIP CATEGORIES

The Coalition has three major categories of membership per the membership matrix following. **All employees worldwide** are welcome to attend all meetings, and will be permitted access to the *Members Only* area of our web site.

Full Membership is appropriate for Workflow and Business Process Management (BPM) vendors, analysts and consultants. You may include up to three active members from your organization on your application and these may be replaced at any time by notifying us accordingly.

	Full Member	Associate /Academic Member	Individual Member	Fellow (by election only)	Visitor
Annual fee	$3500	$1500	$500	$0	$100 per day
Hold office	Yes	Yes	Yes	Yes	No
Nominate somebody for office	Yes	Yes	No	No	No
Committee membership	Yes	Yes	Yes	Yes	Observer
Voting right on standards	Yes	Yes	Active Participants only	Active Participants only	No
Voting right on WfMC.org business	Yes	Current officers only	Current officers only	Current officers only	No
Company reps in Meetings without visitor fee	4 (transfer-able)	1 (transfer-able)	individual only	individual only	Fee required

FULL MEMBERSHIP

This corporate category offers exclusive visibility in this sector at events and seminars across the world, enhancing your customers' perception of you as an industry authority, on our web site, in the Coalition Handbook and CDROM, by speaking opportunities, access to the Members Only area of our web site, attending the Coalition meetings and most importantly within the workgroups whereby through discussion and personal involvement, using your voting power, you can contribute actively to the development of standards and interfaces.

Full member benefits include:

- Financial incentives: 50 percent discount all "brochure-ware" (such as our annual CDROM Companion to the Workflow Handbook, advertising on our sister-site www.e-workflow.org), $500 credit toward next year's fee for at least 60 percent per year meeting attendance or if you serve as an officer of the WfMC.
- Web Visibility: a paragraph on your company services/products with links to your own company website.
- User RFIs: (Requests for Information) is an exclusive privilege to all full members. We often have queries from user organizations looking for specific workflow solutions. These valuable leads can result in real business benefits for your organization.
- Publicity: full members may choose to have their company logos including collaterals displayed along with WfMC material at conferences / expos we attend. You may also list corporate events and press releases (relating to WfMC issues) on the relevant pages on the website, and have a company entry in the annual Coalition Workflow Handbook

- Speaking Opportunities: We frequently receive calls for speakers at industry events because many of our members are recognized experts in their fields. These opportunities are forwarded to Full Members for their direct response to the respective conference organizers.

ASSOCIATE AND ACADEMIC MEMBERSHIP

Associate and Academic Membership is appropriate for those (such as IT user organizations) who need to keep abreast of workflow developments, but who are not workflow vendors. It allows voting on decision-making issues, including the publication of standards and interfaces but does not permit anything near the amount of visibility or incentives provided to a Full Member. You may include up to three active members from your organization on your application.

INDIVIDUAL MEMBERSHIP

Individual Membership is appropriate for self-employed persons or small user companies. Employees of workflow vendors, academic institutions or analyst organizations are not typically eligible for this category. Individual membership is held in one person's name only, is not a corporate membership, and is not transferable within the company. If three or more people within a company wish to participate in the WfMC, it would be cost-effective to upgrade to corporate Associate Membership whereby all employees worldwide are granted membership status.

FELLOWS

The WfMC recognizes individuals from within its existing membership who have made sustained and outstanding contributions to WfMC objectives far and above that expected from normal member representation.

VISITORS

We welcome visitors at our meetings; it is an excellent opportunity for you to observe first hand the process of creating standards and to network with members of the Coalition. Your role will be as an observer only, and you are not eligible for a password, or for special offers available to WfMC members. You must pre-register and prepay your Visitor attendance fee. If you decide to join WfMC within 30 days of the meeting, your membership dues will be credited with your visitor fee.

HOW TO JOIN

Complete the form on the Coalition's website, or contact the Coalition Secretariat, at the address below. All members are required to sign the Coalition's "Document of Understanding" which sets out the contractual rights and obligations between members and the Coalition.

THE SECRETARIAT

Workflow Management Coalition (WfMC)
email: wfmc@wfmc.org / URL: www.wfmc.org
2436 North Federal Highway #374,
Lighthouse Point, FL 33064, United States
Phone +1 954 782 3376, Fax +1 954 782 6365

Workflow Management Coalition Membership Directory

WfMC's membership comprises a wide range of organizations. All members in good standing as of January 2006 are listed here. There are currently two main classes of paid membership: *Full Members* and *Associate Members* (which includes *Academic*). *Individual Members* are not listed. Each company has only one primary point of contact for purposes of the Membership Directory. Within this Directory, many *Full* Members have used their privilege to include information about their organization or products. The current list of members and membership structure can be found on our website, **wfmc.org**.

ACI WORLDWIDE
Full Member
330 South 108th Avenue, Omaha, NE 68154, USA
www.aciworldwide.com
Linda L. Lane, Product Manager
Tel: [1] 800-755-1596 /Fax: [1] 402-333-9725
lanel@aciworldwide.com
Since 1975, ACI Worldwide has provided software solutions to the world's innovators. ACI WorkPoint® is a comprehensive BPM suite that coordinates all aspects of a process—people, rules, tasks and systems—into a cohesive whole. Representing over a decade of development and customer deployment, WorkPoint executes business processes from the simplest to the most complex. Among its many features and functionalities, WorkPoint offers open API's for creating process definitions and instances. WorkPoint also allows you to take advantage of Web services and incorporate disparate legacy applications with new functionality. The WorkPoint product suite also includes a Business Rules Engine (BRE) that enables business users to graphically create sophisticated business rules. WorkPoint can be deployed departmentally or enterprise-wide as an end-user solution. It can also be deployed as an embedded underlying BPM component of a distributed application. And with WorkPoint's Gateway, you can quickly and dynamically deploy user-facing screens and applications. The Gateway requires no scripting, yet provides users with a robust platform for long-term production applications. With the latest release of WorkPoint, the native Microsoft version was migrated from the existing COM+ architecture to a completely .NET-managed version. The existing Java engine and the .NET release run natively, leveraging the strength of their respective architectures.

ADOBE SYSTEMS INC.
Full Member
345 Park Avenue, San Jose CA 95110, USA
Steve Rotter, Senior Product Marketing Manager
Tel: [1] 408-536-6000
srotter@adobe.com
Adobe revolutionizes how the world engages with ideas and information. For more than two decades, the company's award-winning software and technologies have redefined business, entertainment, and personal communications by setting new standards for producing and delivering content that engages people virtually anywhere at anytime. From rich images in print, video, and film to dynamic digital content for a variety of media, the impact of Adobe solutions is evident across industries and felt by anyone who creates, views, and interacts with information. With a reputation for excellence and a portfolio of many of the most respected and recognizable software brands, Adobe is one of the world's largest and most diversified software companies. As demand for digital content skyrocketed, Adobe solutions provided a catalyst for moving ideas from concept through creation to delivery across any digital device. The appointment of Bruce Chizen as Adobe's Chief Executive Officer in 2000 further strengthened the company's market leadership, as Adobe delivered on strategies to move from a desktop software company to a platform provider for enterprises. With its acquisition of Macromedia, Inc. in 2005—developer of the ubiquitous Flash® technology and a pioneer in multimedia and web development—Adobe expanded its strong technology foundation and portfolio of customer solutions.

ADVANTYS
Full Member
1250 Rene Levesque West, Suite 2200, Montreal, Quebec, H3B 4W8

www.advantys.com
Alain Bezancon, President
Tel: [1] 514 989 3700 / Fax:[1] 514 989 3705
alain.bezancon@advantys.com
Established in 1995, ADVANTYS is a leading ISV offering the Smart Enterprise Suite
(SES).The SES provides a modular yet fully integrated set of solutions. Within a single environment organizations of all sizes benefit from a coherent access to features encompassing
content management, collaborative work, workflow and development components.
ADVANTYS' practical approach to technology benefits its broad base of customers worldwide through a range of reliable, scalable, affordable and easy-to-use products. SES full-
web environment uses industry-proven technologies allowing SMEs as well as major companies from all sectors to quickly and easily build their web information systems. As an
active member of international organizations like Workflow Management Coalition or OASIS
group, ADVANTYS demonstrates its technological leadership and its ability to quickly and
practically integrate standards as soon as they become mature and users-beneficial. This
leadership brought Gartner to list ADVANTYS in the Smart Enterprise Suite Magic Quadrant 2004.

AIIM International
Full Member
1100 Wayne Avenue, Suite 1100, Silver Springs, MD, 20910 United States
www.aiim.org
Betsy Fanning, Director, Standards & Content Development
Tel: [1] 240-494-2682 / Fax:[1] 301-587-2711
bfanning@aiim.org
AIIM International is the global authority on Enterprise Content Management (ECM). The
technologies, tools and methods used to capture, manage, store, preserve and deliver information to support business processes. AIIM promotes the understanding, adoption, and
use of ECM technologies through education, networking, marketing, research, standards
and advocacy programs.

Appian Corportation
Full Member
8000 Towers Crescent Drive, 16th Floor, Vienna, VA. 22182 United States
www.appiaan.com
Philip Larson, Director of Product Management
Tel: [1] 703-442-1057
larson@appian.com
Founded in 1999 and headquartered in Vienna, VA, Appian is the first business process
management (BPM) company to deliver advanced process, knowledge management, and
analytics capabilities in a fully-integrated suite. Designed to extend the value of your existing systems, Appian's process-centric, context-driven solutions align business strategy with
execution, and drive quantifiable improvements in business performance. *Fortune* 500
companies, government agencies, and non-governmental organizations have deployed Appian's award-winning platform–Appian Enterprise–to gain unprecedented visibility and control over their strategic business processes and enable customers to make better-informed
decisions about their business.

ARMA International
Associate Member
13725 West 109th Street Suite 101, Lenexa, KS 66215 Untied States
Peter R Hermann, Executive Director & CEO
Tel: [1]913-217-6025 / Fax: [1]913-341-3742
phermann@arma.org

BancTec / Plexus
Full Member
Jarman House, Mathisen Way, Poyle Road, Colnbrook, SL3 0HF, United Kingdom
www.banctec.com
Marlon Driver
Tel: [44] (175) 377-8875
marlon.driver@banctec.co.uk
For over 10 years Plexus has pioneered the development of workflow automation and cur-
rently supports some of the largest workflow implementations in the world. We specialize in
providing core business process automation technology from small scale up to distributed

enterprise wide deployment. Our products are available across a range of Unix, Linux and Windows platforms and support for the database market leaders ensures flexible integration into any environment. Our global presence enables us to partner and provide solutions for a wide range of business cultures and requirements. Our technology partners work alongside us to stimulate the continued product evolution necessary to supply our users with the best tools to harness their information systems as part of the business process.

BEA SYSTEMS
Full Member
2315 North First St., San Jose, California, 95131 United States
www.bea.com
Yaron Y Goland, External Standards Coordination
Tel: [1] 408-570-8000 / Fax:[1] 408-570-8901
ygoland@bea.com

BIZMANN SYSTEM (S) PTE LTD
Associate Member
73 Science Park Drive, #02-05, CINTECH I, Singapore Science Park I, Singapore 118254
http://www.bizmann.com
Ken Loke, Director
Tel: [65] +65-62711911
kenloke@bizmann.com
Bizmann System (S) Pte Ltd is a Singapore-based company with development offices in Singapore and Malaysia, developing business process management (BPM) solutions and providing business process consultation services within the ASIA region. Bizmann develops and implements business improvement solutions based on leading development engine such as award winner BPM software, Bizflow. To further increase functionalities and to provide complete end-to-end deliverables, Bizmann enhance Bizflow development engine by developing additional intelligent features and integration connectors. Bizmann System has set up a Regional PROCESS KNOWLEDGE HUB for the Asia market. Bizmann introduces Best Practices through the Process Knowledge Hub and emphasizes quick deployment. All business process designs/templates are developed by Bizmann as well as imported from the United Sates and other advanced countries to facilitate cross knowledge transfers. Bizmann develops and implements BPM applications across all industries. Unlike conventional solutions, BPM solutions address the fundamental of process challenges that all companies face. It allows companies to automate and integrate real and disparate business processes safely, and securely extend processes to a wide variety of users via the Web. Bizmann BPM solutions rapidly accelerate time-to-value with configure-to-fit process templates and Bizmann's best-in-class business services, designed to address the unique challenges that companies face.

BPM KOREA SOFTWARE INDUSTRY ASSOCIATION [KOSA]
Full Member
Green B/D. 11F, 79-2, Garakbon-Dong, Songpa-Gu, Seoul 138-711 South Korea
www.sw.or.kr
Kwang-Hoon Kim
Tel: [82] (2) 405—4535 / Fax: [82] 2-405-4501
kosainfo@mail.sw.or.kr

CACI PRODUCTS COMPANY
Associate Member
Advanced Simulation Lab, 1455 Frazee Road Suite #700, San Diego, CA 92108
Mike Engiles, SIMPROCESS Product Mgr
Tel: [1] 703-679-3874
mengiles@caci.com

CAPTARIS
Full Member
10085 N.E. 4th Street, Suite 400, Bellevue, WA. 98004 United States
www.captaris.com
Eric Bean, Senior Director, Products Group
Tel: [1] 425-638-4181
EricBean@captaris.com

CCLRC
Associate Member

Rutherford Appleton Laboratory, Chilton Didcot Oxon OX11 0QX United Kingdom
www.cclrc.ac.uk
Trudy Hall, Solutions Developer
Tel: 44]-1235-821900
t.a.hall@rl.ac.uk

CONSOLIDATED CONTRACTORS INTL. COMPANY
Associate Member
62B Kifissias, Marroussi Athens Attiki 15125 Greece
www.ccc.gr
Aref Boualwan, Product Manager
Tel : [30] 6932415177
aboualwan@ccc.gr

DST SYSTEMS, INC.
Full Member
330 W. 9th Street, Kansas City, Missouri 64105 United States
www.dstsystems.com
Bob Puccinelli, Director of Marketing AWD
Tel: [1] 816 843-8148 / Fax:[1] 816 843-8197
rjpuccinelli@dstsystems.com
AWD (Automated Work Distributor) is a comprehensive business process management, imaging, workflow, and customer management solution designed to improve productivity and reduce costs. AWD captures all communication channels, streamlines processes, provides real-time reporting, and enables world-class customer service. AWD clients include banking, brokerage, healthcare, insurance, mortgage, mutual funds, and video/broadband companies. DST has a unique perspective among software vendors: With more than 9,000 AWD users throughout our business process outsourcing (BPO) centers and affiliate companies, AWD is a critical component of our success in the software and BPO markets. DST Technologies is a wholly owned subsidiary of DST Systems, Inc.

FILENET CORPORATION
Full Member
3565 Harbor Blvd. Costa Mesa, CA, 92626, United States
www.filenet.com
Mike Marin
Product Manager, Business Process Management Technologies
Tel: [1] 714 327 5707 / Fax:[1] 714-327-3490
mmarin@filenet.com
FileNet Corporation (NASDAQ: FILE) provides The Substance Behind eBusiness by delivering Business Process Management software solutions. FileNet enables organizations around the globe to increase productivity, customer satisfaction and revenue by linking customers, partners and employees through efficient and flexible eBusiness processes. Headquartered in Costa Mesa, Calif., the company markets its innovative solutions in more than 90 countries through its own global sales, professional services and support organizations, as well as via its ValueNET(r) Partner network of resellers, system integrators and application developers.

FISERV LENDING SOLUTIONS
Full Member
901 International Parkway, Suite 100, Lake Mary, Florida 32746
www.fiservlendingsolutions.com
Chris Berg
Tel: 800-748-2572, ext. 4224 / Fax: 407-829-4270
Chris.Berg@Fiserv.com
Fiserv Lending Solutions is a leading provider of workflow and process management software for the lending industry. Working as a collaborative business partner, we offer comprehensive loan management solutions that enable lenders to increase productivity, integrate key systems, and implement process automation.

FLOWRING TECHNOLOGY CO. LTD.
Full Member
12F,No.120, Sec.2, Gongdao 5th Rd., Hsinchu City, 300 Taiwan
www.flowring.com.
Chi-Tsai Yang, VP and CTO

Tel: [886] 3-5753331 / Fax:[886] 3-5753292
jjyang@flowring.com

FORNAX CO
Associate Member
Taltos u. 1. Budapest 1123 Hungary
http://www.fornax.hu
Mr. Zoltan Varszegi, Business Development Consultant
Tel: [36] 1-457-3000 / Fax:[36] 1-212-0111
zoltan.varszegi@fornax.hu

FUJITSU SOFTWARE CORPORATION
Full Member
3055 Orchard Drive, San Jose, CA, 95134-2022, United States
www.i-flow.com
Keith Swenson, Chief Architect
Tel: [1] 408-456-7963 / Fax: [1] 408-456-7821
kswenson@us.fujitsu.com
Fujitsu Software Corporation, based in San Jose, California, is a wholly owned subsidiary of Fujitsu Limited. Fujitsu Software Corporation leverages Fujitsu's international scope and expertise to develop and deliver comprehensive technology solutions. The company's products include INTERSTAGE(tm), an e-Business infrastructure platform that includes the INTERSTAGE Application Server and i-Flow(tm); and Fujitsu COBOL. i-Flow streamlines, automates and tracks business processes to help enterprises become more productive, responsive, and profitable. Leveraging such universal standards as J2EE and XML, i-Flow delivers business process automation solutions that are easy to develop, deploy, integrate and manage. i-Flow has a flexible architecture that seamlessly integrates into existing environments. This allows you to leverage your IT infrastructure investments and allows you to easily adapt to future technologies.

GLOBAL 360, INC
Full Member
One Tara Blvd, Suite 200, Nashua, NH 03062, USA
www.global360.com
Ken Mei, Director, International Sales Support
Tel: [1-603-459-0924
ken.mei@global360.com
Global 360 is a leading provider of Business Process Management and Analysis Solutions. Global 360 gives you a 360-degree view of enterprise processes and more importantly, the ability to efficiently manage your complete process lifecycle by leveraging our core technologies - content management, process management, goal management, process modeling, forecasting, simulation, analysis, reporting and optimization solutions.

HANDYSOFT GLOBAL CORPORATION
Full Member
1952 Gallows Road, Suite 200, Vienna, VA 22182, USA
www.handysoft.com
Robert Cain, Product Manager
Tel:[1] 703-442-5635
rcain@handysoft.com
HandySoft Global Corporation is leading the way for companies worldwide to develop new strategies for conducting business through the improvement, automation, and optimization of their business processes. As a leading provider of Business Process Management (BPM) software and services, we deliver innovative solutions to both the public and private sectors. Proven to reduce costs while improving quality and productivity, our foundation software platform, BizFlow®, is an award-winning BPM suite of tools used to design, analyze, automate, monitor, and optimize business processes. By delivering a single-source solution, capable of improving all types of business processes, HandySoft empowers our clients to leverage their investment across whole departments and the entire enterprise, making BizFlow the Strategic Choice for BPM.

HITACHI LTD. SOFTWARE DIVISION
Full Member
5030 Totsuka-Chou, Tosuka-Ku, Yokohama, 2448555, Japan
Ryoichi Shibuya, Senior Manager

Tel: [81] 45 826 8370 / Fax:[81] 45 826 7812
shibuya@itg.hitachi.co.jp
Hitachi offers a wide variety of integrated products for groupware systems such as e-mail and document information systems. One of these products is Hitachi's workflow system Groupmax. The powerful engine of Groupmax effectively automates office business such as the circulation of documents. Groupmax provides the following powerful tools and facilities: A visual status monitor shows the route taken and present location of each document in a business process definition. Cooperative facilities between servers provide support for a wide area workflow system Groupmax supports application processes such as consultation, send back, withdrawal, activation, transfer, stop and cancellation. Groupmax is rated to be the most suitable workflow system for typical business processes in Japan and has provided a high level of customer satisfaction. Groupmax workflow supports the Interface 4.

IMAGE INTEGRATION SYSTEMS, INC.
Associate Member
885 Commerce Drive, Suite B, Perrysburg, OH 43551 United States
www.iissys.com
Bradley T. White, President
Tel: [1] 419-872-1930 / Fax:[1] 419-872-1643
sales@iissys.com

INTERWOVEN INC
Full Member
18 East 41st Street, 17th Floor, New York, New York 10017 United States
http://www.interwoven.com/
Linda Watson
Tel: [1] 212-213-5056 / Fax:[1] 212-213-5352
linda.watson@scrittura.com
Interwoven Inc delivers an integrated Java language web-based suite of Business Process Management (BPM), Workflow and Document Management components that are designed to optimize and streamline the legal, trading and operations areas of financial services institutions that are burdened with high levels of complex contractual documentation.

IVYTEAM – SORECO GROUP
Associate Member
Alpenstrasse 9, Zug, 6304, Switzerland
www.ivyteam.com
Heinz Lienhard, Founder; Consultant
Tel: [41] 41 710 80 20 / Fax:[41] 41 710 80 60
heinz.lienhard@ivyteam.ch

IXOS
Full Member
180 Columbia Street West, Waterloo, Ontario, Canada N2L 3L3
Anik Ganguly
Tel: [1[519-888-7111 / Fax: [1] 519-888-0677
anik@ixos.com

KAISHA-TEC
Full Member
c/o G. Long, Kaisha-Tec, Mitaka Sangyo Plaza Annex, 3-32-3 Shimo Renjaku,
Mitaka-shi, Tokyo 181-0013, Japan
Geoffrey Long
www.kaisha.com
Tel: [81] 422 47 2397 / Fax:[81] 422 47 2396
glong@kaisha-tec.com
ActiveModeler/ActiveFlow is a unique workflow combination product based on the No.1 selling process modeler in Japan. Process Visualization is used to create optimized workflows and to speed well-defined development. ActiveFlow provides industrial strength workflow in a Microsoft-centric platform again with some unique features. The workflow satisfies well even the demanding Japanese workflow market including back-office and e-commerce integration.

METODA S.P.A.
Associate Member
Via San Leonardo, 52, Salerno 84131 Italy

Raffaello Leschiera
Tel : [39] 0893067-111 / Fax : [39] 0893067-112
r.leschiera@lineargruppo.it

NEC SOFT LTD.

Full Member
1-18-6, Shinkiba, Koto-ku, Tokyo, 136-8608, JAPAN
www.nec.com
Yoshihisa Sadakane, Sales and Marketing Senior Manager
Tel: [81]3-5569-3399 / Fax: [81]3-5569-3286
sadakane@mxw.nes.nec.co.jp

NORTHROP GRUMMAN (INTEGIC)

Associate Member
14585 Avion Parkway, Chantilly, Virginia, 20151, United States
www.integic.com
Steve Kruba, Chief Technologist
Tel: [1] 703-272-5000 / Fax:[1] 703-272-5053
steve.kruba@integic.com

PECTRA TECHNOLOGY, INC.

Full Member
2425 West Loop South – Suite 200, Houston TX 77027, USA
www.pectra.com
Federico Silva, Marketing Manager
fsilva@pectra.com
Tel: [1] 713-335-5562
PECTRA Technology's award-winning Business Process Management system, PECTRA BPM Suite®, is a powerful set of tools enabling discovery, design, implementation, maintenance, optimization and analysis of business processes for different kinds of organizations. PECTRA BPM Suite® is an application that automates the processes and the most critical tasks in the organization, generating optimum levels of operational effectiveness. It fulfills all requirements demanded by today's organization, quickly and efficiently. Furthermore, it increases the return on previous investments made in technology by integrating all existing applications. Based on BPM technology it incorporates the concepts of: BAM (Business Activity Monitoring) providing management with user-friendly graphic monitoring tools, to follow up any deviation in the organization's critical success factors, with capabilities to control and coordinate the organization's performance by means of graphic management indicators; WORKFLOW offering powerful tools to automate and speed the organization's business processes, improving communication and work-flow between people working in different areas; carrying out the work more efficiently and producing customer satisfaction, lower levels of bureaucracy and cost-reductions in day-to-day operations; EAI (Enterprise Application Integration) enabling integration with all existing technologies in the organization, regardless of their origin or platform, coordinating them to help the organization achieve its goals more efficiently; and B2Bi (Business to Business Integration) enabling the control and coordination of each and every link in the organization's value chain, providing robust tools for business process management, and enterprise application integration, making it possible to totally integrate suppliers, clients and partners in an easy and flexible way.

PEGASYSTEMS INC.

Full Member
101 Main Street, Cambridge, MA 02142 United States
www.pegasystems.com
Rosalind Morville, Sr. PR Manager
Tel: [1] 617-374-9600 ext. 6029
pr@pega.com
Pegasystems Inc. (Nasdaq: PEGA) provides software to automate complex, changing business processes. Pegasystems, the leader in unified process and rules technology, gives business people and IT departments the ability to use best processes across the enterprise and outperform their competition. Our new class of Business Process Management (BPM) technology makes enterprise systems easy to use and easy to change. By automating policy manuals, system specifications and lines of manual coding with dynamically responsive updates, Pegasystems powers the world's most sophisticated organizations to "build for change™." Pegasystems' award-winning, standards-based BPM suite is complemented with best-practice solution frameworks to help leaders in the financial services, insurance,

healthcare, manufacturing and government markets drive growth and productivity. Headquartered in Cambridge, MA, Pegasystems has regional offices in North America, Europe and the Pacific Rim.

PERSHING LLC
Associate Member
One Pershing Plaza, 8th Fl., Jersey City, NJ. 07399 United States
Regina DeGennaro, VP - Workflow Solutions
Tel: 201-413-4588
rdegennaro@pershing.com

SAVVION, INC.
Full Member
5104 Old Ironsides Drive Suite: 205, Santa Clara, CA 95054 United States
http://www.savvion.com
Don Nanneman, Vice President, Marketing
nanneman@savvion.com
Tel: [1] 408 330 3400 / Fax: [1] 408 330 3444
Savvion's award-winning Business Process Management system, Savvion BusinessManager(tm), enables organizations to automate and manage critical business processes by integrating the people and systems that execute those processes. From supply-chain to service management, help desk and employee self-service applications, Savvion enables an organization to define and deploy desktop and mobile solutions to execute a company's business strategies. A GUI designer and a business rules and event management engine, empower business and IT staff to collaborate to define business processes. BusinessManager automatically deploys those applications over fixed and wireless Internets to desktop and wireless devices. Infrastructure, such as SAP, PeopleSoft, Siebel and i2 systems, is then integrated to deliver a complete desktop and mobile solution. Managers gain real time visibility into the status of each process to quickly take action to resolve bottlenecks or re-assign tasks.

SOFT SOLUTIONS
Full Member
2, Allee Lavoisier, Villeneuve d'Ascq, France 59650
http://softsolutionsus.com
Walid Daccache, Project Manager
[Tel : 33] (3) 2 04 14 19 0 / Fax : 33] (3) 2 04 14 19 9
daccache.walid@softsolutions.fr
Soft Solutions was founded in 1989, and has since, built a strong track record of delivering merchandising and marketing solutions into some of the world's largest Retailers. Our solutions include a full range of business applications that support the merchandise functions in the retailer enterprise, including Assortment planning, Pricing and Promotions management, Global Data Synchronization, Forecasting, Advanced analytics, Optimization and Vendor Funds management. These business applications share a common retail business model foundation, the most flexible and comprehensive in the industry. And, in order to insure consistent, auditable execution of business functions, we also provide a fully integrated set of tools such as User and Security Management, Workflow Management, Data integration, Reporting and Translation. Our customers are multi-divisional, multi-format, Tier-1 Retailers including Carrefour, Auchan, Group Louis Delhaize, Intermarche, Casino, FNAC, Monoprix, Kingfisher, Pinault-Printemps-Redoute and Galeries Lafayette. Our suite of applications is completely based on Java/J2EE technology, conforms to the latest industry and technology standards (including GS1) and is compatible with multiple databases, industry application server packages and EAI solutions

SOURCECODE TECHNOLOGY HOLDINGS, INC.
Full Member
4042 148TH Ave NE, Redmond, WA 98039, United States
http://www.k2workflow.com
Leah Clelland
Tel: 1 (425) 883-4200 / Fax: 1 (425) 671-0411
Leah@k2workflow.com

STRATOS S.R.L.
Full Member
via Pavia 9/a 1, RIvoli TORINO 10098 Italy

Luca Oglietti
Tel: [33] 39.011.9500000
l.oglietti@gruppostratos.com

TELECOM ITALIA SpA
Associate Member
Via G. Reiss Romoli 274, Torino, Italy 10148
Giovanna Sacchi
Tel: [0039] (01) 12288040
giovanna.sacchi@telecomitalia.it

TIBCO SOFTWARE, INC.
Full Member
3303 Hillview Avenue, Palo Alto, CA 94304 USA
http://www.tibco.com/software/process_management/default.jsp
Justin Brunt, Sr. Product Manager
Tel: [44] (0) 1793 441300 / Fax : [44] (0) 1793 441333
jbrunt@tibco.com
TIBCO Software Inc is the leading independent business integration and process management software company in the world, demonstrated by market share and analyst reports.
In addition, TIBCO is a leading enabler of Real-Time Business, helping companies become
more cost-effective, more agile and more efficient. TIBCO has delivered the value of Real-
Time Business to over 2,000 customers around the world. TIBCO provides one of the most
complete offerings for enterprise-scale BPM, with powerful software that is capable of solving not just the challenges of automating routine tasks and exception handling scenarios,
but also the challenges of orchestrating sophisticated and long-lived activities and transactions that involve people and systems across organizational and geographical boundaries.

TOGETHER TEAMLÖSUNGEN GMBH
Associate Member
Elmargasse 2-4, Wien, A-1191, Austria
www.together.at
Alfred Madl, Geschaftsfuhrer
Tel: [43] 5 04 04 122 / Fax:[43] 5 04 04 11 122
a.madl@together.at

UNIVERSITY OF MUENSTER
Academic Member
Department of Information Systems, Leonardo-Campus 3 Muenster, 48149, Germany
Tobias Rieke
Tel: [49] 251 833-8100 / Tel: [49] 251 833-8109
istori@wi.uni-muenster.de

VIGNETTE CORPORATION
Full Member
1601 South MoPac Expressway, Building 2
Austin, TX, 78746-5776, United States
www.vignette.com
Clay Johnson, Staff Engineer
Tel: [1] 512-741-1133 / Fax:[1] 512-741-4500
chjohnson@vignette.com
Vignette is the leading provider of content management solutions used by the most successful organizations in the world to interact online with their customers, employees and
partners. By combining content management with integration and analysis applications,
Vignette enables organizations to deliver personalized information wherever it is needed,
integrate online and enterprise systems and provide real-time analysis of the customer experience. Vignette products are focused around three core capabilities that meet the needs
of today's e-business organizations: Content Management - the ability to manage and deliver content to every electronic touch-point. Content Integration - the ability to integrate a
variety of e-business applications within and across enterprises. Content Analysis - the
ability to provide actionable insight into the customer's relationship to a business.

VIZYON NET LTD
Full Member
Tubitak MAM Kampüsü Teknoloji, Gelistirme Bölgesi B Blok No:22

Kocaeli Gebze 41470 Turkey
www.livechainworkflow.com
Fahri Kaan Toker, IT Manager
Tel : (90- 216) 411 17 39 / Fax : (90- 216) 363 13 80
ktoker@vizyonnet.com

Vizyon Net Ltd is a software company with development offices in Istanbul and Tubitak Technological Development Zone, developing workflow, business process management, and document management solutions. Live Chain Workflow Studio is a web based workflow management system, which provides assurance of business process standardization and automation, developed by Vizyon Net. The primary use areas of Live Chain Workflow Studio are managing internal purchase requests, order tracking, time-off & travel requests, production planning, budgeting, project tracking and management, and ISO 9000 types of applications. Live Chain Workflow Studio provides delivery of the right information to the right person and to the right application at the right time. It is modularly structured to allow flexibility and expandability to fit client needs.

W4 (WORLD WIDE WEB WORKFLOW)

Full Member
4 rue Emile Baudot, 91873 Palaiseau Cedex, France
www.w4global.com
Raphaël Syren, Marketing Director
Tel: [33] 1 64 53 19 12 / Fax:[33] 1 64 53 28 98
raphael.syren@w4global.com

W4, one of the leading European software vendors specialized in « Business Process Management », supplies more than 270 customers, serving more than 1 million people. For almost 10 years **W4** has been widely acclaimed for its expertise in **Human Workflow**, which guarantees transparently, via its functional architecture, task follow-up and traceability: who does what, when and how. Whatever the particular need, there is a package available allowing customers to take full advantage of the powerful **W4** technology: **Manage the automation of any kind of process: W4 BPM Suite 2006** is a complete package, from modelling to monitoring, dedicated to the enterprise process automation. This BPM package is capable of managing the automation of complex work procedures involving high volumes of users, as well as support procedures (finance, HR, etc.) and company-specific procedures. Dedicated to end-users, **W4 BPM Suite 2006** provides them with an easy tool for modelling their processes. It also offers managers reporting and supervision functionalities. **Optimize how internal business needs are handled: W4 Ready for Business** are out-of-box packages that capitalize upon **W4 BPM Suite's** powerful and consulting services to deliver applications that correspond well to each individual customer's particular way of doing business. Thanks to **W4 Ready for Business**, companies can optimize how to handle purchase, training and recruitment requests.

Embed an OEM component: W4 Embedded Edition is a collection of embeddable software components for business process management (BPM), targeted at software vendors working on all standard market platforms (ERP, Content management, EAI...) Just some of those who accelerate their business every day thanks to **W4** are Barclays Bank, BNP Paribas, Alcatel Space, Siemens Transportation Systems, Volvo Portugal, EMI Music France, Cap Gemini, Teleca Solutions Italia, TNT, etc.

WORK MANAGEMENT EUROPE

Associate Member
Barbizonlaan 94, 2980 ME Capelle aan den Ijssel, The Netherlands
www.wmeonline.com
Cor H. Visser, Managing Director
Tel: [31] (10) 207 5454 / Fax: [31] (10) 207 5401
cvisser@wmeonline.com

XIAMEN LONGTOP SYSTEM CO., LTD

Associate Member
15/F, Block A, Chuangxin Building, Software Park, Xiamen, 361005, P.R. China
Shou Sheng Ye, R&D Director
Tel: [86] (5) 922-396888
xyyang@longtop.com

WfMC Officers 2006

STEERING COMMITTEE

Chairman	Jon Pyke	Fellow, UK
Vice Chairman (Europe)	Justin Brunt	TIBCO, UK
Vice Chairman (Americas)	Keith Swenson	Fujitsu Software, USA
Vice Chairman (Asia-Pacific)	Yoshihisa Sadakane	NEC Soft

TECHNICAL COMMITTEE

Co-Chairs	David Hollingsworth	Fujitsu Software, UK
	Keith Swenson	Fujitsu Software, USA
Vice Chairman (Europe)	Philippe Betschart	W4, France
Vice Chairman (Americas)	Mike Marin	FileNet, USA
Vice Chairman (Asia-Pacific)	Dr. Yang Chi-Tsai	Flowring, Taiwan

EXTERNAL RELATIONS COMMITTEE

Chairman	Betsy Fanning	AIIM International, USA
Vice Chairman (Europe)	Martin Ader	W&GS, France
Vice Chairman (Americas)	Bob Puccinelli	DST Systems, USA
Vice Chairman (Asia-Pacific)	Dr Kwang-Hoon Kim	BPM Korea, South Korea
SECRETARY / TREASURER	Cor Visser	Work Management Europe, Netherlands
INDUSTRY LIAISON CHAIR	Philip Larson	Appian Corporation, USA
USER LIAISON CHAIR	Charlie Plesums	Fellow, USA

WfMC Country Chairs

ARGENTINA
Federico Silva
PECTRA Technology, Inc.
USA: +1 (713) 335 5562
ARG (BA): +54 (11) 4590 0000
ARG (CBA): +54 (351) 410 4400
fsilva@pectra.com

AUSTRALIA & NEW ZEALAND
Carol Prior
MAESTRO BPE Limited
Tel: +61 2 9844 8222
caprior@ozemail.com.au

BRAZIL
Vinícius Amaral
iProcess
Phone: +55 51 3211-4036
vinicius.amaral@iprocess.com.br

CANADA
Meir Levi
Interfacing Technologies Corp
Tel: +1 514-737-7333
meir.levi@interfacing.com

FRANCE
Raphaël Syren
W4 Global
Tel: +(331) 64 53 17 65
raphael.syren@w4global.com

GERMANY
Tobias Rieke
University of Muenster
Tel: [49] 251-8338-072 -
istori@wi.uni-muenster.de

ITALY
Luca Oglietti
Stratos
Tel. +39.011.9500000 r.a.
l.oglietti@gruppostratos.com

JAPAN
Yoshihisa Sadakane
NEC Soft
Tel: +81-3-5569-3399
sadakane@mxw.nes.nec.co.jp

KOREA
Yeonsoo Yang
HandySoft
Tel: 82-2-3479-5410
ysyang@handysoft.co.kr

SINGAPORE & MALAYSIA
Ken Loke
Bizmann System (S) Pte Ltd
Tel: +65 - 6271 1911
kenloke@bizmann.com

SOUTH AFRICA
Marco Gerazounis
TIBCO Software Inc.
Tel: +27 (0)11 467 3111
mgerazou@tibco.com

SPAIN
Elena Rodríguez Martín
Fujitsu Software, Madrid.
Tel. +34 91 784 9565
ermartin@mail.fujitsu.es

THE NETHERLANDS
Fred van Leeuwen
DCE Consultants
Tel: +31 20 44 999 00
leeuwen@dceconsultants.com

TAIWAN
Erin Yang
Flowring Technology Co. Ltd.
Tel: +886-3-5753331 ext. 316
erin_yang@flowring.com

UNITED KINGDOM
Sharon L. Boyes-Schiller
Skyscape Solutions
Tel: +44 (0)20 8324 1564
sharon@skyscapesolutions.com

USA (WEST)
Bob Puccinelli
DST Systems
Tel: +1 816-843-8148
rjpuccinelli@dstsystems.com

USA (EAST)
Betsy Fanning
AIIM International
Tel: 1 301 755 2682
bfanning@aiim.org

WfMC Technical Committee
Working Group Chairs 2006

WG1—PROCESS DEFINITION INTERCHANGE MODEL AND APIs
Chair: Robert Shapiro, Fellow
Email: rshapiro@capevisions.com

WG2/3—CLIENT / APPLICATION APIs
open

WG4—WORKFLOW INTEROPERABILITY
Chair: Keith Swenson, Fujitsu
Email: kswenson@us.fujitsu.com

WG5—ADMINISTRATION & MONITORING
Chair: Michael zur Muehlen, Stevens Institute of Technology
Email: mzurmuehlen@stevens.edu

WG ON OMG
Chair: Ken Mei, Global 360
Email: ken.mei@global360.com

CONFORMANCE WG
Chair: Michael zur Muehlen, Stevens Institute of Technology
Email: mzurmuehlen@stevens.edu

WGRM—REFERENCE MODEL
Chair: Dave Hollingsworth, Fujitsu
david.hollingsworth@uk.fujitsu.com

WG9—RESOURCE MODEL
Chair: Michael zur Muehlen, Stevens Institute of Technology
Email: mzurmuehlen@stevens.edu

WfMC Fellows

The WfMC recognizes individuals who have made sustained and outstanding contributions to WfMC objectives far and above that expected from normal member representation.

WfMC FELLOW—FACTORS:
- To be considered as a candidate, the individual must have participated in the WfMC for a period of not less than two years and be elected by majority vote within the nominating committee.
- Rights of a WfMC Fellow: Receives guest member level of email support from the Secretariat; pays no fee when attending WfMC meetings; may participate in the work of the WfMC (workgroups, etc), may hold office.

Robert Allen
United Kingdom

Mike Anderson
United Kingdom

Wolfgang Altenhuber
Austria

Richard Bailey
United States

Emmy Botterman
United Kingdom

Katherine Drennan
United States

Mike Gilger
United States

Michael Grabert
United States

Shirish Hardikar
United States

Paula Helfrich
United States

Hideshige Hasegawa
Japan

Dr. Haruo Hayami
Japan

Nick Kingsbury
United Kingdom

Klaus-Dieter Kreplin
Germany

Emma Matejka
Austria

Dan Matheson
United States

Akira Misowa
Japan

Roberta Norin
United States

Sue Owen
United Kingdom

Jon Pyke
United Kingdom

Charles Plesums
United States

Harald Raetzsch
Austria

Michele Rochefort
Germany

Joseph Rogowski
United States

Michael Rossi
United States

Sunil Sarin
United States

Robert Shapiro
United States

Dave Shorter
(Chair Emeritus)
United States

David Stirrup
United Kingdom

Keith Swenson
United States

Tetsu Tada
United States

Austin Tate
United Kingdom

Cor Visser
The Netherlands

Rainer Weber
Germany

Alfons Westgeest
Belgium

Marilyn Wright
United States

Dr. Michael zur Muehlen
United States

Appendix—Author Biographies

LUIS JOYANES AGUILAR

(ljoyanes@fpablovi.org)
Universidad Pontificia de Salamanca, Campus Madrid
Pº Juan XXIII, 3 - 28040 Madrid (Spain)
Phone: (34)667438400

Luís Joyanes Aguilar (Jaén, Spain) holds a PhD in Computer Science (1997) and in Sociology (1996) from Universidad Pontificia de Salamanca en Madrid. He has a bachelor degree en Physics (1977) and Military Sciences (1970). Since 1991, he is the Systems and Languages Department Director and Software Engineering in the Universidad Pontificia de Salamanca en Madrid. Since 2001, he is Director of Master and PhD Programs in this University. Actually he leads the research groups in Multidisciplinary Computer Researches, Knowledge Management and Knowledge Society. He is author of more than 30 books and over 70 communications in scientific magazines and conferences.

VINÍCIUS AMARAL

(vinicius.amaral@iprocess.com.br)
iProcess
Rua Washington Luiz, 820/301, 90.001-460 - Porto Alegre – RS - Brazil
Phone: +55 51 3211-4036

Vinícius Amaral is an active professional and researcher in workflow and BPM areas. He has a large practical experience brought about his participation in several workflow projects development. He received a Bachelor's degree in Computer Science from Federal University of Rio Grande do Sul in 1996 and a Master's degree in Computer Science from Federal University of Rio Grande do Sul in 1999. In 2000, Mr. Amaral founded iProcess (www.iprocess.com.br), a company that is today one of the leaders in the workflow and BPM Brazilian market. iProcess was internationally recognized in 2003 with the Latin America Excellence in Workflow Awards. Mr. Amaral is also professor at the University of Rio dos Sinos (Unisinos).

OLE CHRISTIAN ASTRUP

(ole.christian.astrup@dnv.com)
Project Director, DNV Software
7th floor, Kolon Bld, 36-7, Namchon1-Dong, Suyong-Gu, Busan 613-815, Rep of Korea
Phone: +82 51 610 7790 / Fax: +82 51 611 7172

Dr. Ole Christian's Astrup is currently Project Director and responsible for DNV Sofware's solution sales in Region Korea & Japan. Dr. Astrup has been pioneering the implementation of Best Engineering Practices with some of the largest ship yards in the world targeting their engineering design work processes. In 1987 he obtained his Ph. D in computational mechanics at The Norwegian University of Science and Technology (NTNU). Dr. Astrup has more than 20 years of experience in structural and hydrodynamic engineering from both the marine and general industry.

ARNAUD BEZANCON

(arnaud.bezancon@advantys.com)
Chief Technical Officer, ADVANTYS, Canada
1250 Rene Levesque West, Suite 2200 Montreal, Quebec H3B 4W8

Arnaud Bezancon, IT Engineer (Orsay, France), is the CTO of ADVANTYS. (France) which he co-founded in 1995 with his brother Alain (BBA, HEC, Montreal). ADVANTYS is a leading ISV offering the Smart Enterprise Suite (SES). As a CTO, Arnaud manages the software division of ADVANTYS and launched the SES listed in a Gartner Magic Quadrant in 2004. Arnaud designed ADVANTYS' flagship product—the WorkflowGen workflow management system. Arnaud has developed a pragmatic approach of technology based on real life experience. Actual ADVANTYS' solutions are used by major corporations including Accor, Areva, Deloitte, and Johnson & Johnson.

SASA BOJANIC

sasaboy@prozone.co.yu
Together Teamlösungen
Elmargasse 2-4 Vienna 1010 Austria
Phone: +43 (0) 5 04 04–122 / Fax: +43 (0) 5 04 04-11 122

Education: University of Belgrade, Serbia & Montenegro, School of Electrical Engineering. Skills: Business Analysis, Workflow Analysis and Design, Process Management, Process Modeling, Controlling, Standardization. Work experience includes working with a workflow technologies based on WfMC specifications for more than 5 years. Developed the most popular open-source XPDL graphical editor and workflow engine products. Promoting the use of workflow through educating people, providing consultancy services, implementing workflow systems in various organizations. Actively involved in the development of WfMC standards.

BRUNO BÜTLER

(bruno.buetler@ivyteam.ch)
Co-founder and CTO, SORECOgroup / ivyTeam
Alpenstrasse 9 CH-6304 Zug Switzerland
Telefon direkt: +41 (0)41 726 07 80 / Fax: +41 (0)41 710 80 60

As CTO of ivyTeam, Zug, Switzerland, Bruno is responsible for the architecture and development of ivyTeam's business process management and workflow tools. He is also leading the workflow competence team of the SorecoGroup that initiates and supports the use of workflow solutions in customer projects. As a young engineer in computer science he started his professional career at the central R&D labs of Landis&Gyr Corp., now part of the Siemens group, where he did important R&D work in the field of parallel computing.

CHARLES CHOY, WING-CHIU

(charles.choy@hksme.edu.hk)
Senior Vice President, Hong Kong Small and Medium Enterprises Association Principal, HKSME Association Computer Education Centre
and Chairman of WebForce Limited.
Flat B, 9/F., Prince Industrial Building, 706 Prince Edward Road East, San Po Kong, Kowloon, Hong Kong.

Charles Choy, Wing-Chiu is Senior Vice President, Hong Kong Small and Medium Enterprises Association Principal, HKSME Association Computer Education Centre and Chairman of WebForce Limited. Mr Charles Choy W.C. received his first degree from the Faculty of Engineering in the University of Hong Kong in 1996. He worked for Ove Arup & Partners, a world leading engineering consulting company, and since recognized that BPM/Workflow, document management and decision making process are so beneficial and critical in business operations. Later, Charles founded his own company, WebForce Limited, which aims at introducing the latest and innovative IT solutions and comprehensive customer services to companies in Hong Kong and China. Charles joined the Hong Kong Small and Medium Enterprises Association (HKSMEA) in 2000. And he established the HKSME Association Computer Education Centre in 2001. It has been well accepted with proven success through providing necessary education and training, which helps to increase productivity and improve efficiency, to companies of various industries.

YANG CHI-TSAI

(jjyang@flowring.com)
CTO, Flowring Technology
12F, #120, Section 2, Gongdao 5th Rd., Hsinchu, Taiwan 300
Phone: 886-3-5753331 / Fax: 886-3-5753292

Dr. Yang Chi-Tsai works for Flowring technology as CTO and VP. His research interests include BPM, workflow technology, distributed computing and software engineering. Currently he is working on a 3-year government contract to provide the software industry with workflow applications for CMMi ML2 and ML3 operations.

LINUS K CHOW

linus@handysoft.com
International Director , HandySoft Global Corporation
1952 Gallows Road, Suite 200, Vienna VA 22182 USA
Phone: 1-703-732-7327 / Fax: 1-703-442-5650

Linus Chow is the International Director of HandySoft Global Corporation. He has over 12 years of leadership and management experience in information technology internationally. Currently, Linus, has operational responsibility of the Asia-Pacific, as well as best practice services and support for Europe. At HandySoft Linus has been a senior manager in BPM Services Delivery, Product Management, Marketing, and General Management. He has played crucial roles in expanding the growth of BPM and workflow adoption first in the US and then internationally.

Prior to HandySoft, Linus managed and led IT solutions programs for the US Government in Europe and the US, such as enterprise IT systems implementations for the US Army in Europe, and NIST as examples. He is published and an active speaker on the Best Practices of BPM worldwide. He is very active with the BPM industry frequently engaging with the WfMC, BPMG, IQPC, AIIM, and other industry organizations. A decorated former US Army Officer, Linus has an MBA, an MS in Management Information Systems, and a BS in Mathematics, as well as several industry certifications.

DR. M. ALI CHISHTI

ali.chishti@dha.gov.au
Defence Housing Authority, Canberra, Australia
+61 416 818 510, +61 2 6276 2594

Ali is a solutions / systems architect with extensive experience in software, dot-com, financial and assets based industries. He was the lead Microsoft Architect of one of Australia's leading web portals, and has worked in similar positions (directly or in consulting roles) for various medium to large scale organizations including Hoyts, GlaxoSmith&Kline and Shell Australia. Ali has a bachelor and Master degree in Mathematics and Information Systems respectively and obtained a PhD at the Royal Melbourne Institute of Technology by proposing a contingency model for BPR implementation. His current work at the Defence Housing Authority (in Australia) involves architecting and designing enterprise solutions. He uses UML and open standards to apply IT industry's best practices in his day to day work. Alan McNamara (co-author) and Ali worked together at Defence Housing Authority in Canberra, Australia. They designed the business integration of the major DHA operational systems based on the ASAP services model, and this paper is based on lessons learnt from that practical application of this model.

TADEU CRUZ

(tadeucrz@trcr.com.br)
Consultant, Professor M. Sc.
TRCR KNOWLEDGE
Rua Inhambu, 952 – 111, Moema, Sao Paulo, SP 04520-013, Brazil

Tadeu Cruz has worked in the IT industry since 1973 and has a wide range of skills covering just about every aspect of software development, systems analysis and design, project management, consultancy, BPM analysis and Workflow projects. He holds Bachelor's degree in Business Administration, System Engineering and Philosophy. He holds a M.Sc. in Production Engineering and now pursues his doctorate in History of Science. He attended over one hundred courses of specialization and worked as consultant in various countries. Prof. Cruz, with his son Tiago Cruz, heads his own consulting firm, TRCR KNOWLEDGE, located in Sao Paulo, Brazil, specialized in business process analysis, design and quality improvement. He also introduced several Workflow brands in Brazil. Since 1995, Prof. Cruz has published 14 books in the fields of IT, Information Systems, BPM, ECM, Business Process Analysis and Design, 4 books about Workflow and developed an extensive and rich methodology to capture, document, analyze and improve business processes called DOMP.

DANIEL DE MELLO VIERO

daniel.viero@iprocess.com.br)
Rua Washington Luiz, 820/301, 90.001-460 - Porto Alegre – RS - Brazil
Phone: +55 51 3211-4036

Daniel Viero has a deep experience in business process automation and content management system development. Currently he works as systems architect at iProcess. He is certified as Oracle and Lotus Professional. He received his Master's degree in Computer Science from Federal University of Rio Grande do Sul, Brazil in 2005. His research interests include Workflow, Business Process Management, Enterprise Content Management and Systems Integration.

SHEILA DONOHUE

(s.donohue@crif.com)
Consultant, CRIF Decision Solutions
via M. Fantin 1-3, Bologna 40123, Italy
Phone: +39 3408236575 / Fax: +39 051 417 6111

Sheila Donohue has eighteen years of international experience within the Financial Services and Consulting industries. She is an expert in automating credit decision business processes, having developed several credit approval automation engines for large, global companies, including D&B/AIG, IBM and Hewlett Packard. Currently, she is a Senior Business Consultant with CRIF Decision Solutions in Bologna, Italy, leading project engagements which are focused on automation and control of customer acquisition and portfolio management processes in major financial institutions, mainly in Italy and Eastern Europe. Sheila obtained her Masters of Business Administration in Finance and International Business from New York University's Stern School of Business in 1993. She holds a Bachelors degree in Computer Science and Mathematics from Manhattan College.

CLARENCE (SKIP) ELLIS

(Skip@colorado.edu)
Professor of Computer Science, University of Colorado
Campus Box 430, Boulder, Colorado 80309-0430, USA
Phone: 303-492-5984 / Fax: 303-492-2844

Dr. Clarence (Skip) Ellis is Professor of Computer Science and Director of the Collaboration Technology Research Group at the University of Colorado. At Colorado, he is a member of the Institute for Cognitive Science. He is involved in research and teaching of workflow, groupware, coordination theory, and the Alice programming language. Dr. Ellis has worked as a researcher and developer at MCC, Xerox PARC, Bull Corp, the Institute for the Future, Bell Telephone Labs, IBM, Los Alamos Scientific Labs, and Argonne National Lab. His academic experience includes teaching at Stanford University, MIT, University of Texas, Stevens Institute of Technology, Johannes Kepler Institute in Austria, and at Chiaotung University in China. Professor Ellis is one of the original researchers / developers of Workflow Management Systems (at Xerox PARC in the 1970s, and at MIT before that with Mike Hammer and others). Skip Ellis has published over 100 technical papers, written several books, lectured in more than two dozen countries, and was recently selected as an ACM Computer Society Fellow. He has recently been working and publishing in the area of Workflow Mining.

RAMI ELRON

(rami_elron@bmc.com)
Senior Systems Architect, BMC Software
6 Habarzel Street, Tel Aviv 61581 Israel
Phone: +972-3-7662434

Rami Elron has responsibility for design aspects concerning BMC Software's Identity Management Suite and the solution's next generation architecture and features. An industrial engineer, Rami has over 15 years of experience in computing infrastructure and development environments as a developer, project manager and system architect, and has lectured in academia and at prominent computer industry conferences. Before joining BMC Software, Rami served as VP technologies of a large system integration firm. Rami was appointed by Microsoft to be a Microsoft Regional Director for operating systems, and received several notable awards, including 'Person of the Year' and a special award for the promotion of Microsoft technologies. Rami is an active member of the OASIS PSTC (Provisioning Services Technical Committee) that created the international SPML standard for provisioning and identity management. Rami co-authored a book on Windows XP and has written numerous articles on Windows, security and identity management technologies.

KEVIN ERICKSON

(kevin.erickson@noridian.com)
Information Technology Director, Noridian Administrative Services, LLC
901 40th St S, Suite 1, Fargo, ND, 58103 United States
Kevin Erickson is the Information Technology Director for Noridian Administrative Services, LLC. (NAS). He has over 18 years of experience in systems analysis and design, system administration and application development. As an Open Source advocate and visionary, Mr. Erickson has written papers on the use of Open Source in business and received an award for his paper on the implementation of NAS' Linux-based e-mail system. In his current role, Mr. Erickson drives IT projects that apply technology to improve business operations, reduce costs and improve agility. He is the architect of NAS' initiative to implement business process management and workflow automation company-wide. He is a graduate of North Dakota State University.

LAYNA FISCHER

(layna@wfmc.org)
Publisher , Future Strategies Inc., and Executive Director for WfMC
2436 North Federal Highway, #374, Lighthouse Point, FL 33064 USA
As WfMC's Executive Director, Layna Fischer works closely with the WfMC Committees to promote the mission of the WfMC and is tasked with the overall management of membership logistics, meetings, conferences, publications and websites. Ms Fischer was also the Executive Director of the Business Process Management Initiative (now merged with OMG) and chairs WARIA (Workflow And Reengineering International Association), a position she has held since 1994. She is also the director of the annual Global Excellence Workflow Awards. As president and CEO of Future Strategies Inc., Ms Fischer is the publisher of the business book series *New Tools for New Times*, as well as the annual *Excellence in Practice* volumes of award-winning case studies and the annual *Workflow Handbook*, published in collaboration with the WfMC.

DONGSOO HAN

(dshan@icu.ac.kr)
Information and Communications University/VIsoft
119 Munjiro, Yuseong-Gu, Daejeon 305-732, Korea
Phone: +82-11-338-3440
Dr. Dongsoo Han is associate dean of Information and Communications University, Korea and he serves as president of VIsoft as well. He has led VIsoft's research on workflow and BPM, and has authored numerous papers and articles on workflow systems and Web services for the past 10 years.

MICHAEL HURLEY

(mike@greensquareinc.com)
President & CEO, Green Square, Inc
10835 S. Hoyne Avenue Suite 300, Chicago, IL 60643 USA
Phone: 773-445-0084
Michael Hurley is a recognized expert on the practical application of enterprise content management (ECM), Document Capture and workflow/BPM technologies to the healthcare industry. He founded Green Square in 1997 to focus on vendor independent consulting solutions that connect ECM and BPM with business strategy. Mr. Hurley has directed ECM and workflow/BPM projects for various healthcare organizations including

25 different Blue Cross and Blue Shield plans. He is a frequent speaker on the topic of ECM and BPM strategy as well as the author of a number of articles and papers on the ECM and BPM in healthcare. Mr. Hurley currently serves as chairman of the Healthcare Special Interest Group for the Chicago Chapter of the Association of Information and Image Management (AIIM). Mr. Hurley is a graduate of St. Xavier University and serves on the board of Catholic Charities of Chicago. He is an avid reader, actively working on a goal to read 100 books in a single year and is training to be a brewmeister.

CIRANO IOCHPE

(ciochpe@inf.ufrgs.br)
Federal University of Rio Grande do Sul (www.inf.ufrgs.br)
Institute of Informatics, Av. Bento Gonçalves, 9500 - Campus do Vale - Bloco IV Agronomia - Porto Alegre - RS - Brazil, CEP 91501-970
Phone: +55 (51) 3316-6820 Fax: +55 (51) 3316-7308
Cirano Iochpe is a full professor at the Department of Information Systems, at Federal University of Rio Grande do Sul. His special interests are Geographical Information Systems and Workflow Systems. Mr. Iochpe has several publications in these areas and has also leaded some projects related to these areas. Nevertheless, he is specialist in Software Engineering and Master in Computer Science by Federal University of Rio Grande do Sul. He received his PhD. rer. Nat degree by University of Karlsruhe in 1989.

UDHAI REDDY KAKANI

(udhai_reddy@infosys.com)
BPM Research Head, Infosys Technologies Limited
Electronic City, Hosur Road, Bangalore, Karnataka 560100, India
Phone: +91 9886406860 / Fax: +91 80 28520362
Udhai Reddy has worked extensively on process management and implementation of process change initiatives. He designed and implemented changes at a global level to product management business processes for a FMCG Major. Udhai Reddy also designed the new business processes when an FMCG extended its business from products to services and defined multiple guidelines, frameworks etc., for Infosys around BPM. He designed and built a BPM framework for Infosys BPM consultancy service, built the BPM consultancy toolkit for Infosys, including aspects of BPM in requirements engineering. He has contributed to many seminars and publications, conducted many webinars on BPM and has contributed and presented papers at many seminars and publications.

DR. SETRAG KHOSHAFIAN

(setrag@pega.com)
VP of BPM Technology, Pegasystems Inc.
101 Main Street Cambridge, MA. 02142 United States
Setrag is a recognized expert in Business Process Management, Database Management Systems, and Object-Oriented technologies. Currently he is Vice President of BPM Technology at Pegasystems, Inc. He is a strategic BPM technology, services, and product direction leader at Pega. He is an evangelist of Pega's SmartBPM Suite. He has presented in numerous conferences, sat on variety of industry and technical panels, and participates in standardization initiatives. He is the author of several journal papers, lead author of seven books, as well as whitepapers on various leading features of the award wining PegaRULES Process Commander. Previously he was the Senior VP of technology at Savvion.

KWANGHOON KIM, PH.D.

(kwang@kyonggi.ac.kr)
Collaboration Technology Research Lab.
Department of Computer Science, Kyonggi University, Korea
Tel: 82-31-249-9679
Dr. Kwang-Hoon Kim is Associate Professor of Computer Science Department and Director of the Collaboration Technology Research Laboratory at the Kyonggi University, South Korea. At Kyonggi, he is involved in research and teaching of workflow, groupware, coor-

dination theory, computer networks, software architectures, and database systems. Dr. Kim received the B.S. degree in computer science from the Kyonggi University in 1984. And he received the M.S. degree in computer science from the Chungang University in 1986. He also received the M.S. and Ph.D. degree from the computer science department of the University of Colorado at Boulder, in 1994 and 1998, respectively. Dr. Kim has worked as a researcher and developer at Aztek Engineering, American Educational Products Inc., IBM, and ETRI (Electronics and Telecommunications Research Institute at South Korea). And he is the Vice-President of Workflow and Business Applications technology Forum. He is on the editorial board of the journal of KIPS, and the committee member of the several conferences and workshops. His interests include groupware, workflow systems, CSCW, collaboration theory, distributed systems, software architecture modeling and simulation, e-commerce, and computer networks.

HEINZ LIENHARD

(heinz.lienhard@ivyteam.ch)
Founder of ivyTeam, Soreco-ivyteam
Alpenstrasse 9 , P.O.Box Zug CH-6304, Switzerland
Heinz Leinhard lives and works in Switzerland at the lovely lake of Zug. With ivyTeam he has successfully brought together the web application and the workflow world. He received a Master's degree in electrical engineering from the ETH (Switzerland), a Master's degree in mathematical statistics from Stanford University (California, USA) and the Dr. h.c. from the informatics department of ETH, Lausanne (Switzerland). For many years he headed the central R&D labs of Landis&Gyr Corp., now part of the Siemens group, where he built up important R&D activities in system theory, automatic control, informatics and microtechnology.

ALAN MCNAMARA

(alan.mcnamara@badja.com)
Director, Badja Consulting
Phone: +61 4 12825517
Alan is an experienced technical manager and enterprise and eBusiness architect, and a Director of Badja Consulting. Alan has worked in Finance, Government and Telecommunications industries. His work has covered all elements of Enterprise Architecture, from business process management and requirements gathering to application and technical infrastructure design. Alan's research interest is in developing reference Service Oriented Architectures for Enterprise business infrastructure.

DEREK MIERS

(miers@enix.co.uk)
Industry Analyst, Enix Consulting Ltd
9 Lonsdale Rd London W4 1ND United Kingdom
Derek Miers founded Enix in 1992 to provide strategy and technology consulting to astute blue chip commercial organizations, vendors and system integrators. Over the years he has developed unique perspectives on the use of BPM and other process-oriented technologies ranging from understanding and modeling processes to actively supporting them through modern BPMS environments, enterprise content management and Web Services. From a consulting perspective, Derek has enjoyed engagements with some of the worlds most well known brands, providing a range of training, executive level facilitation and technology selection services. Derek recently undertook a major evaluation of the leading BPM Suites for BP Trends (available free of charge at www.bptrends.com) and prior to that was author of Process Product Watch. As part of his contributing work, Derek has been a regular conference presenter and visiting lecturer at several European universities and business schools. In recognition of his insights and perspectives, Derek was elected as a Director and then Co-Chairman of BPMI.org. He was instrumental in development of BPM Think Tank held in Miami March 2005 and in driving the merger of the organization with the OMG.

ZORAN MILAKOVIC

(zoran@prozone.co.yu)
Together Teamlösungen
Elmargasse 2-4 Vienna 1010 Austria
Phone: +43 (0) 5 04 04–122 / Fax: +43 (0) 5 04 04-11 122
Zoran Milaković is software architect for more than 5 years. He was involved in development of open source software in areas of workflow and document management. He has published various articles in these fields. In the year 2000 he received his University Diploma in areas of Software Engineering in University of Belgrade.

JUAN J. MORENO

(jmoreno@lithium.com.uy)
University Professor / Company Director
Universidad Católica / Lithium Software
Av. Libertador 1532 / 1526, Montevideo 11100, Uruguay
Phone: (598 2)9014071 / (598 9)133 483
Fax: (598 2)9014071
Juan J. Moreno is cofounder and director of Lithium Software, a Workflow and BPM focused company, holding the intellectual property of its DocFlow Workflow Management System. He is professor and researcher at the Engineering and Technologies Faculty of the Universidad Católica del Uruguay. He holds the Degree of Advanced Studies (DEA) in Spain and Europe. He has dozens of technical and arbitrated publications, and he was recognized with the third price of "Innovator of the Year 2003" in his country, Uruguay.

SUNGJOON PARK

(sungjun@icu.ac.kr)
MS student/Engineer, Information and Communications University/Samsung
119 Munjiro, Yuseong-Gu, Daejeon 305-732, Korea
Phone: +82-11-338-3440
Sungjoon Park has been working for Samsung SDS since 1998 and he researched Workflow. Currently he was dispatched to ICU (Information and Communication University) to participate in a strategy brains program.

VLADIMIR PUSKAS

vpuskas@prozone.co.yu
Together Teamlösungen
Elmargasse 2-4 Vienna 1010 Austria
Phone: +43 (0) 5 04 04–122 / Fax: +43 (0) 5 04 04-11 122
Vladimir Puškaš is a member of Enhydra.org development team. He was involved in the development of open source software in many areas, and especially workflow, where he developed one of the most popular open-source XPDL graphical editor and workflow engine products.

JON PYKE

(jpyke@theprocessfactory.com)
Chairman WfMC
CTO, TheProcessFactory
Faris Lane, Woodham Surrey KT15 3DN United Kingdom
Jon was the Chief Technology Officer and a main board director of Staffware Plc from August 1992 until was acquired by TIBCO in 2004. He demonstrates an exceptional blend of Business/People Manager; a Technician with a highly developed sense where technologies fit and how they should be utilized. Jon is a world-recognized industry figure; an exceptional public speaker and a seasoned quoted company executive. As the CTO for Staffware Plc, Jon was responsible for a team of 70 people, geographically split into two countries and four locations. Jon's primary responsibility was directing the product development cycle. Furthermore, Jon had overall executive responsibility for the product strategy, positioning, public speaking etc. Finally, as a main board director he was heavily involved in PLC board activities including merges and acquisitions, corporate

governance, and board director of several subsidiaries. Jon has published a number of articles on the subject of Office Automation, BPM and Workflow Technology. These publications include work for the British Computer Society entitled "Office Automation–The Good News" and the "Workflow Report" for publication by Cambridge Market Intelligence. Jon has authored *Mastering Your Organization's Processes; A Plain Guide to BPM,* with John O'Connell and Roger Whitehead, published by Cambridge University Press. Jon co-founded and is the current Chair of the Workflow Management Coalition. He is an AiiM Laureate for Workflow and was awarded the 2003 Marvin L. Manheim Award for *Significant Contributions in the Field of Workflow.*

Aubrey J. Rembert

(rembert@cs.colorado.edu)
Ph.D. Student, Collaboration Technology Research Group (CTRG)
Computer Science Department, University of Colorado, Boulder, CO 80309
Mr. Rembert earned his B.S. in Computer & Information Systems and his M.S. In Computer Science (emphasis: Software Engineering) from Florida A&M University. Currently, he is pursuing a Ph.D. in Computer Science at the University of Colorado-Boulder. His current interests are data mining, collaborative computing, computational organization theory, and distributed computing.

Steve Rotter

(srotter@adobe.com)
Senior Product Marketing Manager, Adobe Systems Inc
2001 Butterfield Road, Downers Grove, IL 60515 USA
Steve Rotter has been helping organizations with their business process management initiatives for almost 2 decades. Currently, Mr. Rotter is the Senior Product Marketing Manager with Adobe Systems where he leads the business and marketing strategy for Adobe's workflow and process management technologies and contributes to Adobe's overall product strategy for the enterprise market. Prior to joining Adobe, Mr. Rotter was co-founder and Vice President of Marketing of Q-Link Technologies (which Adobe acquired in 2004), one of the pioneers in Business Process Management software. Previously, Mr. Rotter was Managing Partner with Paradigm Research, a business consulting firm specializing in process management and reengineering strategies for the Global 2000. At Paradigm Research, Mr. Rotter led the organization's practice area focused the developing process reengineering methodologies and delivering process re-design solutions. Mr. Rotter has also held numerous industry management positions including Worldwide Marketing Manager within Motorola's Cellular Infrastructure Group where his organization received the prestigious CEO Quality Award. Mr. Rotter is a published author and frequently speaks on the subject of process management at industry events. Mr. Rotter holds a Masters degree from Northwestern University's Kellogg Graduate School of Management and serves as a volunteer on the Marketing Advisory Board and Vision Council for World Vision, a non-profit, Christian relief and development organization dedicated to helping children and their communities worldwide.

Robert Shapiro

rshapiro@capevisions.com
Senior Vice President, Global 360
160 Riverside Dr., New York, NY 10024 United States
Phone: (617) 823-1055 / Fax: (212) 580-1517
In January 2005 Robert Shapiro joined Global 360 as Senior Vice President and remains President of Cape Visions, now a subsidiary of Global 360. As founder and President of Cape Visions he directed the development of Analytics and Simulation software now used by FileNet, Fujitsu, PegaSystems and Global 360 Business Process Management products. Prior to founding Cape Visions, Robert was a driving force in the creation and promotion of graphical techniques for modeling, analyzing and simulating complex systems. As founder and CEO of Meta Software Corporation, he directed the implementation of a unique suite of graphical modeling and optimization tools for enterprise wide business process improvement. Products based on these tools are used by Bank One, Wells Fargo

and other major banks to optimize their check processing operations. As a participant in the Workflow Management Coalition and chair of the working group on process definition interchange, he plays a critical role in the development of international standards for workflow and business process management.

LUCINÉIA HELOISA THOM

(lucineia@inf.ufrgs.br)
Federal University of Rio Grande do Sul (www.inf.ufrgs.br)
Institute of Informatics, Av. Bento Gonçalves, 9500 - Campus do Vale - Block IV Porto Alegre, RS, Brazil, CEP 91501-970
Phone: +55 (51) 3316-616 n5 and 3316-6168 Fax: +55 (51) 3316-7308
Lucinéia Heloisa Thom is an active researcher and professional in workflow area. She received a Bachelor's degree in Computer Science from University of Santa Cruz do Sul in 1999 and a Master's degree in Computer Science from Federal University of Rio Grande do Sul in 2002. Currently, Ms. Thom is working on her PhD-Thesis at Federal University of Rio Grande do Sul where she also collaborates in a workflow lecture. From 2004 to 2005, she developed part of her research abroad at Institute for Parallel and Distributed Systems of University of Stuttgart in Germany. Her research interests include BPM and workflow management systems with a special focus on metamodels, business process modeling and patterns. She has published many articles in these fields.

FRED VAN LEEUWEN

leeuwen@dceconsultants.com
Managing Consultant, DCE Consultants
Wallaardt Sacrestraat 405, 1117 BM Schiphol-Oost The Netherlands
Fred van Leeuwen is an internationally recognised author and speaker on BPM and related subjects. He has been involved with the Workflow Management Coalition since 1996 and is responsible for the Benelux Country Desk. He is a Managing Consultant with DCE Consultants, an independent consultancy company which is part of the Altran group of companies operating on the front line of business management & IT.

MS. CARRINE WONG

(carrine@isid.hk)
General Manager , ISI-Dentsu (ISID) Hong Kong Ltd.
Suite 1101 Central Plaza, 18 Harbour Road, Wanchai, Hong Kong
Ms. Carrine Wong is the General Manager of ISI-Dentsu (ISID) of Hong Kong Ltd. Ms Wong has over 15 years of experience in information technology focusing on knowledge management and business process automation. Carrine has helped many leading organizations such as Bank of Tokyo Mitsubishi, Canon, Toyota Motor and YKK to implement mission critical systems in Asia. Carrine earned a MBA and she joined ISID in 1990. As GM, Carrine spearheads ISID's solutions and services strategy, leads key business initiatives and supports the operations of key business units along with her management team.

ESPEN WØIEN

(Espen.Woien@dnv.com)
Head of Department, DNV Software
7th floor, Kolon Bld, 36-7, Namchon1-Dong, Suyong-Gu, Busan 613-815, Republic of Korea
Phone: +82 51 610 7790 / Fax: +82 51 611 7172
Espen Wøien is currently Head of Department of Software Factory and responsible for the BRIX Workflow Manager portfolio and the common development framework used in DNV Software. He got a Master of Computer Science at the Norwegian University of Science and Technology (NTNU) in 1995.

Index

Additional Workflow and BPM Resources

NON-PROFIT ASSOCIATIONS AND RELATED STANDARDS RESEARCH ONLINE

- AIIM (Association for Information and Image Management)
  http://www.aiim.org
- AIS Special Interest Group on Process Automation and Management (SIGPAM)
  http://www.sigpam.org
- BPR On-Line Learning Center
  http://www.prosci.com
- Business Process Management Initiative
  http://www.bpmi.org *see* Object Management Group
- IEEE (Electrical and Electronics Engineers, Inc.)
  http://www.ieee.org
- Institute for Information Management (IIM)
  http://www.iim.org
- ISO (International Organization for Standardization)
  http://www.iso.ch
- Object Management Group
  http://www.omg.org
- Open Document Management Association
  http://nfocentrale.net/dmware
- Organization for the Advancement of Structured Information Standards
  http://www.oasis-open.org
- Society for Human Resource Management
  http://www.shrm.org
- Society for Information Management
  http://www.simnet.org
- Wesley J. Howe School of Technology Management
  http://attila.stevens.edu/workflow
- Workflow And Reengineering International Association (WARIA)
  http://www.waria.com
- Workflow Comparative Study
  http://www.waria.com/books/study-2003.htm
- Workflow Management Coalition (WfMC)
  http://www.wfmc.org
- Workflow Portal
  http://www.e-workflow.org

Valued Reader Discount 2006

- *Workflow Handbook* series, 2001-2006 Retail $95.00 each
- *CDROM Companion to Workflow Handbook* series Retail $95.00 each
- *Excellence in Practice Series* Volumes I-V Retail $50.00 each

Buy any book or CDROM using *this* order form for instant 50% discount*. Fax to +1 954 782 6365

Year	Title

* Limit one copy of each title. View complete title descriptions online at www.wfmc.org. If ordering online, insert **"Book Order Form 50%"** in the discount code box to get this 50% *Valued Reader Discount* discount.

SHIPPING INFORMATION

Name: _____

Title/Occupation: _____

Company: _____

Address: _____

Phone: _____ Fax: _____

Email: *Please write clearly!* _____

PAYMENT INFORMATION:

No.	COPIES	@ $ each	= $
		FL state tax 6%	= $
		Subtotal	= $
No.	Shipping	(see rates below)	= $
		TOTAL	= $

☐ Check (in US$ drawn on a US Bank to Future Strategies Inc.)

☐ VISA ☐ MASTERCARD ☐ AMEX

Credit Card No. _____ Exp. Date _____

Name on Card _____ Today's Date: _____

Signature _____

Mail or fax this order to:

Future Strategies Inc., Book Division
2436 North Federal Highway, #374, Lighthouse Point, FL 33064 USA
Tel: +1 954 782 3376 / Fax: +1 954 782 6365
email: wfmc@wfmc.org

Shipping: AIRMAIL SHIPPING CHARGES **PER BOOK**: USA Priority Mail $5.95; Canada/Mexico $9.00; UK/Europe $14.00; Pacific Rim $17.00; Africa/South America $19.00 (Distributors/Bookstores/Libraries/Educational Institutions, please call for special discounts and shipping schedule.)

WORKFLOW HANDBOOK ANNUAL SERIES

This annual (since 2000) definitive and one-stop reference work on workflow, standards and business processes is published in collaboration with the *Workflow Management Coalition*, the industry's only standards-setting body devoted to entirely business process management. Contributions come from industry experts and thought-leaders, including WfMC current specifications schemas and examples.

CDROM COMPANION TO THE WORKFLOW HANDBOOK

Each annual CDROM Companion to the Workflow Handbook contains 650MB of valuable information, including:

- Foreword video presentation by Jon Pyke, WfMC Chair
- *Introduction to Workflow* 45-minute video tutorial
- An electronic copy of the entire *Workflow Handbook* in PDF format
- Selected slide presentations to WfMC technical committees
- Workflow product comparative analysis (a substantial subset of the highly acclaimed *Workflow Comparative Study* by Martin Ader)
- Product demonstrations, specifications and literature from selected vendors
- Contributions from industry experts, including WfMC current specifications schemas, examples and WfMC workflow glossary.

EXCELLENCE IN PRACTICE SERIES

What makes a winner? The answer lies in the *Excellence in Practice* series by Layna Fischer, General Manager of the Workflow Management Coalition (WfMC) and Chair of the Workflow And Reengineering International Association (WARIA). To be recognized as winners, companies must address three critical areas: excellence in innovation, excellence in implementation and excellence in strategic impact to the organization.

Featuring the winners and finalists of the annual Global Excellence in Workflow Awards, with guest chapters from leading industry analysts and experts, the profiled case studies provide considerable detail regarding the issues of implementation:

- How these companies managed both their overall technological and business innovations.
- Their system application, the system use, the users; what the job entails
- What were their key motivations
- Their system configuration (number, and type of software, servers, scanners, printers, storage devices, etc., including the vendors and integrators involved)
- How the companies have been impacted by their new system; cost savings, ROI and increased productivity improvements, competitive advantage gained, etc.